RECKONING WITH RACE

America's Failure

GENE DATTEL

ENCOUNTER BOOKS

New York • London

© 2017 by Gene Dattel

First American edition published in 2017 by Encounter Books,
an activity of Encounter for Culture and Education, Inc.,
a nonprofit, tax exempt corporation.
Encounter Books website address: www.encounterbooks.com

Manufactured in the United States and printed on
acid-free paper. The paper used in this publication meets
the minimum requirements of ANSI/NISO Z39.48-1992
(R 1997) (*Permanence of Paper*).

FIRST AMERICAN EDITION

LIBRARY OF CONGRESS CATALOGING-IN-PUBLICATION DATA
Names: Dattel, Eugene R., author.
Title: Reckoning with race : America's failure / by Gene Dattel.
Description: New York : Encounter Books, 2018. | Includes
bibliographical references and index.
Identifiers: LCCN 2017002302 (print) | LCCN 2017022547 (ebook) |
ISBN 9781594039102 (ebook) | ISBN 9781594039096 (hardcover : alk. paper)
Subjects: LCSH: United States—Race relations—History. |
African Americans—History.
Classification: LCC E185.61 (ebook) | LCC E185.61 .D27 2018 (print) |
DDC 305.800973—dc23
LC record available at https://lccn.loc.gov/2017002302

Images sourced by Jill Kelly Fanucci/Griangraf Research
Interior page design and composition: BooksByBruce.com

Dedication

To the Future of America

In the end, to know the past is to know ourselves—not entirely, not enough, but a little better. History can help us to achieve some grace and elegance of action, some cogency and completion of thought, some harmony and tolerance in human relationships. Most of all, history can give us a sense of excitement, a personal zest for watching and perhaps participating in the events around us that will, one day, be history too.

—Robin W. Winks, "The Value of History,"
in *A History of Civilization: Prehistory to the Present* (1995)

Contents

Preface / ix
Acknowledgments / xvii

Chapter One

Racial Attitudes in the North, 1800–1865 / 1

The Antebellum Free States / 2
Lincoln and the Aftermath of War / 35
Reunion / 38

Chapter Two

The Containment of Blacks in the South / 41

Reconstruction: The Setting / 42
The War's Aftermath / 48
The Legal Aspects of Race / 67
The Economics of Race / 69
Northerners in the Cotton Fields / 75
Black Self-Sufficiency: The Montgomery Family / 78
The Education of Freedmen / 83
Theodore Roosevelt and the Northern Privileged Class / 86

Chapter Three

The Great Migration: The Reception of Blacks in Northern Cities / 91

Chicago! / 94
Immigrant in Detroit / 113
Blacks in New York City / 120
The Effects of Philanthropy / 136
From the Farm to the City / 139
Black-on-Black Crime / 140
The Impact of World War II / 142

Chapter Four

The 1960s: Civil Rights and Civil War / 149

A Global Definition of "People of Color" / 152
Black Identity / 153
Integration at Ole Miss / 159
The Struggle for Civil Rights / 163
"The Ivy League Negro" / 173
"Desegregation Does Not Mean Integration" / 174
A Sober Look at an "Alliance" / 183
The Racial Integration Muddle / 187
Black Leaders, from Moderate to Militant / 189
Racial Violence in the North / 197
The War on Poverty / 205
The Private Sector Responds / 208
Another Look at the Sixties / 211

Chapter Five

The Enduring American Dilemma / 215

The Marshall Plan: The Coattail Effect on Black America / 218
Jobs / 224
Still Seeking a Better Education / 230
Self-Examination / 237
The Integration Muddle / 239
Recasting Memorials / 257
Watching the Movies / 261
The Portability of Education / 267
Police and Community / 269
Black Leadership / 281

Chapter Six

From Dream to Reality / 287

Notes on Sources / 295
Index / 313

Preface

We need a frank and honest discussion about race. Or as James Baldwin said in 1964 and as Martin Luther King Jr. put it in 1967, "Tell it like it is." How many times have you heard or read this dictum about America's most sensitive, tragic, and inflammable topic, race? Although the call persists, the conversation never occurs. Instead white Americans are surprised, in fact stunned, by the level of racial tension in America, especially when it turns violent. It fuels the fear of a large, permanent black underclass that will not go away. Fifty years after Baldwin and King, why is the racial divide still our defining social issue?

In the pages to follow I concentrate on what I see as the fulcrum of this issue: the entrance of most black Americans into the economic mainstream. Make no mistake: blacks see economics, exacerbated by past injustice and discrimination, expressed as income gap or poverty as the main cause of black frustration. Economics—which means jobs—is a critical part of the discussion within the black community. And the prerequisite for broad participation in economic advancement is assimilation, denied to blacks until the mid-twentieth century. Assimilation, sometimes considered pejorative, is falsely assumed to deny one's cultural differences. In the word game that has ensued, integration and acculturation are often preferred. Let's be clear: the proper use of assimilation allows for practical and efficient adjustment to common values while retaining different cultural heritages. Without appropriate assimilation, a harmful road to separatism follows.

To assimilate should be a greater priority for blacks than the overzealous pursuit of cultural acceptance. The eye on the prize should be focused on economic improvement, not perceived slights and a separate black society.

For the most part, blacks want more resources thrown at their problems—more public and private funding. Concerned whites agree that money is needed to address issues of housing, education, crime, and single-parent families but want more accountability. Blacks also want more law enforcement against discrimination and more programs run by blacks. They dismiss troubling behavior in the black community, avoiding responsibility and blaming inadequate economic support.

From the birth of the nation, America has relied on assimilation to mold a cohesive society. Assimilation has meant the acceptance of common goals, common values, a common language, and a common legal system that leaves abundant room for cultural heritage. George Washington clearly outlined the country's attitude toward immigrants and their heritage in his 1790 letter to the Jewish community of Newport, Rhode Island. He welcomed the Jews, promising tolerance, protection, and the "good will of other Americans" while reminding them of the obligations and responsibilities of good citizenship.

The Founding Fathers had witnessed the catastrophic results of European fragmentation by land, ethnicity, language, and culture. These were practical men. National unity was the only means of survival. They could also observe firsthand the inherent weakness and vulnerability of the Native American tribal organization, which led to internecine warfare among the tribes and various collaborations with European countries against each other in their battles.

Tribalism and provincialism had to give way to a national identity. As it happens, no other country has attracted so many immigrants from diverse backgrounds and absorbed them into a cohesive unit necessary for the survival of the whole. Immigrants by the millions still come to America for political, religious, and economic reasons but overwhelmingly for a better material life. A large part of their success has been due to America's *adaptable* free enterprise system.

White immigrants left the "old country" and came voluntarily to America. African Americans, involuntary immigrants, arrived in slave ships, first in the seventeenth century, and have been struggling with their identity—national or separate—ever since.

The first Naturalization Act in 1790 specified that "any white alien, being a free white person" was eligible for citizenship. In an America with race-based slavery, where did a free black fit into the assimilation scheme? Although the Fourteenth Amendment in 1868 granted citizenship to blacks, social norms continued to exclude them from the process of assimilation.

Other newcomers to American shores were urged toward assimilation. In 1793 Washington welcomed German immigrants but cautioned them against retaining their "language, habits and principles." Better that they "intermixed," he wrote, "with our people...assimilate to our customs, measures and laws: in a word, soon become one people."

We need to be reminded of the *practicality* of the Founding Fathers' vision. Washington was a land surveyor and real estate investor before he was a general and a president. Thomas Jefferson mastered law, mathematics, horticulture, and architecture; he wanted a distribution of immigrants "sparsely among the natives for quicker amalgamation." Benjamin Franklin was an inventor, discoverer of the electrical conductivity of lightning, printer, advocate of hard work and education, and a self-made man. He, too, advocated the distribution of immigrants among English speakers. The Germans "begin of late," warned the sage Franklin, "to make their Bonds and other legal Writings in their own Language, which—though I think it ought not to be—are allowed good in our Courts." The chaos and inefficiency of allowing multiple-language contracts was obvious then and remains so now.

When Irish-American groups in 1818 applied for a designated section of the Northwest Territory to be set aside exclusively for Irish settlement, Congress, in an emphatic, defining decision, rejected this attempt at separatism. Afterward, new states gained admittance to the union only when they had a majority of English speakers.

The prerequisite for a successful ethnically diverse population living under one roof is assimilation, which leads to a national identity, unity, and the practical means to facilitate social, legal, and commercial interchange. Ethnic cultural heritage can remain a distinct part of identity after concessions are made to assimilation. Prosperous large countries such as Japan, Korea, and those of Western Europe have homogeneous populations. They have not been concerned to develop an assimilation process. Europe is now being tested by its Muslim immigrants, some of whom it sees as incapable of assimilation.

In the American story, the major exception to assimilation, of course, was the exclusion of black America. But the Supreme Court's ending of legal segregation in the 1954 *Brown v. Board of Education* decision marked the beginning of a new era. With restrictions removed, values and merit might now prevail over race and ethnicity. Despite Southern resistance, most Americans assumed that our racial dilemma was thus being solved in the 1960s. The promise of *Brown* seemed to play out in the Civil Rights Acts, the War on Poverty, the end of overt public segregation, and the removal of suffrage barriers. Yet the Northern urban race riots of the sixties, in New York, Watts, Detroit, and Newark, warned of a racial chasm, filled with complex social issues.

Although the 1968 "Report of the National Advisory Commission on Civil Disorders" (now known as the Kerner Report) is the benchmark definition of American racial issues, the number of conferences, commissions, and reports on race in America has been continuing and endless. Daniel Patrick Moynihan's "The Negro Family: The Case for National Action" in 1965 exposed the plight of black family structure, a product of crime, slum housing, and "high rates of alcoholism, desertion, illegitimacy and the other pathologies associated with poverty." Two decades earlier, the sociologist Gunnar Myrdal had explored the problems of black Americans in *An American Dilemma*, and the same issues had been recognized by the black sociologist E. Franklin Frazier in *The Negro Family in Chicago*, a classic study from 1932. Does anyone remember the First Mohonk Conference on the Negro Question, chaired by former president Rutherford B. Hayes in 1890?

The parade continues. In June 1997 President Bill Clinton announced "One America in the 21st Century: The President's Initiative on Race." In 2014 President Barack Obama rolled out yet another program, "My Brother's Keeper." None of these has solved the "Negro Problem." They are highly visible gestures designed to "do something" while generating publicity.

Reckoning with Race investigates five key periods of the African American experience. In each there have been failures, whole or partial, in the assimilation process that is necessary for full participation in the economic mainstream. There have perhaps been missed opportunities, but major discriminatory obstacles have also been at work except for during the last period.

In the first period, from the signing of the Constitution in 1787 to the end of the Civil War in 1865, I consider the frequently overlooked situation of free blacks in the North. In confronting the black experience in

America, all roads lead to the well-charted territory of race-based slavery. But Northern attitudes toward free blacks in the years before the Civil War form an indispensable guide to the African American experience after the war. If blacks, a tiny 2 percent of the Northern population, could not be successfully absorbed, the postwar acceptance of large numbers in the North, after Emancipation, would be impossible. American historians usually omit a critical distinction between the attitude of white Northerners toward race-based slavery and what they thought about free blacks. White Northerners were for the most part vehemently anti-black and obsessively feared a black migration north.

In the second period, from 1865 to World War I, the white North began during Reconstruction (1865–1877) with total control over an utterly defeated adversary before reconciling with the white South. The result was a rejection of any plan to disperse blacks in the North and a direct and indirect containment policy for keeping blacks in the Southern cotton fields. The black population of the North remained at about 2 percent while millions of white European immigrants poured into the country. Historians now seek to view the Reconstruction years as a successful biracial experience. But the small number of temporary white teachers, the black office holders, and the short-term impact of black suffrage did little to advance the newly freed slaves toward equality.

In the third period, from roughly World War I until the 1960s, occurred the Great Migration of blacks north. War-induced labor shortages, not racial tolerance, led blacks to a false promised land of wages, voting rights, and the beginning of a middle and upper middle class but also to the debilitating environment of an urban ghetto and consequent race riots.

The next two stages brought the end of overt legal segregation and the first possibility that blacks might enter the economic mainstream *en masse*. The fourth period was marked by civil rights legislation, violence, the advent of black militancy, resistance to integration in both North and South, and massive programs to assist blacks in the transformation to economic prosperity. The detailed Kerner Report, a reaction to the devastating race riots of the 1960s, outlined for blacks the path to full membership in American society.

In the fifth chapter I recount events of the past fifty years—the structural flaws of black life in America, the real and imagined discriminatory impediments, the evergreen topic of racial difficulties, and a recognition of the only solution: a broad-based effort within black society to truly *prepare*—a word used by the civil rights giants of the 1960s—for the future.

———

In the process of this investigation I encounter a number of myths that need to be busted. For one, both whites and blacks have viewed the South as the exclusive and durable scapegoat in America's racial ordeal. This singular focus on the South may be soothing to white Northern consciences, but it has also provided an escape from the reality of the North's own unenlightened racial world. In fact, the race problem in America has always been a national problem, not exclusively Southern. It is a mistake to think otherwise and leads to flawed responses to the problem. Hence, after the Great Migration and after overt legal segregation in the South disappeared, no racial utopia emerged.

White Northerners reflexively cite odious Southern phenomena—lynchings, legal school segregation, "colored only" signs, and "back of the bus" status. They ignore school segregation in their own communities, race riots, and the large black underclass in Northern as well as Southern cities. Civil Rights museums proliferate in the South while the North predominantly memorializes episodes of racial tolerance. Civil Rights courses generally study the South almost exclusively. Altogether the narrative is scarcely objective. Upon visiting the North, the white Southerner invariably finds a subtle, and not so subtle, racial hypocrisy with an overlay of self-righteousness. Ample evidence, which I present, shows that white Northerners, in the words of one black abolitionist, "best like the colored person at a distance."

I also attempt to clarify the damaging misuse of the term "people of color." Martin Luther King Jr. had some choice words in 1968 about conflating black Americans with foreign "people of color"; he thought some young black militants "are color-consumed and they see a kind of mystique in being colored, and anything not colored is condemned." In his speeches King accepted color-consciousness in American society, though in his "I Have a Dream" speech he famously yearned for colorblindness. The attempt to combine the experiences of various Asian, Middle Eastern,

African, and Latin American ethnicities under the umbrella of a nonwhite brotherhood flouts cultural, economic, and societal distinctions.

In another questionable association, current racial issues are likened to those of the 1960s as a way of cloaking today's problems with the aura of the civil rights movement. In fact, the closest parallel is to the *separatist* ideologies of Malcolm X and the Black Panthers, both of whom have recently gained prestige. Many of the great leaders of the civil rights era, in contrast to black leaders today, understood the need to prepare blacks to enter a competitive world and to recognize and deal with their own "shortcomings."

In the twenty-first century most black spokesmen avoid individual and group self-examination. Instead the black community has developed an immunity to self-criticism that seriously impairs accountability and corrective measures. Black activists have become apologists. They defend black behavior as if it were religious dogma. As an example, the astounding incidence of single-parent families within the black community is viewed as a product of incarceration and poverty or rationalized as an acceptable norm. Destructive black-on-black crime is no longer discussed. The individual has thus become not only a member of a group but subservient to the group. Free will has become subordinate to the legacy of slavery, past injustice, and the current environment. But if historians are correct that even slaves never lost their agency, and if race-based slavery could not eliminate free will, why do blacks wish to surrender their individual self-determination?

In the age of political correctness, hypersensitivity to perceived disrespect has been met by protest rather than objectivity and reliance on the legal system. Separatism is encouraged under the guise of an exaggerated form of multiculturalism. This aberrant strain dominates campus curricula and politics. An appropriate multiethnic approach asks what we have in common; today's iteration dwells on what makes us different. The separatist implications lead to what Marcus Hanson in *The Immigrant in American History* would have pejoratively dubbed a disunited "patchwork nation." The governing political system for this unwieldy collection would necessarily be an autocracy, not a democratic republic.

Does the black community have a vision of the proper level of its integration into American society? Studies indicate that the performance of blacks in schools and the military improves in a racially mixed environment. But blacks cannot agree on how much integration is too much, and the courts now suggest confusing racial percentages—the discredited quota system—in disputed cases of ethnic apportionment. The muddle continues. The requisite concessions to assimilation, which is now labeled a loaded word, are made even more difficult to achieve.

If education is essential to economic advancement, the color-neutral middle-class behavioral norms that I discuss are critical to building a successful educational experience for black children. The results of fifty years of educational and social programs on all levels, from elementary school to graduate studies, need to be highlighted. Black cultural influence is part and parcel of this evaluation process, but the acceptance of Western standards is crucial. Without acknowledging the broader implications of behavioral norms, no policy proposal or specific blueprint for addressing educational inadequacies will be effective, and no alternative has been proffered.

Few of these issues affect those at the pinnacle of black society, where undeniably important and beneficial change has occurred. Opportunities never before possible are now available for those African Americans who have an enabling education. Unfortunately, upper- and middle-class black communities have not been able to influence the large black underclass.

The separatist tendency toward racial self-segregation will prevent large numbers of blacks from scaling the economic ladder. Efforts to establish race-based economic self-sufficiency have not brought broad prosperity to any group. Demonizing Western civilization also impedes assimilation and economic prosperity. The ever quotable Malcolm X inadvertently praised the Western economic model; in 1965 he advised a black church in Rochester, New York, that blacks were moving to England and France because of the "high standard of living" there. The same applies to the United States. Freedom and a high standard of living are products of Western civilization. It is now fully accessible to all who make concessions to assimilation in a nation that holds values more important than race.

Acknowledgments

One of the many fulfilling aspects of writing is the exchange of ideas with others over a long period of time. I have been duly blessed with the thoughts, experiences, insights, and criticisms of many people. It is the historian's pleasure to become acquainted with words and deeds of the past and to test their relevance today. Equally important is the attempt to grapple with current issues and policies. Any faults in the thesis/argument of this book are solely my own. The public forums provided by my previous books, *The Sun That Never Rose* and *Cotton and Race in the Making of America*, were invaluable in gauging the reactions of live audiences to the material's significance. Unvarnished feedback has always been central to my understanding of what was important and what was of interest.

The book's journey owes an enormous debt to my former college professor and friend, the late Robin W. Winks at Yale. His energy, devotion to students, intellectual bandwidth, and facility with comparative history were legendary. It is to him that I owe much of my interest in and respect for racial, economic, and comparative history. My education at Yale was further enhanced by Staughton Lynd's course in Southern history, his thoughtful approach to teaching, and his real-time experience as director of the education part of the Mississippi Freedom Summer of 1964.

The accomplished and experienced editor Ivan R. Dee was instrumental in clarifying my ideas in a book covering a wide swath of history. Although the opinions in the book are my own, his input challenged me to "think through" the most sensitive and complicated social issue in America—race. As such, it was and continues to be a distinct privilege and pleasure to work with him.

A list of those who have made contributions over the decades would be enormous. In addition to Americans, Japanese and Europeans have enriched my perspective. My brothers, Jerry and Richard Dattel, provide support, information, and valued advice. At our college's fiftieth reunion, my classmate Michael Dalby masterfully edited the essay that in part became the book and originated the title *Reckoning with Race*. Conversations with the journalist, author, and teacher Otis Sanford and attorney and civil rights leader Carver Randle Sr. are models for a respectful and vibrant interchange of ideas. I have learned much from Allan Hammons, whose creative and dedicated memorialization of Mississippi Delta cultural heritage for both civil rights and music is a model for others to follow. My publisher, Roger Kimball, has been a fount of knowledge, inspiration, and humor. He and his colleagues at Encounter Books have afforded me the freedom to tackle this evergreen topic with a deeply frank analysis. Their flexibility, guidance, and patience (read: missed deadlines) were truly appreciated.

I am grateful to Rowman & Littlefield for permission to adapt sections of my book *Cotton and Race in the Making of America*.

Most importantly, I thank my wife, Licia, a true partner in life and in work. Her trusted support as a wonderful editor and her generosity in spirit and in love have made the lengthy task of writing this book possible.

Chapter One

Racial Attitudes in the North, 1800–1865

White abolitionists "best love the colored man at a distance."
—SAMUEL R. WARD, BLACK ABOLITIONIST, 1840S

The great fact is now fully realized that the African race here is a foreign and feeble element...incapable of assimilation...a pitiful exotic unnecessarily transplanted into our fields, and which it is unprofitable to cultivate at the cost of the desolation of the native vineyard.
—WILLIAM H. SEWARD, ANTI-SLAVERY ADVOCATE,
NEW YORK GOVERNOR AND SENATOR, SECRETARY OF STATE,
LINCOLN'S "RIGHT HAND," 1860

[Free blacks] have no economy; and waste, of course, much of what they earn. They have little knowledge either of morals or religion. They are left, therefore, as miserable victims to sloth, prodigality, poverty, ignorance, and vice.
—TIMOTHY DWIGHT, PRESIDENT OF YALE UNIVERSITY, 1810

African Colonization is predicated on the principle that there is an utter aversion in the public mind, to an amalgamation and equalization of the two races; and that any attempt to press equalization is not only fruitless but injurious.
—WILBUR FISK, PRESIDENT OF WESLEYAN UNIVERSITY, 1835

[Blacks must] learn trades or starve...and learn not only to black boot but to make them as well.
—FREDERICK DOUGLASS, 1853

White foreigners who are, or may hereafter become residents of [Oregon]...shall enjoy the same rights in respect to the possession, enjoyment, and descent of property as native-born citizens.

No Negro, Chinaman, or Mulatto shall have the right of suffrage.

No free Negro, or Mulatto, not residing in this state at the time of the adoption of this constitution, shall come, reside, or be within this state, or hold any real estate, or make any contracts, or maintain any suit therein; an [sic] the Legislative Assembly shall provide by penal laws, for the removal, by public officers, of all such Negroes, and Mulattoes, and for their effectual exclusion from the state, and for the punishment of persons who shall bring them into the state, or employ, or harbor them.

—OREGON STATE CONSTITUTION, 1857
(THE BLACK EXCLUSION LAW WAS REPEALED IN 1926.)

The Antebellum Free States

The end of slavery in the United States did not change white attitudes toward blacks. From the early nineteenth century, when gradual emancipation began in earnest, the presence of free blacks had presented a problem for the antebellum North. From New England to California and Oregon, whites asked themselves, what shall we do with them? The overwhelming response was that blacks belonged nowhere but in the South.

Race-based slavery was a moral and economic anachronism. For the South, where slavery was implanted in large-scale staple agriculture, morality was an issue, but the advent of the tornado that was cotton gave slavery a vital economic role. In one decade, the 1830s, the South completely revised its rationalization of slavery to account for its economic benefits.

With the growth of slavery due solely to the expansion of profitable cotton agriculture came a gradual shift in the rhetoric of slavery. Nowhere is this more apparent than in the cotton and land boom of the pivotal 1830s. Nat Turner's slave rebellion in 1831 and the growing antislavery movement in the North exacerbated Southern racial fears. In 1831 the Mississippi lawyer and politician Seargent S. Prentiss expressed a commonly held belief: "That slavery is a great evil, there can be no doubt—and it is an unfortunate circumstance that it was ever introduced into this or any other country. At present, however, it is a necessary evil, and I do not think admits of a remedy." Just five years later the quotable Prentiss offered a diametrically opposed view in his recommendation to the Mississippi state legislature:

> Resolved, that the people of the state of Mississippi look upon the institution of domestic slavery…not as a curse, but as a blessing, as the legitimate condition of the African race, as authorized both by the laws of God and the dictates of reason and humanity.…We will allow no present change, or hope of future alteration in this manner.

From a "great" and "necessary" evil to a "blessing" in five years to justify an economic force.

The white North, without the ability to cultivate cotton, had no such economic imperative for slavery, but it nonetheless had to grapple with the existence of a small free-black population in its midst. While Americans have often conflated anti-slavery attitudes with pro-black sentiments, in fact, white Northerners were anti-slavery and also predominantly anti-black. In every Northern state the pattern of responses to free blacks was similar. There was no thought of creating a biracial society based on freedom and equality. White Northerners wanted blacks shipped overseas to Africa, the Caribbean, or Central America via colonization societies or sent to segregated regions within America or placed in designated all-black states or forced into physically separate communities, the forerunners of the modern urban racial ghettos. Above all, after emancipation they wanted blacks contained in the South.

White America's hypocrisy and its true racial attitudes were fully on display in the North. There, racial animosity was rife, and an all-consuming fear of black migration was well entrenched. Northern bigotry played a vital role in curtailing the physical and economic mobility of blacks. Trapped in the South, they were needed as cotton-field laborers, first as slaves, then as free blacks, for with emancipation the economic imperatives of cotton did not go away. The consequence was a separate community of free blacks, first induced by white Northerners, then adopted by the white South after Emancipation, then reinforced by blacks during the long period of compulsory exclusion. Historians generally ignore the North's racial containment policy designed to keep blacks in the South. The policy worked, for on the eve of World War I 90 percent of all blacks in America lived in the South. Only another economic force—a labor shortage in the North—toppled the containment policy.

Black American identity was put to the test early in the North, where slavery was being eliminated by gradual emancipation. The living and social conditions of the small number of free blacks in the antebellum North is well worth reviewing, beginning in the New England and Middle Atlantic states.

Separatism asserted itself early on. As a twenty-six-year-old, Richard Allen, a former slave turned gifted Methodist orator, preached to a small number of blacks in 1786 at St. George's Church in Philadelphia. The young leader was allowed to perform his service at 5 a.m., before the white service. At a later date, either 1787 or 1792, Allen and his fellow black worshipers were told to vacate the white section of St. George's Church. Allen's black colleague, the Reverend Absalom Jones, in a prayer position on his knees, was pulled up by a white trustee. "You must get up; you must not kneel here," the trustee said. The black congregants had been assigned instead to a newly built, racially segregated balcony. Thus provoked, blacks left the church, never to return. "An increase in the black communicants," as W. E. B. Du Bois later wrote, had alarmed the white church and prompted racial segregation. Allen and others would found a racially separate religious entity, the African American Church (Bethel), and a mutual aid society, the Free African Society of Philadelphia. The white North would not be a promised land for free blacks.

In a pattern that would be repeated throughout American history, an increase, or anticipated increase, in the number of blacks in a particular community invariably provoked a policy of forced separation. Historians rationalize the establishment of separate black institutions by Allen and others as evidence of black resilience and ingenuity, but in doing so they ignore the devastating long-term consequences of racial segregation.

Philadelphia, like other Northern cities before the Civil War, offers a glimpse of the "squalid" conditions of most free blacks in the North. In 1862 the English visitor Edward Dicey provided this account of the city:

Everywhere and at all seasons the colored people form a separate community.... As a rule, the blacks you meet in the Free States are shabbily, if not squalidly, dressed; and as far as I could learn, the instances of black men having made money by trade in the North are few in number.... In every Northern city, the poorest, the most thriftless, and perhaps the most troublesome part of the population are free negroes.

"There is...[no] city," wrote Frederick Douglass, the black abolitionist and orator, "in which prejudice against color is more rampant than in Philadelphia." Such was the reality in the "City of Brotherly Love."

By the time Philadelphia's most famous citizen, Benjamin Franklin, was a delegate to the Constitutional Convention in 1787, he had become an abolitionist. Earlier he had owned slaves for thirty years; in 1770 he had lobbied the English government for approval of the state of Georgia's slave codes; in 1779 he had contacted the French police to help recapture Abbe, a female slave owned by John Jay, another of his compatriots living in France. (Jay was a founding member of New York's abolition society when he still owned slaves.) The French police found Abbe and imprisoned her until she "repented her ingratitude." Franklin had also asked the French government to allow his relative, John Williams Jr., to keep a slave in France after the French had abolished slavery.

More important for our purposes, Franklin's ideas for the "improvement" of free blacks were harsh. In the fall of 1789 he issued a formal plan for a committee of Abolition Society members to oversee emancipated blacks. Because he feared a mass of free slaves unleashed on American society, he also recommended that a branch of our "national police...supervise emancipated slaves." A "committee of inspection" would "superintend the morals, general conduct, and ordinary situation of Free Negroes." A "committee of education" was formed to "superintend the children of Free Blacks," who would be taught "moral and religious principles." A "committee of employ" would find "constant employment for those Free Negroes who are able to work, as the want of this would occasion poverty, idleness, and many vicious habits." The jobs contemplated would "require little skill." Apprehensive white abolitionists like Franklin wanted comprehensive white regulation of the lives of blacks after emancipation.

Examples of white Northern racial animosity abound, often with a modern resonance. In the 1790s, residents of New Haven, Connecticut, and Salem, Massachusetts, argued that the movement of blacks to white neighborhoods precipitated a 20 to 50 percent decline in property values. Citizens of South Boston bragged in 1847 that "not a single colored family" resided in the neighborhood. Abolitionist Boston had its segregated "Nigger Hill" when only 1.3 percent of the population was black. Groping for a positive interpretation of this situation, black historians cite examples of Boston blacks and whites living "adjacent to one another." But, in fact, Boston greeted blacks with residential segregation; separate and inferior schools; separate churches, lecture halls, and places of entertainment; and, according to the historian James Horton, "condescension in polite circles." Blacks "held the worst jobs at the lowest pay." Even the Irish, according to Frederick Douglass, were able to push blacks out of their normal occupations. The two decades before the Civil War were a time of economic crisis for Boston's blacks. As the white population doubled from 84,400 to 177,800, the black population held stagnant at 2,261 (1.3 percent).

Historians heap praise on the Massachusetts legislature for banning racial segregation in schools in 1855. The act affected all of fifty children. (When time came for real integration via busing in the 1960s, Boston's resistance, led by Louise Day Hicks, was legendary.) In 1860 only thirty thousand black children out of an American black school population of eighty-six thousand in the free North attended any form of school. A small number attended integrated schools. In contrast, 6.3 million (two-thirds) of white children were enrolled in school.

The absolute numbers of black people residing in a Northern city or state in the antebellum years are critical to understanding racial separation and animosity. They reinforce the distinction made by the white North in opposing slavery but despising the presence of blacks. Blacks constituted a mere 2 percent of the North's antebellum population, and 94 percent of them were not allowed to vote, even with such minuscule numbers. That proportion was preferred even in Boston, the hotbed of abolition and twentieth-century liberal politics. In 1930 the black population in the entire state of Massachusetts was 1.3 percent out of a total of four million. By contrast, as David Cohn has noted, the cotton-dominated Bolivar County, in the Mississippi Delta, alone had the same number of blacks—fifty-two thousand. A hospitable North would have drained the South's labor force after the Civil War.

Connecticut provides a vivid portrait of Northern disdain for free blacks. Slavery was hardly an economic bonanza in Connecticut and was simply not profitable enough to expand. In 1784 the state ended race-based slavery via legislation for gradual emancipation, by which all slaves born after 1784 would be freed at age twenty-five; females were to be freed at age twenty-one. In 1775 the state had had more than 5,100 black slaves, about 3 percent of the population. In 1800, in a population of 451,520, only 8,627 (1.9 percent) were black.

Supposedly, slavery in New England was benign. Still, an article in the *Connecticut Journal* in 1774 exhibited widespread notions of black inferiority. The writer categorized "the Negroes of Africa" as animals to be ruled by white descendants of the biblical Adam.

> God formed [blacks]...in common with horses, oxen, dogs, &c. for the white people alone to be used by them either for pleasure or to labour with other beasts in the culture of tobacco, indigo, rice, and sugar. [This was before the advent of cotton production.]

Connecticut has left an extraordinary record of white attitudes toward free blacks in the antebellum North. In 1800 the Connecticut Academy of Arts and Sciences conducted a survey of more than one hundred Connecticut towns. The major sponsors were Timothy Dwight, the president of Yale College, and Noah Webster. The survey consisted of thirty-two "articles," of which Number 26 dealt with race. Specifically, it wanted to know if a black person born enslaved was different than one born free:

> Free blacks; their number, vices and modes of life, their industry and success in acquiring property; whether those born free are more ingenious and virtuous, than those who were emancipated after arriving to adult years.

The inquiry embodied the optimistic viewpoint that blacks had been degraded by slavery and, once freed, would undergo a transition to "proper" morality and productive citizenship. In Connecticut a brief period between gradual emancipation and the first decades of the nineteenth century evidenced white idealism and a hope that the effects of slavery could be whitewashed from black character. A thorough apprenticeship, similar to Benjamin Franklin's proposal for "improvement," with white tutelage and charity, was envisioned. The goal was the acceptance of white Christian norms. If this transition could not work in Connecticut, what would be the fate of blacks in the rest of America?

The Connecticut town responses were devastating, with a damaging assessment of blacks as lazy and immoral. No distinction was drawn between the character of emancipated blacks and that of freeborn blacks. In all, blacks were recognized in early-nineteenth-century Connecticut as an intractable problem.

Timothy Dwight, the well-educated Congregationalist minister, wrote the report from New Haven in 1811. In one of his own sermons in 1810, Dwight was highly critical of New Haven blacks:

> [T]hese people…are, generally, neither able, nor inclined to make their freedom a blessing unto themselves. When they first became free, they are turned out into the world, in circumstances, fitted to make them nuisances to society. They have not property; nor any skill to acquire it. Nor have they…generally any industry.…They have no economy; and waste, of course, much of what they earn. They have little knowledge either of morals or religion. They are therefore victims to sloth, prodigality, poverty, ignorance, and vice.

In the report of the Connecticut towns survey, Dwight expanded on the destructive behavioral characteristics of blacks.

> Their vices…are usually intended by the phrase "low vice." Uneducated to principals of morality, or to habits of industry…they labor only to gratify gross and vulgar appetites. Accordingly, many of them are thieves, liars, profane drunkards, Sabbath-breakers, quarrelsome idle.…Their ruling passion seems very generally to be…fashionable.

The conservative scholar Thomas Sowell has blamed white Southerners for such destructive traits in blacks. The characteristics— "aversion to work," "neglect of education," "drunkenness," "improvidence," "proneness to violence," love "of fine clothes and good living...more than...a bank account," and "low standards of ability, ambition, and morals"—sound very much like those of early-nineteenth-century Connecticut; yet the erudite Sowell finds that Southern blacks, whom he calls "black rednecks," inherited these habits from white Southern rednecks. There were no white Southern rednecks in Connecticut in 1800 to influence blacks.

In his report, Dwight then describes the white tutelage that will be necessary to bring blacks properly into white society. Two racially separate schools were set up for black children, one of which was funded by charity. For Dwight, education was the only "rational hope of a reformation" for blacks.

But the idea of a black transition to freedom was essentially abandoned by Connecticut. By 1818 the state constitution had disfranchised its tiny black population. By 1820 Connecticut joined the American Colonization Society (ACS), which sought to encourage blacks to leave America for Africa. Short of deportation, this was the ultimate form of exclusion. Few recall that Harriet Beecher Stowe gave a nod to colonization when she sent the heroes and heroines of *Uncle Tom's Cabin* as missionaries to Liberia. The powerful New Haven Congregationalist minister Leonard Bacon in 1823 referred to free blacks as "aliens and outcasts" who should "seek a home on the...shores of Africa." White tutelage had vanished; assimilation was impossible. "You cannot bleach him," wrote Bacon using the color metaphor, "into the enjoyment of freedom."

Connecticut never evolved toward racial tolerance. With a tiny black population, in 1857 the state reaffirmed its disfranchisement of blacks when 76 percent of whites voted against allowing the vote to its 1.9 percent black population. Again, after the Civil War Connecticut voted against ratification of the Fifteenth Amendment to enfranchise blacks.

At the root of this support for colonization and disfranchisement, as elsewhere in the North, was a fear of black migration from the South and an endorsement of separatism. Further evidence may be seen in the Reverend Simeon S. Jocelyn's 1831 proposal that "a Collegiate school [for teaching] a manual labor system" for blacks be established in New Haven. In the years before the Civil War most Northern blacks lived in poverty, typically working as domestic servants or manual laborers. Successful black barbers were an exception.

Jocelyn's school was designed to help blacks "cultivate habits of industry." The clergyman had impeccable credentials as a friend of blacks: he had helped found the anti-slavery society in New Haven, was pastor of New Haven's Temple Church, which had a black congregation, and was actively involved in charities for blacks. Nevertheless, his was a voice in the wilderness. Despite the town's anti-slavery trappings, its citizens had voted heavily against black suffrage in 1857. In a hastily convened town council meeting, the "air ran hot and foul" as New Haven condemned Reverend Jocelyn's proposed school on racial grounds. A resolution passed by the mayor, aldermen, and the Common Council was clear:

> Yale College, the institutions for the education of females, and the other schools [in New Haven]...are important...and the establishment of a College in the same place to educate the Colored population is incompatible with their prosperity, if not the existence of the present institutions of learning, and will be destructive of the best interests of the city....We will resist the establishment of the proposed College in this place by every lawful means.

The proposal died, and thousands of free blacks over the years lost an educational opportunity. Yale certainly had a hand in this. New Haven, like every Northern city, sought to prevent blacks from moving there.

The fear of black migration also derailed a black school founded in Canterbury, Connecticut. The well-documented efforts of Prudence Crandall to educate young black girls in 1831 met with staunch resistance by Canterbury citizens. Connecticut had instituted "black laws" in 1833 to prevent out-of-state blacks from coming into the state for an education. Crandall was accused of violating these laws and was acquitted on a technicality. Afterward her school was the target of vandalism and attempted arson when the citizens of Canterbury descended on the school and destroyed all its windows. The entire episode was brought about because twenty young African American girls were attending Crandall's school. Eventually she abandoned Connecticut for Illinois, an even worse environment of racial intolerance.

Connecticut claims as a daughter Harriet Beecher Stowe, the author of *Uncle Tom's Cabin,* whose emotional appeal was a catalyst for the anti-slavery movement and the Civil War. Hartford boasts the Harriet

Beecher Stowe house, a museum that was once the home of the famous author. Stowe captured the horrors of slavery in her monumental novel that appeared in 1852. Despite her difficulty in finding a publisher, copies of the book literally flew off the press: ten thousand copies in the first week, three hundred thousand in the first year. The book spawned theater productions and other slave stories as its monetary success became widely known.

Stowe's enlightenment had limits. We know what she thought about slavery, but what was her attitude toward free blacks? The reader of *Uncle Tom's Cabin* may easily overlook the book's denouement, the fate of its heroes and heroines—Stowe sent them to Liberia. She deliberately followed the colonization scheme and fictionally deported them to Africa as missionaries. She speaks through George Harris, the former slave. After gaining his freedom, he articulates his future plans:

> I might mingle in the circle of whites, in [America], my shade of color is so slight, and that of my wife and family scarce perceptible....But to tell you the truth, I have no wish to....I have no wish to pass for an American, or to identify myself with them....
>
> We have more than the rights of common men;—we have claim of an injured race for reparation. But, then, I do not want it; I want a country, a nation, of my own.
>
> As a Christian patriot, as a teacher of Christianity, I go to my country,—glorious Africa. I go to Liberia, not as to an Elysium of romance, but as a field of work.

This is a staggering and prescient statement by the author of the most powerful anti-slavery tract ever written in America. Harriet Beecher Stowe sent her characters George, Eliza, and their family and Topsy to Liberia as missionaries to "civilize and proselytize." Here, consciously or subconsciously, was an argument that blacks needed to be separate. It is also the first mention of reparations for the injustice and harm done by slavery, a demand that continues even today. Notably, the white Stowe rejected reparations, as has white America.

In response to Stowe's colonization solution, the black leader Frederick Douglass was indignant. "The truth is, dear Madam, we are *here*, & we are likely to remain." The colonization attempts championed by Abraham Lincoln, by many abolitionists, and by white Southerners are often dismissed as impractical. Indeed, African Americans, despite the harsh reality of the lives of free blacks, thought of themselves as Americans: "Why should we leave this land?" the Reverend Jehiel C. Beman asked in 1835. "Truly this is our home, here let us live and here let us die." When encouraged by an abolitionist in 1853 to consider leaving America through the colonization effort, an Ohio black was adamant: "I would die first, before I would leave the land of my birth."

In 1853 Harriet Beecher Stowe, with her newly minted wealth, rejected Frederick Douglass's proposal for a vocational school for blacks in New Haven, Connecticut. Douglass expressed his "great disappointment" at her response, which had put him in "an awkward position before the colored people." Stowe explained her refusal in a letter to the abolitionist Wendell Phillips:

> Of all the vague unbased fabrics of a vision this floating idea of a colored industrial school is the most illusive. If [black people] want one why don't they have one—many men among the colored people are richer than I am & better able to help such an object.—Will they ever learn to walk?

Stowe thought that blacks should be responsible for their own progress.

After the Civil War, Stowe provided $10,000 for her son Frederick and two of his Connecticut army friends to rent a cotton plantation in Florida, near the St. John's River. She stayed with him in 1866 and described the work ethic of emancipated blacks in her book *Palmetto Leaves*: "As a class they are more obedient, better natured, more joyous, and easily satisfied [than whites]." At the time, conventional white (and some black) American opinion held that blacks were better suited than whites to manual labor in hot climates. Stowe agreed. Blacks seemed at home in the cotton fields:

> The thermometer, for these three days past, has risen over ninety every day. No white man that we know of dares stay in the fields later than ten o'clock.... Yet, the black laborers whom we leave in the field pursue their toil, if anything more actively, more cheerfully, than during the

cooler months. The sun awakes all their vigor and all their boundless jolly....A gang of negroes, great brawny, muscular fellows, seemed to make a perfect frolic of this job which, under such a sun, would have threatened sunstroke to any white man.

For Stowe, education during the transition from slavery to freedom resembled the much-criticized practical philosophy later espoused by Booker T. Washington. Here is the education she envisioned for black children:

The teaching in the common schools ought to be largely industrial, and do what it can to prepare the children to get a living by doing something well. Practical sewing, cutting and fitting, for girls, and the general principles of agriculture for boys, might be taught with advantage.

Unfortunately for Stowe, cotton was easier for her to write about than to grow. The army worm, an insect capable of devastating a cotton field, intervened. Her brave Union captains who had won many military battles were "defeated and routed" over a period of just two days. Only two bales of cotton were harvested from her farm, and she lost her entire $10,000 investment. She returned chastened to the North. Her commitment to black uplift in the South dissipated once there was no easy "golden fortune" in the cotton fields.

Northerners had no use for fiction that portrayed the true lives of blacks in the North. The first novel written in English by an African American was *Our Nig; or, Sketches from the Life of a Free Black* (1859). The author, a black woman named Harriet Wilson, of New Hampshire and Massachusetts, related the brutality and poverty of daily existence for Frado, the black heroine, at the hands of her white custodians. Wilson shows that "slavery's shadows fall" even in Massachusetts. At the beginning of her story, she apologizes for embarrassing her "anti-slavery friends" by revealing the brute racial hatred of free blacks in the North. The six-year-old Frado is abandoned by her mother on the doorsteps of a white family, the Belmonts. During her period of indenture she is beaten repeatedly: at one point Mrs. Belmont "inflicted a blow which lay the tottering ... [Frado] prostrate on the floor ... [and then] snatching a towel, stuffed the mouth of the sufferer, and beat her cruelly." Daily routines included Mrs. Belmont's "spicing the toil with words that burn and frequent blows on [Frado's] head." After running away, Frado is "maltreated by professed abolitionists, who didn't want slaves at the South, nor niggers in their own houses, ... to lodge one; to eat with one; to admit one through the front door; to sit next to one; awful!"

Harriet Wilson's novel lay in obscurity until 1983, a testament to the lack of interest in descriptions of the lives of free blacks in the North. Slavery would sell books, but the sordid condition of free blacks was largely ignored.

To further illustrate the North's distinction between slaves and blacks, consider the case of William Henry Seward, the scruffy but sociable senator and former governor of New York. On May 18, 1860, Seward received 172 votes on the first ballot of the Republican National Convention in Chicago; Abraham Lincoln, the eventual nominee, received only 102 votes. Seward had been the favored candidate from the most populous state in the Union. The awkward Illinois lawyer would go on to win the Republican nomination and then the presidential election with only 40 percent of the popular vote. In Lincoln's administration these two ambitious competitors who earlier had barely known each other would develop a close working relationship. Seward, the most powerful New York politician of the nineteenth century, became Lincoln's secretary of state, his "Right Hand," his "Indispensable Man."

Seward and Lincoln had distinctly different backgrounds. Seward grew up in an affluent family in the small southern New York town of Florida. His father, Henry Seward, was an enormously prosperous farmer, land speculator, and well-connected politician who left an estate worth millions in today's dollars. Henry's access to power allowed him a three-hour visit in 1831 with former president John Quincy Adams. The precocious son, William Henry, was a superb student, and after graduation from Union College and the study of law he traveled to Europe with his father, attending debates in the House of Commons, walking in the

Swiss Alps, and speaking with the aging Lafayette in Paris. By then the son's vision for America was fully formed: "[T]he fearful responsibility of the American people to the people of the nations of the earth, [is] to carry successfully through the experiment which ... is to prove that men are capable of self-government."

Formally educated, cosmopolitan, and well-connected, Seward contrasted sharply with the homespun, self-taught, crafty, pragmatic, opportunistic lawyer from Illinois. The man who wrote and delivered some of America's most inspiring prose had no formal education and used no focus group. Perhaps one element of Lincoln's background needs further comment: he was a corporate lawyer who represented the Illinois Central Railroad on various matters, including taxes.

Seward is best remembered for his consistent anti-slavery position and his realism. The anti-slavery stance is sharply revealed in his famous "higher law" speech of 1850, in which he appealed to "a higher law than the Constitution" in his condemnation of slavery. Seward's "higher law" was handed down by "the Creator of the Universe." Seward the realist foresaw an "irrepressible conflict," a "collision" over slavery: "[T]he United States, must and will ... become either entirely slave-holding or entirely a free-labor nation" (1858). There was no equivocation about his position on slavery.

Seward's attitude toward blacks was also clear. He saw slavery as the paramount issue—it must be abolished for the country to survive; but free blacks were of little concern. Like most other anti-slavery politicians, Seward held blacks, either free or enslaved, in low esteem. In 1860 he spoke of black inferiority and the impossibility of black equality.

> The great fact is now fully realized that the African race here is a foreign and feeble element...incapable of assimilation...a pitiful exotic unnecessarily transplanted into our fields, and which it is unprofitable to cultivate at the cost of the desolation of the native vineyard.

This is a damning statement from the man who was clearer in his attack on slavery than even Abraham Lincoln.

"The North has nothing to do with the negroes," Seward said in conversation in 1866. "I have no more concern for them than I have for the Hottentots. They are God's poor, they always have been and always will be so everywhere." These remarks, published in 1888, are perfectly consistent with Seward's earlier statements. As much as white Americans would like their heroes to be racially enlightened by twenty-first-century standards, they must face the truth of pervasive racial animosity in the North as well as the South.

Seward strongly adhered to the plan (Lincoln's and then Andrew Johnson's) for a swift and lenient integration of the Confederate states into the reconstructed Union. He believed the states, not the federal government, should determine regulations for black suffrage. In a cabinet meeting in 1865 he voted against black enfranchisement. He also advocated vetoing the bill that would have renewed and strengthened the Freedman's Bureau, the agency set up to oversee the welfare of freed slaves. In April 1866 Seward reiterated his views on a prompt reconciliation without concern for blacks, and advocated no federal intervention on their behalf.

> I am ready to leave the interests of the most intelligent white man to the guardianship of his state, and where I leave the interests of the white I am willing to trust the civil rights of the black. The South must take care of its own negroes as the North does.... The North must get over the notion of interference with the affairs of the South.... The South longs to come home.

Seward supported black suffrage in New York State, where "their numbers were negligible," but in 1867 he opposed a bill that enfranchised blacks in the city of Washington because of the size of the potential black vote. Only in time, he thought, would black enfranchisement be appropriate. He also thought that the civil rights legislation of 1866 was "unconstitutional on technical grounds."

Today historians may concentrate on the racial implications of Reconstruction, but Seward and many of his contemporaries were consumed with the grand vision of international trade. According to Seward, commerce was "the chief agent of... advancement in civilization and enlargement of empire." Thus despite his impeccable anti-slavery credentials, he declared that if necessary he would vote to admit California to the United States, "even if she had come as a slave state." In the scheme of economic expansion, the preponderance of free blacks was assigned to their oppressive role of cotton laborers, with highly limited freedom and mobility.

A rather large and imposing statue of William Henry Seward rises on the southwest corner of Madison Park in New York City. By twenty-first-century norms of political correctness, Seward was distinctly anti-black and squandered an opportunity to assist free blacks. His words and actions clearly illustrate the distinction between Northern anti-slavery sentiment and anti-black attitudes.

Seward's New York was decidedly anti-black. In 1790 the total black population of the state, both free and enslaved, was 6.27 percent of the total. A law providing for gradual emancipation intervened in 1799, and on the eve of the Civil War, in 1860, the black population of New York was 1.9 percent—representing an explosive growth in the white population and the numbers of slaves sold to the South. In 1821 New York eliminated a property requirement for white voters while increasing the suffrage qualification fee for blacks from $100 to a prohibitive $250. Thus in 1861 only three hundred blacks in New York City could vote. The state's black voting restrictions were upheld in 1846 by a vote of 224,336 to 85,406. In state constitutional conventions of 1860 and 1869, a majority again defeated black enfranchisement by requiring a property value. In each case black inferiority became a talking point, and delegates overwhelmingly voted against black enfranchisement even with the state's minuscule black population. New York voted against the Fifteenth Amendment, too. As ever, Northerners feared a black migration north.

The *New York Times*, a staunch supporter of Lincoln, advocated the reform of slavery rather than abolition. "We have admitted," the *Times* argued on January 22, 1861, "the impossibility and the folly of immediate abolition of Slavery, [and] pointed out the ruin certain to flow from the sudden release of four millions of ignorant slaves from the dependence and control of masters...." The great need of the South was a modification and amelioration of her system of slavery, which would keep blacks in the region's cotton fields.

As white immigrants poured into New York during the eighteenth century, skilled black laborers were displaced and relegated to menial positions. Free blacks were left with jobs that whites did not want. Some blacks remained as sailors, but most became domestics in private homes, hotels, and boarding houses or worked as chimney sweeps, washerwomen, and "tubmen" (cleaners of privies). The gritty job of crawling down a chimney to remove soot was performed by black children between the ages of four and ten. These jobs, rather than stepping-stones to advancement, were forced steps backward.

Examples of race-based economic conflict illustrate the fragility of the blacks' status. The historian Edgar McManus cited the former slave Austin Stewart's 1857 description of their wretched plight:

> Everywhere Negroes were shunned, cut off from free society, and excluded from most of the skilled occupations. Life held no promise for the Negro, for he was caught in a vise designed to crush, and degrade him.... Great numbers of Negroes sank to the level of pariahs condemned to a bitter existence on the fringe of free society.... The Negroes were in a very real sense a population in quarantine, trapped in a system of racial bondage.

In 1859 the historian Thomas De Voe lamented the plight of New York's black population. Freedom had boundaries, he observed, for blacks were "poor, squalid, dirty, half-dressed, ill-fed and –bred, some...strong with an inclination to be thievish." In fact, blacks were convicted of crimes at a rate three and a half times that of whites. De Voe blamed black poverty on the severe limits imposed by whites. In 1840 the New York State Convention of Colored Citizens described their situation:

> We find ourselves crippled and crushed in soul and ability.... We were translated into the partial enjoyment and limited possessions of freedom.... The prejudice against us in the community has been more potent than the dictates of Christian equality.

Examples of successful black entrepreneurs in the North are scarce. In Philadelphia, James Forten was a well-known sailmaker who in 1929 employed forty workers, black and white. Stephen Smith, a lumber merchant in Philadelphia, had revenues of $100,000 in the 1850s. Among the amazing stories of black business enterprise, a Virginia slave, Robert

Gordon, earned enough money to purchase his freedom by selling a coal by-product, slack, from a coal yard. He then moved to Cincinnati, where he continued building his business and invested in real estate. These and similar stories are inspiring but isolated instances in a prosperous world that was largely closed to antebellum black Northerners.

Despite overwhelmingly anti-black attitudes, white charity on behalf of the black community is a recurring theme in American history. Inspired by humanitarian concerns, such benevolence was so often strictly paternalistic that it led black groups to seek their own destiny. Whites hoped to create an uplifting process by which blacks would be "civilized" and accept Western norms, chiefly in the areas of education, jobs, and morality. One such endeavor, the racially separate African Free Schools, was founded in 1785 by the New York Manumission Society. Its members were heavily involved in the New York City Colonization Society, which began in 1817 and was followed in 1829 by the state organization. Both organizations encouraged sending blacks to Liberia. The Manumission Society also recommended Texas for black colonization because it was a less expensive solution than Liberia and because it was closest to "those states which are overcharged with the descendants of Africa." For white Northerners, black freedom hopefully meant a black exodus.

Yet blacks for the most part rejected colonization. The frustrated black minister Henry Highland Garnet did encourage emigration to the West Indies and Africa in 1858, when he organized the African Civilization Society. In a symbolic but futile gesture, Garnet also promoted the Free Produce movement, which advocated a boycott of slave-produced sugar and cotton.

By the 1830s white New Yorkers had determined that blacks could not be assimilated. In 1839 a group of white women set up the Colored Orphanage Asylum, a racially segregated institution located between Forty-Third and Forty-Fourth Streets along Fifth Avenue. Most of the city's upper-class white women were involved with the colonization society to encourage black emigration to Africa. The Hopper Home, a halfway house for Irish women, was established by the Women's Prison Association in 1854, but it excluded African American women. The Society for the Relief of Worthy, Aged, Indigent Colored Persons began in 1843 as a distinctly segregated entity. In addition, the Colored Home of the City of New York had been established to care for destitute blacks. In all, blacks, with a tiny portion of the city's population, accounted for 20 percent of the people on relief. The Colored Home's 1851 annual report, called "Broken Gloom," was explicitly pessimistic. "For the person of color, no future dawns with brightening ray," the document read, "no star gild his horizon: his doom, if he remains in this his native land, is moral, intellectual and civil inferiority."

Along with economic degradation, blacks in New York also had to contend with violence. White and black abolitionists in New York City were attacked in July 1834. During the Civil War, anti-black sentiment in New York erupted into the most violent civil disturbance in American history to that time. The stage was set in the spring of 1863 as the war was going poorly for the North. The well-chronicled Draft Riots began on July 12. New York's working-class whites, protesting the military draft, rampaged through the city's streets, lynching innocent blacks, roughing up white businessmen, and burning the Colored Orphanage Asylum. At least a hundred people were killed and a thousand wounded in the melee. New York was fortunate in that six thousand Union soldiers returned from victory at Gettysburg on July 4 to help quell the insurrection that had reduced the city to chaos. This was a race riot; white people were killing black people. The label "Draft Riots" should at least be changed to Draft Race Riots.

Through laws and customs, whites in New York pushed the black population into a separate, subordinate society, unfit to enter the assimilation process. Racial segregation was observed in virtually every aspect of life except in working-class taverns. By the opening of the Civil War, housing in New York City was segregated, with 86 percent of New York's African Americans living below Fourteenth Street; fully 75 percent of the city's streets were exclusively white. New York City did not have to wait for a large black migration to put residential segregation in place. When Seneca Village, the only area of significant black land ownership, was taken over by the city in 1857, its residents were poorly compensated and were unable to purchase land elsewhere.

Whites were particularly concerned about amalgamation, interracial sex, and interracial marriage. Lydia Maria Child, a prominent abolitionist, made it clear that she did not wish to violate the "distinctions of society by forcing the rude illiterate [blacks] into the presence of the learned and refined [whites]."

In the mid-nineteenth century, America was bursting at its boundaries, surging across a continent. Cotton was dragging race-based slavery in its westward wake. Slave expansion in the West had its limits because slavery spread only where climate and soil permitted. Nonetheless the free states—those in the North that had abolished slavery—wanted slavery's extension prohibited. The political stakes were high, for the new states carved from the Louisiana Purchase of 1803 were reservoirs of power. The fight over the extension of slavery to the Western territories reached a climax with the presidential election of Abraham Lincoln, who clearly opposed the spread of the peculiar institution.

In portraying westward expansion, history often omits the distinction between black slaves and free blacks. While opposing the extension of slavery, white anti-slavery Northerners were also vehemently anti-black. This attitude toward race would, after emancipation, doom blacks to bondage in cotton production in the South. It was illustrated in the misunderstood Wilmot Proviso of 1846. A little-known Democratic congressman from Pennsylvania, David Wilmot, forever secured his place in American history by introducing an amendment to a $2 million appropriations bill for the Mexican War:

> Provided, that, as an express and fundamental condition of the acquisition of any territory from Mexico...neither slavery nor involuntary servitude shall ever exist in any part of said territory, except for crime...

Americans were an acquisitive lot. Wilmot favored the annexation of Texas, supported the Mexican War, and wanted to buy New Mexico and California. His amendment passed by nineteen votes in the House but was defeated in the Southern-dominated Senate. Although the measure was thereby blocked, it fed the growing controversy over slavery, and its underlying principle helped bring about the formation of the Republican Party in 1854. For Wilmot, the issue was slavery but also race.

> When territory presents itself for annexation where slavery is already established, I stand ready to take it, if national considerations require it, as they did in the case of Texas; I will not seek to change its institutions. I make not war upon the South nor upon slavery in the South. I

will not first ask the abolition of slavery. I have no squeamish sensitivity upon the subject of slavery, nor morbid sympathy for the slave. I plead the cause of the rights of white freemen. I would preserve for free white labor a fair country, a rich inheritance, where the sons of toil, of my own race and own color, can live without the disgrace which the negro slavery brings upon free labor.

Wilmot was not speaking in abstract terms about a technical economic classification of labor, either slave or free. He was voicing brute racial hatred. "By God, sir," he exclaimed, "men born and nursed of white women are not going to be ruled by men who were brought up on the milk of some damn negro wench!" After he switched to the Republican Party and ran for governor of Pennsylvania in 1857, he made it clear that "It is not true that the defenders of the rights of free labor seek the elevation of the black race to an equality with the white. . . . " Wilmot wanted blacks, slave or free, excluded from the annexed territories. In 1857 Oregon was admitted to the Union as a state, having incorporated the Wilmot Proviso's slave prohibition. The white South was extremely upset about the application of the proviso. Oregon also added a black exclusion law to its constitution at a time when the state's black population was 128 people in a total population of 52,337:

No free Negro, or Mulatto, not residing in this state at the time of the adoption of this constitution, shall come, reside, or be within this state, or hold any real estate, or make any contracts, or maintain any suit therein; an [sic] the Legislative Assembly shall provide by penal laws, for the removal, by public officers, of all such Negroes, and Mulattoes, and for their effectual exclusion from the state, and for the punishment of persons who shall bring them into the state, or employ, or harbor them.

The law passed by an eight-to-one majority, greater than the margin to prohibit slavery. The Oregon black exclusion law was not expunged until 1926.

The American West required an enormous flow of new labor but did not want black labor. In a period when millions of white European immigrants were being enticed to come to America and settle in the

West, black labor was specifically excluded. Wilmot's racial antipathy was historically based in the North and would reverberate through the Civil War and beyond, with dire consequences for African Americans.

―――――――――

Lincoln's Illinois and all the states of the Northwest Territory, now the Midwest, followed their Eastern counterparts in disdaining the presence of free blacks. History texts and courses invariably mention that slavery was prohibited by law in the Northwest Territory in 1787. Slavery could not be established in the states of Illinois, Indiana, Ohio, Michigan, Wisconsin, and Minnesota that would be carved out of the territory. But accounts generally fail to mention that the white populations of these states, once admitted to the Union, invariably legislated against blacks. "Exclusion laws" prevented free blacks from even moving there. The new states, like those of the colonial North, according to Eugene Berwanger, "dreaded the thought of a biracial society," slave or free. The legal response to the imagined threat of a black invasion was drastic: exclusionary residence laws, racially segregated schools, denial of suffrage, prohibitions against miscegenation, the banning of blacks from jury service or from testifying against whites, denial of poor relief, flogging, and exclusion from the militia. The North gave the South a blueprint for racial control after emancipation.

Illinois was typical in its fear of a black invasion after emancipation. In 1830 the state had 2,486 blacks (1.6 percent of the population); by 1860 there were 7,698 (0.4 percent of the population). Nevertheless black laws were quickly enacted. In 1813 Illinois territorial laws provided that justices of the peace force every "incoming free black or mulatto" to exit. If a free black or mulatto did not leave, thirty-nine lashes were to be administered every fifteen days while the person was resident. Free blacks had to register with the local court and purchase documents attesting to their freedom.

In 1818, when Illinois was admitted to the Union, anti-slavery literature touted the state's prohibition of slavery in order to avoid the inheritance of free blacks through manumission. In 1823 Governor Edward Coles, a staunch anti-slavery advocate, declared that slavery corrupted the morality of the white population. But his particular concern was miscegenation, "the shameful, the disgraceful, the degrading" practice of sex between the races. By 1829 free blacks had to post a $1,000 bond with proof of freedom in order to enter Illinois. Like Indiana, Iowa, and Michigan, Illinois outlawed interracial marriages and nullified any that had occurred.

Anti-black measures continued into the Civil War years. In 1848 Illinois citizens, by a voting margin of four to one, passed a black exclusion clause. When a black organization proposed in 1852 that the restriction on black testimony against whites be removed, the proposal was tabled. In January 1853 "An Act to Prevent the Immigration of Free Negroes into the State" passed the legislature by forty-five to twenty-three. Under this law, any person who brought a free black or mulatto into Illinois was subject to a fine of $100 to $500 and a jail sentence of one year. Blacks who entered and stayed in Illinois for ten days were subject to a $50 penalty. If the black person could not pay, his services were sold to pay off the fine. Although a black exclusion law was already in effect, Illinois citizens in March 1982, by a two-to-one majority, reinforced it. In August 1862 Illinois voters, by a five-to-one majority, renewed the prohibition on black suffrage—at a time when blacks comprised 0.4 percent of the population.

Like other nonslave states, Illinois wanted black people out of Illinois. Republican senator Lyman Trumbull opposed the extension of slavery as well as "giving Negroes...privileges" equal to white citizens. He favored colonization or any other plan to get rid of blacks "Godspeed." In 1859 he declared, "We the Republican Party, are the white man's party....We are for the free white man." He pondered the fate of emancipated slaves: "What will we do with them; we do not want them set free to come in among us...."

Other Illinois politicians agreed. Republican congressman Owen Lovejoy, brother of the slain abolitionist editor Elijah Lovejoy, opposed slavery but held that blacks were inferior and that the United States was meant exclusively for white people. General (and future governor) John M. Palmer, a Republican, wrote that freedom was not the issue. For him it was "the presence of the negro race; a race which the sentiments of our people doom to a condition of racial and political inferiority beyond the reach of all efforts for their elevation." In 1863 Illinois's Republican governor, Richard Yates, suggested that competition with white labor would lead blacks in the North to a life of "pauperism and neglect." His belief that the benefits of freedom in the South would rid the North of blacks soon became commonplace in the North. The black migration to Illinois did not appear until the labor shortage induced by World War I ignited it. It was then an economic, not a humanitarian, event.

Lincoln, a lifelong opponent of slavery and its extension, was an advocate of both colonization and "diffusion"—the forced distribution of blacks according to population. His hometown Springfield paper, the *Illinois State Journal,* was both Republican and a supporter of Lincoln and offered a strong whiff of prevailing Northern racial sentiment and an endorsement of free blacks only "at a distance."

> The truth is, the nigger is an unpopular institution in the free States. Even those who are unwilling to rob them of all the rights of human- ity and to labor and to enjoy the fruits of their toil, do not care to be brought into close contact with them.... Now we confess that we have, in common with the nineteenth-twentieths of our people, a prejudice against the nigger....

Lincoln has been pardoned for his own racially inspired derogatory comments about blacks. His admirers justify his approach as necessary pragmatism required for winning elections. In 1854, in Peoria, Illinois, Lincoln spoke against black equality: "I am not contending for...political and social equality between blacks and whites." His statement presup- poses an electorate to which racial antipathy appeals. In an attempt to deify Lincoln and remove any racial stigma, he is further exonerated by interpretations of his evolving enlightened attitude toward blacks. Thus he gets a pass on the late-twentieth-century racial litmus test, and there has been no outcry to tear down the Lincoln Memorial. As an example, the historian George M. Fredrickson euphemistically describes the pre- war Lincoln as "clearly a white supremacist, but of a relatively passive or reactive kind." Lincoln knew that slavery was the "root cause" of the Civil War and that cotton was its economic base; he wanted slavery abolished by gradual means, by force if necessary. But he had no plan for the mil- lions of freed slaves.

Colonization, according to V. Jacque Voegeli, was Lincoln's "favorite answer to the race problem." In 1862 he posed the question to a black audience, "Why should the people of your race be colonized?... You and we are different races.... You suffer very greatly by living among us while we suffer from your presence." Lincoln approved a plan to colonize blacks on the Chiriqui land grant on the Isthmus of Panama. His secretary of the interior contracted in September 1862 with the Chiriqui Improvement Company. In August 1862 Lincoln told a group of blacks, "There is an unwillingness on the part of our people, harsh as it may be, for you free colored people to remain with us."

Lincoln signed the Emancipation Proclamation on January 1, 1863. A day earlier he had signed a bill authorizing $500,000 to fund colonization schemes. One such plan, presented by the promoter Bernard Kock, would have removed five thousand blacks from America to Ile Vache, an island owned by Haiti, at a cost of $250,000. The first four hundred black colonists left in 1863; the surviving 368 returned in 1864 after the attempt failed. The man whom America credits for freeing the slaves also wanted them out of America. Lincoln was not alone in seizing the colonization solution. Republicans John A. Bingham, Owen Lovejoy, and George Julian voted for $500,000 in federal funds to finance the "removal of freed slaves freed in the District of Columbia" and the South.

Again, historians attribute Lincoln's colonization comments and concrete efforts as clever maneuvering to gain political support in the border states and elsewhere in the North. Eric Foner, for example, points out that Lincoln never mentioned colonization after the Ile Vache fiasco. Foner considers this an example of Lincoln's pragmatism and evolved position and proof that he was never a true supporter of colonization. In reality, Lincoln realized that colonization was impractical and impossible.

His search for ways to deal with free blacks led Lincoln to a "diffusion" policy. Like most white Northerners, he was concerned with a mass migration north. In 1862 he paid homage to the diffusion principle by which "Equally distributed among the whites of the whole country... there would be but one colored to seven whites.... Could the one, in any way, disturb the seven?" In the North, Lincoln overlooked the fact that across the region and throughout the nineteenth century, a ratio of even one black person to one hundred whites already greatly disturbed white populations.

Diffusion made its way into proposed legislation. In April 1864 Kentucky senator Garrett Davis proposed that Congress redistribute blacks to Northern states in "proportion to their white population," but the Senate "scorned" his plan. In June that year a "milder form" of dispersal was presented by West Virginia senator Waitman T. Willey and met with an equally negative response. Willey wanted to give the Freedmen's Bureau permission to contact Northern governors and city leaders to arrange sending freedmen north. This, Senator Willey thought, would relieve labor shortages and provide guidance for the freedmen.[1]

Abolitionist Massachusetts was very much against having blacks distributed to their state. The Radical Republican Charles Sumner thought that dispersal was "entirely untenable." His Massachusetts colleague Senator Henry Wilson thought the diffusion idea would "have a bad influence in the country." Radical Republicans recognized that the white North wanted no free blacks despite a labor shortage—except in the one case of supplying blacks for the Union Army to help the Northern states fill their draft recruitment quotas.

The day of reckoning for Massachusetts and the Northern states came in 1862. No longer could they attack the institution of race-based slavery without confronting the question of the disposition of free blacks. As the Union Army marched through the South, tens of thousands of enslaved blacks were freed as plantations were abandoned. The federal government had no policy with regard to the destitute thousands whom they had set free. Plans evolved by necessity in different areas of the South, each policy subject to interpretation, violation, and different degrees of enforcement.

---

1 There is a current ring to the diffusion policy. The founding father of Singapore, Lee Kuan Yew, an ethnic Chinese, in 2013 recommended to the United States a policy of diffusion. Singapore, a multiracial entity—Chinese, Tamil, and Malay—did not employ diffusion because of its small area, but it had adopted English as the national language in order to promote social cohesion and discourage ethnic competition. Lee thought that large numbers of Hispanics, if they settled in one area such as California, would threaten the successful Anglo-Saxon culture there. He was not speaking about race or the complete negation of Hispanic heritage. "If they come in dribs and drabs and you scatter them across America, then you will change their culture," Lee continued, "but if they come in large numbers...and stay together in California, then their culture will continue, and they may well affect the Anglo-Saxon culture around them." Lee, an admirer of American society and values, had a keen sense of the proper place of culture within ethnic groups. His aim was the social cohesion necessary for a nation to function effectively.

The diffusion idea was also raised during the 1960s civil rights era by Georgia senator Richard Russell, who suggested that blacks be distributed to the states in proportion to their population.

The containment policy, a form of domestic colonization in the South, evolved as the white North faced racial judgment day. Thousands of freed slaves, designated as contraband, appeared behind the lines of the Union Army in Virginia. General William Tecumseh Sherman viewed them as a nuisance, "an irritating distraction from winning the war." But the question of what to do with freed slaves in Confederate territory was no longer abstract. A precipitating event occurred in September 1862 when General John Dix, an anti-slavery Union commander in Virginia, requested that the governors of Massachusetts, Rhode Island, and Maine accept two thousand needy former slaves. Massachusetts governor John Andrew rejected the plea. Andrew had optimistically expected that free blacks in the North would gravitate south, where their "peculiarities of physical constitution" were better suited.

> For the … [former slave refugees] to come here for encampment or asylum would be to come as paupers or sufferers into a strange land and climate—a trying event to its habitués … to a busy community where they would be incapable of self-help—a course certain to demoralize themselves and endanger others.

Governor Andrew is best known to American movie audiences for his role in supporting the placement of black soldiers in the Union Army in the movie *Glory* (1989). But the film does not mention that less than a year before Andrew's authorization of the legendary black Fifty-Fourth Massachusetts Infantry Regiment, he had denied asylum to black refugees. Western governors likewise warmly supported the policy of keeping black refugees in the South.

In February 1864, however, Governor Andrew changed his tune. He wrote to President Lincoln complaining that Union commanders in Virginia refused to allow contraband to emigrate to Massachusetts, where there was a labor shortage. The governor's real agenda—pursuing blacks in order to fill Massachusetts's military quotas—was transparent. Lincoln replied with undisguised sarcasm.

> If I were to judge from the letter, without external knowledge … I would suppose that all the colored people of Washington were struggling to get to Massachusetts; that Massachusetts was anxious to receive them

as permanent citizens; and that the United States Government here was interposing and preventing this. But, I suppose these are...[not] the facts. If...it be true that Massachusetts wishes to afford permanent home within her borders, for all, or even a large number of colored persons who will come to her...I would not for a moment hinder [them] from coming.

The conscription of Northern troops, as we have seen in New York, was a combustible burden. Driven by expediency, Andrew had initiated a meeting of governors at Altoona, Pennsylvania, to demand the recruitment of black troops. Iowa's governor, Samuel Kirkwood, did not mince words when he insisted on some "dead niggers" in addition to dead white men on the battlefield.

The West had to face a similar situation. When the accumulation of black refugees in the lower Mississippi Valley—in Tennessee, Mississippi, Louisiana, and Arkansas—prompted federal action, in September 1862 the Union Army began sending freed slaves north. Many were sent by Union commanders to Cairo, Illinois. Secretary of War Edwin Stanton validated this policy by requiring the Union general in Cairo to care for the blacks. In one of America's extreme racial ironies, Illinois still had a black exclusion law. More important, Stanton was turning a blind eye to racial animosity in the state. As the railroad began carrying trainloads of black refugees to Illinois, white reaction there was instantaneous and predictable. Pike County citizens attacked Secretary Stanton for resettling a "worthless negro population" in their midst. At Olney, Illinois, black refugees were halted and forced to return to Cairo. The mayor of Chicago refused to set up a committee to help resettle the freed slaves. According to the *Chicago Tribune*, Republican governor Yates declared that the "scattering of those black throngs should not be allowed if [it] can be avoided.... The mingling of blacks among us will mean that we shall always have trouble."

On October 13 Stanton countermanded his order, halting the shipment of black refugees to Cairo. Stanton's brief foray into the racial cauldron of the white North has been described as a tactical "blunder." In fact, the secretary of war had inadvertently exposed America's racial nerve. Lincoln and Stanton learned a hard lesson about Northern white hostility in Illinois, the "Land of Lincoln," and also in

Massachusetts, the land of Charles Sumner, William Lloyd Garrison, and John Andrew.

In the wake of this experience in Illinois and Massachusetts, the federal government settled on a "containment policy": freed slaves would be kept in the cotton fields of the South. The new policy was enunciated publicly by the army's adjutant general, Lorenzo Thomas. He outlined his plan to Secretary Stanton on April 1, 1863, leaving no doubt as to why it was necessary.

> It will not do to send [the black refugees] in numbers into the free states, for the prejudices of the people of those states are against such a measure and some of those states are against such a measure and some have enacted laws against the reception of free negroes.... You all know the prejudices of the Northern people against receiving large numbers of the colored race.

Instead the freedmen were put to work on abandoned cotton plantations, where they were often exploited by Northerners who rented the land. Some ex-slaves leased abandoned plantation land, with mixed results.

As Ohio, Indiana, Minnesota, Wisconsin, Michigan, and Iowa demonstrated, Illinois's racial animosity was no aberration. Ohio in 1810 counted 1,889 blacks (0.8 percent) in its population; by 1860 there were 36,673 blacks (1.5 percent) in a total population of 2,302,838. Soon after admission to statehood in 1803, Ohio passed a series of "black laws" designed to prevent blacks from coming into the state. An 1804 law required blacks or mulattoes to prove they were free before they could enter Ohio. An 1807 law mandated that blacks and mulattoes post a $500 bond to ensure "good behavior and self-support." In 1832 an Ohio legislative committee described "free blacks" as without "moral constraint" and "more idle and vicious than slaves." Free blacks were considered a "distinct and degraded class" who "demoralized whites simply by association." Anyone with one-quarter black blood could not join the militia, vote, serve on a jury or testify against a white person in Ohio. In 1859 the

Ohio Supreme Court ruled that any child who had "any visible taint of African blood" could not attend a school for white students.

Cincinnati, a major trading city of the Old Northwest, was a scene of frequent racial strife. In 1829 violence erupted when the city's trustees demanded that blacks pay the $500 bond or leave the city within thirty days. When blacks did not comply, a riot ensued. Mobs of whites, who could not be controlled for three days, attacked blacks, murdered some, and damaged homes. Almost a thousand blacks fled for Canada, where they founded the town of Wilberforce. In 1841 yet another race riot exploded in Cincinnati.

Blacks in Cincinnati found solace in their own communities. Some managed to accumulate property. The riots provoked them to build their own schools. In Cincinnati as in other Northern cities, education was, the historian Carter G. Woodson noted, the "greatest problem" for blacks. By 1856 they were allowed to elect trustees of their own schools. One black school, the Gilmore High School, was used by white Southern planters to educate their mulatto children. Although the black exclusion laws were repealed in 1849, the city's "black laws" stood basically unaltered until after the Civil War, when fear of a black migratory invasion subsided because of government policy designed to keep blacks in the South.

Despite some changes, the black populations of Ohio cities remained in dire straits after the Civil War. Peter Clark, a respected Cincinnati black community member, noted that racial animosity "hampers me in every relation of life, in business, in politics, in religion, as a father or as a husband." Anti-slavery Cleveland was also a hostile environment for free blacks. The prominent black John Malvin "found every door closed against the colored man... excepting only the jails and penitentiaries, the doors of which were thrown wide open to him."

Ohio indulged in the "most extensive colonization" rhetoric during the 1840s. In 1849 Ohio citizens pledged $11,000 to fund an "Ohio in Africa" resettlement. A bill providing $25 each for up to fifty black people a year failed to pass when legislators realized that there was no way to monitor blacks who might enter Ohio expressly to collect the money. The legislature did petition the federal government to establish a black reservation on land recently obtained from Mexico.

If blacks could not effectively be excluded or deported, white Northerners—either Eastern or Western—wanted them to remain in the South or move there. If this could be accomplished there would be no need for further worry about a black migration north. The Ohio Democrat Jacob Brinkerhoff wanted slavery excluded from Western territories, but his views were essentially racial: "I have selfishness enough greatly to prefer the welfare of my own race to that of any other and vindictiveness enough to wish...to keep the South with the burden which they themselves created." The Republicans George Julian of Indiana, Albert G. Riddle of Ohio, and Thaddeus Stevens of Pennsylvania, as well as Salmon P. Chase, governor and senator from Ohio before he became Lincoln's secretary of the treasury, voiced hope that emancipation would "drain" the tiny Northern black community southward. Democrats and Republicans were aligned at least on the notion of keeping free blacks out of the North.

The important Ohio Republican senator John Sherman, brother of the Union general, declared matter-of-factly that Ohioans were both antislavery and anti-black. Ohioans, according to Sherman, were "opposed to having many negroes among them," and blacks in general "were spurned and hated all over the country North and South." Sherman supported colonization. In June 1852 he worried that an emancipation bill "would have made Southern Ohio uninhabitable or driven us to the enactment of harsh and cruel [exclusion] laws." He spoke of the impossibility of assimilation and the immutable "law of God.... The whites and blacks will always be separate, or where they are brought together, one will be inferior to the other." After emancipation, Senator Sherman wrote to his brother, "No one cares about the negro except [that] as...he is the cause of the war he should be made useful in putting an end to it." The senator was advocating the drafting of blacks into the Union Army.

Salmon P. Chase gained visibility in Ohio by defending fugitive slaves. Later, as chief justice of the US Supreme Court, he admitted the first black lawyer to practice before the court. He had been a strong anti-slavery advocate and supported black suffrage, yet he wanted blacks out of the North, "at a distance." In July 1862 he encouraged General Benjamin Butler, commander of the Union forces in the Gulf States, to emancipate the slaves in his territory. Chase's motive was to make the area attractive to Northern blacks. After emancipation, he reasoned, blacks would gravitate toward the more appealing Southern climate.

Ohio's newspapers were outspokenly anti-black. In 1862 the *Cincinnati Enquirer* vehemently opposed "confiscating," the term used for freeing the slaves: "The hundreds of thousands, if not millions of slaves it will emancipate will come North and West, and will either be competitors with our white...laborers, degrading them by the competition, or they will have to be supported as paupers and criminals at public expense." The *Columbus Crisis* raised the specter of miscegenation, suggesting that Ohio's "farmers and mechanics were not prepared to mix up four million of blacks with their sons and daughters..." Ohio's Western Reserve, in the northeastern part of the state, was reputed to be relatively tolerant, yet a Republican editor there who had opposed black exclusion laws voiced his desire to rid Ohio and the country of blacks: "We have no special affection for negroes. We neither desire their companionship or their society.... We would be glad if there were not one in the State or one in the United States."

Ohio's involvement with the Underground Railroad that helped fugitive slaves in their journey to freedom in Canada has been widely acknowledged by historians, historical memorials, and a museum in Cincinnati. None give the full story of Ohio's antipathy toward blacks. American historians and heritage professionals in general focus on slavery and the South rather than the crucial impact of Northern racial hostility. The Underground Railroad was a transit line to carry fugitives through the state, not welcome them as residents. In 1862 an Ohio farmer waxed proudly about his state to an English visitor but added, "There is but one thing sir, that we want here, and that is to get rid of the niggers."

White Northerners occasionally made insincere gestures about bringing free blacks north. During the Civil War a Minnesota minister advocated bringing "ten thousand Negroes" to his state. The black migrants would be forced to work for their employers, who would pay the cost of their trip. The benevolent minister would have the free blacks "fined or imprisoned" if they did not fulfill their contract with their sponsor. Nothing happened. At the time Minnesota had fewer than three hundred blacks (0.2 percent of the population); fifty years later, Minnesota's black population totaled seven thousand (0.3 percent of the population).

Meanwhile the white population of Minnesota was exploding, rising from 169,000 during the Civil War to more than two million in 1910. Neighboring Wisconsin had a similar growth trajectory with blacks intentionally almost invisible. Wisconsin's black population in 1860 numbered 1,171 (0.1 percent) and was still denied suffrage by an over-whelming vote. The state had been admitted to the Union in 1848; by 1855 the Wisconsin State Colonization Society was established to send its thousand-plus blacks to Africa. Strapped for money, the Society managed only to pass an ineffectual resolution. The intent was nonetheless clear: Wisconsin wanted no blacks. Wisconsin Republican newspapers cited fears that emancipation would produce a "Negro infestation." Wisconsin Democrats raised the specter of miscegenation. If blacks could vote, they asserted, black men would "marry our sisters and daughters and smutty wenches... [would marry] our brothers and sons." Republican senator James R. Doolittle favored colonization in order to "keep our Anglo-Saxon institutions as well as our Anglo-Saxon blood pure and uncontaminated." Doolittle wanted blacks colonized in Florida.

Ultimately the fallback position of Northerners was the containment of blacks in the South. In 1863 the Wisconsin Assembly determined that the most effective way to keep blacks out of the state was to ensure that they had "freedom, homes and employment" in the South. Northern blacks, it was thought, could be coaxed into the South. They could not compete in the North because the Northern boss was an "exacting task-master" while the Southern manager "has less repugnance to the black man's shiftless ways. They understand each other better."

Even as Wisconsin and other states in the North were excluding or discouraging black settlement, they were attempting to augment their sparse populations by actively promoting white European immigration. Wisconsin formalized its white immigration policy in an 1852 law that established an immigration commissioner to be located in New York City. (Iowa passed a similar law in 1860.) The commissioner's office was a conduit for information about Wisconsin to white European immigrants and worked with a Dr. Hildebrandt, a Wisconsin native who represented America in Bremen, Germany. The office dissemi-nated thirty thousand German-language brochures, half of them to Europe. Wisconsin continued to publish these brochures throughout the nineteenth century.

Thousands of immigrants sought information at Wisconsin's New York office. The orchestrated effort involved contact with foreign con-suls as well as railroad and steamship companies. Immigration to the state surged. In 1853 Wisconsin received the following white European immigrants: 16,000 to 18,000 Germans; 4,000 to 5,000 Irish; 3,000 to 4,000 Norwegians; and 2,000 to 3,000 others. The recruitment efforts succeeded; by 1900, 710,000 (34 percent) of Wisconsin's two million people were of German lineage. There was never an attempt to entice blacks from the South.

Each of the states of the Old Northwest followed the same pattern of black exclusion, either by law or by custom. In 1860 Iowa had a truly inconsequential black population of 1,059 (0.2 percent) in a total of 673,844 residents, yet exclusion laws appeared as early as 1827. Iowa demanded from entering blacks a $500 bond and proof of freedom; intermarriage was made illegal; blacks could not serve in the militia; jury service was prohibited; nor could they vote. In 1857 Iowans voted 49,511 to 8,489 against black suffrage. The state's colonization society encouraged formal recognition of Liberia so that Iowa's black residents would be tempted to move there. "As long as blacks are here," declared J. C. Hall at the Iowa colonization convention of 1857, "they must be treated as outcasts and inferiors." As the threat of black migration eased, Iowa abandoned its exclusion laws in 1864.

Michigan's anti-black, anti-slavery stance was similar to that of its neighbors. By 1860 the state had 6,799 black residents (0.9 percent of the total population). A $500 bond requirement for entering blacks was passed in 1827; black suffrage was prohibited in 1836 with the comment, "[T]he negro belonged to a degraded caste of mankind." A law against miscegenation followed in 1846. The Radical Republican senator Jacob M. Howard was upset when confronted in 1862 with the possible relocation of 123,000 freed slaves to Michigan. After it became apparent that blacks would be contained in the South, Senator Howard voiced his opinion that freed slaves "ought to be created as equals before the law." He promoted black equality only when they were "at a distance." The city of Detroit suffered its first race riot in 1863.

Lincoln and the Aftermath of War

The abolition of race-based slavery, the close of the Civil War, and the tragic death of Abraham Lincoln concluded an era. The posthumous Lincoln has been given supernatural powers by historians. Despite their efforts to divine what Lincoln's Reconstruction policy might have been, they shed little light on postwar events.

Lincoln did, however, espouse the very American view that "every man should have the means and opportunity of benefiting his condition." To deprive anyone of the "fruits of their labor," he declared, was tyranny. The black man therefore had a "right to eat the bread, without the leave of anybody else, which his own hand earns, [in that regard] he is my equal ... and the equal of every living man." Lincoln was adamant about the need for work; his philosophy of "root, hog, or die" applied to blacks as well as whites. But he was noticeably silent on specifics. He expressed no views on land redistribution and the famous concept of "forty acres and a mule" for the freedmen.

Frederick Douglass and other blacks, in anticipation of Booker T. Washington, echoed the self-help and economic independence philosophy of Abraham Lincoln. "Learn trades or starve," advised Douglass in 1853, "and learn not only to black boots but to make them." In 1831 black state and national conventions recommended "their people to shift from menial jobs to mechanical and agricultural pursuits, to form joint-stock companies, and mutual-savings banks ... to pool capital for the purchase of real estate, and to patronize Negro-owned businesses." More adamantly, the "Negro Convention" of 1848 antedated Booker T. Washington's views on the critical nature of economic self-sufficiency: "To be dependent is to be degraded.... Men may indeed pity us, but they cannot respect us." Black attitudes, according to the historian Leon Litwack, held that "it was nonsensical for Negroes to prate about political and social equality" without economic independence. Avoiding the dependency trap meant understanding the values of business and proper training.

Historians have pushed the idea of the "evolving" Lincoln beyond the boundaries of nineteenth-century America's racial realities. Lincoln's last public address, on April 11, 1865, is said to foreshadow his intent to deliver full citizenship with political and economic equality to the freed slaves. Lincoln said he would "prefer that [suffrage] were now conferred on the very intelligent and those who serve our cause as soldiers." This was not a dictum or ultimatum, it was a recommendation to the state of Louisiana. This limited endorsement of suffrage for freedmen has been given broad and speculative meaning that has had a soothing effect on the conscience of later generations of white Americans.

Lincoln's nod to the "very intelligent" black is a recurring theme in American history, where one can find a pattern of recognition by white America of a black elite. The few blacks accorded this status were useful to white America as role models for progress as well as persons of influence within the black community. In the 1830s Alexis de Tocqueville, that most famous of all foreign observers of America, remarked on the separation of the races and on the possibility of an individual attaining equality. He was convinced that "the white and black races will [never] ... be upon an equal footing." Tocqueville does allow that an "isolated [black] individual may surmount the prejudices ... of his race ... but a whole people cannot rise above itself." And the exceptional individual would have little impact on the whole of society. Lincoln's invitation to the powerful black abolitionist, orator, and writer Frederick Douglass to visit the White House for a meeting in 1862 acknowledges white America's recognition of a black elite. This instance, and later when Theodore Roosevelt hosted Booker T. Washington for dinner at the White House, were gestures to the black community of the esteem for a few exceptional individuals.

On February 26, 1865, the *New York Times* candidly predicted and endorsed black separatism in the South and the possibility of the occasional exceptional black: "White ingenuity and enterprise ought to direct black labor," editorialized the *Times*. "Northern capital should flow into these rich cotton-lands on the borders of the Atlantic and Gulf. . . . The negro race . . . would exist side by side with the white for centuries being constantly elevated by it, individuals of it rising to an equality with the superior race. . . . [Cotton production requires] the white brain employing the black labor. . . . "

The tendency to select gifted individuals from the black masses continues in the twenty-first century. The white psyche has always had room for a black elite. During the 2008 presidential race, the Senate Democratic Majority Leader, Harry Reid, referred to the candidate Barack Obama as notably "light-skinned" and having no black dialect "unless he wanted one." In the same year, then Democratic senator Joe Biden extraordinarily remarked, "I mean, you got the first mainstream African American who is articulate and bright and clean and a nice-looking guy. . . . I mean that's storybook, man."

Some in the black community have recognized the limits of Lincoln's racial enlightenment. The black journalist Lerone Bennett Jr.'s book

Forced into Glory: Abraham Lincoln's White Dream (1999) describes the reactionary nature of Lincoln's actions. The book, published by the black media giant Johnson Publishing Company, also the publisher of *Ebony* magazine, has been widely criticized by white historians. In his 1965 book, Robert Penn Warren asked some black "big brass" what they thought about Lincoln. "I think that Lincoln is vastly overrated," said Harlem congressman Adam Clayton Powell. "I think that he did nothing at all except that which he had to do, and he did it in terms of winning a war." Roy Wilkins, the venerable executive director of the NAACP, was more nuanced: "I have mixed feelings about Lincoln. . . . I think that you'd have to judge Lincoln in the context of his climate, and in that context I still would give him . . . credit." Malcolm X thought Lincoln "did more to trick Negroes than any other man in history." Malcolm put Kennedy, Franklin Roosevelt, and Eleanor Roosevelt in the same category as Lincoln. Interestingly, in 1964 the White Citizens' Councils exalted Lincoln as the "patron saint" of racial segregation. "Negro colonization," wrote historian John Hope Franklin, "seemed almost as important to Lincoln as emancipation." Lincoln, according to Franklin, hoped for colonization until the end of the war.

Lincoln's greatness needs no exaggeration. Without Lincoln, America would have splintered. He saved the Union and hastened the end of America's most enduring tragedy, race-based slavery. White historians wince when blacks challenge Lincoln's racial credentials. But Lincoln, despite the efforts of historians, did not conform to the racial standards of the twenty-first century.

Reunion

The closing scene of the Civil War and the practical end of race-based slavery occurred at Appomattox, Virginia, on April 9, 1865. The Emancipation Proclamation could now take full effect. The surrender ceremony had none of the drama of the bloody war or the struggle for human dignity and human rights in the land of the free and the home of the brave. There was no conversation; the signing of documents took twenty-three minutes. The cordial and respectful interaction between the victor, General Ulysses S. Grant, and the vanquished, General Robert E. Lee, was symbolic of the reunion of white America. Black America would remain excluded from the American mainstream.

What transpired at the small courthouse would be quite instructive for the black experience after Emancipation. The meeting of the opposing generals is particularly noteworthy because of the current demonizing of Confederate symbols, including statues of Lee. Both Lee and Grant were antagonists in a war that felled hundreds of thousands of soldiers, but the scene at Appomattox was anything but vengeful. Both generals had been graduates of the US Military Academy. Grant would become president of the United States for eight years of the postwar Reconstruction period; Lee would live a quiet life as president of what is now Washington and Lee University.

Lee was immediately paroled. Despite the fact that Grant viewed the Confederate cause as immoral, his respect for the Confederate general was genuine. Grant recorded that his "own feelings were sad and depressed."

> I felt like anything rather than rejoicing at the downfall of a foe who had fought so long and so valiantly.... [Lee and I] soon fell into a pleasant conversation about old army times.... [O]ur conversation grew so pleasant that I almost forgot the object of our meeting.

In the annals of military history, the discussion between and the disposition of the two warring combatants at this surrender was arguably unique. On June 13, 1865, a mere two months after Lee surrendered, Grant ordered a pardon application for Lee with his personal "earnest recommendation." Within five years the leader of the secessionist army would be hosted in the White House by President Grant. Again, the friendly invitation by the victorious head of state to his defeated foe is unusual, to say the least.

As the historian C. Vann Woodward wrote, "... when the chips were down, the overwhelming preponderance of views of the North on [black equality] were no different from those of the South—and never had been." But the key difference between North and South was that four million black people lived in the South before the Civil War, compared with only 250,000 in the North; and unlike the North, the South depended on black labor for cotton production.

Black America would remain excluded from the American mainstream. A combination of white Southern racial intransigence and white Northern racial antipathy would effectively chain blacks to the cotton fields until World War I. Though unstated, a racial containment policy was in effect, sanctioned by white America. The issues of equality, black political and social rights, separation, exclusion, and economic independence had uncomfortably surfaced in the white antebellum North. Only the question of race-based slavery had been put to rest. America would struggle to resolve its myriad remaining racial problems.

Chapter Two

The Containment of Blacks in the South

If the freedman does not work in the cotton field, "let him starve and exterminate himself if he will, and so remove the negro question,—still we must have cotton."

—EDWARD ATKINSON, BOSTON ABOLITIONIST
AND SUPPLIER OF ARMS TO JOHN BROWN, 1861

...these imperturbable darks.... The more I see of them, the more inscrutable do they become, and the less that I like them.... It is discouraging to see how utterly wanting in character and conscience these people [the freedmen] seem to be, and how much more hopeful they appear at a distance than near to....

—IDA HIGGINSON, WIFE OF UNION SOLDIER
HENRY LEE HIGGINSON, BOSTON ABOLITIONISTS,
DESCRIBING FREE BLACKS ON HER GEORGIA FARM, 1866

Cannot a nation that has absorbed ten million foreigners into its political life without catastrophe absorb ten million Negro Americans into that same political life at less cost than their unjust and illegal exclusion will involve?

—W. E. B. DU BOIS, 1900

Race measured by race, the Negro is inferior, and his past history in Africa and in America leads to the belief that he will remain inferior in race stamina and race achievement.

—ALBERT BUSHNELL HART, HARVARD PROFESSOR,
TEACHER AND MENTOR OF W. E. B. DU BOIS, 1910

I know the negro fairly well. I have seen him at close quarters in the
Yazoo Delta, where he formed ninety percent of the population, and
where universal suffrage in his hand is the veriest criminal farce.

—THEODORE ROOSEVELT, 1906

Meet a Reconstruction stalwart, Ohio Radical Republican
Benjamin Franklin Wade. Senator Wade, an abolitionist, supported black suffrage but personally loathed black people and favored
colonization. In 1863 the Ohio senator asked, "If we are to have no more
slave states, what the devil are we to do with the surplus niggers?" Wade's
political career ended partly because of his forthright advocacy of allowing black men to vote in Ohio. In a referendum held in Ohio's 1867 general
election, black suffrage was trounced, and Wade soon faded away. In 1851
he described Washington, DC, as a "god forsaken Nigger ridden place,"
where the food was "all cooked by niggers until I can smell and taste the
nigger." In 1873 he sought to hire a white servant because he was "sick and
tired of niggers." He abused a black attorney by calling him a "damned
Nigger lawyer." In 1871 he traveled with Frederick Douglass to explore the
annexation of Santo Domingo (now the Dominican Republic) as a home
for freed slaves. This juxtaposition of support for black voting rights for
small numbers of Northern blacks and the desire to remove them from
the neighborhood was common in the Northern states. And if blacks
could not be coaxed into leaving the United States, at least they could be
a Republican voting bloc, confined to the South.

Reconstruction: The Setting

W. E. B. Du Bois may have called Reconstruction, the period between
1865 and 1876, "a splendid failure," but it was a failure nonetheless. This
was the time allotted for the adjustment of the slaves to their new freedom. Why was Reconstruction a failure? The facile explanations—lack of
political will in the North, President Andrew Johnson's racial prejudice,
and Southern resistance—gloss over the real determinant: Northern
and Southern racial attitudes. Until this overriding fact is acknowledged, America will never confront its racial dilemma. Remember, no
other group has been asked and encouraged to leave the country by

establishment organizations and leaders in both the North and the South. These removal organizations—colonization societies—were founded to send the black population abroad.

Following the South's capitulation, the race-based slavery system that most of the Founding Fathers had hoped would "wither away" was officially dead. Frederick Douglass, the black abolitionist, rhetorically asked, "What shall we do with the Negro?" His famous and oft-quoted answer was "Do nothing.... Give him a chance to stand on his own legs! Leave him alone!" Douglass feared that state intervention might raise the specter of blacks as "wards of the state." He thought that ensuring suffrage, civil rights, general property rights, and an end to discrimination were sufficient protection. Very few Radical Republicans, as we shall see, were committed to the extended use of force in reforming the South so as to protect the freedmen. But they did seek a deep government involvement, even land redistribution.

It was never possible that white Northerners would shed white Southern blood for black civil rights. While the story of white Southern resistance is firmly ensconced in history textbooks and heritage events, the critical force of white Northern racial attitudes is a deliberately neglected part of American history. The lame excuses for white Northern apathy during Reconstruction—lack of will and a preoccupation with material concerns—ignores the American consensus about the place of blacks in the society. All the issues of Reconstruction circle back inexorably to the attitude of the white North toward blacks.

Despite the North's dominant position, at the close of the war no firm plan for Reconstruction existed. Political leaders acknowledged the need for a transitional phase for the freedmen, an apprenticeship period or a civilizing status between slavery and freedom. The British post-slavery apprenticeship for its slave colonies thousands of miles away, in the 1830s, was no guide. Moreover, the humanitarian aura of British emancipation was dealt a severe blow when in October 1865 British authorities brutally repressed the bloody Morant Bay, Jamaica, racial insurrection, in which two hundred blacks were murdered. Afterward the British colonial secretary suggested that Jamaicans were "idle, vicious and profligate"; and a British journal thought that the black Jamaican population was moving "back to its ancestral barbarism." There was no model here for Reconstruction.

The standard story of the postwar years is as follows: The South convinced the North that the Reconstruction governments, in which blacks played a large role, were corrupt and needed to be forcibly removed. Similarly the South successfully created the myth of the "lost cause," which fostered nostalgia and white reconciliation and minimized the role of slavery as the cause of the conflict. Was the North really this gullible? After all, the North had condescendingly viewed the white Southerner as honor-bound, emotional, indolent, and devoid of commercial skills. It is difficult to imagine that the stereotypical white Southerner could dupe the North. Yet historians claim that white Southerners, a discredited group recently trounced in war, could influence the minds of Northerners.

A more plausible explanation returns to the economic imperatives. For white Americans in the North, the Civil War was a necessary distraction to preserve the Union and abolish race-based slavery. After the war the nation was free to pursue its material goals and populate a continent, both of which had been defining American characteristics from the beginning. The inability of white America to focus on black civil rights cannot be blamed on a *sudden* attraction to wealth. White Northerners had made an extensive effort to build commercial relations with the South before the war. Northern rails and cities vied for Southern business. Northern economic dominance of the South, some argue, was akin to colonialism.

In the wake of the conflict, King Cotton was a bit shaken but remained on the economic throne. America needed cotton's export power and fuel for the burgeoning textile industry in the North and subsequently in the South. American cotton would soon provide three-quarters of the world export market for the "indispensable product." How could America not determine that the future of free blacks was in the cotton fields of the South? The financial system and credit requirements of cotton production did change—to sharecropping, instead of bank borrowing by the landowner. In theory, sharecropping was an arrangement for equity participation by the black farmer; in practice, the black farmer could be easily defrauded because he had no legal recourse. The arrangement was purely arbitrary. Slavery was only the first chapter of the link between African Americans and cotton. Beginning in 1800, slaves cultivated cotton for sixty years, but free blacks were cotton laborers for nearly a hundred years after Emancipation.

The inability to understand the failure of Reconstruction survives. A *New York Times* editorial of March 2016 distilled the doom of Reconstruction to two events: "Washington's decision to no longer enforce the rights of African Americans" and "the rise of the Ku Klux Klan." But racial attitudes in the white North prevented any sustained federal action to protect free blacks. Even the passage of civil rights legislation and constitutional amendments grew out of the need to keep blacks in the South. Eric Foner's description of blacks in the North is hardly a paean to racial enlightenment. Northern blacks, according to Foner, were "trapped in urban poverty and confined to inferior housing and menial and unskilled jobs (even here their foothold, challenged by the continuing influx of European immigrants and discrimination by employers and unions alike, became increasingly precarious)." Under such circumstances, blacks had no "viable strategy" for economic progress.

In addition to white Northerners' dread of a black migration, they feared that former slaves would refuse to work in the cotton fields. Edward Tobey, an influential Bostonian, warned that "If… [the freedmen] refuse to work, neither shall they eat." The abolitionist Henry Ward Beecher declared that "The black man is just like the white… —he should be left, & obliged to take care of himself & suffer & enjoy, according as he creates the means of either." Boston anti-slavery advocate Edward Atkinson supplied the militant Kansas abolitionist John Brown with rifles. And he organized the Shaw Monument Fund, which raised money for the Saint-Gaudens statue that honored Robert Gould Shaw, the Boston officer who commanded the black Fifty-Fourth Regiment. But Atkinson agreed that the free black must remain in the South to produce cotton. If not, "Let him starve and exterminate himself if he will, and so remove the negro question…" In 1889 Atkinson was given an honorary degree by the University of South Carolina for his service to the South.

One needs only to read the pages of the *New York Times* during the late nineteenth century to see why Reconstruction was doomed from the outset. In 1863, in the midst of the war, the *Times* noted the "vast and most difficult subject of making [freedmen] work" after emancipation. In 1865 the *Times* wrote that free blacks should be cotton laborers under the supervision of "[w]hite ingenuity." Further, the *Times* noted the need to civilize the freedmen over centuries, with some black individuals rising to equality with the white man. In 1883 the *Times* supported the dismantling of civil rights legislation. And it opposed special rights for blacks who "should be treated on their merits as individuals precisely as other citizens." In 1874 the *Times* favored the racial integration of schools in sparsely settled areas of the country where there were few blacks. But in 1890, when a significant number of blacks were involved in a desegregation suit, the newspaper called blacks "foolish" for insisting that their children attend a white school. "Whoever insists upon forcing himself where he is not wanted," thundered the *Times*, "is a nuisance, and his offensiveness is not in the least mitigated by the circumstance that he is black."

Since the Union had not been sundered by the Civil War, and the country saved from the brink of self-destruction, it must have been asked, Who would assist the freedmen? Would their committed, long-term ally be Congress, the president, the Supreme Court, the Republican Party, the white soldiers of the Union Army, white Northern philanthropists, or Northern state governments?

Attitudes produced consequences. White Southern resistance to black equality immediately sought a racial caste system; white Northerners maintained their belief in black inferiority and second-class or, at best, probationary citizenship. Whites North and South in effect helped create a subordinate role for black Americans.

The former slave was trapped in the cotton South, unable to move in great numbers to the industrial North until the economic demands of World War I. In 1914, 90 percent of all African Americans lived in the South; 50 percent were involved with cotton production. If conditions in the South were so deplorable, why was there so little movement north? Now that they were free, why didn't blacks flee the lands to which they had been chained for generations? Why didn't they flock to Detroit, New York, and Chicago?

W. E. B. Du Bois, the black activist and giant of African American history, regarded the North as racially inhospitable. From 1865 until World War I, the white North imposed a containment policy that maintained the black population in Northern states at less than 2 percent. "Cannot a nation that has absorbed ten million foreigners into its political life without catastrophe," wrote the prolific Du Bois, "absorb ten million Negro Americans into that same political life at less cost than their unjust and illegal exclusion will involve?" The white North dictum of keeping blacks "at a distance" persisted. Despite Emancipation and a brief phase of political enfranchisement, America's pattern of racial animosity remained the same.

A consistent theme among the abolitionist Republicans who favored containment was expediency. The influential Massachusetts Republican congressman George S. Boutwell wrote, "Next to the restoration of the Union, and the abolition of slavery, the recognition of universal suffrage is the most important result of the war." What did he really mean? In 1866 he warned that if black people were not given rights they would move north with disastrous consequences for white workers.

> I bid the people, the working peoples of the North, the men who are struggling for subsistence, to beware of the day when the southern freedmen shall swarm over the borders in quest of those rights which should be secured to them in their native states. A just policy leaves the black man in the South.... An unjust policy on our part forces him from home [to the North], to the injury of the black man and the white man both of the North and the South. Justice and expediency are united in indissoluble bonds....

Translation: If the freedmen are given rights, they will not move north. Boutwell even labeled the policy expedient! He further acknowledged that America's racial dilemma was intractable, recommending that Georgia, South Carolina, and Florida be given exclusively to the freedmen. Boutwell was saying, in effect, that blacks could not be assimilated.

Reconstruction witnessed the passage of an impressive amount of legislation that supported the rights of freedmen. With these laws, the federal government (still dominated by white Northerners) attempted to impose rules and values that its own constituencies—even with their tiny black communities—had not accepted. The legislation had to be tested locally in states with large black populations, not in the North. It had to be interpreted through the judicial process; the new laws would require enforcement.

Abstract concepts of freedom and citizenship, embedded in

Reconstruction legislation, were crushed when applied to the real world of nineteenth-century America. Reconstruction's accomplishments—the fostering of public education for blacks and whites in the South, and the introduction of blacks to political and civil life—were overshadowed by subsequent events. The political rights of freedmen were taken away; their economic livelihood was chained to cotton production and an arbitrary legal system; and their physical and economic mobility within America was denied.

The result was an extension of the separation policy dictated by white America—from colonization abroad to segregated communities within towns, to containment in the South. The future would bring another form of separation—the urban ghetto in both North and South.

As the decades passed, what changed? How do the stories of some of the major actors in this ongoing drama illustrate themes—civil rights, economic progress, education, priorities, racial attitudes, relations between North and South? What, if anything, was reconstructed? Where did black America fit?

The War's Aftermath

In April 1865 the South was devastated; the terms of Lee's surrender to Grant at Appomattox Court House were unconditional. In theory, the white North could dictate terms and conditions to the utterly defeated South, which it had occupied. In just four years of fighting, 265,000 men of productive age in the white South were dead or incapacitated. In Mississippi alone, of the seventy-eight thousand soldiers and officers that the state provided to the Confederacy, 35 percent perished. Transportation and infrastructure throughout the South were disrupted as the war destroyed towns and cities, roads, railroads, and bridges. Farms were in disrepair. Large numbers of freedmen were destitute. One tiny but poignant statistic of devastation may be found in the Mississippi budget: in 1866, 20 percent of all state revenues were spent on artificial limbs for Confederate veterans.

The capture of the Confederate president, Jefferson Davis, on May 10, 1865, presented an intriguing issue for the United States government. For two years Davis was incarcerated at Fort Monroe in Hampton, Virginia. Initially Northerners branded him a traitor and demanded his trial as a war criminal. The cabinet wanted to indict him as a conspirator in the assassination of President Lincoln, but no connecting evidence ever materialized. Abram Dittenhoefer, the self-proclaimed confidant of Lincoln, wrote that the president had intended to "let him die in peace on his Southern plantation." Lincoln "would not permit any punishment to be inflicted on Jefferson Davis unless it were absolutely demanded by the American people."

But President Andrew Johnson and his cabinet were eager to punish Davis, who had hired an able defense lawyer, Charles O'Conor. The war's military tribunals had been discontinued, so Davis would have to be tried in a civilian court system. The attorney general James Speed "had grave doubts" about winning the case. He warned that the federal government might "end up having fought a successful war, only to have it declared unlawful by a Virginia jury." Legal questions centered on the states' right to secede.

President Johnson then suggested a pardon for Jefferson Davis, who proudly refused to accept it. A pardon, he said, "would be a confession of guilt." Davis relished the idea of pleading the justice of his cause in a courtroom, with the nation as an audience. He was finally indicted in May 1866. The prosecutors who joined the case, William H. Evarts and Richard Dana, replaced the original indictment for complicity in the assassination of the president with a new one accusing Davis of treason. Even with the new charge, Evarts and Dana had serious doubts about obtaining a conviction. The government did not want the embarrassment of a defeat in court. When the case came to trial in May 1867, a postponement ensued.

The judge, John Underwood of the US District Court of Virginia, allowed the defendant to be released on bail of $100,000. The sum was guaranteed by an unlikely group of abolitionists—Horace Greeley, editor of the *New York Tribune*; Gerrit Smith; and Cornelius Vanderbilt. Each guaranteed $25,000, and ten others contributed $2,500 each. The day after Davis's release, a banquet was held in Richmond. At the festive affair, journalists from New York, Boston, London, and Richmond toasted both Confederate and Union generals. Greeley, who had attempted to shorten the Civil War by compromise, wanted a peaceful reunion. He attended the trial in person and afterward spoke to a group of blacks and whites at the African Methodist Church in Richmond. The editor asked the assembly to forget:

> I entreat you to forget the years of slavery, and secession, and civil war
> now happily past.... forget that some of you have been masters, others
> slaves, some for disunion, others against it, and remember that you are
> Virginians, and all now freemen.

Gerrit Smith, the abolitionist supporter of John Brown and sponsor of the ill-fated black colony of Timbuctoo in New York, now placed
equal blame for slavery on both North and South. "A sufficient reason
we should not punish the conquered South is that the North was quite
as responsible as the South for [slavery], the chief cause of the war ... the
mercenary North."

Chief Justice Salmon P. Chase devised a legal strategy for avoiding
the prosecution of Davis, one derived from the Fourteenth Amendment.
Because Davis had already been punished by prohibiting him from holding public office, a new trial would amount to double jeopardy. Fearing
Davis's ability to perform before the Supreme Court, prosecutor Evarts
offered to drop the case if Davis would not ask the Supreme Court to
review. On February 26, 1869, Evarts informed Davis that all indictments
would be dropped. Davis was a free man. In other words, the federal
government could not prosecute the man who had led the rebellion for
fear of losing the case.

Honor-bound, Davis had outwitted the federal government. In 2016
public opinion has belatedly passed judgment by provoking the removal
of statues of Jefferson Davis from various sites. In 1869 the leaders of the
Union preferred union over revenge.

Only one high-ranking Confederate official was in danger. That was
Judah P. Benjamin, who at various times held significant positions in the
Confederacy—secretary of war, attorney general, and secretary of state.
The multilingual Benjamin, a brilliant lawyer who had argued before the
Supreme Court on numerous occasions, was forced to leave the country
because his Jewish ancestry made him vulnerable to American anti-
Semitism. He fled to England where he pursued his legal career.

Another beneficiary of post-conflict cordiality was Raphael Semmes,
the colorful captain of the famous Confederate raider *Alabama*, who was
not prosecuted. Like its sister ships, the *Shenandoah* and the *Florida*, the
Alabama had preyed on American merchant ships and virtually decimated the fleet. All the Confederacy's war vessels had been purchased on

cotton credit; all were built in England with full knowledge of the British government, by British employees of British companies, with British materials, and were manned by British seamen, much to the consternation of the American government.

Semmes, an American who was essentially a pirate, was arrested for treason on December 15, 1865, but was released without a trial. Afterward he taught literature and philosophy at what is now Louisiana State University before returning to his native Mobile, Alabama, to practice maritime law.

If America had any hope of enforcing black rights, a significant military presence in the South would have been necessary after the war. In the spring and summer of 1866 serious race-related riots broke out in Norfolk, Vicksburg, Nashville, Charleston, Memphis, and New Orleans. Because the federal government viewed these disturbances as a possible incipient insurrection, it imposed a form of martial law that entailed dividing the South into military districts overseen by the United States Army.

This show of force sounds impressive, but reality reveals otherwise. It involved little commitment to protect the freedmen. During this period of military occupation, the army was reduced to a mere shadow of the fighting machine that had won the Civil War. Clearly the Republicans, the white Northern population, and President Grant were aware of the widespread racial violence in the South. They knew that troops had to manage a vast area in the enforcement of newly enacted laws. Yet Republicans presided over the dismantling of the Union Army in the South, which was reduced from 1 million men on May 1, 1865, to 152,000 by the end of the year. By the time of the 1868 elections it numbered 20,000; by 1871, 8,000; and at the close of 1876, 6,000. Other than a few aggregations in cities, the troops were dispersed in small units. In 1869 there were only 716 Union soldiers in Mississippi; Texas had 4,600, of which 3,000 were occupied with American Indian problems.

What attempts were made to guarantee legal protection for blacks? The Thirteenth Amendment, which abolished slavery, did not gain the requisite majority in the House of Representatives in April 1864. It finally passed by three votes on January 31, 1865, with copious doses of bribes and the pardons of Confederates. Thaddeus Stevens quipped that "the greatest measure of the nineteenth century was passed by corruption." Even at that late date there was difficulty in providing a constitutional guarantee of freedom.

The Radical Republicans rode to victory in the elections of 1866 on the backs of Southern violence, the restrictive Black Codes enacted in the South, and the unpopularity of Andrew Johnson, the stubborn, irritable, anti-slavery, Southern-leaning Democratic president. Johnson was ultimately impeached by Congress, though he was found not guilty by one vote in the Senate. Nonetheless he lost his authority. He was succeeded as president by Ulysses S. Grant, who held office from 1869 to 1877. There remained plenty of time to execute an effective Reconstruction; Johnson was hardly to blame for Reconstruction's failure.

After 1866, legislation provided a form of citizenship to the black population—but reality made a mockery of legislative language. Three compelling reasons propelled the enactment of black rights: (1) Protection would induce blacks to remain in the South. (2) Black suffrage would provide Republicans with an unassailable voter base in the South. (3) Black suffrage would not affect the North because of the small black population.

But the Reconstruction interlude was rife with hypocrisy. Republican (and sometime) Democratic congressman Samuel W. Moulton of Illinois supported civil rights legislation in order to contain freedmen in the South. "Whenever the colored man is completely and fully protected in the southern states," Moulton reasoned, "he will never visit Illinois, and...every northern state will be depopulated of colored people as will Canada."

In 1866 Roscoe Conkling, a New York senator and author of civil rights legislation, clearly pointed to the need to keep blacks in the South:

> Four years ago, mobs were raised, passions were roused, votes were given, upon the idea that emancipated negroes were to burst upon the North. We then said, give them liberty and rights at the South, and they will stay there and never come into a cold climate to die.

The expedient support of white Northerners for black equality could hardly be expected to withstand sustained Southern resistance.

After Grant's election to the presidency in 1868, a new leader became the target of Southern antagonism. The former commanding general of the victorious army was a former slaveholder and a recent convert to black rights. Unafraid of risking the lives of his troops in the cause of preserving the Union, he had presided over an army that had lost hundreds of thousands of soldiers to combat and disease. How many lives would he now risk to preserve black rights? The answer is none.

A variety of legislative efforts sought to outline the civil and political rights of freedmen during the Radical Republican ascendancy. The Fourteenth Amendment (1868), through its famous due process clause, broadly ensured that rights could not be taken away; the Fifteenth Amendment (1870) guaranteed the right to vote; the Civil Rights Act of 1875 provided for equal treatment in public accommodations and prevented the exclusion of citizens from jury duty "on account of race, color, or previous condition of servitude."

Grant's rhetorical and legislative advocacy of black issues was solid. He applied pressure to secure passage of the Fifteenth Amendment and was ebullient in his message that announced ratification:

> A measure which makes...4,000,000 people who were heretofore declared by the highest tribunal in the land not citizens...is indeed a measure of grander importance than any of the kind from the foundation of our free Government to the present day.

Later, as with other events, Grant would express second thoughts about the Fifteenth Amendment. At the close of his frustrating second term, he announced to his Cabinet that the Fifteenth Amendment "had done the Negro no good, and had been a hindrance to the South, and by no means a political advantage to the North."

During Grant's presidency the federal government confronted repeated acts of violence and intimidation against freedmen in the South. Congressional hearings on the activities of the Ku Klux Klan and other white-supremacy organizations led to the Enforcement Acts, which gave the president power to intervene militarily on behalf of the freedmen. Grant occasionally authorized military force to curtail "lawlessness, turbulence, and bloodshed," but he failed to intervene in the pivotal 1875 Mississippi election that effectively ended Reconstruction in the state. In the end, Grant gave the freedmen no foundation for future security. Most federal expenditures under the Enforcement Acts were spent in the North, not the South. In effect, the Republican Party used federal money to gain political advantage in the Democratic cities of the North.

In order to combat the Ku Klux Klan in South Carolina, Grant warned the South that he would "not hesitate to exhaust the [presidential] powers...whenever it should be necessary to protect the rights of citizens." In 1871 he suspended habeas corpus in nine counties in South Carolina, sent troops, and made hundreds of arrests. In North Carolina and Mississippi there were also hundreds of arrests but no convictions. In 1872 Grant ordered troops into New Orleans to protect the Republican regime; in 1873 he ordered troops to Louisiana in response to the massacre of blacks in Colfax.

But suppressing resistance in the South was ultimately ineffective. Troop reductions, as noted earlier, had left the army understaffed. Southerners persisted in vigorously challenging federal authority and reestablishing white rule. The white South was not deterred. In a nod to priorities, the federal government actually expended vastly more time, money, and men in subduing and placing Indians on reservations in the West than it did in enforcing laws to protect freedmen in the South.

The actions of white America, rather than the words of a very few Republicans, demonstrated that black equality was not a priority in a country obsessed with land expansion and railroads, rife with racial animosity, and devastated in 1873 by financial panic and depression. The political and economic opportunists who ventured south were resented by the defeated region. In Mississippi, a state where blacks constituted a significant and in some places a majority of the population, the restoration of white rule was tantamount to a "racial-political" war.

A close look at the Mississippi election of 1875 reveals the predictable lack of white Northern commitment. In that state contest, white Mississippians violently intervened to prevent blacks from voting. In addition, the Mississippi Democratic congressman L. Q. C. Lamar worked assiduously to rid the state of Republican political control. Henceforth white Mississippians would control the state government without black participation.

Grant refused a request by the Republican governor, Adelbert Ames, for federal troops to supervise elections in Vicksburg. The president famously responded through his attorney general, Edwards Pierrepont: "The whole public are tired out with these annual autumnal outbreaks in the South and the majority are ready to condemn any interference on the part of the [federal] government." Translation: White Northerners did not care about black rights in Mississippi.

Governor Ames provides a useful example of the lack of dedication by Northern Republican officials. He was forced to curtail his summer holiday in cool New England to tend to the volatile situation in 1875. A Maine native, Ames was a political opportunist whose main objective in Mississippi was to gain a seat in the US Senate. He supported the civil rights of his constituency, the black population, but he had no long-term commitment to remain in Mississippi to fight for the rights of freedmen. While Lamar was energetically campaigning for the Democrats during the summer and fall of 1875, Ames was ensconced in the governor's mansion in Jackson. There he whiled away his time reading Anthony Trollope's novel *The Way We Live Now* (about a ruthless, corrupt financier who promotes a fraudulent railroad investment in the United States). In August a frustrated Ames confided to his wife that he had given up: "I am fully determined not to accept the Senatorship if I can get it. I do not like anything in the life I lead here."

Reconstruction was thus effectively overthrown in Mississippi. Governor Ames retreated to the private sector in Minnesota and New England, where there were few blacks. Grant's defeat in the 1875 battles of Vicksburg, Yazoo City, and other Mississippi venues was arguably as significant as his victory in the Battle of Vicksburg during the Civil War.

According to John R. Lynch, the able black congressman from Mississippi, Grant admitted that political expediency had impelled his inaction. Congressman Lynch, during an audience with Grant in November 1875, asked the president why he had not intervened in the Mississippi election, "a sanguinary struggle" that was practically an insurrection against the state government. Lynch suggested that prominent Ohio Republicans had warned Grant about sending troops to Mississippi because such an action would jeopardize their own prospects in October elections. Grant confessed that he had taken the expedient path. The bold general, in this instance, had become a political hack.

The most significant of the initial Southern acts of reconciliation between the North and the South featured Congressman L. Q. C. Lamar's eulogy for the abolitionist Massachusetts senator Charles Sumner, author of the Civil Rights Act. Lamar had written the secessionist document for the state of Mississippi. Yet after Sumner died on March 11, 1874, the Massachusetts congressional delegation asked Lamar to "deliver a memorial address" to Congress. Lamar's oration resonated within the Senate and across the North. He had genuine respect for Sumner and used the opportunity to promote reconciliation. He praised Sumner, a man universally disliked in the South. As he finished, his tribute gave way to a deafening silence and then to thunderous ovation. "Democrats and Republicans alike, melted in tears," one observer noted. "Those who listened sometimes forgot to respect Sumner in respecting Lamar." The secessionist supporter of slavery had become the reconciliatory and rhetorical supporter of black suffrage. The Northern press was rapturous.

Congressman Lynch, who had significant interaction with his fellow Mississippian Lamar, figured prominently in the Reconstruction period. Lynch was the son of a white planter and a slave mother, and grew up in Natchez. In 1869 the ambitious, self-taught Lynch was elected to the Mississippi House of Representatives at the age of twenty-two. Like his black colleagues, he emphasized public education, black suffrage, black civil rights, and economics based on self-help. He tried unsuccessfully to put a compromise school integration clause in the state constitution, by recommending that school districts whose small population could support only one school should be integrated. A similar plan was approved in some Northern locales where there were few blacks, but it was unattractive in the South with its large black populations.

An aggressive young politician and master parliamentarian, Lynch managed to be selected speaker of the Mississippi House over the opposition of white Radical Republicans. He delivered on his promise to be fair to all men "who are alike entitled to equal rights and privileges."

He was noticed by a *New York Times* reporter, who admiringly wrote of the "astonishing…coolness and sagacity with which he disposed of all points." A white Mississippi newspaper went so far as to declare its support of white candidates only if they were equal to Lynch in "intelligence, moral worth and integrity, which virtues we give [him] credit." Elected to Congress in 1872, Lynch was defeated in 1876.

Lynch retreated to Natchez to establish a law practice, purchase farm land, and pursue an influential role in Republican politics. He would ally with Lamar's supporters as some black Republicans and some Democrats formed a so-called fusion political movement. This fragile alliance was based on political jockeying by whites and blacks, and the implicit recognition by blacks of their increasingly weak position. It was hardly biracial cooperation, but it did allow Lynch to be reelected to Congress. Defeated after one term, he would never run for public office again.

The Reconstruction world of Mississippi threw together black senator Blanche K. Bruce, black congressman John R. Lynch, and white congressman and senator L. Q. C. Lamar. They often disagreed but enjoyed an amicable relationship and sometimes worked together. In 1885 Lynch visited Lamar, who was secretary of the interior in Grover Cleveland's Cabinet. Lynch had come to "pay him my respects and tender him my congratulations upon his appointment." Lamar greeted Lynch and introduced him to his other visitor, Mayor William Russell Grace of New York.

After the mayor left, an extraordinary conversation ensued between the two Mississippians. As disclosed in Lynch's memoirs, it provides a rare glimpse of behind-the-scenes racial politics. Lamar's position allowed him to dispense patronage jobs. The Democrat Lamar offered to the Republican Lynch a job that paid a generous annual salary of $2,250. Lynch had not solicited any form of employment for himself. He declined the offer but added his respect for the secretary of the interior.

Lynch had come to submit a list of "colored" department of interior employees whom he hoped Lamar would retain. Lamar agreed upon seeing the names. As the dialogue continued, Lynch mentioned two sensitive cases, "[one] a colored man, a physician; the other a white man, a lawyer." The "colored man" was married to a white woman, the "white man" was married to a black woman. Lamar rejected the white man married to the black woman because the case had drawn public attention and was highly charged; the black physician's case was not well known, and Lamar accepted it. He was not concerned about intermarriage but did not wish to "antagonize public opinion."

Lynch then asserted that "opposition to [racial] amalgamation is both hypocritical and insincere." Lamar agreed but offered a candid qualification:

> My sympathies are with your friend and it is my desire to retain him.... But when you ask me to openly defy the well-known sentiment of the white people of my State on the question of amalgamation, I fear you make a request of me which I cannot safely grant, however anxious I may be to serve you... although in the main, I recognize the force and admit the truth of what you have said on that subject.

Lamar regretted that he could not act on the proposition that Lynch had "so forcibly and eloquently suggested." The "white man" with the black wife was not retained: the "colored physician" continued in his position. Such was the convoluted world of racial norms practiced in the South and in the North.

Reconstruction officially ended with the compromise that followed the disputed presidential election of 1876, in which the Republican candidate, Rutherford B. Hayes, agreed to withdraw remaining federal troops from Southern states. The Democratic and anti-black candidate, Samuel J. Tilden from New York, had won the popular vote, but the electoral votes of Florida, South Carolina, and Louisiana remained in doubt. Hayes's bargain allegedly called for removal of troops from the South and government support for a transcontinental railroad through the region in return for the contested electoral votes. Often not mentioned is the fact that had Tilden been elected, the situation of blacks would have worsened.

The racial attitudes of Rutherford B. Hayes, the anti-slavery Ohio congressman, governor, Union Army general, and US president from 1876 to 1880, vividly illustrate the transition from Reconstruction to reconciliation. After the Civil War, Hayes supported black suffrage with platitudes: "Our government has been called the white man's government. Not so. It is not the government of any class, sect, or nationality or race." Education, Hayes thought, was the only long-term solution to the acceptance of blacks in American society. After his presidency, as chairman of the Slater Fund, he underwrote programs "to assist the education of young able blacks." Hayes's agenda incorporated a heavy dose of white control and paternalism; in essence he and like-minded Americans sought to "civilize" the freedmen.

Expediency was an integral part of Hayes's politics. He understood that a black vote was a Republican vote, hence his support of the Fourteenth Amendment was based not on equal protection but on the clause that denied representation where black voting was restricted. When Cincinnati blacks voted for the first time, Hayes gleefully announced, "They vote Republican solid." But his actions contradicted his rhetoric.

Despite the bargain that secured his presidency in 1876, Hayes had made his decision about troop withdrawal from the South and reconciliation well before the election. By 1876 he had moved away from Radical Reconstruction. In 1875 he had replied to a Kenyon College classmate, "As to Southern affairs, the let-alone policy seems to be the true course.... The future depends on [the] moderation and good sense of [white] Southern men." Hayes was aware that a removal of the remnant of federal troops would leave freedmen at the mercy of white Southerners. Nevertheless, after he received the Republican nomination for president, he confided to his friend Guy Bryan, a Texan, "You will be almost if not quite satisfied with my letter of acceptance—especially on the Southern question." On the use of federal troops in the South, the candidate wrote to Republican senator Carl Schurz, "There is to be an end of all that." In February 1877 he was ready to do away with the North's "injudicious meddling." In September that year, as president, Hayes spoke to a Georgia group that included blacks. "[N]ow my colored friends,... After thinking it over, I believe your rights and interests would be safer if this great mass of intelligent white men were left alone by the general government."

In 1880 Hayes anticipated Booker T. Washington's famous social metaphor at the Atlanta Exposition of 1895. The occasion was the twelfth anniversary of the all-black Hampton Institute. Hayes, now the former president, spoke:

We would not undertake to violate the laws of nature.... We are willing to have these elements of our population separate as the fingers are, but we require to see them united for every good work, for national defense, one as the hand.

To his nineteenth-century audience, the meaning was unmistakable: social separation and inequality. In 1878 he had recorded in his diary that "the blacks, poor, ignorant and timid, can't stand alone against the whites." Hayes knew that the black man would lose any struggle in a white America that adhered firmly to racial separation and racial hatred.

Where was Frederick Douglass during the postwar period? Douglass was indisputably the most prominent black leader of the antebellum and Civil War periods. His abolitionist writings and lectures were widely known, powerfully expressed, and highly effective. He edited and published the influential *North Star* (1847–1851), which later became *Frederick Douglass' Paper.* In a precedent-setting event, Abraham Lincoln hosted Douglass in the White House in 1862. Despite Lincoln's attention, Douglass knew that Lincoln was "the white man's president"; blacks "were only his stepchildren."

The drama and violence of Douglass's early life—escape to freedom, the abolitionist movement, the Civil War—had given way to Emancipation; continuing violence and a slide into racial second-class citizenship dominated the second phase of his life. The fiery orator and writer died in 1895, thirty years after the end of the war. His oratory and writing skills had not diminished, but his effectiveness had waned. With the end of slavery, Douglass found his rhetoric helpless in the face of white America, not just the South. His penetrating eyes and determination leap from the photographs and paintings of the younger man; a resignation born of frustration and disappointment seem to characterize the older giant of black history.

Frederick Douglass was clear about treatment of the freedmen. He thought that ensuring suffrage, civil rights, general property rights, and the end of discrimination would be sufficient protection. Douglass never espoused land reform. He advocated self-reliance and hard work, which together would bring land ownership. He emphatically viewed the South as the freedmen's home. He knew all too well the Northern fear of "vagrancy, and criminality from the freedmen."

Like many revolutionaries, Douglass lost his radical force after the revolution. Nowhere is this more explicit than in his role in the Freedmen's Bank, an entity created within the Freedmen's Bureau to help encourage thrift among the emancipated slaves. On March 3, 1865, the Freedmen's Bureau, or as it was formally named, the Bureau of Refugees, Freedmen and Abandoned Lands, was chartered by the federal government to act as a guardian for the freedmen in matters of education and relief, and protection in earning a living. The goals were to further an orderly transition to a free society and reestablish cotton production. Thus it was essential to safeguard the freedmen "from abuse...foil the selfish designs of northern speculators, and...transform the South from a plantation economy to an economy of small, family-owned farms." The Freedmen's Bureau was expressly designed to be temporary; it ceased to exist in 1869 except for responsibilities in education and payments to blacks who were Union Army veterans. Even these duties ended within a few years. President Lincoln had not given "much attention to the Freedmen's Bureau." Its basic purpose for "white America," according to the historian William McFeeley, was to prevent the kind of black violence that had occurred with the end of slavery in the Caribbean.

The newly appointed commissioner of the Freedmen's Bureau upon its creation was General Oliver Otis Howard, a fervently religious thirty-five-year-old from Maine who had lost an arm in combat and had never been an abolitionist. Howard, the battle-tested veteran, told a black audience in New Orleans, "You must begin at the bottom of the ladder and climb up." He wanted blacks to "return to plantation labor...and work their way out of the wage earning class" to become landowners. In this approach he was merely echoing fears that freed slaves would be idle. He did not consider a black person equal "and never advocated equality," McFeeley writes, "except by law and justice." During the war, Union soldiers under the command of Generals Sherman and Howard had showed "contempt" for freedmen in South Carolina. After his bureau experience, the pious general was next assigned the task of chasing the Nez Perce Indians away from their homeland in the Wallowa Valley in Oregon. Howard, the well-intentioned Sunday school teacher, took his black servant, Washington Kemp, to Maine to become a landowning farmer. Instead Kemp became a "subsistence farmer," known for his minstrel appearances throughout the state. Nonetheless Oliver Otis Howard's name lives on in Howard University, the premier historically black college in America.

The auxiliary of the Freedmen's Bureau, the Freedmen's Bank, was chartered in 1865 with a main office in Washington, thirty-five branches, and an asset base of $3 million. The bank was established to foster savings habits among the freedmen. The founder, John W. Alvord, a Congregationalist minister and abolitionist, had no banking experience. The institution became riddled with mismanagement, fraud, and poor loans, all overseen by its white directors.

Frederick Douglass was appointed president of the failing bank in March 1874, in the financial institution's dying days. Douglass had no chance of rescuing the bank, but he enjoyed the prestige of being called the "president of the Freedmen's Bank." The towering figure yielded to symbolism rather than substance. The former slave, in awe of the physical structure, was fooled.

> [The building was] one of the most costly and splendid buildings of the time, finished on the inside with black walnut and furnished with marble counters.... I often peeped into its spacious windows, and looked down the row of its gentlemanly and elegantly dressed colored clerks with...their buttonhole bouquets in their coat-fronts....I was amazed with the facility with which they counted money....The whole thing was beautiful.

An icon of American history, Douglass marveled at his rise from impoverished slave to "President of a bank counting its assets by the millions."

But he had not the slightest notion of the bank's business and condition, and rather than trying to learn, he spent his time promoting civil rights legislation. The perils of having a political activist manage a business were thus on display. What was actually transpiring in these luxurious accommodations? A black cashier, "Daddy" Wilson, was the "figurehead used by the white financial committee to endorse" fraudulent business activity. The depression of 1873 aided the bank's demise. It folded in July 1874, a few months after Douglass had been named president. Thousands of freedmen lost their savings when the bank met an ignominious death in bankruptcy.

No movie about Reconstruction will feature the debacle of the Freedmen's Bank, but the impact was psychologically severe. W. E. B. Du Bois in 1901 highlighted the significance of the failure. "Not even ten years of slavery could have done as much to throttle the thrift of the freedmen," wrote Du Bois, "as the mismanagement and bankruptcy" of the Freedmen's Bank. Others have cited the formation of black banks as evidence of Du Bois's exaggeration. Du Bois may have been hyperbolic, but there is a major lesson to be learned. Of 134 black banks formed between 1888 and 1934, seventy failed in the Depression of the 1930s, and only four were in existence in 1996, according to Juliet E. K. Walker's *The History of Black Business in America*. A thriving, self-sufficient black business community could not survive outside the economic mainstream. Separatism, whether voluntary or involuntary, will not bring material success to a broad group.

Douglass advocated black advancement through farming. Fundamental and prescient was his understanding of white Northern antipathy toward blacks. He predicted the growth of black urban ghettos occasioned by a black migration to the North. The result, he wrote, would leave blacks "crowded into lanes and alleys, cellars and garrets, poorly provided with the necessities of life."

As for the South, Douglass believed that there the black person held a monopoly on the labor supply. "He is there, as he is nowhere else, an absolute necessity," Douglass wrote. The economics of the cotton field were never far from Douglass's thoughts. "Neither the Chinaman, German, Norwegian, Swede," he observed, "can drive [the African American] from the sugar and cotton fields.... The climate of the South makes such labor uninviting and harshly repulsive to the white man."

Although Douglass emphasized suffrage, he knew, as did Booker T. Washington, that economic power was vital for black progress. The freedman's labor in the cotton field was worth more than "sword, ballot-boxes or bayonets. It touches the heart of the South through its pockets." But because the freedman was a captive, with no option to move north, blacks had no bargaining power. Had the white North been receptive to black migration, blacks might have had economic leverage; white Southerners would have had no choice but to acquiesce to black civil and economic rights. Such was not the case.

Douglass was drawn into two episodes of the black separatist quandary. First, in a variation of the colonization scheme, he was appointed in 1871 to visit Santo Domingo to explore annexation. In a broad sense, President Grant was not at all sure what to do about the freedmen. He thought that annexation of Santo Domingo would provide a safe haven for blacks who wished to leave the country. In effect, Grant recognized the nation's inability to assimilate blacks. The Santo Domingo plan might have forced white Southerners to be more accommodating because of a labor shortage, but Grant was admitting that America could not absorb four million freedmen. He wanted to "secure a retreat for the portion of the laboring class of our former slave states, who find themselves under unbelievable pressure." He continued:

> The present difficulty in bringing all parts of the United States into a happy unity and love of country grows out of the prejudice to color.... The colored man...with a refuge like Santo Domingo his worth here would be soon discovered and he would soon receive such recognition as to induce him to stay: or if Providence designed that the two races should not live together, he would find a home in... [Santo Domingo].

Douglass favored the idea of annexation as a safety valve for black Americans. In his final message to Congress on December 5, 1876, Grant maintained his support of Santo Domingo as a home for blacks. According to the president, it would be a "congenial home" for the freedmen, "where their civil rights would not be disputed and their labor much sought after." As early as 1871, racial separation was Grant's stated preference; Santo Domingo was yet another variation of schemes to remove or resettle black people. Implicit was the understanding that they would not move to Northern states. The black alternative was Santo Domingo, not New York, Massachusetts, or Ohio. Grant's scheme led a tortured existence before it died at the hands of the Senate.

During his entire postwar life, Frederick Douglass clung to his hope that white and black Americans could live together peacefully. His keynote speech at the dedication of the Emancipation Memorial in Washington's Lincoln Park in 1876 was the highlight of a life whose crowning moment was the abolition of slavery. The statue shows a slave in chains on his knees in front of Lincoln—hardly an introduction to freedom. At the celebration, Douglass referred to Lincoln, the Great Emancipator, as the "white man's president."

The champion of emancipation did have a role model: the Jews. He advised blacks to imitate the Jews, who were "worst situated than you are" but "have fought their way up." He rejected the exodus metaphor by citing Jewish example:

> A Hebrew may even now be rudely repulsed from the door of a hotel, but he will not on account get up another exodus as he did three thousand years ago, but will quietly "put money in his purse" and bide his time, knowing that the rising tide of civilization will eventually float him.

A bronze statue of Frederick Douglass stands on the steps at the side entrance of the New York Historical Society; Abraham Lincoln is around the corner, adorning the front entrance of the museum. A block away, Theodore Roosevelt sits astride a horse with an American Indian below him on the steps of the American Museum of Natural History. Roosevelt wrote that universal suffrage was a farce; if enacted, the South would resemble the dysfunctional Haiti. Douglass would not have been pleased.

The only major attempt at mass black migration to the North after the Civil War was the "Exoduster" movement of the late 1870s, in which Southern blacks were enticed to go to the promised land of Kansas. Most conventional discussions of the Exodusters focus on the oppression and destitution of Southern blacks, in the midst of a depressed cotton market, as impetus for the first black-initiated domestic migration of freedmen. In 1854 "Bleeding Kansas" had suffered a conflict to determine whether it would be admitted as a free or a slave state. By 1870 the Kansas population had grown to more than a million and continued to grow, but at no time did blacks account for more than 5 percent of the population. By the spring of 1879, thousands of Southern blacks were pouring into Kansas.

Kansas prided itself on being anti-slavery before the war, and for John Brown's stand there against slavery. But the state's anti-black sentiment was as strong as its anti-slavery feeling. The door was shut very quickly on the poor black migrants. The Lawrence city council raised money to "send these undesirables to some other city." Humanitarian efforts stalled. A few of the Exodusters eventually enjoyed better lives than they had had in the South, but Kansas was no promised land and certainly no haven for large numbers of blacks.

In May 1879 Frederick Douglass famously recommended to a black group that freedmen stay in the South. He viewed Kansas as yet another false Canaan, along with Haiti and Liberia. The "dumping" of thousands of impoverished blacks, he cautioned, would reinforce the image of "that detestable class from whom we are not so free—tramps."

The overworked and misleading allusion to the biblical exodus would ring hollow except in song. When the Israelites left Egypt for the promised land, they created their own country where assimilation issues were irrelevant. The Exodusters, however, remained in an America where they were not wanted. Even the South did not want them, but no alternative cotton workers could be found. Mississippi cotton farmers tried diligently but unsuccessfully to recruit Europeans, particularly Italians, and Chinese to labor in the cotton fields.

Kansas, like many Northern states, experienced a huge demand for white immigrants. From 1861 to 1890, 11.3 million white immigrants—primarily from the United Kingdom, Germany, and Scandinavia—arrived in America. Most of them were destined for the North and the West, precisely those areas where few blacks lived. Between 1879 and 1881, while a few thousand blacks made their way to Kansas, more than a half-million Germans immigrated to the Midwest. From 1800 to 1920, 18.2 million people arrived mainly from Southern and Eastern Europe. When white immigrants were available, states could find no refuge for blacks.

The Kansas slave-versus-free dichotomy is best illustrated by its anti-slavery Republican senator, John J. Ingalls. On May 28, 1893, Senator Ingalls was quoted in the *Chicago Tribune* as advocating physical separation and repatriation to Africa to solve the race dilemma. (Sixty-one years later the Supreme Court upended legal segregation in *Brown v. Board of Education of Topeka*. For Kansas it was closure of a kind.)

The Legal Aspects of Race

The impressive extent of civil rights legislation passed during Reconstruction was no match for reality. The legislation was ignored, circumvented, and violated in the South and the North, and sometimes did not survive the tests of the judicial process. Former slaves soon found themselves devoid of rights and at the mercy of the states. White Republican-appointed Supreme Court justices decimated national legislation and constitutional amendments that had been passed during Reconstruction.

Grant's appointments to the Supreme Court played a key role in the nullification of Reconstruction legislation. After the *Slaughterhouse Cases* (1873) restricted the due process clause of the Fourteenth Amendment, *United States v. Cruikshank* (1876) demolished the Enforcement Acts. Grant's appointee, Chief Justice Morrison Waite, issued the *Cruikshank* opinion. Waite, a strong defender of states' rights and a former Ohio corporate lawyer, consistently voted against black rights in his fourteen years on the bench.

In 1883 the Supreme Court dealt a fatal blow to the Civil Rights Act of 1875, which stated that "all persons within the jurisdiction of the United States shall be entitled to the full and equal enjoyment of the accommodations" in "restaurants, theaters, hotels, and railroads." Lawsuits alleging that black citizens were denied "equal enjoyment" arose in Kansas (1875), California (1876), Missouri (1877), and Tennessee (1879). These cases, joined as the Civil Rights Cases, reached the Supreme Court in 1883. In the San Francisco case, a black man named George M. Tyler was denied entry to Maguire's Theatre after he had purchased a ticket because he was "of the African or negro race, being what is commonly called a colored man, and not a white man."

Justice Joseph Bradley, a Grant appointee, wrote the opinion in the civil rights cases. Bradley was a railroad lawyer who had arrived on the bench with a record of hostility toward equal rights for blacks. In his opinion he reasoned that depriving "white people of the right of choosing their own company would introduce another form of slavery." The court, eight to one, ruled that the black plaintiffs in these situations were not protected under the Thirteenth and Fourteenth Amendments. Justice Bradley's opinion amounted to a lecture to blacks, whom he said were no longer "to be a special favorite of the law." The Radical Republican senator George Hoar of Massachusetts, in his memoir, described Justice Bradley as a "most admirable appointment." But John R. Lynch attributed the failure of Reconstruction to President Grant's Court appointments of Joseph Bradley and Morrison Waite, whose votes condemned civil rights legislation.

The Supreme Court's decision in the civil rights cases was applauded by the establishment Northern press. *Harper's Weekly* called it "an illustration of the singular wisdom of our constitutional system." The *New York Times* observed that "The Court has been serving a useful purpose in thus undoing the work of Congress." According to the *Times,* blacks "should be treated on their merits as individuals precisely as other citizens are treated in like circumstances." In the 1890s the *Times* elaborated, declaring that civil rights legislation had been responsible for sustaining "a prejudice against negroes...which without it would have gradually died out." The newspaper proposed "self-help and reliance." It suggested that blacks follow the leadership of "eminent leaders of the white race in the South."

Other racial landmark cases continued to flow from appointments to the Supreme Court by the anti-slavery Republican Party. In 1896 *Plessy v. Ferguson* formally enshrined racial segregation in public accommodations, provided that the facilities were separate but equal. The decision was quickly interpreted as applying to all aspects of American life, including schools.

A man defined as black, Homer Plessy, had been arrested for violating a state law by sitting in the "white section" of a New Orleans train. According to Louisiana's definition of "black," Plessy qualified. He was an octoroon—a person whose parentage was one-eighth black. (The court agreed that a state could determine who was black.) Plessy died in obscurity in 1925, but his name resonates in American history.

The *Plessy* opinion was written by Judge Henry B. Brown, an appointee of Republican president Benjamin Harrison. Brown wrote that "separation of the two races," in and of itself, did not convey a "badge of inferiority" upon blacks.

> If the two races are to meet upon terms of social equality, it must
> be the result of...a mutual appreciation of each other's merits and

voluntary consent.... If one race be inferior to the other socially, the Constitution... cannot put them on the same plane.

Therefore the states were free to legislate separation. In the seven-to-one decision, Justice John Marshall Harlan, a former slaveholder from Kentucky, is given credit for his dissent, in which he said the "Constitution is color-blind." No attention is given to Justice Harlan's authorship of the opinion in *Cumming v. School Board of Richmond, County, Georgia* (1899), which allowed unequal funding for black schools. *Plessy* was finally overturned by *Brown v. Board of Education* (1954), which held that segregation is inherently unequal. (By 2016, however, de facto and self-segregation were present in every aspect of American life.)

The final nail in the coffin of black suffrage, it could be argued, was the 1898 Supreme Court decision in *Williams v. Mississippi*, which upheld Mississippi's 1890 constitution that had effectively disfranchised blacks. The consequences of that constitution were striking. In 1880, 110,113 whites and 130,606 blacks were registered to vote in Mississippi. In 1896, 108,998 whites and 16,234 blacks could vote in the state. In its consideration of the constitutionality of Mississippi's law, the court's opinion was written by Justice Joseph McKenna, an appointee of Republican President William McKinley.

The Economics of Race

Was political or economic power more important for the freedmen? The question resonates in the twenty-first century, when blacks have political power but still lack broad representation in the private sector of the economy. Could a separate black economy prosper in American society where racial separation, both North and South, was deeply embedded? The controversy between two major black leaders, Booker T. Washington (1856–1915) and W. E. B. Du Bois (1868–1963), centers on the correct approach to black success in America and remains enormously relevant. Both Washington and Du Bois recognized that blacks were confined to the South; neither forecast the Great Migration north that began during World War I.

Booker T. Washington, born into slavery and educated at the vocational Hampton Institute in Virginia, had experienced physical labor. He was an apostle of self-help, racial pride, racial self-sufficiency, vocational training, and the prioritizing of economic over political goals. In 1881 Washington founded the Tuskegee Institute in Alabama, a vocational institution that derived its plan from the Hampton Institute. He was the most visible and important black leader of his time, a recognition crowned by the famous invitation from President Theodore Roosevelt to dine at the White House.

Washington rose to national prominence when he spoke at the Cotton States Exposition in Atlanta on September 18, 1895. There he paraphrased Rutherford Hayes, who had dismissed social equality with whites as a goal for blacks. "In all things that are purely social," Washington declared, "we can be separate as the fingers, yet one as the hand in all things essential to mutual progress."

"[N]o race can prosper," said Washington, "until it learns that there is as much dignity in tilling a field as in writing a poem." He recommended preparation in agriculture, mechanics, commerce, domestic service, and in the professions—a recognition of the obvious geographic and vocational restrictions placed on blacks. Respect, Washington believed, would come only with economic success: "No race that has anything to contribute to the markets of the world is long in any degree ostracized."

But he acknowledged that a precondition of racial cooperation was a just administration of the law. He chafed under the humiliation of the racial strictures of his day and foresaw that the *Plessy* decision meant unequal funding for black schools. He thought the inconvenience to the Negro was temporary, but he often worked silently to help those who challenged the system. He rightly observed that legal segregation "was inconsistent in placing no corresponding segregation on whites, and would widen the breach between the races." He correctly prophesied—but decades too early—that the courts would find "segregation laws illegal."

In order to build Tuskegee, Washington needed money, and that led him to ingratiate himself with white philanthropists. Andrew Carnegie gave him an enormous donation of $600,000 in 1903 with a nod to cotton production. Carnegie was explicit: "It is certain that we need more cotton."

> Without money there would have been no Tuskegee..., and with it and its educational contribution black suffrage would someday be

restored through the increased capacity of blacks to perform in duties of citizenship.

John D. Rockefeller spoke of Tuskegee as "the most important contribution yet found towards the solution of the race problems of this country." Rockefeller supported the General Education Board (GEB), which sponsored much of black educational philanthropy. What was the attitude of Northern philanthropists? Wallace Buttrick, executive director of the GED, unabashedly declared, "I recognize the fact that the Negro is an inferior race." A GED trustee, the wealthy Philadelphia department store owner Robert Ogden, noted that blacks were "thriftless, careless, shiftless, and idle by disposition," with "childlike qualities." "Our great problem," Ogden said, "is to attach the Negro to the [Southern] soil and prevent his exodus from the country to the city."

Today Washington's reputation is that of an appeaser, race traitor, and "accommodationist." He has been vilified for his practical strategy, an alleged capitulation to white America. But it is difficult to imagine that white America needed any justification or support for its denial of black equality. And Washington had no choice if he wished to build Tuskegee.

Washington sought to construct an economic stepping-stone. The "Wizard of Tuskegee" envisioned an evolution from black laborers to entrepreneurs, who would "rise to the level of owning stores, operating factories, owning bank stocks, loaning white people money, and manufacturing goods that the white man needs."

How were the freedmen supposed to earn a living? We know that they were confined to the South; we know that cotton production was their destiny after, as well as before, the Civil War. America decided that white Southerners, not freedmen, should be entrusted with land ownership to ensure the production of the indispensable product.

Washington was famously challenged by W. E. B. Du Bois, who from an early age seemed destined for an intellectual life. As a youth from Great Barrington, Massachusetts, he aspired to Harvard but was steered to the all-black Fisk University in Nashville, Tennessee. After graduation he received a Ph.D. from Harvard and joined a small black elite.

Du Bois would write effectively about civil rights issues. He helped found the NAACP and edited its publication, *Crisis,* where he concentrated on discrimination, politics, and the inequality of race in America. He was in no mood to compromise over civil rights temporarily, as Washington advocated. The dispute between the intellectual Du Bois and the practical Washington was only one manifestation of their different philosophies. Du Bois did subscribe to a concern for helping blacks "earn a living," but he wanted training in the liberal arts for leadership and power.

Economics was not his focus, nor did he dwell on vocational solutions for black participation in the mainstream economy. But Du Bois proudly described his dreamy novel, *The Quest for the Silver Fleece* (1910), as "an economic undertaking of some merit." This work, set in the cotton South, espoused his fuzzy brand of Marxism, the centrality of cotton, and the importance of economics in daily life. His villain was industrial capitalism; his solution was socialist redistribution, as described by one of his characters: "...folks ain't got no right to things they don't need." Du Bois's elitist ideal world recoiled at the dirty world of American profit and commerce; his black world could contribute values and spirit that were lacking in the Anglo-Saxon sphere: "We black folks is got the spirit." The capitalist "manipulated the cotton market," wrote Du Bois's character, "while black men who made the cotton in Alabama and the white men who bought it froze in Siberia." Racial cooperation was the antidote to capitalist enslavement. "Durned if I don't think these white slaves and black slaves," one of his characters spoke, "had ought to get together."

Du Bois, in 1908, warned of black family structural problems, a condition that would reverberate into the twenty-first century. Twenty-five percent of all black births, he estimated in 1900, were "illegitimate" and "only one-half [of all blacks were] observing...monogamic sex mores." For whites, he wrote, the numbers were 2 percent for "illegitimate births" and 90 percent were living in monogamous relationships. He was deeply concerned about the morals of the mass of blacks, as distinguished from the elite. The problem of morals, he thought, was a vestige of slavery. Du Bois noted the importance of "economic hindrances to [the] sound moral life ..." of the black person.

Du Bois, by 1900, had identified an elite black community separate from the masses—"a large and growing class...equal to the best in the nation." Du Bois would track the elite in his famous phrase and article, "The Talented Tenth" (1903). Of the 2,079 black college graduates in 1899, he tabulated the following occupations: teachers (53.4 percent), clergymen (16.8 percent), physicians (6.3 percent), students (6.3 percent), lawyers (4.7 percent), government service (4 percent), business (3.6 percent), farmers (2.7 percent), and a few miscellaneous categories. The occupation options would be enlarged over the twentieth century, but the private sector would remain underexploited by the black community.

"The majority of black churches," wrote Du Bois in 1914, were "financial institutions catering to a doubtful round of semi-social activities." He admonished the black church to "adopt a new attitude towards rational amusement and sound moral habits." Would the church remain a business well into the twenty-first century?

In *The Souls of Black Folk* (1903), Du Bois tackled the unavoidable issue of assimilation. For him, the black American had two souls, "an American, a Negro," which produced a "double-consciousness." This tension endowed the "Negro" with "a second-sight into the American world," for he not only had to know himself but to see himself through white eyes. What, then, was the proper identity of blacks? Du Bois wanted to "merge the two souls" while retaining both.

> [The black person] would not Africanize America, for America has too much to teach the world and Africa. He would not bleach his Negro soul in a flood of white Americanism, for he knows the Negro blood has a message for the world. He simply wishes to make it possible for a man to be both a Negro and an American, without being cursed and spit upon by his fellows, without having the doors of Opportunity closed roughly in his face.

This description was born of the early twentieth century, with a black population confined to the South and chained to cotton production. Du Bois straddles the abstraction of "two souls," which avoids dealing with real-life situations of assimilation. The identity issue for blacks would remain a problem even after the elimination of overt legal discrimination, after blacks had left the South and gained political power, and when American universities and corporations were actively seeking their participation.

The context of the times produced both Washington and Du Bois, but their controversy continues. Washington stayed in the American South, where black people lived; Du Bois finally abandoned America for Ghana. At the age of ninety-four he belatedly apologized to Washington, whom he had considered a racial turncoat. The dapper intellectual, now confined to his wheelchair, responded to one of his Ghanaian university students who asked if Booker T. Washington was still considered "the classical traitor to the cause of black freedom." The writer Conor Cruise O'Brien, present at the exchange, recounted Du Bois's response: "When I was a young man, I once said something like that." But his aunt rebuked him, he said, reminding her erudite nephew that Washington had been a slave and had served under "a very different condition. . . . his object is essentially the same [as yours]: more education and more freedom for black people. . . . So I hope I never again hear you speak disrespectfully of Booker T. Washington." To which Du Bois concluded, "And, I never did."

Washington raised hundreds of thousands of dollars to create a lasting institution; Du Bois needed a few thousand dollars to fund his editorial work. Washington played the hand he was dealt in a particular time and place. His work was constructive while doing no harm to black efforts. Unlike Du Bois, he had a realistic notion of the importance of economics, but self-sufficiency, the only open avenue for blacks, was doomed.

During the Civil War, General William T. Sherman attempted the famous "forty acres and a mule" experiment, a misunderstood promise that the freedmen thought would make them landowners. On January 16, 1865, General Sherman, for the sake of expediency, authorized the distribution of "not more than forty acres of tillable land" south of Charleston to each ex-slave family among refugees from Savannah. Sherman's Special Field Order No. 15 became the basis of the oft-discussed and lamented claim of forty acres and a mule. The order derived not from the general's charitable instincts but from a desire to rid himself of black refugees, whom he viewed as "an irritating distraction from winning the war." Sherman would soon disavow any intention to convey land title to the freedmen. Within a few months, forty thousand freedmen had occupied four hundred thousand acres of land in the area specified by Sherman, land that white farmers were forced to leave. The order conveyed no title and was subject to government approval. The land was soon restored to its former owners.

Thaddeus Stevens was the most vocal advocate of the confiscation of white Southern land for distribution to freedmen, as a retribution of sorts. Southern plantations, according to Stevens, "must be broken up and relaid" in forty-acre plots for the freedmen. Stevens's concept was consistent with Republican notions of keeping blacks in the South. A bill for granting Western lands to freedmen was never considered; and despite rhetoric about confiscation, no enabling legislation was passed in Congress. Instead President Johnson, Secretary Seward, General Grant, and a large cast of characters favored pardons for a broad range of Confederates, including Robert E. Lee and Raphael Semmes. Pardons were granted others in exchange for favors or money, or because of past friendships. The sordid affair of pardons degenerated into bribes and arrangements made by well-placed pardon brokers who charged $150 to $500 per transaction.[1]

Northerners in the Cotton Fields

Some white Northerners journeyed south after the war, lured by the prospect of making money when the price of cotton rose. Some also wished to assist the freedmen. Former Union officers were aware of smugglers' profits during the war; none had the slightest knowledge of production issues—weather, insects, black labor, credit requirements, price, and the once-a-year payment. Many such ventures, like Harriet Beecher Stowe's, were financial debacles.

Would white Northerners transform the lives of freedmen? One such

---

1 "Forty acres and a mule" lives on as a metaphor. The perennial clarion call for reparations to address slavery, discrimination, and Northern and Southern versions of segregation has been sounded since 1989 by Congressman John Conyers of Michigan. He has repeatedly introduced House Bill HR-40, calling for a federal commission to examine and determine the relevance of slavery, the legacy of slavery, and racial discrimination in the lives of black Americans. The number forty refers once more to "forty acres and a mule," which Conyers and others mistakenly cite as America's post–Civil War promise to former slaves. Conyers includes monetary reparations when "warranted."

candidate was Major Henry Lee Higginson. Boston native, Harvard educated, and a Union soldier, the naive Higginson dreamed of cotton wealth
and the prospect of teaching the freedmen the lessons of white Northern
success. At the end of the war the former abolitionist was faced with the
challenge of earning a living. For this Bostonian, the South seemed like
a "carpet-bagger's paradise": "Making money there is a simple question
of being able to make the darkies work." Again, "free labor, Northern
capital, and Northern energy," he thought, would reform the inefficient
Southern labor system. Like others, he succumbed, he admitted, to "a
sort of after-the-armistice intoxication."

Higginson's financial and moral adventure began with the collabo-
ration of two army and Harvard buddies, Channing Clapp and Charles
Morse. Higginson and his wife, Ida, the daughter of famed Harvard
scientist Louis Agassiz, moved to Georgia. In 1865 they quickly spent
$30,000 to buy a five–thousand-acre Georgia farm called "Cottonham."
Higginson's acquaintance with cotton farming was based on his reading
of three books: Frederick Law Olmsted's *Sea Board Slave States*, Fanny
Kemble's *Journal of a Residence on a Georgia Plantation in 1838–1839*, and,
of course, *Uncle Tom's Cabin*. On November 15, 1865, Higginson outlined
his rosy projections in a letter to his father. He calculated a $5,633 profit—
an enormous sum—for each of the three partners.

His freedmen employees, according to Higginson, would submit
because only "work or starvation was before them." He dismissed the
idea of a possible federal grant of forty acres to each freedman as "chi-
merical." Instead his plan was to offer a wage of $370 per year for a man
and a woman, and the prospect of a school for the freedmen's children.

On the farm Higginson was careful to set an example as a diligent
worker. "Bye and bye, when [the freedmen]…see us plough and chop
and hoe, and drive mules and clean horses…, they will feel still more per-
suaded to do their work." His idealism was immediately tested. In January
1866 the freedmen on his farm struck for higher wages. Ida noted in her
diary that the "darkies do not understand that they will not be paid if
they strike.…They still do not understand the value of work and wages."

Higginson was clearly frustrated. "As for the blacks…their future is a
mystery as dark as their skins," wrote the young New Englander, "…their
moral perceptions are deficient, either from nature or from habit or
from ignorance. They know that it is wrong to steal and lie, but they do

it continually." Rain and insects destroyed Higginson's crop; in the end, he "lost a great deal of money."

The Higginsons abandoned the dream of cotton and Georgia in a hasty retreat to Massachusetts. Ida had quickly concluded that "if left to themselves...[the freedmen] would [not] have energy enough to be thrifty and prosperous...they seem to need supervision...." She added, "These imperturbable darks...The more I see of them the more inscrutable they become and the less do I like them...." Utterly defeated, she concluded:

> It is discouraging to see how utterly wanting in character and conscience these people [the freedmen] seem to be, and how much more hopeful they appear at a distance than near to....

This echoed the sentiments of the black abolitionist Samuel R. Ward, who noticed that white abolitionists generally "love the colored man at a distance." Massachusetts abolitionists were at the forefront of the anti-slavery movement, but they recoiled when faced with the freedmen. They certainly made no effort to encourage them to move to Massachusetts.

The days of discouragement for Henry and Ida Higginson did not last long. They would enjoy financial, social, and philanthropic success in the cozy world of Boston and Harvard. Major Higginson attained wealth by selling bonds for the family's financial firm of Lee, Higginson and Company. He was able to realize his passion for music by organizing the Boston Symphony Orchestra in 1881 and was its main benefactor until 1918. As befitting a sports enthusiast, in 1890 he donated to Harvard a thirty-one-acre tract of land called Soldiers Field, in honor of six friends from Harvard who had died in the Civil War. At the dedication of Harvard's football stadium built on the land, he praised Confederate soldiers:

> No men of any country ever displayed more intelligence, devotion, energy, brilliancy, fortitude, in any cause than did our Southern brothers.... Today these Southern brothers are as cordial and kindly to us as men can be.... [T]here is no Kentucky, no Virginia, no Massachusetts, but one great country.

Massachusetts, in 1890, had yet again demonstrated its reconciliation with the white South.

Black Self-Sufficiency: The Montgomery Family

Was it possible for a black person or a black community to succeed in the cotton South if white oppression and a white-administered labor system were removed? Here we have the perfect test case, the Yazoo-Mississippi Delta town of Mound Bayou, an all-black community. Mound Bayou was perhaps the most significant experiment in black separatism and self-sufficiency in late-nineteenth-century America. The community was populated by blacks and governed by blacks, and the surrounding land was farmed by blacks without white Southern intervention.

One of many all-black towns established by freedmen, Mound Bayou was the best known of the all-black agricultural communities. Booker T. Washington, the proponent of self-help, racial consciousness, and racial separatism, himself wrote, "Outside of Tuskegee [the college he founded]...there is no community in the world that I am so deeply interested in as I am in Mound Bayou." President Theodore Roosevelt, who paid a personal visit to the community in 1907, described Mound Bayou as an "object lesson full of hope for the colored people."

Mound Bayou was the creation of the Montgomerys, an educated, experienced, willful, and confident black family. Its patriarch, Benjamin, had been born into slavery in Virginia; his son Isaiah was born into slavery in Mississippi in 1847 and died in 1924, in the Yazoo-Mississippi Delta. During the period between the end of the Civil War and the demise of cotton farming in the 1930s, the Montgomerys became at one point the largest black landowners in America.

This remarkable story begins with Joseph Davis, older brother of Jefferson Davis. Born in Georgia in 1784, Joseph Davis set out to make his fortune in the rich cotton land of western Mississippi. As a slaveholder, in short order he amassed land at Davis Bend, Mississippi, and considerable wealth in addition to a thriving law practice. On a trip in 1825, Davis shared a nine-hour coach ride with the Welshman Robert Owen, who was responsible for the communal settlement at New Harmony, Indiana. The well-read Davis, influenced by Owen, adapted notions of a cooperative environment to his own plantation. It was slavery but of a different form. Davis developed a vision of a cohesive, communal black society that he passed on to his slave Benjamin Montgomery. As a child Benjamin had learned to read and write from his playmate, the white son of his owner.

Benjamin Montgomery proceeded, incredibly as a slave, to develop a myriad of mechanical, business, and intellectual skills. While a slave, he opened a retail store that expanded as Davis acted as credit guarantor. White Mississippians traded in the store, and the enterprising owner soon established his own credit. Montgomery also acted as an agent for Davis in purchasing supplies and shipping cotton. He became the business manager for Davis's Hurricane plantation as well as Jefferson Davis's Brierfield plantation. Jefferson Davis, as a United States senator, even applied for a patent for Montgomery's boat propeller for a steamboat.

On his eleven thousand acres Joseph Davis practiced chattel slavery, but he established a form of "self-government" for the 345 slaves. He instituted a judicial system whereby slave complaints were heard by a slave jury, and slaves were allowed to testify. The court met on Sundays in a building called the Hall of Justice. There could be no punishment without a conviction by jury peers. An overseer's complaint was also subject to the court's review. Jefferson Davis adopted a similar court system at Brierfield.

During the Civil War, Benjamin Montgomery moved to Cincinnati and was technically emancipated; he returned to Mississippi in the summer of 1864. When, after the war, he confronted the Freedmen's Bureau with plans for developing a self-contained black community, an acrimonious relationship ensued. Meanwhile the Montgomerys continued to operate a retail store as they had before the war. Montgomery & Sons supplied 80 percent of the merchandise for the Davis Bend freedmen and charged a 20 to 25 percent markup on its goods.

When Joseph Davis received his pardon from the federal government in March 1866, his confiscated lands were returned. On November 19 that year he sold the Davis plantations to Montgomery and his sons. The experiment of a large-scale black community began with sixteen hundred freedmen who rented land from the Montgomerys.

Benjamin Montgomery immediately made it clear that his interests were economic, not political. He believed enfranchisement and political involvement to be distractions: "Regarding the suffrage question as of doubtful and remote utility, the discussion of it and other political topics as more likely to produce contention and idleness than harmony in the community, such discussions will be discouraged." This did not inhibit Montgomery from suing whites in legal disputes. Joseph Davis, on the other hand, supported the benefits of black suffrage.

The Northern press, white and black, followed events at Davis Bend closely. In December 1866 the *New York Times* endorsed Montgomery's avoidance of political activity and viewed him as a successful model for freedmen. The *Times* was impressed with Montgomery's knowledge of freedmen, with "whose foibles he [was] entirely familiar." The proper way for the freedmen to succeed, said the *Times*, was by "making themselves an indispensable industrial power."

The Davis Bend operation was subject to the vagaries that confronted all cotton farms: fluctuating cotton prices, unpredictable weather, floods, labor shortages, and insects, and all were partly responsible for the Montgomerys' failure to make interest payments to the Davis brothers. Just as important, the Montgomerys were not buttressed by a financial infrastructure. Their ability to operate a large business operation outside the economic mainstream was tenuous at best, though some of the results were gratifying. In 1870 Davis Bend produced twenty-five hundred bales of cotton, which might have given the Montgomerys a $50,000 profit. They won state contests "for the single best bale of long staple cotton" and the highest rating by the credit-rating firm of R. G. Dun. Nevertheless in 1881 the Montgomerys lost their land to Jefferson Davis in judicial proceedings.

After Benjamin Montgomery died in 1877, Isaiah Montgomery adhered to his father's philosophy of the primacy of economic interests in an environment where political rights were unattainable. He pursued his father's dream of a black-owned cotton community by orchestrating the purchase of land from the Louisville, New Orleans, and Texas Railroad, which had completed a railroad line through a fertile 7,200 square miles in the frontier area of northwest Mississippi known as the Delta. In 1887, accompanied by his cousin Benjamin Green, an astute businessman, Isaiah led fifteen Davis Bend freedmen to the settlement of Mound Bayou, Mississippi, and there a black colony was born.

Mound Bayou was nonetheless tied to the roller-coaster cotton world and had no financial infrastructure to absorb the attendant and inevitable shocks. By 1907 the community had achieved a fragile and superficial prosperity. It was a self-sustaining community with four hundred families and four thousand blacks. The town contained a railroad station (with a small waiting room for whites), a timber mill, thirteen stores, two cotton gins, a hospital, schools, and churches. For Booker T. Washington, Mound Bayou became living proof that the self-help philosophy in a racially separate community could work. After a mortgage default, a lenient renegotiated loan allowed the colony to continue.

During the early years of Mound Bayou, Isaiah Montgomery committed a visible, infamous act for which he is most remembered. As the only black among 134 delegates at the Mississippi Constitutional Convention of 1890, he voted for a constitution that codified white dominance and effectively disfranchised most black voters and some white voters. President Grover Cleveland applauded Montgomery's position. Despite some Republican opposition, the North embraced Montgomery's stand as a way to end the "southern problem." But most of the black response was scathing.

Frederick Douglass issued a harsh rebuke. "[W]e must denounce the policy," Douglass thundered, "but spare the man." Douglass demanded that "The South must let the Negro vote" or lose its congressional representation. Yet earlier Douglass had questioned the readiness of blacks for public office. "Slavery was a poor school in which to develop statesmen," he said, "and colored legislatures proved that." It is worth noting that a decade earlier Douglass had emphasized the priority of economic over political power.

What were Isaiah Montgomery's motives? Was he a classic traitor? Certainly he sought the favor of white leaders in order to protect Mound Bayou. His fledging black community existed amid a dominant white environment that was hostile to the very existence of a black enclave. The forty-three-year-old Montgomery was conversant with white America's racial attitude toward blacks; he could expect no help from white Northerners. He was not naive in assuming that assimilation with whites was a possibility. In nineteenth-century America a self-segregated community was his only option. He even boasted that "Not a single white person resides or owns property within [Mound Bayou's]...limits." Black political power had already been lost in the fallout from Reconstruction; black political presence was ineffective. Most likely a symbolic protest at the Mississippi Constitutional Convention, either in refusing to become a delegate or in assuming a role as a protest delegate, would have been a futile gesture.

Montgomery did have a bold plan for the future of blacks in Mississippi. In a revealing letter to Booker T. Washington, he outlined an ambitious project—to establish a credit company that would loan money to black farmers. It would further the expansion of a black-owned "vast territory," which would include most of the northern part of the Mississippi Delta. The area would consist of portions of Tunica, Coahoma, Quitman, Tallahatchie, and Washington counties. Mound Bayou would be its financial and industrial capital. Montgomery's scheme encompassed more than a multitude of black yeoman farmers with "forty acres and a mule." Rather than a modest, self-contained black community, he envisioned a large economic unit that could function as an independent black political entity. Isaiah Montgomery, like his father, knew that political power meant little without economic muscle.

Montgomery is often associated with Booker T. Washington's maligned policy of appeasement. Yet the choices for Montgomery and Washington were either militant protest as individuals outside the South or attempts to improve the plight of millions of black cotton farmers within an existing system. The white North's containment policy had trapped 90 percent of the black population in the cotton fields. In reality, both Washington and Montgomery had no alternative if they wished to build black institutions in the South. In bowing to "power realities of [his] time and place," the historian Neil McMillen wrote, Montgomery realized that "conciliation was a more promising path to black progress than confrontation."

Mound Bayou had to create a town with viable mercantile concerns, an educational system, functioning financial institutions, an appropriate municipal government, and effective contacts to the white environment. The Delta, with its cheap, fertile land, provided the venue. Cotton was the commercial linchpin that would determine the colony's fate. But Mound Bayou, and the theory of Mound Bayou, failed when confronted with reality.

The fluctuations of the cotton world severely bruised the community. Its shallow, fragile, and short-lived prosperity has been exaggerated. Because of national publicity, Mound Bayou became a symbol of black hope, but by the early 1920s the town was economically moribund. Both its bank and its loan company failed. Great swings in the price of cotton were a large factor in the demise. The white Delta towns were subject to the same trauma, but a more secure financial infrastructure allowed them to prosper modestly for another forty years. The progeny of the white Delta community, unlike that of the black population, whether in Mound Bayou or elsewhere, had the mobility to find other economic opportunity.

Montgomery's legacy draws both ire and praise. He is sometimes belittled as an elitist. In contrast, the late Milburn Crowe, a Mound Bayou native and historian, revered Isaiah Montgomery. The elaborate tombstone erected at Montgomery's gravesite was a gift from white Delta men. Walter Sillers Sr., an influential white planter and friend, delivered a eulogy at Montgomery's funeral. Sillers remarked that Isaiah Montgomery was "one of the greatest of his race...and like Moses, he carried his people from slavery to their new freedom in the wilderness."

Mound Bayou and the Montgomery family saga provide an abject lesson in the futility of black economic hopes after the Civil War, even with black ownership and black political control. Despite glowing rhetoric, Mound Bayou demonstrated the limits of racial independence in a white economic world. And in the commercial world, where interaction with the economic mainstream is a prerequisite for success, racial separatism simply could not work effectively. This theme would recur repeatedly into the twenty-first century.

The Education of Freedmen

Education was the prerequisite for black advancement and entrance into the economic mainstream. The plight of black education in the South after the introduction of public schools is well known. Second-class citizenship included underfunded, racially segregated schools and a vocationally dominant curriculum. The goal was to train productive cotton workers and skilled manual labor. The most optimistic proponents, such as Booker T. Washington, viewed this as an intermediate phase before the access to more sophisticated occupations. The South was the venue.

Meanwhile, what was the educational trajectory for the minuscule numbers of black Northerners? When the Great Migration began during World War I, was the condition of black Northerners the future model? With 20-20 hindsight we know that something was very wrong in the North. The plight of black education there is well documented in Davison Douglas's *Jim Crow Moves North: The Battle over Northern School Segregation, 1865–1954.* The dichotomy between anti-slavery and anti-black attitudes remained pronounced even where small numbers of blacks lived.

As described by Douglas, legislative efforts to merge black and white schools in the North could occur only when there were few blacks. Racial enlightenment did not propel anti-segregation legislation. By 1865 abolitionist Massachusetts alone—with a black population of less than 1 percent—had ended legal school segregation. Black students in Maine, New Hampshire, and Vermont, all with black populations of less than 0.2 percent, were allowed to attend integrated schools. Connecticut and Rhode Island, with black populations of less than 2 percent, enacted desegregation legislation in the 1860s. Douglas notes that Midwestern states with tiny black populations—Wisconsin (0.2 percent), Minnesota (0.2 percent), Iowa (0.5 percent), and Michigan (1 percent)—also desegregated in the 1860s. Between 1870 and 1890 each of these states *lost* black population. Several school districts allowed blacks to enroll in integrated schools after challenges by black parents. All had small numbers of black students.

The prime motivations for combining dual black and white school systems were "political expediency" and "cost," not racial enlightenment. In Ohio the cities of Columbus, Cleveland, and Cincinnati were keenly aware of the price of two school systems. It was calculated in 1882 that a merger could save Cincinnati 90 percent of the $50,000 spent on separate schools. When segregated schools were mandated by Ohio in 1863, the *Cleveland Leader* balked at the expense "entail[ed] upon taxpayers." In 1872 McLean County, Illinois, built a distinct school building for two black children. San Francisco ended its dual school system in 1875 because of the cost of keeping eight black students separate. Oakland in 1872 had established only one school because of the prohibitive cost of separately educating a few black students. In 1874 Pittsburgh repealed its school segregation laws because of the expense of operating its one black school.

Each area had a different racial story. Philadelphia's anti-segregation legislation, passed in 1881, was circumvented: many black children were not allowed to attend white schools. Philadelphia officials were quite open in discouraging integration. School board member Henry J. Halliwell candidly charged that "Negroes are lazy and shiftless and avoid hard work.... [T]hat will keep them out of the schools." Exceptions were made for light-skinned blacks. Particularly instructive was this comment made by a Philadelphia school board member:

> I think it is very doubtful if there are many colored students who can submit for the course of studies and discipline of the regular public schools.... For one thing, they have not the same mental oversight at home and by nature they are not partial to restraint.

New Jersey's results were mixed. Paul Robeson, the actor, writer, and activist, attended segregated schools in Princeton. One community built a new school for blacks, which appeased the black community.

New York's integration effort was similarly skewed. Where there were few blacks in upstate, one school sufficed. Brooklyn and Queens, on the other hand, experienced resistance to integration. An 1875 court case in Brooklyn ruled that separate black schools would be "highly conducive to the welfare of black students."

Pushback also came from elements within the black community who advocated segregated schools. Black parents in Cincinnati and New York complained of "mistreatment" by whites in integrated schools. Black teachers were concerned about their jobs as few of them in Boston, Chicago, and Cleveland were able to teach in integrated schools. Anti-segregation laws would "virtually [dismiss] all the colored teachers for the profession," argued an Ohio black teacher in 1887. Indiana blacks opposed 1897 anti-segregation legislation on the grounds that "many colored men and women" would be deprived "of their livelihood." Their fears were well founded. After Pittsburgh shuttered its only black school in 1875, "no black teacher would teach in Pittsburgh again until the 1930s."

As one may easily recognize, these themes—racial integration (as opposed to desegregation), displacement of teachers (blacks in Chicago and New Orleans in the twenty-first century), racial funding parity versus integration, white flight in anticipation of black influx—are very much alive in the twenty-first century. The courts, the media, and educational politics reflect an abundance of unsolved issues from the nineteenth century.

Theodore Roosevelt and the
Northern Privileged Class

The doyen of the Progressive Era, Theodore Roosevelt, was decidedly opinionated about blacks. It might be assumed that he was racially progressive when, as New York governor in 1900, he supported school desegregation legislation that held that "No person shall be refused admission from any public school...on account of race or color." But Roosevelt thought that Reconstruction was a "mistake," that it proved how "federal legislation in itself could not solve the racial dilemma." He wanted blacks to lower their expectations and not hope for the impossible or be "led away, as the educated Negro so often is...into the pursuit of fantastic visions."

On numerous occasions Roosevelt elaborated his thoughts on black inferiority. He had a detailed correspondence with his Harvard friend Owen Wister, the author who popularized the Western literary genre with his novel *The Virginian*. In 1906 Roosevelt responded to Wister, "I entirely agree with you that as a race, and in the mass, the [blacks] are altogether inferior to whites." He distinguished between elite blacks, whom he held in high regard, and the black masses. He admired Booker T. Washington, whom he famously hosted at a White House dinner in 1901. No other invitations to blacks were forthcoming.

Roosevelt viewed the black person as a child: "I do not believe that the average Negro...is as yet in any way fit to take care of himself...for if he were, there would be no Negro race problem." He abhorred the lynching of blacks (and whites) in the South, but he never made a public anti-lynching pronouncement. He associated rape with black men: "This worst enemy of the colored race is the colored man who commits some hideous wrong, especially if that be the worst of all crimes, rape..." At Tuskegee he warned black students about descending into crime and told them that blacks were a "backward race."

In politics TR thought most of the black population was unqualified to hold public office, but he wanted others to be given an opportunity to succeed: "If ninety-five percent of the blacks were unfit to hold office...rule those ninety-five out, but not the five percent simply because of the color of their skin." He was proud that while reducing the number of black appointments to public offices in the South he had upgraded the quality of his selections. As such, his support of his black appointments—Minnie Lee Cox as post office mistress in Indianola, Mississippi, and William Crum to the board of customs in Charleston, South Carolina—attested to his sincere conviction. He held the Republican Party in the South with disdain as a "set of black and white scalawags, with few decent men." He was wary of black suffrage; he believed that certain sections of the South "would become another Haiti if the ballot was given to blacks without qualification." "Universal suffrage" for blacks he regarded as a crime and a joke.

Roosevelt's deeds spoke as loudly as his words. In November 1905 black soldiers stationed in Brownsville, Texas, were accused of killing a white saloonkeeper, shooting a white police officer, and running rampant through town. An exhaustive investigation revealed no evidence that the soldiers were guilty. Roosevelt nevertheless resolved to discharge 167 of the 170 men accused, many of them decorated combat veterans. He was vindictive because no black soldier had divulged the name of a perpetrator.

Roosevelt thought of the white man as a tutor to blacks and other races. While denouncing "social intermingling," he favored "elementary justice" for blacks. In order to deserve it, they had to exhibit "thrift, sobriety, self-control, respect for the rights of others…and intelligence to work to a given end."

Roosevelt's biographers blame his racial attitudes on his Georgia-raised mother. In general, and where possible, white Americans view anyone with a drop of white Southern blood as potentially racially biased by twenty-first-century standards. Theodore Roosevelt was raised in New York City and went to Harvard.

As it happens, Roosevelt's assessment of black inferiority was similar to that of the white Northern scions of anti-slavery families, untainted by white Southern blood. Charles Francis Adams Jr., Harvard educated, a Union officer, grandson of John Quincy Adams, and son of Civil War ambassador to London Charles Francis Adams Sr., was a railroad businessman and author. He was emphatic about black inferiority: "The Southern people have the dead weight of Africanism tied to them." He labeled the "African…a distinct alien" who disrupted the American goal of assimilation. In 1907 the president of Harvard, Charles W. Eliot, advocated racially segregated schools if Boston's black population were to grow. Abraham Lincoln's son, Robert Todd Lincoln, a railroad attorney for the Pullman Company, refused to respond to a complaint by W. E. B. Du Bois about poor treatment of black officials aboard a Pullman Company car.

Then there was Harvard professor Albert Bushnell Hart, who carried a sound abolitionist family pedigree. The influential Hart, often described as the founding father of professional history in the United States, served as president of both the American Historical Association and the American Political Science Association. He considered the average black man a "moral and social cripple." He was pessimistic about their "intellectual...power.... Genuine friends and well-wishers of the Negro feel the irresponsibility of the race." This Harvard intellectual's summary of the race issue in 1910 was devastating and offered little hope:

> The main issue must be fairly faced by the friends as well as the enemies of the colored race. Measuring by the white people of the South..., the negroes, as a people, appear to be considerably below the whites in mental and moral status. There are a million or more exceptions, but they do not break the force of the eight or nine millions of average negroes. Race measured by race, the Negro is inferior, and his past history in Africa and in America leads to the belief that he will remain inferior in race stamina and race achievement.

Yet one of Hart's brightest students was W. E. B. Du Bois. Hart placed mulattoes such as Du Bois in a special class that might at times reach the potential of whites. One historian has branded Hart with the perplexing label of "liberal racist."

Lincoln, Theodore Roosevelt, and Albert Bushnell Hart were among those who could identify a black elite with whom they could relate, separate from the black population. W. E. B. Du Bois later identified a similar elite in his phrase "Talented Tenth," referring to a percentage of blacks whose excellence distinguished them from the black masses.

———

Between Emancipation and World War I, white America, both North and South, refused to assimilate African Americans into the broader society and, most important, into the economic mainstream. Millions of white immigrants, with some struggle, successfully made their way through America's route to assimilation. Blacks were denied this quintessential American rite of passage. A white Northern containment policy effectively entrapped freedmen in the South with no mobility, even while the black population in the North remained less than 2 percent from 1865 to World War I. The white North breathed a collective sigh of relief in avoiding a mass black migration north; the white South accepted the black presence in order to fill its critical need for cotton laborers.

The white North's distinction between its abhorrence of race-based slavery and its disdain for free blacks was exposed. Frederick Douglass recognized this in 1864. The outspoken black leader cited the North's recognition of slavery as a "stupendous crime against nature," which had to be dealt with by war, but he also noted that second to anti-slavery attitudes was a "national prejudice and hatred toward colored people of the country." After Emancipation, nothing fundamentally changed in white America's wish to separate itself from blacks.

A poignant anecdote of two conspicuous women serves as a powerful example of the nation's reunion. On June 23, 1893, the *New York Times* front-page headline read "Celebrated Women Meet." The article referred to the beginning of a warm friendship between Julia Dent Grant, the widow of Ulysses S. Grant, and Varina Howell Davis, the widow of Jefferson Davis. Both women were living in New York when Mrs. Grant called upon Mrs. Davis. Their subsequent carriage ride together in Central Park drew media attention. White America had reconciled. The American family was united except for one member, the black community.

Chapter Three

The Great Migration: The Reception of Blacks in Northern Cities

The authors... [of *Black Metropolis*] know that violent events will soon flare forth, prompted either by whites or blacks; and they know that white America will stand transfixed in bewilderment at the magnitude and sanguinity of these events.
—RICHARD WRIGHT, INTRODUCTION TO *BLACK METROPOLIS*, 1945

It was the winter of 1927 that I first glimpsed Chicago through the naive eyes of a young Mississippi Negro to whom the South Side loomed as the promised land, the longed-for Mecca. Instead of cotton fields, muddy streets and shacks, I looked with amazement upon vast stretches of street and stone, towering factories and wide straight streets thronged with trolley tracks.... Instead of the scent of magnolias, I smelt the stench of the stockyards, and the odor of gas fumes.

Ten years later, in 1937, I had become saturated with Chicago's reality of gang murders, corrupt politics and the depression. Like most Americans seeking a broader vision of life, I packed my suitcase and struck out for other parts.
—RICHARD WRIGHT, "THE SHAME OF CHICAGO," *EBONY*, DECEMBER 1951

So far, most [white] Chicagoans view Negro-white relations negatively—solely in terms of preventing a riot.
—ST. CLAIR DRAKE AND HORACE CAYTON, *BLACK METROPOLIS*, 1945

Education means an assimilation of white culture. It decreases the dissimilarity of the Negroes from other Americans. Increasing education provides theories and tools for the rising Negro protest against caste status in which Negroes are held.... [E]ducation has a symbolic significance in the Negro world: the educated Negro has, in one important respect, become equal to the better class of whites.

[In the North] the American Creed permeates instruction, and the Negro, as well as the white youths, is inculcated with the traditional American virtues of efficiency, thrift, and ambition. The American dream of individual success is held out to the Negroes as to other students.

—GUNNAR MYRDAL, *An American Dilemma:*
The Negro Problem and Modern Democracy, 1944

We're not the NAACP. We're a business.

—JOHN H. JOHNSON, FOUNDER AND PUBLISHER, *Ebony*

The lives of Franklin and of Lincoln, my patron saints, are the strongest agency for Americanization known today.

—MICHAEL (MIHAJLO) PUPIN, "THE REVELATION OF LINCOLN TO A SERBIAN IMMIGRANT," 1926

Tornado By-Passes Negroes

—*CHICAGO DEFENDER,* 1940S

In their attempt to establish or define or foster a separate identity, blacks have developed a tendency to view matters exclusively through a racial lens. Clearly this derives from W. E. B. Du Bois's notion of a "double consciousness"—that of a black as well as an American—and it misleads the viewer in subtle or crucial ways.

In the 1940s the influential black daily newspaper the *Chicago Defender* used two thousand "agent-correspondents" to report personal hometown stories of "births, weddings, and deaths and then sold the paper to their fellow townspeople." From 1941 to 1945 the *Defender*'s white national editor, Ben Burns, was directed to make sure that articles exhibited a "pro-Negro" slant. Because he was white, the *Defender* placed Burns inconspicuously in a second-floor corner of the newspaper office, at an "unobtrusive desk" where no one would notice him. He masqueraded as a black person in a column called "Let My People Work." Burns recounts one absurd "hometown" case involving a destructive tornado.

It was exclusively rendered racial with a "three-inch 'scare' headline": "Tornado By-Passes Negroes."

This sort of perspective easily becomes excessive and less benign. W. E. B. Du Bois would sometimes be trapped by racial bias, or racial blindness, in his praise of Japan's fascist activity in the 1930s. Because he grossly erred in assuming a unity among all peoples of color, he completely rationalized Japan's brutal invasion of China. The recurring interpretation of the world when isolated by the blinders of race would grow even more pronounced in the twentieth century.

What happened when the dreaded black migration to the North finally took shape? The chief motivating factor was economics: a plain old-fashioned labor shortage finally broke the chains that bound blacks to the cotton fields. The need for labor created by World War I, and the interruption of the flow of white immigrants, propelled the Great Migration of Southern blacks. In turn it provoked the great *white* migration, otherwise known as white flight—the movement of whites out of residential areas when blacks moved into them. America's racial legacy would remain.

When factory jobs beckoned, Southern blacks who sought to escape the South were easily motivated to journey north. When industry beckons anywhere, whether in nineteenth-century Great Britain or twentieth-century China, people leave the farm for the city. For Southern black tenant farmers, industrial work in the North meant regular wages as opposed to the once-a-year unpredictable farm payment. Yet another "promised land," the American North loomed on the horizon, and Chicago, the bustling industrial giant, became a conspicuous Canaan. That this saga finally arrived at Chicago's racial impasse in 2016 is relevant, but that story must wait its chronological turn.

In the booming wartime economy, the number of unemployed nationally dropped from 8.5 percent in 1915 to 1.4 percent in 1918. Employers were desperate for workers, even black labor. Fears of a black invasion gave way to the recruitment of blacks by agents who offered free transportation. Between 1916 and 1919, half a million Southern blacks moved to the North; by 1930 another million followed the steel tracks of the railroad, on the way to various Northern cities in pursuit of jobs.

Racial discrimination in the South played a secondary role in guiding the blacks north.

For white Northerners, the black person was no longer "at a distance." The anti-slavery white North's anti-black views were now on full display. The migration momentum continued so that by the 1940s racial demographics had changed substantially. Between 1920 and 1940 the black population of Detroit grew from 40,000 to 149,000, Cleveland from 34,000 to 84,000, New York from 152,000 to 458,000. Still, abolitionist New England's black population amounted to little more than 1 percent. The cotton kingdom of the Mississippi Delta retained a population of 400,000, of which 300,000 were black.

In the years bookending the world wars, Chicago received a tenth of all migrating Southern blacks. The city became a natural terminus for blacks because of the Illinois Central Railroad, which paralleled the Mississippi River from New Orleans. As a consequence, Chicago's black population consistently rose in each decade of the twentieth century, from 44,103 in 1910 (2 percent), to 109,458 in 1920 (4 percent), to 337,000 in 1930 (9.4 percent). It was Chicago that W. E. B. Du Bois selected as the setting for his 1928 political novel *Dark Princess*, a tale of the evolving black migrants' political participation. Du Bois was indeed prescient. In 2008 Chicago's adopted citizen Barack Obama became the first black president of the United States.

Chicago!

America's "Second City" was unprepared for these men and women. An anti-slavery stronghold in antebellum America, Chicago had had a minuscule black population of 1 percent at the turn of the century. The historian William Tuttle wrote, "The larger the black community [in Chicago], the more insoluble appeared the problems." De facto segregation followed when black numbers mushroomed.[1]

In 1917 the *Chicago Tribune*, whose antebellum abolitionist stance did not extend to racial tolerance, called the black migration a "huge mistake" and shouted, "Black man, stay South." The *Tribune* described

---

1 In 2016, after five years as Chicago's mayor, Rahm Emanuel, a close ally of President Obama, became enmeshed in a racially charged police, education, and housing quagmire. He had either willfully overlooked the consistent racial tension and anger in the city's segregated environment

black migrants as "lazy, shiftless ne'er do wells, surely to be a burden on the city." The newspaper often used condescending terms in referring to blacks: "Half a Million Darkies from Dixie Swarm to the North to Better Themselves."

As tens of thousands of blacks poured into the city, pressures rose for blacks to seek housing beyond their traditional boundary lines. Alarmed whites responded with bombs, threats, laws, and organized resistance. Between July 1917 and March 1918, whites exploded fifty-eight bombs at black residences in previously all-white neighborhoods. In 1919 a six-year-old black girl was killed by one of the bombs. As early as 1897, homeowners in the Woodlawn neighborhood had coerced white landlords to stop renting to blacks. Even then, Chicago had a "black belt," which would eventually become a black ghetto called Bronzeville. At the time, the [Chicago] *Property Owner's Journal* had launched a caustic salvo:

> There is nothing in the make-up of a Negro, physically or mentally, which should induce anyone to welcome him as a neighbor. The best of them are unsanitary...ruin alone follows in their path....Niggers are undesirable and entirely irresponsible and vicious.

In 1917 the Chicago Real Estate Board passed a resolution that encouraged whites on every block to defend their territory from black incursion. Before "white flight" became a common expression in the 1960s, panicked whites sold their property at a loss to escape quickly. The poet and rising journalist Carl Sandburg reported of a white society woman who, faced with black encroachment, sold an apartment for $14,000 that she had purchased for $26,000. Rents, despite lower home prices, soared for the entrapped blacks, who were exploited by other blacks as well as by whites. Editor Ben Burns of the *Defender* recounts the story of a wealthy black attorney who in the 1940s illegally subdivided two apartments into six and collected an exorbitant rent from his "black brothers." It turns out that the attorney had been part of a legal team that challenged restrictive covenants. The NAACP won its lawsuit against restrictive covenants, but the Supreme Court did not rule that the covenants were *illegal*. Instead

---

or did not understand racial history beyond the soliciting of black votes. In 1945 St. Clair Drake and Horace Cayton had written, "So far, most [white] Chicagoans view Negro-white relations negatively—solely in terms of preventing a riot." Much had not changed.

the court in 1917 held that each case must be tried individually. The result was a virtual quarantine of blacks in racially segregated Chicago neighborhoods.

Wealthy black businessman Joseph Binga's home was the most conspicuous bombing victim in this period. Binga had come to Chicago penniless three decades earlier and had built a small black empire in banking and real estate. The rising star was now the public face of black business potential. Yet when his house was destroyed, the *Property Owner's Journal* attacked him for having "wormed his way into a white neighborhood." Binga's fate would be determined by the "business cycle," which made blacks even more vulnerable because they were the "weakest link" in America's commercial chain. He became a victim of the 1929 crash and subsequent Depression. Convicted of embezzlement, the former magnate was sentenced to jail and paroled in 1940 in the custody of a Catholic priest. He was then employed as a janitor in a Bronzeville Catholic church and died broke in 1943.

For the most part, black housing in Chicago amounted to slum conditions. Toilets were located in "hallways, yards, and basements." Overcrowding was commonplace; apartments lacked proper ventilation and lighting. Landlords did not make repairs. Health statistics were consistent with housing conditions: infant mortality, life expectancy, illegitimate births, and incidence of disease were disproportionately skewed in the "black belt." In 1925 the death rate for blacks in Chicago approximated that of Bombay, India. Vice and crime proliferated.

By 1929 the *Chicago Defender* was telling blacks, for the first time, to stay "in the South." Although white-owned banks were failing, life outside the economic mainstream was (and remains) especially precarious. The assimilationist path, unavailable to Mound Bayou's Isaiah Montgomery or Chicago's Joseph Binga, would yet again prove necessary for a group's broad economic advancement.

In every aspect of Chicago life from 1919 to 1925, blacks met with discrimination and ostracism. Was an existence in Chicago better than one in Mississippi? Certainly a steady (though low) wage, the right to vote, the prevalence of a somewhat fair legal system, the absence of fear of white-on-black vigilante violence, and a better educational system were advantages. But the shock of entering a segregated urban ghetto would leave lasting scars.

In the Chicago school system, principals practiced a form of racial segregation by assigning black students to a "substandard branch," which might be 90 percent black. White parents in the Wendell Phillips school district, on the city's South Side, formally asked for a new school because "white children should not be compelled to sit with colored children." Frequent racial clashes occurred at Wendell Phillips High School, which had a majority of black students. Parks, playgrounds, and beaches were "unofficially segregated," and whites used violent means to keep the parks segregated. Public accommodations, theaters, restaurants, and stores routinely treated blacks discourteously.

All these conditions were tolerated by blacks because of the possibility of employment. Before World War I, Chicago's major industrial companies—Armour, Swift, Pullman, and International Harvester—hired only white workers, but in wartime white exclusivity was no longer possible. In 1900 approximately 65 percent of black men and 80 percent of black women in Chicago had been domestics or servants. Only 8.3 percent of the men and 11.9 percent of the women had held manufacturing jobs, most of them unskilled. But wages at the meatpacking plants and steel mills were attractive to field hands and sharecroppers. In 1910 blacks accounted for only 6 percent of the workforce at the meatpacking plants; by 1920, 32 percent of the workforce in these unsanitary, debilitating jobs was black. Factories were forced by labor shortages to ease their policies, and factory work became the main source of employment for blacks. Between 1914 and 1919 the employment situation was plagued by layoffs and rampant inflation that saw prices rise in Chicago by 75 percent. Blacks were last to be hired and first to be fired. Factory work, when stable, provided wages, but for the most part it did not provide the stepping-stone to a better life. There was a ceiling.

As the black population grew and as blacks became strikebreakers, racial friction escalated. On July 27, 1919, the racially combustible city drew the spark that ignited one of America's worst race riots. On that day a black teenager, Eugene Williams, swam into a section of Lake Michigan's South Side beach that was understood to be for whites only. The youth drowned after he was pelted with rocks by angry whites. The ensuing massive violence lasted fourteen days and required the deployment of the state militia. Of 38 people killed, 23 were black; of 537 injured, 342 were black. The Chicago race riot should not have been a surprise as it had been preceded by numerous racial skirmishes. The *Chicago Tribune* now predicted far greater segregation:

> Despite the possible justice of Negro demands, the fact is that the races are not living in harmony.... How long will it be before segregation will be the only means of preventing murders?

If blacks could not be confined to the cotton fields, they would be consigned to the ghettos. A new era in racial tension had begun, this time in the "promised land." And blacks would fight back.

Soon after the riots, Carl Sandburg published an account of the conflagration. In a bizarre phrase Sandburg referred to events as a "so-called race riot." Yet there was nothing "so-called" about the racial battle. Sandburg repeatedly blamed the race riot on poor "housing, transportation, and education, not skin color." This, he wrote, was a "national problem," and he recommended that a commission "be appointed to investigate and make recommendations."[2] (Fifty years later an Illinois governor, Otto Kerner, would chair a task force to dissect other American race riots. The Report of the National Advisory Commission on Civil Disorders, or the Kerner Commission, appeared in 1968 after massive race riots had occurred in Newark and Detroit. White America was terrified in 1968 as it had not been in 1919.)

The social conditions of Chicago blacks were well chronicled by the black sociologist E. Franklin Frazier, a University of Chicago PhD, in *The Negro Family in Chicago* (1932). Frazier explored the demoralization of the black family as it collided with urban life. The family structure of most lower-class blacks, he wrote, "lacked continuity and roots...fading memories of relatives and life in the South were all that remained of a shattered social life." One unmarried mother whom he questioned about "her family background" responded, "I ain't got no history." "Negro life," wrote Frazier, "appeared casual, precarious, and fragmentary." His chapter titles were straightforward: "Desertion and Non-Support," "Illegitimacy," "Juvenile Delinquency."

---

2 Chicago had to wait until 2009 for a small memorial to this terrible event. A small bronze plaque was placed by Elmhurst High School on the Lake Michigan shore. America had decided that race-related troubles should be commemorated and highlighted only in the South.

Disproportion was Frazier's operative word. By 1921, with only 4 percent of the Chicago population, blacks accounted for 15.6 percent of the "cases of desertion brought before the Court of Domestic Relations." The numbers would grow substantially. Blacks in Chicago and most Northern cities, according to Frazier, "furnish a disproportionate number of [juvenile delinquent] cases in most cities for which statistics are available." One case tells the story of a mother whose son joined a gang at twelve, dropped out of school, and turned to a life of crime. In the 1920s, at the Cook County Hospital in Chicago, "about 50 percent of the illegitimate births were Negroes." Cincinnati and Philadelphia blacks had correspondingly high illegitimate births:

> Illegitimacy was found to be an aspect of the general breakdown in the urban environment of the customary controls which characterized the rural and simple communities from which a majority of the persons involved have come... and a well-nigh complete demoralization of the individual.

Thus the disorganization of the black family was under way well before the oft-cited Moynihan Report of 1965.[3]

Race in Chicago was vividly on display through the intertwined relationship of three men—a black novelist, a white editor of black publications, and a black publisher. The men were Richard Wright (1908–1960), the black author of *Black Boy* (1944) and *Native Son* (1940); Ben Burns (1913–2000), the relatively unknown but highly influential white editor at the *Chicago Defender* and at *Ebony* magazine; and John Johnson (1918–2005), the black publisher of *Ebony* and founder of the powerful Johnson Publishing Company. These strong personalities knew one another, collaborated, and ultimately collided in the racial

---

3 Moynihan's report was titled "The Negro Family: The Case for National Action." Then an employee of Labor Department, he warned that "the family structure of lower-class Negroes is highly unstable, and in many urban centers approaching complete breakdown." Ensuing government welfare programs, said some conservative observers, exacerbated the disintegration of lower-class black families. The percentage of single-parent black families, already disturbingly high, skyrocketed after the vast expansion of government welfare programs in the 1960s.

reality of their segregated world and the rough-and-tumble arena of black publishing.

The best known of the three men is the angry, militant novelist and ultimately foreign exile Richard Wright. Born near Natchez, Mississippi, Wright made his way to Chicago in 1927. Like many disillusioned blacks and whites, in 1933 he joined the Communist Party, which he later abandoned. Wright and Ben Burns, the white editor, became acquainted at Communist Party meetings in Chicago.

For Wright, Chicago was the most compelling example of the urban black situation. His best-known works of fiction and his important nonfiction introduction to *Black Metropolis* were written in and about Chicago. *Native Son* is a brutal fictional account of the life of Bigger Thomas, who migrated north as a youth. Thomas's tragic story, reflecting the devastating impact of Northern urban ghetto life, stunned white America.

The twenty-year-old fictional Thomas—a gang member, high school drop-out, and petty crook—epitomized the dysfunctional product of the Northern ghetto. After obtaining through a charity a job as a chauffeur for a wealthy white Chicago family, Thomas drives the daughter Mary Dalton to a rendezvous with her Communist boyfriend. The two patronizingly include their driver, the uncomfortable Thomas, on a drunken spree.

A racial horror story follows. Thomas, whose involvement is by chance, must carry the inebriated heiress upstairs to her bedroom. When Mary's blind mother enters the room, a hapless Thomas is overcome with fear, hate, and resentment as he realizes that he will be caught in the bedroom of a white woman who has passed out. The petrified Thomas covers her face with a pillow and inadvertently suffocates her. The blind mother senses only the smell of alcohol and leaves. Terrified beyond belief, Thomas disposes of the body in the basement furnace, first dismembering the body parts, including the head, in order to fit them in.

In a catatonic state, Thomas leaves the Dalton house and flees to the apartment of his black girlfriend, Bessie. She and Thomas have a relationship of convenience, not love or respect. Thomas proceeds to rape Bessie, bludgeon her to death with a brick, and force the body down a ventilation shaft.

As these crimes are discovered, Chicago is in a state of panic. White mobs loudly call for Thomas's lynching, and he is captured by a dragnet of thousands of Chicago policemen. Soon, accompanied by ubiquitous press coverage and the intimidation of blacks and Communists, Thomas is brought to trial. The death penalty is assumed.

Thomas is defended by Boris Max, a Jewish Communist. Through Max's arguments, Richard Wright indicts white America for creating Bigger Thomas and thousands of blacks through the oppressive, intolerable conditions imposed upon them. Max refuses to allow an insanity plea. He argues that Thomas is not responsible for his actions because he has no free will—a theme that later becomes pervasive. His actions, according to Wright (and later others), are reflexive reactions to a culmination of conditions, beginning with slavery and graduating to the urban nightmare of poverty, exploitation, restriction, discrimination, and condescension. Thus even murder can be tolerated. The "limits" and "restrictions" on black life, says Max, are everywhere. "Multiply Bigger Thomas twelve million times," wrote Wright through Max's voice, "…and you have the psychology of the Negro people."

Through Max, Wright presciently describes the impending racial violence that would engulf America in the 1960s. "Kill…[Bigger Thomas] and swell the tide of pent-up lava that will some day break loose," pleaded the lawyer Max, "not in a single, blundering, accidental, individual crime, but in a wild cataract of emotion that will brook no control." The massive race riots of Watts (1965), Newark (1967), and Detroit (1967) would vindicate Wright's prediction within a decade after the author's death. "[T]welve million blacks," he wrote, "constitute a separate nation, stunted, stripped, and held captive *within* this nation…." One stinging phrase identifies the root of America's racial catastrophe: blacks are "excluded from, and unassimilated, in our society." For Wright, assimilation was America's racial solution.

Boris Max's strategy of pleading for life imprisonment for Bigger Thomas does not work. Thomas gets the death penalty. Bewildered by the world he inhabits, the antihero is unrepentant.

Black Boy, Wright's other best-known book, purports to be a memoir. But even the Library of America edition of the book cautions the reader about "the reliability of Wright's memory." It is difficult, perhaps impossible, to distinguish between "fiction and fact" in this autobiography. Instead the publisher praises Wright's "stunning imagination and mythic power" and, curiously, refers to "the challenge of being Southern, black, and male in America" without noting the plight of a black male in Chicago. In this respect, Wright's *Native Son* and his introduction to *Black Metropolis* offer better material than *Black Boy*.

The strident Wright captured the devastating black experience in Chicago in his introduction to *Black Metropolis: A Study of Negro Life in a Northern City* (1945), written by the anthropologist St. Clair Drake and the sociologist Horace R. Cayton, both black and both trained at the University of Chicago. This unvarnished appraisal of Chicago's black community and its relationship to the white community set the stage for the racial turmoil of the 1960s long before violence and the Moynihan Report. The connections and issues relate directly to the 1960s and the twenty-first century.

In his introduction to their work, Wright declared that the "decisive and pivotal centers of Negro life in America" had shifted to the Northern urban cities. Indeed, Chicago had produced "the most incisive and radical black thought." Riots in New York, Detroit, Los Angeles, and Mobile, all occurring in 1943, were fresh in Wright's mind. He warned of more "violent events" to come and strived to explain "the racial outbreaks that plague America." These were a prelude, he thought, to a maelstrom of race violence. "[V]iolent events," he quotes Draken and Cayton, "will soon flare forth prompted either by whites or blacks.... White Americans will stand transfixed in bewilderment at the magnitude... of these events."

For Wright, black oppression grew from white roots. The black man's degradation and alienation—his conduct, personality, and culture, his entire life—were created by "conditions imposed upon him by white America." The American black, in Wright's view, was the "victim" of an almost "complete rejection" by white society.

Wright's white people, whether South or North, simply did not understand the "Negro problem." Twenty-first-century Americans bemoan the absence of a frank conversation about race and prefer dialogues about reconciliation. But even in Wright's time, he complained that the groups dealing with racial issues "have consistently diluted the problem, blurred it, injected foggy moral or sentimental notions into it." He accused the "political Left" of gyrating and squirming, reducing race to "fit rigidly into a class-warfare frame of reference, when the roots... lie in American culture as a whole." He rejected the oversimplification of class conflict. The "political Right," he charged, practiced avoidance by "regarding Negroes as individuals...ignoring the inevitable race consciousness which three hundred years of Jim Crow living has burned in the Negro's heart."

Wright assigned no individual responsibility for black actions, no matter how heinous. And his viewpoint persists today among blacks *and* whites. The individual has been subsumed by the group. Wright was a harbinger of twenty-first-century black denial of responsibility for one's own behavior and a surrender to group thought. Ironically, historians today assiduously claim that even slaves had "agency," or individual free will. Acts of resistance within the harsh strictures of race-based slavery are cited as prime examples of distinct personal behavior. Yet according to black authors from Richard Wright to Ta-Nehisi Coates, blacks have been forced by a brutal discriminatory environment to seek shelter in a racially defined group.

Richard Wright's long-term friendship with Ben Burns began in the 1930s when both worked at the *Daily Worker*, the Communist newspaper in Chicago. Burns soon woke up to the foibles of communism and looked elsewhere for employment to support his family. Because of his Communist background and his commitment to racial equality, he landed a job with the *Chicago Defender*. A dark-skinned Jew, Burns was often mistaken as black. He could go into the black world incognito, just as Walter White, the blond, blue-eyed, light-complexioned black head of the NAACP, could masquerade or "pass" for white. Walter White could move into the white world to discover and report the reality of its treatment of and attitudes toward blacks.

Black racial pride dictated that during his sojourn at the *Defender* (1941–1943) and at *Ebony* (1945–1954), Burns worked in relative obscurity to avoid being "spotted as the 'white boss' of a Negro publication."[4] He was given no masthead credit at the *Defender*, yet he was wholly responsible for most of the twenty-four-page national edition. Burns was dismayed to find that many of the *Defender*'s reporters received "payoffs" for planting favorable stories. Both at *Ebony* and at the *Defender*, Burns found that he was more "racially knowledgeable than most of the staff." He acquiesced

---

4 Burns's full account is delivered in his autobiography, *Nitty Gritty: A White Editor in Black Journalism* (1996).

to racial slights and hostile treatment as a price to pay for his dedication to racial equality. In retrospect he had no regrets in his lifelong adventure in black journalism, despite having been fired unceremoniously and without cause by both publications.

John Johnson, the third actor in this racial drama, was an enormous entrepreneurial success story, made even more stunning because he was black. A poor Arkansas youth, he boarded the Illinois Central train in Memphis with his mother in 1933 and arrived in Chicago at the age of fifteen. In 1942 he borrowed $500 by using his mother's furniture as collateral. With the money he started a magazine, *Negro Digest*, patterned after the popular *Reader's Digest*. Skeptics, like Roy Wilkins, then editor of the NAACP's magazine the *Crisis*, remarked that Johnson "would never make it." There had never been a successful major black publication. But then, Wilkins did not know a great deal about the private sector and business entrepreneurship. Later, as executive director of the NAACP, Wilkins admitted, "Johnny...I gave you some bad advice." Johnson, who had met Ben Burns while both were working on a political campaign, employed the white journalist as the freelance editor of *Negro Digest*.

Johnson did very well over the next fifty years. Aggressive and clever, he was good at cutting corners in an energetic, obsessive pursuit of wealth and black publishing independence. "I made hundreds of millions of dollars," Johnson wrote in his "autobiography," *Succeeding Against the Odds* (1987). *Ebony* had a formula: it copied *Life* magazine. It avoided racial controversy and sought to present black happiness and achievement, to "entertain and educate," as an escape from the difficulties of daily black life. "*Ebony*," its opening editorial in the autumn of 1945 proclaimed, "will try to mirror the happier side of Negro life—the positive, everyday accomplishments from Harlem to Hollywood."

Black journalism in the 1940s, as Burns noted, was "synonymous with racial militancy." *Ebony* chose a different path, which meant there would be no coverage of race riots, lynchings, or political protests. As an example, Johnson encouraged Burns to write an article called "Why Negroes Buy Cadillacs," which would rationalize conspicuous consumption. Burns complied: "The fact is that a Cadillac is an instrument of aggression, a solid substantial symbol for many a Negro that he is as good as any white man." Still, the initial success of *Ebony*, wrote Burns, was predicated on "four basic subject areas: interracial marriage, Negroes passing as whites, sex, and anatomical freaks." Advertising, as in white publications, tilted toward alcohol and cigarettes. To supplement revenues, Johnson entered the black beauty business: he created a cosmetics brand called Beauty Star. His labels were attached to containers for skin lighteners (Star Glow) and hair straighteners (Raveen), which he advertised in *Ebony*. It worked. Within twenty years Johnson was a very wealthy man.

In November 1945 the first issue of *Ebony* hit the newsstands with twenty-five thousand copies and immediately sold out. The new magazine was largely the handiwork of Ben Burns, who happened to be white. His tools were a Royal typewriter, a pica ruler, copy pencils, scissors, and rubber cement. Articles from freelance writers and photos were put together on the kitchen table of Burns's Jackson Boulevard apartment. He was, in his own words, the entire editorial staff, just as he had been for Johnson's *Negro Digest*.

Race, personalities, and viewpoints now enter this seemingly cohesive biracial relationship. Johnson wanted a feel-good magazine; Burns wanted a platform to promote racial equality and serious journalism. They butted heads often but spent time together socially with their wives, Esther Burns and Eunice Johnson. To Burns it seemed that Johnson ignored the "forgotten man," the black who lived in the ghetto with little money. "I've been a Negro all my life," Johnson countered, "and you're still new at it." Burns thought *Ebony*'s total emphasis on black pride was excessive.

Johnson shied away from racially controversial material. In 1946 European papers were writing about black soldiers fraternizing with German women, and Burns wanted to cover the story. Johnson approved. Burns hired a French photographer, Ilya Gregory, to photograph black GIs embracing German women on beaches. One scene showed a topless blond woman performing before black GIs. After the photographs were confiscated by American customs officials, Johnson killed the article.

Johnson's avoidance of negative racial stories was also on display when he rejected Richard Wright's article about racial reality in Chicago. Wright had moved to Paris in 1947. In 1950 he reunited with his friend Ben Burns in Chicago, where portions of *Native Son* were being filmed for the movie version of the best-selling book. (A French director was shooting most of the movie in Argentina after Wright refused a Hollywood offer that stipulated that Bigger Thomas be portrayed as a white man.) Burns offered Wright $500 to write about his return to Chicago, and the now famous author, in need of cash, accepted. An acrimonious publishing tale began.

Wright submitted a scathing indictment of race, which he called "The Shame of Chicago," to the upbeat *Ebony*. Johnson immediately rejected the piece. After incessant pleading by Burns, Johnson relented. But, not wishing to alienate advertisers, he stipulated that Burns write an "editorial rebuttal... based on Johnson's own racially moderate views." Burns, who agreed with Wright's damning assessment, violated his own principles and beliefs by agreeing to write the "scurrilous editorial... one that I wrote with a sickening sense of dejection." The article and editorial were published in the December 1951 issue of *Ebony*.

Wright had left Chicago in 1937, ten years after he first arrived. Now he recounted that he "had become saturated with Chicago's reality of gang murders, corrupt politics and the depression." "How," he asked, "does Chicago strike one after twelve years? Truthfully, there is but one word for it: ugliness." The slums had left their mark on black dwellers. World War II had brought a degree of prosperity to blacks, as Wright could see Cadillacs parked next to piles of garbage. When he tried to reserve a room for his black producer, the Palmer House refused; Wright had been able to get his own room under the name of the Council on Race Relations. The filming on site required the bribing of Chicago policemen.

Despite material improvements, black life in Chicago was distinctly oppressive, Wright thought. He reported a conversation with a white friend well versed in Chicago's racial situation: "Negroes in Chicago are surrounded by daily conditions of incipient riot.... When racial violence breaks, the cops are on the side of the white hoodlums, openly so." Relative to white Chicago, the South Side was "distinctly hopeless. Meaning this: Chicago whites grudgingly withhold from the Negro the right to living space, full citizenship, job opportunities; but the Negro within these hopeless limits, is making progress in material standards of living..." It was worth noting Chicago jazz, *Ebony*, and some other advancements.

Burns's rebuttal, which he called "difficult and painful to formulate," accused Wright of ignoring the "better side of Negro life in Chicago." Black Chicagoans, Burns fabricated, had a higher standard of living than Parisians. Burns later asked Wright to do an article about his experience in Paris. The resulting piece, "Why I Chose Exile," was summarily rejected by Johnson, who said that Wright had moved from attacking Chicago to attacking America. In his own memoir, Johnson never mentions the Richard Wright rejection episode.

Throughout the story of Wright and Burns and *Ebony*, it's clear that Burns wanted to report harsh racial reality while Johnson wanted pleasantry and progress. The ultimate clash was inevitable: Burns was fired in 1954.

While they worked together, Burns and Johnson had more than an editorial relationship. In 1950 Johnson asked Ben and Esther Burns to accompany him and his wife to Europe. The two couples spent several weeks traveling in France and Spain together. On their tour Johnson discovered that racial harmony in Europe was a myth. The two couples were seated at the black table on the ship to Europe. (Like her husband, Esther Burns was dark-complexioned and easily mistaken for black.) Hotel reservations were not honored when the Johnsons appeared.

Johnson, seemingly confident and self-assured as a black leader, was uncomfortable with whites. When he was invited to lunch with white businessmen, he would eat beforehand. When Eleanor Roosevelt dined at *Ebony*, the menu was changed from fried chicken to steak. Burns pressed Johnson to solicit major white corporate advertisers, explaining that the contact should be between chief executives. Burns even devised Johnson's pitch—patriotism and "nondiscriminatory practices." Johnson, the consummate salesman, in short order captured ad revenue from Elgin Watch, Zenith Radio, and Quaker Oats.

Burns was a keen observer of racial issues that would continue to trouble Americans in the twenty-first century. In the 1940s he knew that crime was an "immutable fact of black life in America." His black friends did not immediately blame "ghetto poverty" for the cause of black crime; rather, it was part of the "nefarious web of racism." The emerging middle class of law-abiding citizens on the "bedeviled South Side" of Chicago, alongside the "underclass" (a sociological term not yet coined in the 1940s), were inured to black crime. Burns had real doubts that poverty and "slum misery" were the sole causes of it. "Why," he asked, "did so many black gangs thrive while committing mayhem against their own people?"

———————

One of *Ebony's* important areas of interest was the question of racial identity through interracial marriage and the common practice of "passing," or moving, by virtue of skin color, secretly and sometimes officially into the white world. *Ebony's* interracial sex-related articles were more than sensation or gossip; they concerned questions of black pride and identity. Articles such as "Famous Negroes Who Married Whites" increased sales by fifty thousand copies. In 1957 E. Franklin Frazier observed that black women feared competition for their own men from white women. That fear, Frazier said, was exacerbated by the lack "of eligible Negro men." He was writing well before mass incarceration was touted as the cause of their being so few marriageable black men.

Later in the century Lawrence Otis Graham, black and a Princeton and Harvard Law School graduate, was equally engrossed with black men who married white women. Graham, who once wrote about his plastic surgery to reshape his nose to a more Caucasian style, was a lawyer and chronicler of the black upper class who named high-profile interracial couples in his book *A Member of the Club* (1995). Franklin Thomas, president of the Ford Foundation; Harvard professor Orlando Patterson; Walter White of the NAACP; Massachusetts senator Edward Brooke; Virginia governor Douglas Wilder; Lena Horne; Clarence Thomas; and Henry Louis Gates were among black leaders who had married outside their race. Blacks, wrote Graham, were even suspicious of Frederick Douglass, who in 1884 married his white secretary.

At the core of these marriages, according to Graham, was a feeling that such a union would reduce the black person's commitment to black causes. (But Thurgood Marshall, for example, then head of the NAACP Legal Defense Fund, continued his aggressive pursuit of racial equality.) Graham noted that "materially successful black men" who married white women thereby stigmatized black women as inferior or "physically unattractive." He observed that 71 percent of interracial marriages involved black men and white women.

According to Graham, blacks who read profiles of successful blacks in *Ebony, People,* or *Business Week* would routinely check the race of the subject's spouse. This was the "litmus test of loyalty to the race." Blacks feared that interracial marriage would deprive black children of "black mentors and role models." If powerful blacks married whites, it was assumed that financial resources and wealth would be compromised, thus reinforcing negative stereotypes about blacks. Then too, there would be confusion about the racial loyalty of biracial children. The Urban League in fact opposed federal government attempts to classify mixed-race children as biracial. In 1993 the NAACP objected to adoptions of black babies by white parents. At stake was the supposed loss of "unique black culture."[5]

Graham, the elite Ivy League black, married an Ivy League black woman. His parents surrounded him with images of important, visible blacks. He was exposed to haute black social clubs and surrounded by copies of *Ebony, Jet, Sepia, Black Enterprise,* and *Essence.* The family vacationed in the fashionable black enclaves of Oak Bluffs on Martha's Vineyard and in Sag Harbor, Long Island. These were and remain important self-selected vehicles for the black upper class.

Anti-miscegenation laws in many states continued to prohibit interracial marriage until the famous 1967 Supreme Court decision in *Loving v. Virginia* invalidated such laws. Societal attitudes can be an even more potent obstacle. Varying shades of skin color make racial distinctions difficult. The most extraordinary example of such a case occurred in White Plains, New York, a suburb of New York City, in 1927. There at the Westchester County courthouse, spectators gathered to hear deliberations of the county's supreme court in the Rhinelander case.

Leonard "Kip" Rhinelander, scion of a wealthy family, in 1924 had married a dark-skinned woman, Alice Jones. Rhinelander's family pressed their son to have the marriage annulled, but Alice Jones refused to accept the annulment and a lawsuit followed. The Rhinelanders alleged that Alice Jones had deceived Kip Rhinelander about her race. The argument centered on deception, not the legality of a mixed marriage. The

---

5 Movies elaborated this theme, notably 1949's *Pinky,* which described the troubles of a biracial woman whose elite white fiancé terminated their relationship upon discovering her black ancestry. The movie produced Academy Awards for Ethel Waters and Ethel Barrymore. Of note is that the black actresses Lena Horne and Dorothy Dandridge were rejected for the starring role of *Pinky* in favor of the white actress Jeanne Crain.

Rhinelanders' counsel, former New York Supreme Court Justice Isaac Mills, considered mixed marriages a violation of "civil society, [and] nature." Alice Jones's attorney, Lee Parsons Davis, influenced her to partially disrobe in the jury room in front of an all-white male group of lawyers, jurors, and the judge. If she had been obviously black, Davis argued, Rhinelander, who had seen her exposed before the marriage, would not have been deceived. In fact, the jury ruled that no deception could have occurred. Alice won the case. Rhinelander eventually was granted a divorce. In the midst of the appeal process, a bill was unsuccessfully introduced in the New York legislature to ban marriages between blacks and whites.

Extensive media coverage of the sensational trial appeared in both black and white papers and journals, especially of the disrobing episode. The *New York Times* headlined "Rhinelander's Wife Admits Negro Blood." The black *Amsterdam News* applauded the results: "womanhood in general and Negro womanhood in particular" had been protected. "[I]f Rhinelander had used his girl as concubine or prostitute," carped W. E. B. Du Bois in the NAACP's *Crisis*, "white America would have raised no word of protest."

Many light-skinned blacks have secretly entered the white world and silently renounced their racial origins. The process of "passing" is the ultimate form of rejection of black identity. "Passing" has long been a common topic in the black community. In his memoir *Sand against the Wind* (1966), John C. Dancy, head of the Detroit Urban League, noted the "Negro[es] . . . [who] elected to go white and gotten away with it." *Ebony*'s pages were no stranger to this "best-selling feature." In 1948 Roi Ottley published a controversial piece, "Five Million US White Negroes," which claimed that "between 40,000 and 50,000 Negroes 'pass' into the white community yearly and between 5,000,000 and 8,000,000 persons in the US possess a determinable part of Negro blood." Ben Burns thought that Ottley's "facts were solid," but they are scarcely verifiable and highly suspect.

By 1954 *Ebony* magazine had a circulation of five hundred thousand; all of Johnson's publications had a circulation of 2.6 million. But the three men who had dedicated themselves to racial equality had become estranged.

John Johnson had moved, astonishingly, from a Southern migrant on welfare to the *Forbes* magazine list of the four hundred wealthiest Americans. In 1982 his net worth was $100 million (equivalent to $250 million in 2017), with later estimates at $200 million. "I earned it," Johnson said. And he did. His memoir is festooned with the usual photos of the author with celebrities ranging from presidents to entertainers. The proud, determined, impeccably dressed Johnson liked to view himself as a consummate salesman in addition to his shrewd business acumen. He had a list of do's and don'ts for his advertising salesmen in their dealings with black customers. No. 4 is pertinent: "In conversation, don't use the term 'nigger,' 'Negress,' 'darky,' or 'boy.'"

The tension-filled relationship between Johnson and Burns was unfortunate. Burns had borrowed $4,000 from Johnson in order to buy a middle-class house in a white neighborhood. As a gesture, Johnson forgave the loan when he fired Burns. The intellectual and lapsed Communist Jew never wavered in his devotion to racial equality, despite being harassed and demeaned by many of his black colleagues. He became the invisible white in a black world.

During one of his exiles from black publishing, Burns had to enter the corporate world in the form of a public relations firm. Communists, at times, have a knack for capitalism, and such was the case with Burns. While "leafing through a neighborhood newspaper...in 1957," he came across a "new drive-in chain restaurant ad"—the company was beginning a franchising effort. A cold call resulted in an interview with Ray Kroc, head of the fledging McDonald's. The burger icon became a client, and Burns's company, Cooper, Burns & Golin, eventually became the major public relations firm of Golin/Harris International.

Burns found the groveling aspect of the PR business distasteful and had another stint at the *Chicago Defender* beginning in 1962. He encountered the usual anti-white resentment about being "too critical and too demanding." Finally he realized that a white editor-in-chief would never be welcomed at a black publication. He left the *Defender* in 1963.

Richard Wright had a more circuitous and painful journey than either Johnson or Burns. Having made his literary mark in Chicago, in 1937 the angry and disaffected Wright decamped for New York. A brief sojourn there was followed by permanent emigration from America to Paris in 1946. Five years later he submitted to Burns a piece called "I Choose Exile."

"I Choose Exile" expressed Wright's bitterness toward America. "I live in voluntary exile in France," he wrote, "and I like it. There is nothing that I miss..." Wright exalted the freedom available to him and to the French in general. He recounted how in 1946 he had attempted to buy a farmhouse in New Hampshire but was informed by the real estate broker "that the white owner did not want to sell his house to a Negro." That, he said, was when he decided to move to Paris. After much wrangling, the former Communist received a passport and took his family to France. "I Choose Exile" was never published by *Ebony* or any other American magazine; it languishes in the Kent State University Library. Wright's enchantment with France would wane; his dispute with fellow black novelist James Baldwin exposed fissures in the racial solidarity among disenchanted black expatriates. Wright sought to move yet again, but Great Britain rejected his attempt to resettle.

Wright poetically recalls his departure from the South:

I was leaving the South To fling myself into the unknown...I was taking a part of the South To transplant in alien soil, To see if it could grow differently, If it could drink of new and cool rains, Bend in strange winds, Respond to the warmth of other suns And, perhaps to bloom.

Wright never bloomed, though, never found the "warmth of other suns" in his journey from the South to Chicago, to New York, to New Hampshire, or to Paris. Without describing Wright's failed attempts, the use of the quotation is a distortion.

Richard Wright viewed the world through a lens tainted by race. He called for the unity of people "of color" while briefly involved with Asian and African politics and the remnants of European colonialism. He died in 1960 without witnessing the failure of the Bandung Conference (Indonesia) as the showcase of the unity of "people of color." The illusion was revealed. Culture, values, and economic living standards, not race, were (and remain) the determinants of successful economic and political maturation. By the end of the twentieth century, millions of immigrants from the countries represented at the Bandung Conference were banging on the door of their colonial oppressors to gain entrance to functioning countries, Western values, and economies that yielded an adequate living standard.

Similarly, the judgment of W. E. B. Du Bois was not only blurred but blinded by his hatred of America and capitalism, and, most important, by his tendency to rationalize destructive behavior in the name of race or economics. Du Bois was enamored of the dictatorships of Russia and Germany and the colored people's fascism of Japan. He studied in Germany in the mid-1930s and later traveled to Japan. Aware of the Nazis' anti-Jewish policies and practices, including the Nuremberg Laws of 1935 and the *Kristallnacht* attack on Jewish businesses, he maintained an affection for Nazi Germany. The "scientific" approach to government and the centralized economies of Russia, Germany, and Japan appealed to Du Bois, the naive intellectual and Marxist admirer. He found German persecution of the Jews "legal" but white America's treatment of blacks "unconstitutional." The result of Nazi-Japanese cooperation could be, wrote Du Bois, "increased freedom and autonomy for the darker world, despite all theoretic race ideology."

A persistent strain characterizes the vision of life through the racial lens, as evidenced by Johnson, Burns, Wright, and Du Bois. It severely hampers accountability and constructive criticism. Real grievances and good intentions give way to a failure of objectivity and self-examination.

Immigration in Detroit

During the Great Migration, how did America at the same time assimilate or absorb white European immigrants who came by the millions? The process of cultural adaptation of the newcomers had a name: Americanization. The boom town of Detroit in the time of World War I offers a powerful example. The acceptance of white immigrants there was distinctly different from the greeting received by blacks in the Great Migration. And, important to note, a significant number of the white Europeans came from functionally illiterate agricultural backgrounds.

The huge labor demand of Detroit's nascent automobile industry fostered immigration as well as migration. Fueling this influx was Ford Motor Company's announcement on Monday, January 5, 1914, that it would henceforth pay five dollars a day to its workers, including blacks—roughly twice the wages paid by its competitors. Within twenty-four hours, ten thousand men appeared at Ford's employment office in nine-degree weather.

Today it may be difficult to imagine that Detroit, having filed for America's largest municipal bankruptcy in 2013, was ever a thriving industrial power. But the media's feeding frenzy on the woes of Detroit fails to note that the city was once dubbed the "Arsenal of Democracy" for its sheer productive capacity in military materiel. Detroit was everything that the South was not: the Motor City was an industrial juggernaut that combined labor with technology.

In the early part of the century Detroit's population, because of the automobile industry, exploded from 285,704 people in 1900 to 993,678 in 1920 to 1,568,662 in 1930. The city was a magnet for foreigners: in 1910, 344,820, or 74 percent of the population, were either foreign-born or children of foreigners. An astounding 43 percent of the population were born in non-English-speaking countries or were progeny of non-native English speakers. The sheer size and timing of this influx of immigrants challenges the imagination.

In 1915 Detroit charged Raymond E. Cole of the Committee for Immigration to America to analyze the city's influx. The goal, according to Cole, was "to assimilate the immigrant into the body politic of the city and so into American life." The process had to be "primarily protective and educational in nature." Immigrants must shed the remnants—clothes, language, politics—of the old country and adapt. Cole wanted to conserve the "desirable qualities and energies of the immigrants" while "maintaining American standards." The operative word was "Americanization"; as many as six thousand Ford employees marched in a 1915 Americanization Day parade.

A Ford document, "Helpful Hints and Advice to Employees," of that year cogently set forth the goals of citizenship:

> The Company believes it to be for the best interest of all employes (sic) born in other countries that they become citizens of the United States as soon as possible, in order that they may enjoy the benefits and protection offered by this form of government, and to take an intelligent part in the conduct of its affairs.

Ford's legal department was mandated to "advise employees as to the quickest and easiest... [manner] of obtaining citizenship." Workers could avail themselves of Ford's lawyers "from 8:00 A.M. to 5:00 P.M. daily, except Saturdays."

Of utmost importance was rudimentary proficiency in English. Motivation came both from workers and from the company. As a practical matter, English skills promoted efficiency and safety in the factory. The Ford English School used 163 company volunteer instructors who taught without pay. Successful matriculation was rewarded with an official diploma. Thousands of Ford employees took advantage of this program, which averaged six to eight weeks. The federal government and the industries of Detroit recognized the Ford English School as a step toward citizenship.

As described by David Allan Levine in *Internal Combustion*, the graduation ceremony, dubbed "Ford English School Melting Pot," was an extravaganza. Thousands of spectators gathered in an auditorium. A large ship was placed on the stage. The newly minted English speakers dressed in their native garb filed into the ship. Each carried a flag designating their country of origin—Syria, Poland, Austria, Russia, Norway, and so on. Transformed in the melting pot, the immigrants emerged dressed appropriately in American attire, and, of course, they were waving American flags. A banner emboldened with the words "E Pluribus Unum" hung from the rafters of the auditorium.

Similarly, from 386 Detroit industrial firms thousands of employees seeking citizenship took English courses in the evening at public schools. In addition to the workplace, English was deemed essential for "Americanization" as a deterrent to the transplantation of foreign ideas of "anarchy and socialism," and to enable the immigrant to function in the American economy. When children of immigrants checked out a book from the public library, they were given a note that asked whether their parents spoke English well. Directions to language classes were appended. In slack business periods, preference was given to those workers who could demonstrate proficiency in English. The Packard Motor Car Company, according to Levine, even required a test to determine if job applicants could "speak, read and write English... [and] jobs depended on regular attendance at night school." Ford and other Detroit firms, motivated by practical necessity, thus created a systematic approach to transitioning the immigrant to American society. The private sector, in cooperation with local government and civic organizations, was able to accomplish the monumental task of absorbing a huge number of non-English-speaking immigrants.

Ford's scheme for immigrant workers, dubbed a "profit-sharing plan," had highly intrusive, almost forgotten strings attached. The section "Home Comforts and Sanitation" of the employee handbook mandated cleanliness and included graphic contrasting photos to illustrate proper and improper behavior. The message was unmistakable. Details included "bathing frequently," the proper use of garbage cans, reliance on sermons to form children's habits, the practice of dental hygiene, and the necessity for "all children between the ages of 7 and 16 years to attend school." Employees were required to save part of their "profits." Bank accounts were encouraged. John Lee, a Ford executive, was explicit: "no man was to receive the money who could not use it advisedly and conservatively...it was within the province of the company to take away his [money]" by dismissal.

These were no idle suggestions. Inspectors from the Ford Sociological Department were charged with "teaching Ford employees how to live." These inspectors could place employees on probation and monitor improvement. If faults were not rectified, the five-dollars-a-day "profit" could be reduced on a sliding scale. If the employee failed to reform after six months, he would be fired. Ford exercised complete social control.

No legal obstacles, based on civil rights interpretations, would annul the paternalistic and heavy-handed intervention of the Ford Sociological Department. Labor unions, a nonfactor in 1915 Detroit, would never have conceded the absolute power necessary for a private corporation to exert extensive social control over workers.

Yet there are lessons to be learned from Detroit's historical experience. People enthusiastically abandoned the Balkanized countries of Europe; Detroit wanted unity at the factory and in the community, not a replica of a fragmented Europe. The descendants of immigrants who felt the intrusive hand of Ford did not complain about ancestral oppression. Detroit in 1915 understood that basic communication in English was a stepping-stone to the economic mainstream.

Michael Pupin (1858–1935), a non-English-speaking peasant from Idvor, a small village in Serbia, became the poster boy for early-twentieth-century immigrants. Arriving in the United States at Castle Garden, the New York clearing house for immigrants, in 1874, the sixteen-year-old entered his new country penniless and without family or relatives. He was immediately cheated. With his last nickel he bought a prune pastry that turned out to be a fake filled with prune pits. The resilient youth persevered, worked in a biscuit factory, learned English, and mastered the admission requirements for Columbia University, which he entered in 1879. "The Americanization process which was going on within me," wrote Pupin in his memoir, "was very much speeded up by what I saw at the [Philadelphia] Centennial Exposition" in 1876. There the impressionable young man was mesmerized by the painting *Men of Progress— American Inventors,* a celebration of American men of science in the 1850s. In addition to becoming a fine oarsman at Columbia, Pupin won the freshman prize in Greek and mathematics. He graduated in 1883 with honors in mathematics and physics. The renowned scientist and Columbia University president Frederick Barnard "beamed with joy when he handed...[Pupin] his diploma." A scholarship took him to Germany, where in 1889 he was awarded his PhD from the University of Berlin.

There followed a staggeringly prolific career that began as a professor in physics at Columbia, in the new Department of Electrical Engineering. His field, electromagnetic science, helped him achieve thirty-four patents—and wealth. His work in long-distance telephone technology earned him the title of the "man who connected the world." One of his early accomplishments was an improvement in x-ray technology for which one of his colleagues, Professor Butler Hall, proposed "to establish a fellowship" at an exclusive arts club, the Century Association, which would entitle Pupin to "two toddies daily for the rest of his life." The Century Association rejected the offer.

Pupin's love and respect for his adopted country and its history knew no bounds. While he never forgot his native country, his patron saint was Abraham Lincoln. A traveling storyteller had regaled the nine-year-old Serbian boy about the American president. From his days in Idvor he was equally taken with Benjamin Franklin. "The lives of Franklin and of Lincoln, my patron saints," wrote Pupin, "are the strongest agency for Americanization known today." Pupin's memoir, *From Immigrant to Inventor* (1923), won the Pulitzer Prize for biography. The Columbia physics building is named for him. This extraordinary man remembered Serbia through his visits, his philanthropy, and his aid to Serbian technological education. His statue adorns his village, Idvor, and a school of technology in Serbia, the Mihajlo Pupin Institute, is named for him.

The attitude toward assimilation and Americanization in the early twentieth century would become vastly different by the year 2000. Michael Pupin demonstrated that it was possible to embrace American norms without sacrificing one's native cultural heritage.

By any measure, Detroit's formula for immigrants worked well except for African Americans. Like all Northern cities, Detroit continued to keep blacks "at a distance" by entrapping them in enclosed areas separated from the white city. This exclusion from the process of assimilation has rendered blacks vulnerable in major American cities to the present day. The isolation of Detroit's blacks in ghettos and a separate world illustrates the perils of a malfunctioning adaptive system. Citizenship was not the issue; full participation in the American economy depended on assimilation.

The racial situation in Chicago and Detroit would be replicated in every major urban city where the black population expanded—and expand it did. In 1910 the black population of Detroit was 5,741 (1.2 percent of the total); by 1920 an increase to 40,838 (4.1 percent of the total) brought real problems; in the 1930s blacks numbered 120,066 and racial tension exacerbated; before 1950 the presence of 300,506 (16.2 percent) ignited a race riot; and before 1970 a black population of 660,427 (44.5 percent) led to a major racial conflagration. In 1922, three thousand five hundred new black migrants were arriving in each of the summer months. Gaining momentum at the same time was the Detroit Ku Klux Klan, whose membership grew from three thousand in 1921 to twenty-two thousand in 1923. Racial flash points—in housing, health, jobs, crime, and education—would be long-term staples of black migration to the North, where wages and suffrage rights, unlike in the South, were available.

Housing obstacles appeared early on in the form of restrictive covenants, white antagonism, overt discrimination or credit-driven mortgage scarcity, crowded and unsanitary conditions, and exorbitant rents. White Detroit was not subtle. The Detroit Real Estate Board could not sell a home to a black in a "strictly white neighborhood." Realtors were obliged to follow Article 34 of the Code of Ethics of the National Association of Real Estate Boards (1924), which stated: "A Realtor should never be instrumental in introducing into a neighborhood...members of any race...whose presence will clearly be detrimental to property values..." Rents skyrocketed. A black family paying $4.60 per month for rent in 1916 would pay $9.27 by 1920; house rentals moved from $20 per month in 1915 to $100 by 1920. Multiple roomers boarded for $4 to $6 per week. Both black and whites would take advantage of the new migrants. The Detroit Board of Commerce's Americanization Committee met with John Dancy, the head of Detroit's Urban League, in 1919 and were appalled by the conditions, but no remedies were initiated.

Violence followed obstacles. In 1925 a black physician, Alexander Turner, was stoned when he moved into a white neighborhood. Five thousand angry whites had surrounded his house. In effect Dr. Turner was evicted. Another black doctor, Ossian Sweet, purchased a home in a white section with resulting violence, murder, and a highly publicized trial.

A highly educated black migrant from Orlando, Florida, through energy and perseverance, Sweet had worked a series of menial jobs to graduate from Wilberforce University and Howard University's medical school. Then, in 1921, he had begun a practice in Detroit. Anticipating trouble when he moved into his home in a white neighborhood, Sweet informed the police and occupied the residence with seven other blacks, including his brother Henry, who were heavily armed with rifles, shotguns, revolvers, and pistols. When a mob surrounded the house, gunshots followed. Two white men were hit and one was killed, though it was impossible to determine who had shot him. Sweet and his brother were arrested and tried for murder.

This civil rights showcase trial began on October 30, 1925. Clarence Darrow, the renowned defense attorney, was asked to defend the Sweet brothers. Darrow may have been a champion of the underdog, but he was not shy about asking for exorbitant fees. He requested $50,000 from the

NAACP, which was supervising the defense. He settled for $5,000. The famous lawyer was just returning from his theatrical performance at the Scopes trial in Dayton, Tennessee.

Darrow was especially effective in defending both Ossian and Henry Sweet, who were acquitted after a hung jury in the first trial. Darrow put "prejudice" on trial rather than murder. In his closing argument he concluded: "I believe the life of the Negro race has been a life of tragedy, of injustice, of oppression. The law has made him equal but man has not." In the wake of the trial a disheveled Darrow also addressed fifteen hundred blacks extemporaneously for two hours at the Detroit YMCA. "It may be," he said,

> that without slavery, your race would never have had its chance for civilization. You might still be savages in Africa—and you might be better off there. But still I think that civilization is worth the price we have to pay for it.... You'll have to work harder—harder than the white man—because you're on his home grounds.... There is no inherent difference between your capacity for growth and that of any other man, whatever his color.

Racial violence in Detroit did not end with a favorable verdict in the Ossian Sweet case. On June 20, 1943, a series of racial incidents in Belle Isle Park ignited a full-scale race riot, resulting in eighteen hundred arrests, five hundred injuries, and thirty-four deaths. Thirteen hundred of the arrests were blacks; twenty-five blacks and nine whites were killed. Major destruction occurred on Hastings Street in the Detroit ghetto. The street was described by John Dancy, as having "bad housing, congestion and filth...[and was] densely populated by Negroes." Small shops on Hastings Street, mainly owned by Jews, were stoned and looted. On June 21 federal troops finally took control of the city. Dancy suggested that Detroit had "paid the price for its economies and omissions in the field of race relations." The events of 1943 would be a prelude to a massive riot in 1967.

Blacks in New York City

The black experience during the Great Migration would fit neatly into the historian Daniel Boorstin's description of black ghettos as "cities within cities." Inevitably the "Negro problem" surfaced when sizable numbers of blacks entered. New York City was no different. The black population there increased from 60,666 (1.76 percent of the population) in 1900 to 327,706 (4.73 percent) in 1930 to 1,087,931 (13.98 percent) in 1960. It was largely concentrated in Harlem. Predictably, local commissions and review boards were established in response to racial problems. Reports ensued.

Residential segregation patterns were as evident in New York City as they were in Chicago and Detroit. Whites would flee neighborhoods when blacks arrived. In a 1925 essay, "Harlem: The Culture Capital," James Weldon Johnson, a black author and educator, explored the white reaction to the migration of blacks into the area: "[T]he whole movement [of blacks into Harlem] in the eyes of whites, took on the aspect of an 'invasion'; they became panic stricken and began fleeing as from a plague." Housing was deliberately segregated. In 1947 the Metropolitan Life Insurance Company opened Stuyvesant Town, a housing complex for some nine thousand middle-income white families in Manhattan. Black families were not allowed. Three years earlier the same company had proposed to fund Riverton Houses, a residential complex for blacks in Harlem.

Residential separation brought school segregation and racially gerrymandered school populations. After World War I, residential segregation in New York increasingly concentrated black students in black schools. The biracial Commission on Conditions in Harlem (1935) did not acknowledge school segregation, even though by 1934 thirteen schools in Harlem were "virtually all black" because of segregated housing. Yet another commission on the Condition of Colored Urban Population (1939) "found no intentional segregation," according to Davison Douglas. In 1940 New York City redrew districts to "preserve" racially segregated schools. White children in the Washington Heights section of New York were bused "to avoid attendance at a nearby predominantly black school..."

Education has always been regarded as the key to upward economic mobility, especially for blacks. New York City's struggle with black education illustrates the difficulty of integration in the face of segregated classrooms, whether the segregation is self-imposed or de facto. For the NAACP's Walter White, ending school segregation in the North was essential. "Unless we can win out in the North," White wrote in 1924, "we shall never be able to win in the South." Du Bois concurred, noting in 1925 that residential and school segregation was growing quickly in the North as a result of the black migration. There were arguments against desegregation in the North—the paucity of black teachers, the treatment of black students in mixed classrooms, and the performance of black students in integrated settings. Du Bois recognized these problems but believed they were outweighed by advantages. Later he would have second thoughts about integration.

African Americans were acutely aware that integration likely meant the elimination of many black teachers. Blacks in Brooklyn supported segregated schools in order to augment the number of black teachers. In nineteenth-century Ohio black teachers had opposed desegregation: a teaching career was vital to educated blacks. In 1910 half of all black college graduates became teachers; the figure was still over 40 percent in 1930. Desegregation would jeopardize opportunities in a major area of black advancement, and it would cost jobs.

Furthermore, in New York City's de facto segregated schools black students were routed to courses that were geared to low-level jobs. Black girls were often restricted from taking "commercial courses" because they would find no opportunities outside menial labor or domestic work. Courses in "Domestic Science" meant "cooking, sewing, and manual shop work," a formula that strongly resembled vocational training in the South. This "dumping ground," according to the 1936 Mayor's Commission on Conditions in Harlem, was necessary because of "the traditional belief concerning the capacity of the Negro" and labor union barriers to a wide range of job prospects.

Within the black community, data dueling began in earnest over the relative merits of integrated versus segregated education. Studies began to appear in the 1920s that showed that attendance rates and graduation rates in segregated schools (Washington, DC; Baltimore; and St. Louis) were greater than those of legally desegregated schools (New York, Boston, and Philadelphia). Then there were opposing views offered by Howard University's Charles Johnson when he compared desegregated Cleveland schools to Baltimore's separate schools. The enormous success of all-black Dunbar High School in Washington, DC, with its all-black faculty and rigid discipline, was a model used by both supporters and detractors of segregation. Briefly, the integrationists argued that reform along Dunbar's lines would create a better learning and life experience; separatists were pessimistic about the survival of racial mores in an integrated world. In any event, Dunbar's highly regimented approach was peculiar to its circumstances and not replicated within the African American community. It never became a viable example for mass use.

New York was not alone in segregating its schools. One could find the same discriminatory practices in Cleveland. As black students were sequestered into separate schools by deliberate gerrymandering, "severely overcrowded" schools resulted. In 1948, 1,395 black students attended the Hayes School with a capacity for 800 students; 1,635 black students attended the Kinsman School with a capacity for 750. The Cleveland school board refused to send black students to nearby white schools, but white students with large numbers of black students in neighborhood schools were allowed to "transfer to predominantly white schools."

The Supreme Court's unanimous decision in *Brown v. Board of Education* (1954) brought an end to state-sanctioned segregation in American schools. The court held that the "separate but equal" doctrine of *Plessy v. Ferguson* was inherently unequal. *Brown* was the culmination of a long series of court cases beginning in the 1930s and led by the NAACP. The early cases were carefully selected attacks on state-sanctioned school segregation in border states. The strategy was led by Thurgood Marshall and the underappreciated attorney Charles Hamilton Huston. *Brown* was directed at legal school segregation in the South, but its impact was resounding in the North, whose de facto segregated school systems were unequal in practice. Initially restricted to ending legal segregation, *Brown* has now been expanded to include preferential treatment to ensure diversity and make amends for past treatment. The decision clearly supports Charles Evans Hughes's 1907 speech in which he said that "the Constitution is whatever a judge says it is." Legal wrangling over racial quotas, diversity, busing, school funding, and the enforceability of integration across racially separate neighborhoods has been a perpetual feature of the court system in the years since *Brown*.

Discriminatory funding, both North and South, was also called into question by the *Brown* decision. In 1954 New York City allotted three times as much for building-related expenditures for white elementary school students as for black and Puerto Rican students, and eight times as much for "instructional equipment." Total expenditures for white students were three times that for black and Puerto Rican students. Most districts in the North and South attempted to equalize funding as a way to deal with *Brown*.

Massive resistance to the *Brown* decision in the South is well chronicled and well commemorated. Not so in the North. The North's reaction was white flight, a form of massive resistance to racially mixed schools. In 1950 "whites comprised a majority of students," Davison Douglas writes, "in all the nation's largest school districts except Washington, DC." By 1965 "the percentage of black elementary school students attending majority black schools in Detroit, Chicago, and Philadelphia ranged from 87 to 97 percent." In 1980 every big-city school district in America became two-thirds to three-fourths minority. Daniel Patrick Moynihan, in his famous report on the Negro family, noted that the number of New York City schools that were 90 percent black or Puerto Rican had increased from 64 in 1957 to 134 in 1963.

As a result of the *Brown* decision and racial tension, New York City was forced to acknowledge its own segregated dilemma. The mere size of the city's school system boggles the mind. In 1959 it involved more than eight hundred public schools, almost a million students, forty-five thousand employees, and a $400 million ($3.3 billion in 2016) budget. After *Brown*, few know that New York City scrambled (unsuccessfully) to integrate. On December 23, 1954, New York City's Board of Education declared "racially homogeneous public schools...educationally undesirable" and asked that a plan to "prevent the further development of such schools" be put in place. New York City schools would be forced "to integrate...as quickly as practicable." The board proceeded to do what boards always do—generate another commission. On the same day, December 23, the Committee on Integration was established to reckon with the details of residential separation and a highly charged busing policy. A series of reports culminated in the final assessment, titled "Toward Greater Opportunity," presented in 1960.

The need to minister to the problems of underprivileged (now called "at risk") children was also daunting. According to the sociologist Nathan Glazer, underprivileged students were undernourished, "perhaps physically abused," improperly cared for, and hampered by a language deficiency in English and in vocabulary. Glazer wrote in 1964 of the consequences for the children: "apathy, outrageous behavior, resistance." Classroom discipline would suffer to the point of continual disruption; an army of people and enormous funding would be required to cope.

In 1958 a group of black mothers calling themselves the Little Rock Nine of Harlem began a boycott of three Harlem junior high schools, charging inferior education. By 1960 the black community in New York City advocated a school strike supported by James L. Hicks, the black editor of the *Amsterdam News*, who blamed white people: "All I know is that Negro children are entitled to the same things white children are entitled to and they are not getting them." On February 3, 1964, almost half a million black and Hispanic students boycotted New York City schools.

The influential study *An American Dilemma* (1944), written by the Swedish sociologist and economist Gunnar Myrdal, chastised American race relations, particularly in the South. The keys to "Negro" advancement, Myrdal thought, were education and assimilation. Education meant "an assimilation of white culture," which would break the bonds of the racial "caste system." Education also meant absorbing the "American virtues of efficiency, thrift and ambition" to win access to the "American dream of individual success." The "educated Negro, in one important respect, [would] become equal to the better class of whites," Myrdal wrote.

In his concentration on the South, Myrdal was oblivious to inferior educational opportunities for blacks in the North. "[T]here is [but] little difference," he suggested, "between Negro and white schools in the North, either in quality of instruction and facilities or in the content of the courses." Myrdal is widely read and remembered for his influence on the *Brown* decision, but his little-known and utterly mistaken view of race relations in the North would return to haunt America until the present.

Brown only intensified the complexity of racial desegregation and integration in the North and South. The court decision of nine judges was the simplest part of the problem. Thereafter America struggled with the meaning of colorblindness versus color consciousness, white flight, desegregation suits, model inner-city schools, affirmative action, quotas and curricula, residential racial segregation, charter schools, and black ambivalence.

The Harlem Renaissance of the 1920s in New York is celebrated for its artistic achievements. But the era that produced the Cotton Club, black intellectual ferment, and artistic endeavor that is still admired failed to nurture self-sufficient businesses within the black community or promote access to the economic mainstream. The historian David Levering Lewis summarized this stunted economic underdevelopment:

> Unlike their Jewish models...the Afro-American leaders tended to minimize or to ignore the grimy aspects of migrant Jewish business success as a basic condition for the perpetuation of collective achievement. Hence, the Harlem Renaissance literally took place in rented space—in a Harlem they did not own. Racial aristocrats steeped in liberal arts educations, they missed the significance of the butcher and tailor shops, the sweatshop, the pawn shops, and the liquor stores...

Coincidentally, the black leaders of the time were out of touch with the masses. In 1940 Ralph J. Bunche, later to be the first African American representative to the United Nations, wrote that there existed a "tremendous gap" in the attitudes between the "Negro elite...and the black mass." The absence of structure, a dearth of entrepreneurship, a lack of predisposition toward commerce, little enabling group cooperation, poor educational background, exclusion from labor unions, and limited access to credit—all these factors inhibited the base so necessary for private-sector success. And fully entrenched discriminatory regulations and practices were major obstacles to those blacks who wished to enter the economic mainstream outside the black ghetto.

There existed, according to Lewis, "a proud self-confidence in Harlem"—with no economic foundation. Black publications like the *Amsterdam News* and the socialist *Messenger* exalted success stories and Horatio Alger rags-to-riches tales. But exaggeration and misinformation crept into such stories. The venerable Urban League was guilty of a misleading boosterism at the expense of reality when it reported in 1927 that 75 percent of the real estate in Harlem was "under colored control." It neglected to mention that "white landlords" owned the property that was only "controlled" by black managers. Fully 80 percent of Harlem's wealth was owned by white people. In a section of the community in 1931, the NAACP's *Crisis* reported, whites owned 83 percent of the 2,308 businesses. Only 29 percent of these businesses employed blacks, who were used in "menial, low-playing positions." The dangers, yet again, of looking exclusively through a racial lens could lead to dangerous conclusions. The fragile economic condition of black America would be exposed over and over again. In 1934, during the Great Depression, 43 percent of Harlem's black families depended on public welfare.

The business prowess of a few was nonetheless widely publicized. Most conspicuous was Madam C. J. Walker (formerly Sara Breedlove), who created a cosmetics empire. Madam Walker was born in Louisiana and moved to Mississippi before settling in Indianapolis where she built a line of hair products that were marketed door-to-door by thousands of saleswomen. This was an entirely black operation, with the products manufactured, advertised, and sold by blacks to blacks. In 1916 Madam Walker moved to Harlem, where she would become a fixture in the black community. She befriended Booker T. Washington and W. E. B. Du Bois while bestowing large philanthropic gifts on Tuskegee Institute and other causes. She was also a social and political activist, the keynote speaker at the National Negro Business League conference in 1912, and a member of the NAACP executive committee by 1917. Touted as the first self-made female millionaire, upon her death in 1919 she was found to be worth only $600,000. Nonetheless this remarkable woman is memorialized by a museum and by the resurrection of her brand. A cosmetics company called Madam C. J. Walker Beauty Culture was established in 2016.

Of considerable fame, but not at Madam Walker's level, was Pigs' Feet Mary. By 1925 she had parlayed a street-vending business in Harlem into a small fortune of $375,000. The enterprising woman pushed a baby carriage from which she sold "chitterlings, corn, hogmaw, and pigs' feet." She grew this into a newsstand and some residential property. If her tenants were late in paying rent, she informed them by letter, "Send it, and send it quick."

The Harlem business crossroads often pitted blacks against Jewish landlords and shop owners. The Jewish presence in Harlem had begun in the late nineteenth century. During World War I, 178,000 Jews lived in Harlem, though by 1930 there were only 5,000. Meanwhile 172,000 blacks had moved into the community. Jews actively resisted black settlement. Adolph B. Rosenfield of the Property Owners Improvement Association, according to the historian Winston C. McDougall, was "somewhat successful" in preventing black encroachment in Harlem. Harry Goodstein of the West Side Property Owner's Association sought to "limit black advancement." Brooklyn witnessed a violent confrontation between Jews and blacks in 1927 over black movement into Jewish neighborhoods.

Despite their residential move out of Harlem, Jews maintained an extensive business presence there. Blacks were their customers, but few Jews employed blacks, who attempted to boycott their stores. The boycotts occurred in thirty-five cities, beginning in 1929 in Chicago. The black slogan "Don't Buy Where You Can't Work" was aimed especially at Jewish merchants. Three-fourths of the stores in Chicago's Bronzeville were owned by Jews. Particularly vitriolic anti-Semitic outbursts against Jewish shops in Chicago occurred in 1938. One of the most vociferous verbal assaults in Harlem was led by Bishop Amiru Al-Minin Sufi Abdul Hamid, whose jobs crusade, according to Cheryl Greenberg, branded Jews as "exploiters" and the "worst enemies of black people." The colorful Hamid—imposing at six feet three inches and 225 pounds, dressed in a white turban and black, crimson-lined cape and green velvet blouse— would stand on a stepladder urging people to stop buying in Jewish stores that did not hire blacks.

Meanwhile the Harlem Economic Association promoted black patronage of black businesses as a "racial duty." Some Harlem merchants sold "Race Loyalty" buttons for ten cents each. Each button featured a Sphynx [sic], a clear indication of "Negro ancestry." The symbol would appear in the form of buttons, clothes, hairstyles, and slogans. From the pulpit, the Reverend John H. Johnson preached that "we must spend our money among our own people."

In Harlem, race patronage did not work. Jewish merchants had better merchandise, lower prices, and more credit. "Shop Black" and "Employ Black" efforts permeated black communities and organizations with scarce impact. Koch's Department Store, Harlem's largest, founded by a

Jew in 1890, closed in 1930 "rather than employ African Americans." It reopened in 1934 under a new owner, Morris Weinstein, who agreed to employ some blacks in clerical positions. Likewise, another Jewish store, Blumstein's, in 1934 agreed to hire thirty-five blacks.

In the overall picture of business in Harlem, these victories may have been symbolic—but pyrrhic. The prominent black journalist Louis Lomax recalled stopping by to listen to a black speaker in Harlem on a Saturday night in 1958. His anti-Semitic rant was followed agreeably by the crowd.

> "I want you to understand how the white man, particularly the Jew, keeps you in the economic locks. Am I right or wrong?"
>
> "You right," the crowd shot back.
>
> "You get up early every morning with roaches and rats running round you bed.... You stumble over to your child's bed to make sure the rats ain't done bit his ears off. Is that right?"
>
> "That's right."
>
> "... You go down to the garment district to meet the man... and this is where the lock come in: you go downtown to work for Mr. Eisenberg.... You work all day, eight hours a day, five days a week for forty-four dollar.... Mr. Eisenberg is watching you sweat and grunt and he makes forty-four hundred dollars.... You come back up to Harlem and buy your clothes from Mr. Gosenberg.... You buy your jewelry from Mr. Fineberg.... You get borrowed money from a finance company headed by Mr. Weinberg. Now what you don't know is that Mr. Eisenberg and Mr. Gosenberg and Mr. Fineberg and Mr. Goldberg and Mr. Weinberg is all cousins.... They got you working for nothing, and then they take back the little nothing you make before you can get home with it. That's how they got you in the economic locks."

Lomax had just witnessed black nationalism. It had morphed from racial pride and separatism to an extreme form, which he called the "Muslims."

Black nationalism, an extension of racial pride, became another attempt to define black identity in America. By its nature it embraced self-segregation. Its prophet was Marcus Garvey, who arrived in the United States from Jamaica in 1916 to become Harlem's self-appointed messiah of black America. Garvey, the leader of the Universal Negro

Improvement Association (UNIA), even advocated repatriation to Africa. He was deported in the late 1930s and was living in London. The interesting and not surprising bedfellows of Garvey-type black nationalism were white supremacists like Earnest Sevier Cox and the race-baiting Senator Theodore G. Bilbo of Mississippi. As described by the historian Charles Morgan, Bilbo joined forces in 1933 with a splinter group of the UNIA, the Peace Movement of Ethiopia (PME), led by Mittie Maude Lena Gordon of Chicago. The PME and Bilbo jointly asked for federal financial assistance to support black repatriation to Liberia in the proposed Greater Liberia Act of 1938. Bilbo even tried to get official permission for Garvey to be allowed to return to America. When Bilbo advocated for funding of black repatriation in the Senate for three hours, black supporters filled the galleries.

In the black quest for identity, another candidate appeared in 1930 with the founding in Detroit of the Nation of Islam, a group made up chiefly of African American Muslims. The founder, Wallace Fard Muhammad, while professing to be the incarnation of Allah, espoused black pride (often interpreted as black racial superiority) and the Islamic religion. By 1934 the leadership had passed to Elijah Muhammad, whose judgment as filtered through the racial lens was distorted. The leader of the Nation of Islam served time in prison because he refused to register for the draft during World War II—he did not wish to fight against the nonwhite Japanese enemy. He died in 1975.

Race music provided a particularly fascinating nexus of blacks and Jews. In the 1940s and 1950s Jews in the urban ghettos became involved in managing and owning the record labels of black musicians. This was true in Harlem with the Apollo, Old Time, and Atlantic labels, and in many other American cities. Jews, according to the historian Jonathan Karp, gave black musicians "unprecedented opportunities to record and acquire fans." But "almost invariably," he continued, Jews "exploited black artists who were doubly vulnerable..." The well-known black disc jockey Nathaniel "Magnificent" Montague was clear in his judgment: "We knew...from being ripped off by Jews in the record business, that there were as many sinners as saints in this marriage..."

The relationship between Jews and African Americans has been deemed special because of the putative "joint suffering," a phrase often used. Lomax's opinion about Jews was conflicted: "[T]hey are a people with a tradition which...offends the Negro.... Of all the ethnic suburban groups...the Jewish communities were the most adamant about keeping Negroes out." He described Jews as "more than just white." Black historical figures—Frederick Douglass and Booker T. Washington, as we have seen—used Jews as models. Washington was explicit: the race problem could be solved by copying the Jew who had "entwined himself about America in a business or industrial way."

Jews especially cite the historical connection between them and the civil rights movement: Arthur Spingarn, national president of the NAACP; Jack Greenberg, lead attorney for the NAACP Legal Defense Fund; board members of the NAACP and the National Urban League; the philanthropist Julius Rosenwald, who funded black schools in the South; the participation by left-oriented Jews, particularly in the 1960s, including two of the three students killed in the Freedom Summer of 1964 in Philadelphia, Mississippi. But black resentment toward Jews surfaced in the urban North when blacks were in close business contact with Jews. In fact the Jewish-black alliance theory is fraught with problems and must be examined on an individual rather than a group basis. As we shall see, the fault lines in this relationship would continue.

Blacks noticed Jewish traits—mainly a propensity for saving and commercial savvy—that propelled them to success outside Jewish enclaves. Very little was said about Jewish attachment to education. Besides Frederick Douglass, Louis Armstrong noticed the Jewish habit of saving. As a youth, the jazz great worked for the Karnofsky family, who plied a junk and coal trade in the red-light district of New Orleans. Armstrong recalled, "Speaking of my job with the Karnofsky Family, the profit...wasn't such a big idea, but the Jewish people always managed to put away their Nickels and Dimes, Profits which they knew would Accumulate into a *Nice* little Bundle some day."

Jewish immigrants absorbed the need for assimilation in the crowded tenements of the Lower East Side of New York. Abraham Cahan, editor of the *Forward*, the prominent Yiddish newspaper, wrote numerous columns instructing Jews how to become Americans and "embrace their new country's modernity." His advice featured "table manners, matrimonial difficulties, and baseball." Cahan's classic novel, *The Rise of David Levinsky* (1918), explored the hardships, success, and failures of the immigrants. His advice to immigrant parents whose children would be born in America rings true: "We should...especially not raise our children so that they will grow up to be foreigners in their own birthplace."

Harlem brought into focus the contrast between these two very different immigrant groups, both with a history of persecution but with unlike traditions. Jews would find success materially and influentially without a political power base. But they came voluntarily. Blacks, in the words of the historian Carl Degler, were "involuntary immigrants."

Widespread racial violence arrived in Harlem on March 19, 1935, when a riot roared down Lenox Avenue, its main thoroughfare. Thousands of Harlem residents vandalized a segment of the business district; shops were looted; three blacks were killed and scores injured. The arrest of a teenage black Puerto Rican, Lino Rivera, for shoplifting and subsequent false rumors of police having beaten him to death sparked the incident. New York's Mayor Fiorello La Guardia immediately called for a biracial Mayor's Commission on Conditions in Harlem. Headed by E. Franklin Frazier and with a staff of thirty, the commission concluded with the familiar list of needs to address: preventing discrimination; assuring employment opportunities, health care, and housing; and addressing the high crime rate. The popular Mayor La Guardia attracted a crowd of twenty thousand black supporters for his 1941 reelection rally in Harlem. He was returned to office. Nevertheless, Harlem erupted in another major race riot on August 1, 1943.

Harlem's racial turmoil was not isolated; Detroit and other cities also experienced disorder. "Hell Breaks Loose in Eight Cities" headlined the *Amsterdam News* on June 26, 1943. In Harlem a black man shot by the police during a disturbance ignited widespread vandalism and theft. The historian Dominic J. Capeci Jr. records six blacks killed, 185 injured, most of them black, and "more than 550 blacks...arrested for burglary or for receiving stolen goods." More than 1,450 stores reported damage. Harlem's congressman Adam Clayton Powell Jr. attributed the frustration to economic conditions, noting that of five thousand retail employees in

Harlem, barely one hundred were black, and those were mainly porters and maids. President Franklin Roosevelt, preoccupied by war, refused to create a national commission to study racial issues, but Mayor La Guardia responded by forming yet another one, this time titled the Mayor's Commission on Unity. Tensions would burst again in the 1960s.

Beneath the gloss of the Harlem Renaissance and the promise of the black migration from the South lay the reality of black life in the inner city and an increasing dependence on governmental largesse. In addition to a lower class, however, the Great Migration produced a black middle class and a small elite. Opportunities for wealth accumulation did exist in cities with regular wages and access to a less restrictive but limited educational system. This was of course true anywhere industrial employment supplanted work in subsistence agriculture.

In *Black Bourgeoisie* (1957), E. Franklin Frazier concentrated his attention on the emergent middle class. Integration, he found, meant that black economic advancement occurred within a separate society. America's private business sector, the *sine qua non* of mass economic advancement, remained restricted. Black doctors, lawyers, and dentists operated for the most part in the "Negro community." Black wealth, according to Frazier, was "too inconsequential for the [black middle class] to exert any political power." He thus annoyed the black press by addressing "the real economic position of the Negro." But his comparison of banking assets was unassailable. The total assets of all "Negro banks" amount to "less than those of a single small white bank in a small town in the State of New York."

As noted earlier, white America had early on acknowledged the existence of a black elite. This small but conspicuous group would develop its own social milieu. The Jack and Jill of America organization was formed in 1938 to bring together children of the black elite; the Boule organization identified potential black leaders. The black elite in every large city, as recorded by Lawrence Otis Graham, could be easily identified because of their small size and visible presence.

Black churches, too, were stratified along class lines. In Detroit, Graham noted the Plymouth Congregational Church as home to intellectuals and St. Matthew's Episcopal Church as popular with the elite. These congregations were distant from the storefront churches that catered to Detroit's poor. This division by class within race resembled the social distinctions within white society. Wealth and privilege induced a form of isolation that also paralleled white social distinctions.

Interestingly, Frazier used a Southern city, Durham, North Carolina, as an example of a positive black middle class. He praised the growth of Durham's black private sector of banks and financial institutions. He lauded the black community's middle-class traits of hard work, frugality, "abstemious" behavior, and a "stable family life" as propellants for success.

The prerequisites for entry into the economic world—capital formation, entrepreneurship, a saving mentality, an educated elite that provides a model for private-sector advancement, and a mindset emphasizing commerce—were never developed in the restricted black world. One could find exceptions; Chicago's John Johnson and Madam C. J. Walker surmounted obstacles. But the absence of structure, which affected education, jobs, and high crime rates, was due to both internal cultural traits and external discrimination and forced separatism. Urban black society provided no stepping-stone for the masses to enter the American economic mainstream.

Frazier was eager to dispel the myth of a possible "separate Negro economy" in mainstream America. "Negro banks" could not survive in such an economy. White philanthropy's attempt to foster black private enterprise was equally doomed. In 1928 John D. Rockefeller founded and funded the Dunbar National Bank in Harlem, the only bank in the community. It was one of the few banks that hired black clerical help. It may have been "called a Negro bank," Frazier noted, "but was controlled by whites." In 1938 the Dunbar National Bank became a casualty of the Depression, as did many white-managed financial institutions. Other mainstream financial institutions survived; few black ones endured. A prerequisite for the accumulation of wealth was assimilation into American society as a whole. This was impossible in America, both North and South, in the racially separate world. No form of black pride or black nationalism could surmount this obstacle. Later appeals to black separatism would only delay or hinder movement into the economic mainstream. The failure of the Mound Bayou, Mississippi, experience—a separate black economy—was replicated in the Northern cities.

Black churches have been hugely influential in social and political matters to the present day. In 1945 the Phelps-Stokes Fund reported 38,303 black churches in the United States, including 5,660,616 communicants, 35,021 Sunday Schools, 2,424,800 Sunday school pupils, and $200 million in church property. The number of congregants indicates an enormous potential for influencing behavioral norms, conduct, parental standards, and family structure. No other institution in black society has a comparable scope. A 2003 study by the *Chronicle of Philanthropy* revealed that blacks contribute as much as 25 percent more of their disposable income than whites. Ninety percent of their donations are made to the church.

In the twenty-first century the black church remains an obligatory way station for political candidates, white or black. The concentration of blacks in certain cities and states and their characteristic tendency for bloc voting is a powerful political lever. Statistically, blacks are considered a minority in the United States at large. But when the actual density of black communities is considered, it is misleading to call blacks a minority. In various cities and states they are far from an inconsequential minority and hence can exercise important voting clout.

Politicians are supremely aware of the influence of black churches. As a young lawyer, Barack Obama seized the opportunity to increase his visibility by joining Reverend Jeremiah Wright's Trinity United Church of Christ on Chicago's far South Side. The controversial Wright's congregation, numbering in the thousands, was an appropriate platform for the launch of a political career. President-elect Obama even invited Reverend Wright to give the invocation at his inaugural in January 2008. When Wright's derogatory remarks about America and whites created a media backlash, Obama "disinvited" his mentor and pastor. Later he jettisoned Reverend Wright as a political liability.

In 2015 the *New York Times* chronicled in articles and photographs the white Democratic office seekers who were attending black churches and soliciting black ministers. The awkward scene of presidential candidate Bernie Sanders of Vermont, a state with a 1 percent black population, is the epitome of opportunism. Despite Sanders's belated attempts to flash his civil rights bona fides, in the primaries he lost heavily to Hillary Clinton in black districts. She rode to victory on the coattails of a white

Southerner, William Jefferson Clinton, an enormously popular politician within the black community.

The Effects of Philanthropy

By the late nineteenth century white educators, businessmen, and politicians had begun to target black America for philanthropic contributions. Initially their interests lay in the South, and their objective was to help blacks move into the workforce through education. As blacks moved north in the Great Migration, philanthropy shifted to the urban cities of the North.

Booker T. Washington's approach, labeled the Tuskegee-Hampton idea, was the model seized upon by whites. Both Tuskegee and Hampton Institutes emphasized practical vocational skills rather than a classical education. President William McKinley lauded Tuskegee for its concentration on "practical industry." Theodore Roosevelt, who served Washington as a trustee for nine years, praised the Tuskegee-Hampton approach. Harvard's president, Charles Eliot, added his accolades. John D. Rockefeller Jr. thought the Tuskegee-Hampton model was the best way to solve the "race problems in this country."

Along with praise came Northern money. A Baptist seminary for women in Atlanta was renamed Spelman College in honor of John D. Rockefeller Sr.'s wife after a substantial donation in 1884. The General Education Board (GEB) was founded in 1902 with a $1 million gift from the Rockefellers, who by 1921 had contributed $129 million. Part of its mission was to help black schools in the South. Some philanthropy carried a strong undertone of racial inferiority and an unstated goal of producing labor for cotton production. Robert Ogden proposed a New York City vocational school that would train blacks to be domestics.

Julius Rosenwald's ambitious foray into black primary education in the South was particularly noteworthy. His fortune, a product of his brilliant management of Sears, Roebuck and Company, was the basis of the Rosenwald Fund. Between 1914 and 1932 the fund was responsible for the construction of 5,357 educational buildings—public schools, shops, and teachers' homes—at a cost of $28.4 million, in 883 counties in the rural South. Contributions came from Rosenwald (15 percent), local whites (4 percent), blacks (17 percent), and public tax funds that were mainly collected from blacks (64 percent). Rosenwald's seed money coaxed almost $23 million or 81 percent from a poor black base. In one Alabama town, "One old man, who had seen slavery days, with all of his life's earnings in an old greasy sack, slowly drew it from his pocket and emptied... [$38] on the table" for the Rosenwald program.

By the 1940s white philanthropies had lost their ideology of racial inferiority. Citing Gunnar Myrdal's research, the Phelps-Stokes Fund report of 1946 clearly stated that previous assumptions of biological inferiority had been scientifically disproved. Myrdal "opposed the doctrine of inherent inferiority" after decades of research had produced "a veritable revolution of scientific thought on racial characteristics of the Negro." Myrdal did say that the "Negro today [in 1946] is generally speaking [not] as advanced as the white man." "Climatic and historical factors, including the white man's sins of commission and omission," were responsible, according to the Phelps-Stokes report, for the condition of the black man, whose capabilities were equal to those of the white man. As a symbol of progress, Phelps-Stokes noted that for the first time in 1930 the *New York Times* had capitalized the word "Negro." Of equal importance to Phelps-Stokes was the shift to the use of the term "Negro American" rather than American Negro. First used by James Weldon Johnson in 1934, the description signified that a black was primarily an American and secondarily a Negro.

Ebony targeted white philanthropy as an unacceptable form of dependency. The emphasis on black identity, expressed through racial pride, racial independence, and racial separatism, was the essence of a 1949 *Ebony* editorial titled "Time to Stop Begging." The article argued that "zooming tax rates" and union militancy would undercut the "cornerstone" of financial support for black institutions. Just as important, *Ebony* condemned the philanthropists' control of black recipients such as Meghary Medical College and Fisk and Hampton universities. White philanthropists, according to *Ebony*, had excluded blacks from senior positions. Independence required that black institutions be supported by black philanthropy.

The "Negro," continued *Ebony*, "has made his mark in every field" and "has attained... racial pride, dignity and militancy." "Negro income" was estimated to be more than $10 billion annually. The magazine chastised the "many monied Negroes" who were too "nearsighted and greedy" to help their people. Despite this call for racial pride and racial liberation from whites, *Ebony* nonetheless wanted white support of black institutions, but without strings attached. The editorial concluded with a warning: the black person will never be equal without financial independence.

> [Wealthy Negroes] have yet to learn that when any Negro goes begging, he is not only degrading himself but his whole race. The sooner Negro Americans can stand financially on their own feet taking care of their own, the sooner will the day of true equality come for all Negroes—rich as well as poor...

Money, whether derived from white, black, public, or private sources was and remains a critical goal for black assimilation. Booker T. Washington's truism was embedded in the *Ebony* editorial.

Black objections to dependence on whites may also be seen in the NAACP's attitudes toward their lawyers. Key players in the civil rights struggle, these attorneys had their own internal bout with racial separation, racial pride, and racial control. The organization was uncomfortable having to rely on white lawyers. Few black lawyers could be found when the NAACP began its crusade: in 1910 only 795 of the nation's 114,000 lawyers were black. Fewer still lived in the South. Black businessmen, complaining that "black attorneys lacked competence," preferred white lawyers. Likewise the NAACP relied heavily on white attorneys like Moorfield Storey, president of the NAACP, and Louis Marshall. "There were not ten Negro lawyers," wrote William H. Hastie, who would become the first black federal judge, "capable of handling civil rights litigation, engaged in practice in the South." Clarence Darrow, as noted earlier, was asked to litigate the 1925 case of Dr. Ossian Sweet in Detroit. Walter White, then an assistant secretary of the NAACP, "expressed a low opinion of...[the Detroit] Negro lawyers" and lobbied for Darrow and Arthur Garfield Hayes to defend Sweet.

By the 1920s qualified blacks were being educated at Ivy League schools. Chief among them were Harvard Law School graduates Hastie and Charles Hamilton Houston, who became dean of the Howard

University Law School and Thurgood Marshall's professor. Houston joined the NAACP legal staff in 1935 in the transition from white to black control. He led the brilliant litigation of graduate school desegregation cases in Missouri, Maryland, Oklahoma, and Texas. These cases, in essence, proved the inherent inequality of "separate but equal," the foundation of overt legal segregation. The NAACP lawyers, according to the historians August Meier and Elliott Rudwick, were influenced by "racial pride." To depend on whites "was an admission of inadequacy and an implied criticism of the black bar." Yet following Thurgood Marshall as director of the NAACP Legal Defense Fund (which had become an entity distinct from the NAACP) was a white, Jewish, Brooklyn-born attorney, Jack Greenberg. He presided over the organization from 1961 to 1984. The NAACP still relied heavily on white counsel during the golden years of the civil rights revolution. During racial turmoil between blacks and Jews in the Ocean Hill–Brownsville section of his native Brooklyn, Greenberg presided over the NAACP's legal arm.

From the Farm to the City

The adjustment from rural Southern life to Northern urban ghetto existence created another set of obstacles for blacks. Clearly they were radicalized by the urban environment. *Ebony*'s article "Urbanization and Family Breakdown" (August 1979) outlined the "correlation between City Life, Crime," which "most Black experts... [viewed as] self-evident." Life in the South, in addition to discrimination, violence, and hardship, did entail nurturing via extended family, a closely knit community, role models, better supervision, and "social control." Instead of the promised land in the North, "blacks found crowded housing, communities devoid of family or friends, welfare lines, Northern racism and daily stress," all prime conditions "to turn a susceptible person to a life of crime."

Welfare was also a prime culprit. Billy W. Pugh, president of the Black Probation Officers Association, associated family disintegration directly with crime. He described "welfare" as "two-faced": "[O]n the one, deter[ring] crime by offering money for the necessities of life... on the other hand, foster[ing] crime by removing the incentive and drive that make a person feel complete." Welfare was "one of the most abiding urban problems... [which] creates a cycle of crime by depriving Black youngsters of positive role models." Lloyd Sealy, the first highly ranked black police officer in the New York Police Department and a professor of criminal justice at John Jay College, was dismayed by the lack of "social control" within the black community. "Black urban neighborhoods" were literally breeding grounds for steering youths into "juvenile gangs and crime." All of which contributed to "spiraling crime rates."

The deprivations of life in the South were balanced by a cohesiveness that was absent in the urban North.

Black-on-Black Crime

Black crime in America has been treated in a separate category beginning with the few numbers of free blacks in the North before the Civil War. The massive move to urban areas in the North and South in the early twentieth century exacerbated the problems associated with black crime. The special conditions in the cities—poor housing, unemployment, discrimination, poor nutrition, family disintegration, inadequate educational facilities, and police brutality—are usually blamed. This argument would suggest that blacks have had no free will, self-determination, or self-development. But these traits, a form of human agency, are the same characteristics that allowed blacks to survive the horrors and demeaning experience of race-based slavery. There would appear to be a contradiction.

Observers commonly cite a propensity toward criminal activity at the first stage of immigration, whether among Italians, Irish, Eastern Europeans, or Jews. Mobility then ensues with traditional stepping-stone patterns—except for blacks, who remain isolated by racial restrictions and white hostility. Moreover, blacks did not enjoy the institutional structures that would help them surmount obstacles and take advantage of opportunities when overt legal discrimination was eliminated and subtle discrimination was mitigated. Crime was a factor in the poor immigrant experience, but the extent of intra-racial homicides is a distinct feature of the black experience. The Irish and the Italians benefited enormously from parochial schools. Jews inherited a literate tradition and an entrepreneurial background. The black community, church, and family were inadequate to the task.

Urban anonymity both replaced the closely knit communities of the black South and led to radical behavior. Gangs, and their attendant destructiveness, filled a void for black males. Chicago's Black P. (Pharaoh) Stone Nation gang, formed in 1958, was still active in the tragic murder of nine-year-old Tyshawn Lee in November 2015. By the 1930s, examples of gang activity abounded, captured in Richard Wright's fictional *Native Son* or in E. Franklin Frazier's sociological work. By the end of the century, friction with police became a focal point of the black community rather than black-on-black crime, which was either ignored or blamed on exogenous factors.

The tension between the greater need for police involvement in high-crime areas and the antagonism between blacks and predominantly white urban police forces has been a continuing saga in American history. Encounters between police and blacks have consistently generated publicity and legal action. Despite the police responsibility to ensure safe neighborhoods, black cooperation with law enforcement officials has been lax.

In the 1950s Louis Lomax reported several commonplace examples of police errors and abusive treatment of blacks. When a black plain-clothes Detroit officer was sent to investigate an illegal gambling operation in 1955, a white cop mistakenly thought he was a perpetrator and beat him. In Chicago a black man, James Monroe, and his family were aroused by police at 5:00 a.m., insulted, and physically assaulted. Monroe sued, claiming unlawful entry, and received a $50,000 judgment against the police. In Cleveland a white policeman shot a twenty-three-year-old black man who he thought was reaching for a gun. Surprisingly, Lomax quotes a civil rights commission document that "adduced evidence that police in the non-South were the worst offenders."

While at *Ebony*, Ben Burns wondered about black silence in the face of black-on-black crime. Ultimately he surrendered to the rationalization that crime is "a subtle form of revolution." Later in life he was interested in the response to the problem by Benjamin Ward, New York City's first black police commissioner. In a conversation reported in the *New York Times* on July 27, 1987, Ward "blamed most of the city's crime on young black men." He told black ministers that black-on-black crime is "our little secret" and added, "[Young black men] are committing genocide against their people. They are ripping off the neighborhoods...killing innocent people as they fight over their drug locations." The black New York State Supreme Court judge Bruce Wright was equally blunt: "If you don't talk about it, it will remain a dirty little secret." "No white person comes into Bedford-Stuyvesant and rapes a grandmother," added the black Brooklyn College professor Carlos Russell.

In 1982, 85.6 percent of black homicide victims, as reported by the New York Police Department, were killed by other blacks. A 1985 *New York Times*/WCBS poll reported that 71 percent of whites and 51 percent of blacks would be frightened if they saw "rowdy black male teen-agers on a subway car."

In response to Ward's candor, Reverend Jesse Jackson accused Wall Street, not blacks, of perpetrating "the biggest criminal acts" in New York in 1987. But Hazel Dukes, president of the New York State chapter of the NAACP, differed: "I am more worried about the people who take the subway from Wall Street to Brooklyn, than people who work on Wall Street." Black representative Charles Rangel diverted the conversation to abusive police behavior. (Today this dialogue would be virtually the same except that generally black police commissioners and no representatives of the NAACP would dare speak candidly about intra-racial crime.)

Today the "dirty little secret" remains basically ignored by black leaders in deference to the drama and symbolism of abusive police behavior and the group response of Black Lives Matter.

The Impact of World War II

The first test of mass forced racial integration came in the armed services. Officially President Harry S. Truman issued an executive order on July 26, 1948, ending segregation in the military. By the summer of 1952, segregation in the armed services had been virtually eliminated.

In 1950 Columbia University president Dwight D. Eisenhower, the former general and soon-to-be president, established the Conservation of Human Resources Project to study manpower issues in the United States. The cooperative research effort was funded by American business. Its director was Eli Ginzberg, professor of economics at Columbia and adviser to presidents, whose study of black soldiers in World War II resulted in *The Negro Potential* (1956). The significance of Ginzberg's work can be measured by both the data and the context. It is a fascinating account of racial opinions at the time. The disintegration of the black family that would later be presented in the Moynihan Report (1965) was already apparent in *The Negro Potential*.

At the start of World War II the army had concluded from studies of World War I that "any large-scale inflow of Negro manpower" would present enormous difficulties. World War I had proven that "Negro manpower was poorly endowed mentally... for future efficient utilization." Other problems were related to "military discipline and public relations." At the onset of World War II, blacks represented only 2 percent of the regular army. Between 1920 and 1940 only one black had graduated from West Point. By the end of the war in 1945, almost seven hundred thousand blacks were on active duty out of a total of 8.3 million servicemen and women. Of seven hundred thousand whites and blacks who were rejected for "mental or educational deficiency," 45 percent were black, and 73 percent of them were categorized as "below average" or "least capable."

Performance in combat was mixed. Black divisions were "described as at best, fair." General Mark Clark concluded that his Ninety-Second Division's black troops' "accomplishments were less favorable than any of the white divisions." But he did note "many instances of individual heroism and successful action by smaller units." Combat support units he described as generally demonstrating "a high degree of efficiency." Black troops who fought "in platoons alongside white soldiers did well." Of special recognition was the "outstanding record" of the "Negro airman."

Studies indicated that a "high proportion" of black troops caused disciplinary problems; "passive resistance" against authority was a frequent occurrence. Ginzberg recognized that a significant number of army officers held "strong opinions about the inferiority of the Negro."

Segregation, education, and family background played a role in hampering the effectiveness of black soldiers. "It would be difficult," Ginzberg wrote, "to exaggerate the influence of segregation on the training and utilization of Negroes in the Army during World War II." He recommended better officers for black units, the integration of units, and balancing the units with men of "varying aptitudes and skills." "Military planners realized," Ginzberg concluded, "...that if the Negro was to fight, he had to fight on an integrated basis."

That opportunity came quickly in 1950 when General Matthew Ridgway, commander-in-chief in the Far East during the Korean War, asked permission to integrate army training centers. Although integration was achieved by 1952, still 55 percent of "Negro registrants" were rejected by the armed services in 1953–1954 for "mental or educational deficiency." The black soldier would eventually achieve equality in the military. Two years after *The Negro Potential* was published, a young black man was promoted to second lieutenant; in 1989 this lieutenant, now General Colin Powell, became chairman of the Joint Chiefs of Staff.

As a by-product of their experience in the military, many former black soldiers became active in the civil rights movement. One such individual, Aaron Henry of Clarksdale, Mississippi, became head of the Mississippi chapter of the NAACP. Henry, a pharmacist and a stalwart in the struggle for voting rights, was later elected to the Mississippi House of Representatives.

In *The Negro Potential*, Ginzberg went on to analyze the preparedness of blacks for employment. He began with basic preparation for education and work, which he suggested must come from within the family, and a set of values and goals: "The Negro must alter many of his values before he will be able to cope effectively with [economic opportunities]."

Among blacks, family stability, the key to a proper value system, was in crisis. Of special concern were single-parent families and male desertion. Ginzberg quoted at length E. Franklin Frazier's 1950 observation:

> The incidence of desertion on the part of the male...is much greater among Negroes than any other racial or ethnic [group]....Since family disorganization is so widespread, the family environment of a large number of Negro children is precarious and fragmentary....They do not even acquire the domestic work skills necessary to make a living....
>
> Negro children from disorganized families often exhibit little interest in the knowledge and skills provided by the public schools....The lack of family discipline and a failure of the disorganized family to provide models...of the values of the community are partly responsible at least for the irregular work habits and lack of ambition among many Negro youths....

These children began school with an inadequate vocabulary, little understanding of the world, and no sense of the "pleasure of learning." Given the handicaps of family and environment, the child was likely never to perform adequately. The school, according to Ginzberg, could not compensate for these deficiencies. The impact of poverty, bad schools, a dysfunctional family, and a dangerous slum neighborhood would take its toll on intellectual and moral development. Children were seriously stunted before they reached school age.

Ginzberg's objective was "speed of assimilation of the Negro into American society." In that process, he noted, the main burden and responsibility for "Negro preparation for work falls on the Negro community itself." Assimilation demanded cultural adaptation, which called for better knowledge among blacks of the values and behavior of the middle class. This meant close association, a difficult task because of segregated housing. Blacks could not find their way to the proper workplace if they had not "lived, played, and studied with [whites] ... in childhood and young adulthood." Segregation and separation, Ginzberg thought, would surely impede black economic progress. Education would be the path to the economic mainstream.

Beginning with World War I, the Great Migration of blacks to Northern cities brought them a jarring adjustment: an end to overt segregation (but not segregation itself), an ability to earn factory wages, the right to vote, access to public accommodations, and a trickle into the middle and upper middle classes. The move also prompted residential and educational segregation, race riots, enormous frustration, lack of penetration in the private sector, tension with police, restricted access to credit, and the radicalization of youth. In short, two racially separate societies developed. Social, economic, and residential mobility, fundamental American traits, were severely restricted. A form of self-segregation developed. The basic structures of black life for coping with the transition—family, community, and church—did not evolve. Assimilation did not happen.

In the 1950s two events shattered legal segregation. The landmark *Brown v. Board of Education* decision ended the legal foundation of racially segregated school systems. Still, racially separate neighborhoods, the failure of school busing, white flight from neighborhoods after black penetration, and black self-segregation continued to thwart the racial integration of secondary schools. In 1964 in New York City, a black student was likely to attend a school that was 90 percent nonwhite. Despite its Commission on Integration, New York was more racially segregated in 1966 than at the announcement of the *Brown* decision.

When the demure, reserved Rosa Parks refused to move to the "colored" section of the bus in Montgomery, Alabama, in 1955, the incident prompted blacks to boycott the city's bus system, and one aspect of overt legal discrimination was doomed. The Civil Rights Act of 1964 specifically eliminated discrimination in public accommodations, and the practice ended within a few years. A statue of Rosa Parks now stands in the National Statuary Hall of the US Capitol.

But though she became a symbol, Rosa Parks was still a human being. On August 30, 1994, the eighty-one-year-old was mugged, robbed of $103, and hit several times by a black assailant, Joseph Skipper. The attack on the symbol was, of course, major news. Had the victim been a mere elderly black woman rather than a person of note, the crime would have gone unreported. The attack on Rosa Parks, the symbol, angered *New York Times* columnist Bob Herbert, a champion of real and perceived racial discrimination. Five days later, he wrote forcefully about strict law-and-order measures to combat this type of black-on-black crime: "It is time to grab the felons and let them know...they will not be allowed to capture the soul of the civil rights movement." Black-on-black crime would, Herbert thought, be the primary challenge of the next phase of the civil rights struggle. But by 2016 blacks had forgotten the need for bold law-and-order measures.

The desire for self-determination and self-sufficiency among blacks led to greater pressures against discrimination but also, as with the Nation of Islam, a favorable view of racial separation. While the moderate NAACP pursued legal means and assimilation, as espoused by Roy Wilkins, its executive director, the Nation of Islam, through the voices of Elijah Muhammad and Malcolm X, preached hatred of whites, a rejection of integration, and an absolute demand for racial, economic, and physical independence—in other words, a nation within a nation. The Black Muslim diatribe against white persecution and oppression would become a continuing fundamental message of black society. Louis Farrakhan, leader of the Nation of Islam, called the white man the "greatest trouble-maker...the greatest peace-breaker...the greatest murderer on earth." Malcolm X proclaimed that white people were "devils."

In the wake of the Great Migration and its consequences, black attitudes toward the future were mixed. On the one hand, despite the failed utopia of the "free" North, there was optimism. *Ebony* magazine consistently touted black advancement. Yet Richard Wright's angry prose would prove to be prescient, and Gunnar Myrdal's *An American Dilemma* explored "The Negro Problem and Modern Democracy." Racial violence during the period was evidence of enormous frustration. Black discontent boiled over in protests involving education, housing, and employment inequality. Persistent friction between blacks and police became a fixture of urban life. Black anger fueled the extreme rhetoric of the black militants.

Just ahead, the 1960s in both North and South would feature large-scale civil disruption.

Chapter Four

The 1960s: Civil Rights and Civil War

On our part Negro citizens must redouble their efforts to educate and train themselves for the new responsibilities which equal opportunities will require of them. They must march not only to the picket lines but to the libraries: they must prepare themselves for the stiffening competition of a no-holds-barred marketplace. They must make a special effort to eradicate the disorganization which has afflicted the lives of so many families. They must overcome not only subtle barriers of discrimination but their own shortcomings as individuals, and must make the effort incumbent on any pioneer group to move on higher emotional, spiritual and educational levels.

—WHITNEY YOUNG JR., EXECUTIVE DIRECTOR,
NATIONAL URBAN LEAGUE, 1964

When the thrust changes from desegregation to integration...one of [the black person's] chief responsibilities is to prepare himself to live in an integrated society.... We must be able to face up honestly to our own shortcomings.... We seek integration based on mutual respect.

—MARTIN LUTHER KING JR., 1965

[T]here is no [racial] moral distance, no moral distance...between the facts of life in San Francisco and the facts of life in Birmingham; one has to tell it like it is.

—JAMES BALDWIN, *TAKE THIS HAMMER*, 1964

I'm not coming in here to speak as a Baptist or a Methodist or a Democrat or a Republican...not even as an American.... I am speaking as a Black man. The new type of Black man, he doesn't want integration.

Not segregation, [but] separation.... Separation is when you have your own; you control your own economy; you control your own politics; you control your own society; you control your own everything.... We don't think as Americans any more, but as Black men.
    —Malcolm X, at Michigan State University, January 23, 1963

Negroes have continued to flee from behind the Cotton Curtain, but now they find that after years of indifference and exploitation, Chicago has not turned out to be the new Jerusalem. There will be fewer overt acts to aid us here; naive targets such as the Jim Clarks and George Wallaces will be harder to find and use as symbols.
    —Martin Luther King Jr., Chicago, June 1965

The Negro is not free in the North. He is at the bottom of the economic ladder, often without a job and with inadequate educational opportunities.
    —Martin Luther King Jr., Cleveland, Ohio, July 27, 1965

It's not the bus, it's us.
    —Julian Bond, in response to white resistance to forced busing to achieve integration, 1960s

In the turbulent sixties the post–World War II calm would be tested by the civil rights movement and the Vietnam War. Gender equality and a cultural revolution would follow. How would America adapt? For blacks, what would change and what would remain unsolved in the twenty-first century? How would change affect black identity, racial separation, or racial integration? What obstacles would remain in the quest for full black participation in the economic mainstream? America would discover what could be fixed, what would remain mired in complexity, and what would become perhaps unfixable. Overt legal segregation would end, but racial strife would encompass the entire country. The quandary of separation versus integration would continue to haunt America.

The 1960s began with the election to the presidency of the charismatic John F. Kennedy. At forty-three years of age, Kennedy, the youngest elected president in the nation's history, personified the boundless energy and promise of America. He came out of an Irish Catholic family that had attained wealth and power. Harvard educated, he embodied American cultural adaptability and assimilation. His ambitious father Joseph Kennedy's ruthless pursuit of business success led ironically to his appointment by Franklin Roosevelt as the first chairman of the Securities and Exchange Commission—the fox had been asked to guard the chicken coop. Joe Kennedy, who knew the foibles of Wall Street, surprisingly proved to be an able government regulator. His son Jack was able to fulfill the father's quest for power. Like Abraham Lincoln, Jack Kennedy would be "forced into glory" by race.

The American economy in the sixties was considered to be globally hegemonic. General Motors, the engine of American industry, ruled the vital industrial base. The automaker's power, considered great enough to be a threat to competitors, provoked anti-trust inquiries designed to prevent destructive monopoly control. The French author Jean-Jacques Servan-Schreiber, in his book *The American Challenge*, forecast the virtual takeover of Europe by American industrial power. "The present European generation has only a few years," wrote the celebrated historian Arthur Schlesinger Jr. in the foreword to Servan-Schreiber's exaggerated tale, "to decide between restoring an autonomous European civilization or allowing Europe to become a subsidiary of the United States."

The Dow Jones Industrial Average (DJIA) on January 1, 1962, was 649. America's changing economy could easily be understood by the composition of the DJIA: only six of the thirty companies comprising the index in 1962 were still in the DJIA in 2016. Wall Street designated a group of stocks, the "Nifty Fifty," supposedly possessed of limitless growth potential because of the momentum and business acumen of their companies. The arrival of *Institutional Investor* magazine in 1968 heralded a new force in the securities markets, exemplified by public employees' pension funds. In ensuing decades the size and obligations of these funds would critically limit local and state government budget options, a condition that would severely strain expenditures in largely black inner cities. The preeminence of American businesses would be severely challenged by domestic and foreign competitors; the business world is never static.

Costs of education were manageable. Even at the elite Yale University, tuition, room, and board for an undergraduate cost only $3,500 per year ($28,000 in 2017 dollars).

In July 1969 the United States displayed its technological prowess when two astronauts walked on the moon. America's social problems, too, were considered solvable by science and rational government planning and intervention. The War on Poverty commenced in the midst of the civil rights revolution and the Vietnam War. The initials VC stood for the Communist-led Vietcong as well as for the high-tech financing of venture capital; both entered the American lexicon at roughly the same time.

A Global Definition of "People of Color"

In the sixties the nonwhite, non-Western nation of Japan would begin the economic assault on America the Leviathan. Utterly defeated in World War II, Japan was occupied by the victorious Americans. But rather than exact revenge on either Germany or Japan, the Allies supervised the rebuilding of the former fascist enemies. Creating democratic societies, not colonial oppression, and reestablishing American overseas markets were mutually complementary goals. The United States allowed Japan to recover its former status as an industrial power. General Douglas MacArthur, who had been trounced by the Japanese in the Philippines and whose men had borne the brunt of Japanese cruelty, became supreme commander of the occupying American forces. He ruled efficiently and benignly from an elaborate office in the Dai-Ichi Insurance building. (Today Dai-Ichi company officers continue respectfully to offer tours of MacArthur's office to visiting US executives.)[1]

Soon the Japanese would again attack America, but this time in the consumer marketplace. Once-powerful Detroit would feel the brunt of the prowess of a "people of color"; black Detroit would bear the greatest burden. In 1953 a young electrical engineer had negotiated a license from Western Electric to make transistors in Japan. His name was Akio Morita, and his company would become the giant Sony. By 1964 Tokyo

---

1 In 1953 C. Vann Woodward, the distinguished historian of the South and a Southerner himself, was invited to teach a semester on Reconstruction at the University of Tokyo. The Japanese wanted to know about the South's experience of being ruled by the American North. The most popular movie in Tokyo at the time was *Gone with the Wind*.

would host the Olympics. Japan would shatter a monolithic image of "people of color," the myth of the unity of nonwhites—an assumption of shared goals, similar culture, same aptitude for economic advancement, and common antipathy toward the West. This notion of "people of color" was thought to be the basis of concerted progress and action. It wasn't. Globalization was brought home to America by a nonwhite, non-Western nation.

Black Identity

In the United States, questions about identity and assimilation shadowed attempts to formulate and implement public policy on race. America no longer had the luxury of ignoring problems of forced integration and self-segregation. Black integrationists envisioned an assimilated society once overt legal segregation had been toppled and government regulations were established; black separatists, on the other hand, had given up on assimilation and proposed a self-contained black society. Even black integrationists did not know how much integration was appropriate. It was clear that earlier attempts to form an economically self-sufficient black community had failed.

The identity conundrum penetrated the classroom of Spelman College, a historically black women's college (HBCU) in Atlanta. In the early 1960s the radical historian Staughton Lynd had taught at Spelman. In his first class in 1962, a survey course in American history, Professor Lynd began with the pilgrims at Plymouth Rock. A young woman in the class asked, "What does that got to do with me?" Lynd had previously had little contact with American blacks. He had known "almost no black people growing up [in New York City] ... [other than] a black cook." The next year, 1963, Lynd began with the slave ships. This time a young woman asked, "How come you're teaching us this special history?"

The classroom questions had devolved into one of fractured personal identity. Where does a black person fit in American society? To what extent is an African American exclusively part of a separate group and treated specially? To what extent is there a shared American background with common values?

Some blacks now looked to Africa for identity and guidance. African independence movements fueled optimism about black progress. The most influential black intellectual, W. E. B. Du Bois, moved to Ghana in 1963 and became a citizen there. His interest in Africa and people of African descent was well established.

At their most extreme, black separatists like Marcus Garvey had advocated the resettlement of black Americans in Africa. Malcolm X now extolled the virtues of Africa and the superiority of African values and culture against those of the "white devils." Several of his speeches between 1963 and 1965 clearly indicate his separatism, his thinly veiled call for violence, his spiritual and misguided optimism about Africa, and the vague nature of his policy recommendations. In 1964 Malcolm, through racial lenses, looked to Egypt and Ghana for economic progress. The delusion of a surge in Egyptian and Ghanaian progress was typical of the uninformed, fuzzy, racially obsessed thought patterns of Du Bois and Malcolm. Du Bois described plans for a TV station and a publishing plant in Ghana. Tema, on Ghana's Atlantic coast, he envisioned as a major industrial city. Both Malcolm X and Du Bois rejected American capitalism in favor of a socialist approach; both argued that economics was key to equality. In reality, the only unifying theme for black separatists was—and remains—real and imagined white oppression and discrimination.

Malcolm knew that the large-scale movement of American blacks to Africa was scarcely feasible. Yet, according to Malcolm, the black man in America owned nothing. He wanted blacks to own land and to run their own economy. Malcolm saw the black man as a victim of exploitation by whites who owned stores where blacks shopped and who owned the homes in which blacks lived. Blacks were victims of "economic and political exploitation." The white man, Malcolm declared, "keeps the Black community in the image of a criminal....It's a science...to make the victim look like a criminal." In 1964 this "image making" falsely "depicted the [Harlem] rioters as hoodlums, criminals, thieves, because they were abducting some property." But really, Malcolm advised, politicians, white merchants, and white landlords were the thieves who had stolen property from the black community. Translation: It's all right to steal and burn down the neighborhood. Black activists from the 1960s to the twenty-first century have often justified looting and wanton destruction as a form of compensation and revenge—even when they are burning their own neighborhoods. (In 2016 blacks openly supported the phrase "In Defense of Looting.") An appeal to violence was persistent, though sometimes disguised, in much of Malcolm X's work. He avoided discussing black-on-black crime, as do black leaders today.

In 1964 Malcolm spoke at Michigan State, not as "an American" but as "a Black man." He considered racial integration a form of tokenism to appease black integrationists like Thurgood Marshall and Roy Wilkins. He accurately noted: "[T]here is no real integration anywhere in North America—North, South, East or West, not even in San Francisco, Oakland, or Berkeley...." White liberals "have been making a great fuss over the South only to blind us to what is happening in the North." The failure of residential and housing integration, he thought, as did Barry Goldwater, would prompt "Negro leaders" to demand a forced "quota, or percentage of white people's jobs."

For Malcolm the real criminal was the "white liberal, the political hypocrite...who pose as our friends, [and] force us into a life of crime." Blacks were "migrating" to England and France, Malcolm noted, because of "the high standard of living." He should have asked *why* there was a "high standard of living" there and might have concluded that assimilation into Western civilization, rather than separation, was beneficial.

At the University of California in 1963, Malcolm blamed white liberals for lowering the "moral standards" of the black masses. The result, he thought, was clear:

Our young girls, our daughters, our baby sisters become unwed mothers before they are hardly teens. Our community has tens of thousands of unmarried mothers who have no hope of ever getting a husband. And our community has tens of thousands of little babies who have no father to act as their provider or protector.

These comments, similar to those of E. Franklin Frazier, were made before Daniel Patrick Moynihan's devastating report on the black family. Malcolm blamed white America for black unemployment and poverty, which had forced his people into a life of crime. Upper-class blacks did not escape his wrath. The "Negro community...trapped in the slums" was "trapped in a vicious cycle of ignorance, poverty, disease, sickness, and death.... The wealthy, educated Black bourgeoisie... never reach back and pull the rest of our people out with them...." Blacks, he thought, no longer feared the white man and had stopped "turning their nonviolent cheek to the violent white man." He predicted a "bloody race war."

The "permanent solution" for Malcolm X was separation, with reparations. The US government, he said, should pay for travel to "our homeland" and the equipment to farm—echoing several proposals since the Civil War to make land available for separate black settlement. Alternatively the government should "divide a separate part of the country into which our people can migrate." Financial support would last only for "twenty to twenty-five years until we are in a position to be completely independent." In 1989, a third-year law student at the University of Minnesota would write a column demanding that blacks would be given Arkansas, Alabama, Georgia, Louisiana, and Mississippi as a black region. The student, Keith Ellison, writing under the pen name Keith E. Hakim, is currently a congressman from Minnesota and deputy chair of the Democratic National Committee.

The Jews, "who got what they wanted," were Malcolm's role model. He chastised Jews for pretending they were friends of blacks. If Jews would shed their hypocrisy, Malcolm said, they could genuinely help blacks by showing them how to "solve the problems" of segregation. The University of California audience laughed and applauded when he appealed to economics, not protest:

> [Jews] haven't been sit-in or Freedom Riders, they usually go in with an economic weapon. They bought Atlantic City, and now they can go there. They bought Miami Beach and now they can go there.

When Malcolm X became disenchanted with his leader Elijah Muhammad, he left the Nation of Islam. In February 1965 he was assassinated in New York City by members of the Nation. Much of Malcolm's doctrine lived on in Stokely Carmichael's Black Power movement, the Black Panthers, and today's black militancy. But this approach to racial unity was predicated on grievance, not constructive policy. In retrospect,

Malcolm was well suited to inflame blacks rather than prepare them for entrance into the economic mainstream.

The black journalist Louis Lomax was also interested in African and black identity, but from the different perspective of integration. Lomax traveled to Africa in 1960 to explore "the mystical thing called black brotherhood," and wrote a book titled *The Reluctant African*. Before his trip he met in Harlem with a man whom he identified only as "a gifted African-American intellectual and former lecturer at New York University." When Lomax "suggested that multiracialism was the better part of common sense," he was told, "You are going to die from an overdose of integration." But Lomax had an "irrevocable commitment" to it.

Separatism was in the air during Lomax's journey. In Egypt his taxi driver, pointing to a diesel engine in a store window, proudly told him it was made in Egypt: "Black man made that." Gamal Abdul Nasser, the Egyptian dictator, had implemented Africanization and Egyptianization. There were no street signs in English.

Lomax stopped in Paris, where he saw Richard Wright. Five years earlier Wright had praised the vague concept of the unity of colored people at the Bandung Conference. Now he criticized Africans for their "snobbish," "imperious," and "arrogant" attitudes toward "American Negro intellectuals." And he bitterly attacked the African nations that begged for money from the white nations. Business deals with whites constituted a "dependency mentality," said Wright. Hatred of the white man was shaky ground for unity and economic progress.

The productive Lomax, ever in search of black identity, was appalled by the emerging separatism of American blacks. In his 1960 book *The Negro Revolt*, he worried about "the emerging tribe mentality of blacks." "All American Negroes 'pay dues,'" Lomax wrote. "[I]f you are a writer, 'dues' is the price you pay for being relegated to 'Negro' themes when your real interests…lie someplace else…if you are a college professor on an 'integrated' campus, 'dues' are what you pay when students make you a specialist on the Negro and approach you with sympathetic condescension." It seemed indisputable to him that blacks "are becoming more tribal."

We had come together as a tribe for negative, not positive, reasons; we were bound together by the animus of the white man, not by historical customs and traditions such as those that have fashioned the world's peoples into culture groups.

Tribalism, or separatism, remains a highly destructive path within American society. In 2005 John Hope Franklin, the twentieth century's most distinguished black historian, would reiterate Lomax's warning: "African-American scholars have repeatedly been cast or pushed into the field of black studies even when they were not inclined to go that route." Franklin was infuriated when the equally eminent historian C. Vann Woodward, a close friend, categorized Franklin as an historian of African American studies. Franklin wanted to be known as an historian, not as a specialist historian of black subject matter. The friendship was permanently frayed. Franklin wrote that "Negro scholarship" was the "victim, that there was some 'mystique' about Negro studies, similar to the view that there was some 'mystique' about Negro spirituals which required a person to possess black skin in order to sing them." The integrationist Franklin viewed the "mystique" as degrading, suggesting an inability to compete.

"Africans are Africans, not Negroes." Thus spoke an African to Louis Lomax in 1960. By then the identity search had moved to the nature of a name, with history yielding several possibilities. "I am a Negro, and proud of my race," declared Mississippian Blanche K. Bruce, the first elected black person to serve in the US Senate, in 1875. Marcus Garvey, the modern founder of a separatist black community, proudly called his organization the United Negro Improvement Association. W. E. B. Du Bois thought "Negro" was acceptable as well as "black," but "colored" was adopted by the NAACP.

In November 1967 *Ebony* magazine explored the debate in Lerone Bennett Jr.'s article "What's in a Name?" According to Bennett, there were three camps. The first group preferred "Afro-American," in order to shed the perceived master-slave connotation of "Negro." The second group wanted to continue to use "Negro," arguing that a debate over naming would distract from real problems. The Black Power contingency wanted to apply "black" to those who wanted emancipation, and contemptuously referred to integrationists as "Negroes." For the black actor Ossie Davis, "A black man means not to accept the system as Negroes, but to fight hell out of the system as Malcolm did." In an earlier and tragic period, the black abolitionist Henry Highland Garnet had dissented altogether: "How unprofitable it is for us to...debate upon the questions which we shall be called..."

In June 1968 *Ebony* proceeded to conduct a naming contest. The results showed that 48 percent of readers favored "Afro-American," 23.3 percent "black," 12 percent "African American," 8.1 percent "Negro," 3 percent "colored," and the remainder mixed. The magazine, substantially agreeing with Henry Highland Garnet, de-emphasized the significance of a name in preference to the progress of black America. Yet even today conflicts over black identity remain distracted by the sensitivity of symbolism over substance.

Whether in the North or the South, the white attitude of keeping black people "at a distance" has yielded two separate worlds. Millions of mostly poor white immigrants abandoned Europe for economic and political reasons; most successfully assimilated into American society. A trip to the Tenement Museum in New York offers a vivid picture of the life of Eastern European Jewish immigrants in the early twentieth century. The vast majority of these people rose to middle class or higher status via the stepping-stone route. There was no such path for the black participants in America's Great Migration.

Integration at Ole Miss

Mississippi was undoubtedly the South's most extreme example of overt legal segregation. In September 1962 a black air force veteran and native Mississippian, twenty-nine-year-old James Meredith, set out alone to break the status quo. His target was the state's flagship school, the University of Mississippi (Ole Miss), which denied entrance to black students. Meredith was not taken seriously by the *Chicago Defender* when he appeared at their offices in the spring of that year.

James Meredith's racial awakening had "matured" between 1957 and 1960 when he was serving in the air force and stationed in Japan. Sergeant Meredith was inspired by Japan's values—"pride, stoicism, reverence for nature, industriousness, and the sanctity of the family." These values, he expressed, were identical to those of his own closely knit family. He began to think of himself as human, as not being different simply because he was black. The natural courtesy of the "nonwhite" Japanese conveyed "respect and equality." He did not feel inferior; white superiority, he thought, was an American phenomenon.[2]

Meredith began his quest to attack personally a fortress of racial segregation without institutional help. His decision to integrate Ole Miss was his decision, not that of the NAACP or the federal government. He applied for admission to the school on January 21, 1961, and was rejected. When a court process ensued, Meredith asked for help. In a letter to Thurgood Marshall, then director of the NAACP's Legal Defense Fund, he described his goal of admission to the racially segregated university: "I am familiar with the probable difficulties involved... and I am fully prepared to pursue it all the way to a degree." He wanted to do this "for the benefit of (1) my country, (2) my race, (3) my family, and (4) myself." In a telephone conversation, Marshall and Meredith "didn't hit it off," the would-be student thought. Marshall kept asking him about his "legitimacy" in the undertaking. Meredith, thinking that Marshall was questioning his integrity, hung up on the future Supreme Court justice. A few weeks later Marshall, having developed an interest in the case, reestablished contact with Meredith. The case for Meredith's admission to Ole Miss wound its way to the Supreme Court, where Justice Hugo Black, a former Ku Klux Klan member, removed all obstacles to Meredith's acceptance.

Because of the duplicity of Mississippi governor Ross Barnett in his conversations with President Kennedy and Attorney General Robert Kennedy, all hell broke loose when Meredith physically attempted to enter the school in September 1962. The world watched the campus riot via television. Eventually five thousand soldiers and national guardsmen were deployed to restore order. Two people were killed and scores of others injured. But Meredith entered the university, enduring persistent harassment during his two semesters there. He graduated on time.

Cynical blacks mocked Meredith's achievement. Malcolm X ridiculed the need for thousands of troops to assist a single black man. This was, in his view, tokenism and an illustration of the failure of integration. W. E. B. Du Bois, by then a resident of Ghana, rejoiced but added, in his

---

2 The Japanese are indeed polite to non-Japanese, a practice which can be misinterpreted as genuine when in fact it is a superficial product of their culture. Japan is arguably the world's most separatist society. A little more than a decade before Meredith arrived in Japan, the Japanese military was in the process of slaughtering millions of nonwhite Asians. The homogeneous and hierarchical nature of Japan is both a strength and a weakness.

elitist style, "[W]hy would anyone want to be admitted to the University of Mississippi?"

When James Meredith opened the door for black students, Ole Miss was forever changed. In light of the nation's racial turmoil, the Kennedy brothers were generally despised in Mississippi. Yet on March 18, 1966, fewer than four years after the conflagration over Meredith's integration of the school, Senator Robert F. Kennedy was greeted by thunderous applause from five thousand students, faculty, and guests who were crammed into the basketball arena at Ole Miss to hear him speak. This triumph of free expression occurred in Mississippi's "closed society."

The instigators of the Kennedy appearance, Ole Miss law students Ed Ellington, Gerald Blessey, and Frank Thackston, all native Mississippians, wanted first of all to clear the university's image. They were both clever and persistent. Blessey, through his friend Cleveland Donald, the second black Ole Miss undergraduate, delivered the invitation to Senator Kennedy. To their surprise, he accepted. The university administration then tried unsuccessfully to force the students to disinvite him.

Upon his arrival on the bucolic campus in Oxford, Mississippi, Robert Kennedy was greeted "as a celebrity, if not an old friend," according to the *New York Times*. Enthusiasm about his appearance and demands for additional space grew exponentially. The venue was changed twice before the largest building on campus, the basketball arena, was enlisted to hold the crowd.

In his introduction of the senator, Ed Ellington mocked Yale's refusal to allow Alabama governor George Wallace to appear on its campus. A university should be an open forum, Ellington said. When Kennedy approached the podium, the audience erupted in applause and cheers. (The decibel level of this tumultuous reception can only be grasped by listening to the recording on the accessible file at the Ole Miss archives.) Kennedy's prepared remarks, punctuated by noisy approval, lasted for twenty minutes.

By 1966 the New York senator was well aware of the American, rather than merely Southern, context of racial strife. "Racial injustice and poverty," he said, "are to be found in the streets of New York and Chicago and Los Angeles, as well as the towns and farmlands of Mississippi."

The critical underlying motivation for Kennedy's visit emerged during the Q&A session following his talk. The law students aimed to cripple the buffoonish Ross Barnett's campaign for reelection. Similarly, Kennedy was eager to expose the governor for his hypocrisy and lying, which had led to the 1962 integration debacle. In the hardened racial atmosphere of the 1960s, Barnett had portrayed himself as a staunch resister of the federal government and the Kennedys. He couched his alleged defense of segregation and states' rights in heroic terms. In reality, Barnett was well aware that his actions were pure theater.

Frank Thackston, later the editor of the law review at Ole Miss, was assigned to ask Kennedy about the conversations among himself, President John Kennedy, and Governor Barnett before Meredith's enrollment. Kennedy was well prepared. He expounded for thirty minutes on the "negotiations" and the interchanges with Barnett. Before the episode, Kennedy said, he had had twenty-five conversations (President Kennedy had participated in two calls) with Barnett, who wished to save face. Barnett even asked that the federal marshals draw their weapons to simulate a mock confrontation. Barnett wanted a charade. His assurance of a strong presence of state law enforcement officials was a lie. The battle of Ole Miss could be laid at Barnett's feet.

This discussion during Kennedy's Q&A session reduced Barnett to ridicule. His reelection campaign was destroyed in the primary. The law students played a key role in the removal of Barnett from politics.

There is no better example of the importance and cleansing process of free speech on campus than Robert Kennedy and the band of students at Ole Miss. The experience was prelude to a lifetime of achievement for the aspiring lawyers. All proceeded to prominent legal careers in Mississippi. Ellington became a federal judge; Blessey was elected state senator and mayor of Biloxi; Thackston became a respected lawyer in Greenville.

On May 14, 1978, Senator Ted Kennedy of the formerly despised Kennedy family gave the commencement address at Ole Miss. "I am honored to be here at Ole Miss today," said the junior senator from Massachusetts before acknowledging Mississippi senator James Eastland: "Few, if any, Senators in Washington have a greater commitment and dedication to public service and to the citizens of their states than Jim Eastland. Senator Eastland is remembered as previously a staunch supporter of racial segregation." But it was Eastland who had appointed the recently elected senator Ted Kennedy to his coveted committee assignments—among which was the Civil Rights Committee.

Ole Miss had changed.

The Struggle for Civil Rights

With fifty years' hindsight we can see what happened legally and practically to end the ossified racial caste system that had evolved after Emancipation. The South's overt legal segregation and its resistance to integration, voting rights, and racially discriminatory laws are well-trodden territory. The fifty-year anniversary commemorations in the form of ceremonies, museum exhibitions, books, TV series, and movies about the 1960s civil rights era repeatedly show the often violent and stark images of a struggle long in coming. A partial checklist is familiar: the callous murders of Emmett Till in 1955 and Medgar Evers in 1963; the travesties of justice with failed prosecutions and ultimate convictions; the taunts, physical assaults, and humiliations that accompanied the 1960 lunch-counter sit-ins; the 1961 burning of the Freedom Riders bus; the violence-plagued admission of James Meredith to Ole Miss; the 1963 March on Washington and Martin Luther King Jr.'s "I Have a Dream" speech; the Birmingham church bombing with young girls murdered; the Selma march; the brutal slaying of three civil rights workers in Mississippi in 1964 during Freedom Summer; and the assassination of King in 1968. Extensive coverage and TV and documentary footage of conspicuous images—"Whites Only" signs, photographs of lynchings, dogs and fire hoses in Birmingham—provided drama, moral clarity, and instant recognition. As overt legal segregation gave way to the complexity of de facto segregation and urban ghettos, the distinct lines of good and evil blurred. The twin dragons of slavery and legal segregation had been slain, but what next?

Discrimination in public accommodations and resistance to voter enfranchisement were eliminated with difficulty, but within a generation the oppressive Jim Crow system cracked. Simultaneously, not sequentially, events in the North exposed the true depth of the racial divide. Racial violence was not an exclusively Southern phenomenon.

In the summer of 1964 an adventurous group of one thousand black and white college students journeyed to Mississippi to organize and encourage voter registration and educational projects. Stanford and Yale supplied many of the volunteers; Staughton Lynd, the soon-to-be history professor from Yale, directed the preparatory education segment of the action. Freedom Summer, as it was called, became infamous when three of the student volunteers, two white and one black, were murdered in June in Philadelphia, Mississippi. Without doubt these deaths gave impetus to the passing of the 1964 Civil Rights Act under the aegis of President Lyndon Johnson. The events of the Mississippi Freedom Party's invasion of the 1964 Democratic Convention is well known in print and film. Today blacks hold more elective offices in Mississippi than in any other state. To what extent the impact of the students' deaths and the publicity generated by the Freedom Summer played a role in the winning of black suffrage is debatable, but that battle, despite current disputes over voter identification, is over.

The concept of Freedom Summer originated within the Southern Nonviolent Coordinating Committee (SNCC, pronounced "Snick"), a militant (despite its moniker) and separatist collection of frustrated blacks. SNCC wanted to flood Mississippi with students to draw attention to racial conditions. Important to note, it was an organization that espoused black self-sufficiency and wanted white volunteers in order to generate publicity if they were harmed; black deaths, for SNCC, seemed to go unnoticed. Eventually SNCC would kick out all white members and marginalize the charismatic black Mississippi activist Fannie Lou Hamer. By the early 1970s SNCC had disintegrated.

The educational element of Freedom Summer involved essentially more than forty Freedom Schools for blacks throughout the state of Mississippi. The radical Staughton Lynd did not know why he, not a black person, was selected to coordinate the program. For the idealistic young Yale professional, the experience was both exhilarating and frustrating. He oversaw the schools with perhaps two thousand students who studied French, wrote poetry, produced plays, and discussed black history in a variety of venues, including church basements. He remembers the support of the black community and the poignant examples of blacks greeting him after church services with "crumpled" bills for financial support.

Over time the impact of the Freedom Schools was negligible. No massive grassroots movement for education materialized. Lynd was enamored with the prospect of building an alternative to existing inadequate schools. Then reality arrived. He admitted:

Despite the glow and the publicity of that summer, we did not have sufficient unity as a movement because... of [the lack] of all the qualities of institutional staying power to have made the alternative substantive.

He analogized his brief sojourn with that of a trade union movement "where the organizer blows into town, accomplishes miracles... and then the election... [W]in or lose, the organizer takes off." That model, he and his accomplished wife, Alice, came to realize, was "ridiculous." In order to effect change, one had to work through an institutional structure with a commitment to stay for an extended period of time. Large numbers of students could not achieve functional literacy without an effective structure.[3] The "order," according to Lynd, "must come from above." Staughton and Alice Lynd wanted a "regimented" process.

Structure, the key, was absent. Neither the public school, the family, nor the church provided the necessary prerequisites for giving black children the opportunity to succeed by endowing them with an appropriate skill set. Lynd fully subscribed to Daniel Patrick Moynihan's analysis of the core problem, the absence of the intact black family. Lynd blamed government welfare programs for exacerbating the absent-father problem by making it easier for the wife to live without him. The denigration of women in black rap music baffled him.

Other observers have lauded the Freedom Summer. Doug McAdam wrote of eighty volunteers "who decided to say in Mississippi indefinitely," but he did not say how long they stayed or what they did. He didn't "specifically focus" on commitment to blacks in Mississippi after the summer. We can be sure that few maintained a long-term involvement in the state after what can best be described as a brief, idealistic, youthful adventure. The volunteers do appear at reunions to recall their exploits. McAdam describes the volunteers as "finding themselves regarded as conquering heroes... by activist subcultures" such as the militant Students for a Democratic Society and Vietnam War protesters. The poster child for the "conquering heroes" was Mario Savio, leader of the Free Speech Movement at the University of California, Berkeley.

---

3 Interestingly, the armed services provide such a theoretical model for successful assimilation and education within the black community.

While the media and academics were focused on Freedom Summer in Mississippi, blacks in Chicago and New York were mounting protests against inferior schools and inadequate school funding. On October 22, 1963, 225,000 students, most of them black, had boycotted Chicago's schools. The boycott leaders had organized "freedom schools" in churches and other venues to provide a serious appearance. In February 1964, the spring before the Mississippi Freedom Summer, almost five hundred thousand black and Hispanic students, shouting "Jim Crow must go," boycotted New York's public schools. They screamed about New York City, not Mississippi. The ever-present Malcolm X smiled at the cameras with an I-told-you-so look. Again, "freedom schools" were set up in churches. On June 11, 1965, one hundred thousand students, most of them black, again boycotted Chicago schools in defiance of the "injustice of segregation" in Chicago.

These events presaged the continuing protests and dissatisfaction of blacks and Hispanics into the twentieth century. The nightmare that is now Chicago's public school system has yielded protests without improvement. New York undergoes periodic fits of reform with little change except for increased school budgets.

What happened to SNCC after it organized Freedom Summer? From the early 1960s SNCC was destined to become a separatist, black-only organization. In 1963 it reluctantly conceded the need for white students to participate in the Mississippi drive for voter registration and for black education. This concession recalls the approval of white Northerners in using black soldiers in the Civil War. In 1863 whites preferred that blacks be killed; in 1963 SNCC wanted the publicity of whites exposed to violence.

Fannie Lou Hamer, the charismatic grassroots leader from Ruleville, Mississippi, often disagreed with SNCC. Hamer, who had a limited formal education, a beautiful voice, and a knack for phrasemaking, was a committed integrationist. According to the journalist Kay Mills, Hamer "didn't care whether the young people were white or black." "If we're trying to break down the barrier of segregation," she wisely reasoned, "we can't segregate ourselves."

But after Freedom Summer SNCC reverted to form, and its effectiveness soon dissipated. By the fall of 1964 it had fallen into disorganization. Clayton Carson wrote of the closing of Freedom Schools and community centers because of the "absence of dependable personnel." Others observed the increase in "drinking, personality clashes, inefficiency and anti-white outbursts." At one point a SNCC member described SNCC "factions" squaring off against each other with "pool cues, baseball bats, knives and a couple of pistols." They were arguing over "whether people at a conference could be admitted to breakfast without a meal ticket."

By 1966 the black separatists had taken control. A year earlier SNCC had purposely marginalized the integrationist Fannie Lou Hamer by inserting a high school education requirement for board members. Some of the separatists would say that she was "no longer relevant." Hamer, who had only a sixth-grade education, dissociated herself from the group. Stokely Carmichael, now the SNCC chairman, delivered his famous Black Power speech on June 16, 1966, in Greenwood, Mississippi. "We want black power," he shouted five times to a crowd. Whites were officially expelled from SNCC by the end of the year.

Carmichael would lead a peripatetic life. He was born in Trinidad before moving to New York, where he graduated from the prestigious Bronx High School of Science. After his chairmanship of SNCC, he asserted his African identity by changing his name to Kwame Ture and in 1969 moved to Africa where he would become involved with African politics in Guinea and Ghana. There he was spiritually and intellectually captivated by the failed leaders Sekou Toure and Kwame Nkrumah. And, like W. E. B. Du Bois, Richard Wright, and Malcolm X, the radical young Carmichael was a proponent of an ill-defined and fuzzy version of Marxism. He even spent a few days in a Guinean jail. Always enjoying a crowd, he returned to speak at his alma mater, Howard University, to large groups. He succumbed to prostate cancer in 1997 after blaming his illness on "American imperialism."

Ultimately Carmichael was a frustrated ideologue. When he saw that elective office was no complete solution to the social and economic problems of black America, he meandered into the vague world of socialist revolutionary politics and the spiritual elixir of Pan-Africanism. His unabashed Marxism absurdly led him to resent the rise of the black middle class; he wanted a classless society devoid of capitalist distinctions.

For SNCC, an obsessive emphasis on black power, black pride, the threat of violence, and otherworldly Marxism could be temporarily comforting emotionally, but the organization lacked the framework and long-term commitment to move blacks into the economic mainstream. A philosophy based almost exclusively on grievance, anger, egos (SNCC colleagues referred to Stokely Carmichael as Stokely Starmichael), frustration, and racial separatism was—and is—counterproductive in addressing the practical realities of policy, implementation, and accountability.

The remarkable story of Fannie Lou Hamer has been oft-told. Biographies by Kay Mills and Chana Kai Lee relate her life in detail. She was born in poverty, worked as a sharecropper and clerk on a Mississippi Delta farm, was fired from her job when she became active in the civil rights movement, was beaten by a law official in Winona, Mississippi, and tirelessly toiled for voter registration drives. Her memorable testimony and appearance at the alternative Mississippi Freedom Democratic Party convention in 1964 have been duly memorialized in print and video. She went on numerous speaking tours in the North to raise funds and an awareness of Southern conditions. In 1964 Malcolm X introduced her at the Audubon Ballroom in Harlem as "the country's number one freedom fighting woman." She recounted her tale of poverty, suffering, shooting, and intimidation to enthralled audiences. She knew how to work a crowd.

Hamer was initially captivated by SNCC's alignment with the black masses rather than the middle class. She even went to West Africa with a SNCC group in 1964. Her enchantment with Africa grew when her host, President Sekou Toure of Guinea, greeted the group personally. In their 1960s enthusiasm for the independent countries of Africa, Hamer and her colleagues could hardly imagine the extent of the brutal Toure's dictatorship, his imprisonment and torture of political prisoners, and the mass graves used to bury the detractors of his regime. Nor would they witness the denouement and descent of the African countries into a political morass. Hamer's infatuation with West Africa had its limits; the integrationist Delta woman wanted to fix things in America. She would not move to Africa "until Italians went back to Italy, and Germans back to Germany." She was an American original.

Although Hamer could effectively inflame Northern audiences by focusing on the misdeeds of the South, she knew very well that the racial dilemma was nationwide. In this—but not in his attitude toward violence—she agreed with Malcolm X, who was unequivocal: "America is Mississippi.... There is no such thing as the South—it's America." Hamer put it this way: "The problem is not a Mississippi problem. This is America's problem." When a white woman on a train in Connecticut refused to let Hamer sit next to her, and then allowed a white woman to occupy the seat, Hamer experienced Northern racial enlightenment firsthand.

By the 1960s Fannie Lou Hamer, the poor Delta native, was attacking the rarely discussed class distinctions within the black community. She was scathing in her indictment of the educated, middle-class NAACP. She renamed it the National Association for the Advancement of Certain People. "There ain't nothing," she asserted, "that I respect less than the NAACP." The feeling was mutual. The sophisticated executive secretary of the NAACP, Roy Wilkins, a major architect of the civil rights movement, had no use for Hamer. At the 1964 Democratic National Convention he told her, "You don't know anything, you're ignorant, you don't know anything about politics.... You people have put your point across, now why don't you pack up and go home."

White liberals, too, found Hamer irritating. The future Democratic presidential candidate Hubert Humphrey delivered LBJ's refusal to allow her to speak at the convention: "The president [Lyndon Johnson] will not allow that illiterate woman to speak from the floor of the convention." LBJ would sign civil rights legislation, but grassroots black speakers were not welcome at his convention. SNCC, allegedly representing the black masses, belittled Hamer and essentially eliminated her from the organization. She had disagreements with Martin Luther King Jr. and his organization, the Southern Christian Leadership Conference (SCLC). She did not attend King's funeral because she "couldn't remorse around the hypocrites [who] were there."

Revolutionaries have difficulty after the revolution. Hamer failed in her attempt to build an organization to foster education and child development. Her rhetorical skills, appeals for white support, reliance on grassroots black political power and the election of black officials, and revolutionary language were of little use in her two projects, the

Pig Bank, a farm cooperative, and the Child Development Group of Mississippi (CDGM). Her idea of a Freedom Farm to provide jobs and food for black farmers was noble. In 1968 she formed the Pig Bank with the purchase of thirty-five gilts (females) and five boars (males). The Pig Bank would lend the gilts to families, and they would be returned to the bank after paying dividends to the borrowers in the form of piglets. Projected production was three thousand new pigs by the third year. The Freedom Farm planned to grow vegetables, soybeans, corn, greens, sweet potatoes, and eventually cotton. By 1971 Hamer had purchased almost seven hundred acres of land for the farm. The ambitious undertaking included an "Afro-Boutique" that would manufacture African clothing.

Hamer's abundant contacts and national stature brought funding. She appeared on *The David Frost Show* to appeal for contributions. Harry Belafonte was active. A Midwestern group, Measure for Measure, was her main source of funds; the Young People of Harvard University raised donations. The National Council of Negro Women was a sponsor.

But the Freedom Farm faltered from the beginning. No one in the organization had ever run a business, hence bad management was apparent. The bookkeeper, Nora Campbell, was fired for "failure to stop drinking in the office" and "failure to report to work on time." The records were a mess. Also, Hamer had commingled funds from her other endeavors—"Voter Education Projects, independent political campaigns and demonstration[s] in the name of social justice." One supporter blamed Hamer's reluctance to accept government funding on her fear of white control. The Freedom Farm tried belatedly to reorganize in 1973, then ceased operation in 1974.

Hamer's efforts on behalf of the Child Development Group of Mississippi (CDGM) met a similar fate. In 1965 the Hamer-backed CDGM received a grant from the Office of Economic Opportunity (OEO). But among various organizations vying for other federal funds, the CDGM lost out. It didn't help that one of Hamer's supporters, Annie Mae King, explained her qualifications for helping children: "Everybody know how to raise their children—they done raised up all the white children." Many more poverty programs, most controlled by blacks, were later begun in the Delta.

By 1972, after she had unsuccessfully run for the state senate, Hamer's national support had evaporated. Even the National Council of Negro

Women dropped her from the payroll. According to Kay Mills, "National leaders, the press, even state politicians stopped visiting." Her husband Pap was angry about the treatment of his wife. He had to pay people to stay with her during her last days. People would merely use her to get "clothes, food, or money."

Despite her public denunciation of racial injustice, particularly in the South, Hamer as well as other blacks had personal relationships with Delta whites. In a small rural environment, blacks and whites lived cheek and jowl. There was no anonymity. Hamer was close to Pascol Townsend Jr., a white lawyer in Drew, Mississippi. Civil rights attorneys were baffled by this "odd couple, the courtly white southern lawyer and the stout, black former sharecropper." In 1969 Townsend arranged for the legal adoption of Lenora and Jacqueline, Hamer's two daughters. He did legal work for the Freedom Farm, and Hamer spent a good deal of time in his office. She served as a reference when Townsend was considered for a federal judgeship, which he did not get.

The racial calculus of the Delta could reveal fascinating ironies. The black Reverend Edward Thomas recalled his job as a youth in Inverness, Mississippi, where he worked for Roosevelt Stapleton, a black man who owned a service station. The only other service station was owned by Bill Tinnin, a white man. The two service station proprietors would occasionally discuss business. Once, Bill Tinnin, the white owner, said he had a problem—his black customers paid on time, but his white customers did not. Roosevelt Stapleton replied that he had the opposite situation—his white customers paid on time and his black customers didn't. Such was the intertwined world of race in the Delta.

On March 29, 1970, her hometown declared Fannie Lou Hamer Day and Banquet in Ruleville. The mayor, C. M. "Fisty" Dorrough, had clearly tried to discourage her civil rights activities only a few years before. But things had changed. Dorrough wrote to her in obvious sincerity:

> You have put up a valiant fight for those things you truly believe in and have obtained results that you should be recognized for. . . . The results of your battles are now a matter of public record, and more benefits are

coming each year. If more Americans gave of themselves as you...ours would be a better nation....The history books of tomorrow will record your efforts and the results, but I am sure you are more interested in...a better, more comfortable way of life for those you love. May I add my commendation for you and the job you have done.

Hamer had deep religious convictions, but she was not a friend of black ministers, whom she sometimes called "chicken-eating preachers." She wanted black men to be more active in their community. Families without fathers were of special concern. Black men, she thought, abnegated their responsibilities. Still, she was vehemently against abortion and contraceptives, which she considered genocide and sinful; her stance against "out-of-wedlock births" was clear.

Mayor Dorrough was right. History did treat Hamer respectfully and admiringly. She lived to see the end of both racially segregated public accommodations and voting restrictions. But the severe social issues that she confronted remain very much with the nation in the twenty-first century, despite a plethora of government and private programs, particularly in her own Sunflower County. The civil rights revolution addressed clearly defined discriminatory problems; other more complex problems remain.

Underlying economic trends, often forgotten, are important in the recording of history. The coincidence of the civil rights movement in the rural South and the full implementation of farm machinery and chemicals finally displaced the blacks in the cotton fields. No longer was cotton farming labor intensive; the link between black America and the "indispensable" crop was finally broken. This worried urban Northerners, who sensed another Great Migration. Manhattan's borough president Percy Sutton, who was black, became involved in May 1967 elections in the small rural Mississippi towns of Sunflower and Moorhead. "[All] New Yorkers have an interest," Sutton reasoned, for the displacement of black farm workers might send them scurrying to the urban cities of the North. If blacks could vote, he argued, "industry would flow into the South and displaced blacks could be absorbed."

Sutton's absurd rationalization notwithstanding, white and black Northerners emphatically did not want Southern blacks as neighbors. On the day of the Sunflower County elections, Sutton, the dapper young black New York State assemblyman Charles Rangel, New York City councilman Paul O'Dwyer, and *New York Times* journalist Walter Rugaber descended upon Sunflower, a town of five hundred people. Fannie Lou Hamer from nearby Ruleville was also heavily involved. The black candidates lost the election, but black elected officials subsequently dominated Sunflower's political landscape. Despite Sutton's prediction, no industry ever arrived in Sunflower, which is yet another moribund Delta town whose white population has departed. The majority black population remains mired in poverty and hopelessness. The New York politicians, having gotten their publicity, never returned. Another politician, the then Senator Barack Obama, traveled to Greenville, Mississippi, in the Delta on his presidential campaign. After breakfast at a black-owned restaurant, Bucks, the *New York Times* (March 12, 2008) reported Senator Obama's comments to the crowd: "I promise when I'm president of the United States, I'll come back to the Delta." During his presidency, President Obama never returned to the Delta.

"The Ivy League Negro"

Fannie Lou Hamer represented the lower end of the black social and economic spectrum in the 1960s; meanwhile the black middle and upper classes were growing and becoming more defined. Entrance to an elite Ivy League school was a sure sign of black social advancement, but it carried its own problems. In the August 1963 issue of *Esquire* magazine, William Melvin Kelley, a black student at Harvard, considered his situation in a confessional article, "The Ivy League Negro." There were ten blacks in Kelley's class; the Yale class of 1966 would have five. Soon Ivy League schools would begin recruiting blacks in earnest. Foremost on Kelley's mind was his "ambiguous" racial identity. Was he part of a racially conscious black group, or was he an individual who happened to be black? To be fully part of a "mythical racial unity," Kelley thought, one had to agree to "hate all white people."

Kelley's newfound status was established during a summer job while at Harvard. Wearing a laborer's dirty garb, he entered a Boston bank to open an account. The bank officials treated him with condescension until he mentioned his address, "Adams House, A-24, Harvard College." The tone of the conversation changed immediately to one of respect: "Why don't you sit down, Mr. Kelley."[4]

Kelley's experience at Harvard nurtured an air of superiority. As he explained, a Harvard student, white or black, "comes to believe in a quiet way, that Harvard is the best school in the country and therefor that he is select. Yale Negroes feel the same way." In twenty-first-century parlance, "select" would be synonymous with "privileged"; Kelly's black privilege, conferred by the Harvard stamp, would equal white privilege. Kelley had become an individual: "Everything at Harvard is geared to make a man think for himself. He formulates his own ideas. Blind devotion to race does not stand up against analysis."

At Harvard, Kelley's social life was circumscribed because there were so few black undergraduate women to date. He worried abstractly about his obligations to blacks and carried some guilt, for he felt "closer to the educated white man than to the uneducated Negro." In general, Kelley wrote, "The Ivy League Negro, and most educated or upper-class Negroes, have an ambiguous attitude toward the uneducated, lower-class Negro." When he saw a drunken black beggar he felt ashamed because of the man's race, not because of his condition. The tension between "negro consciousness" and the "individual" would follow most black students to the Ivy League.

"Desegregation Does Not Mean Integration"

The landmark desegregation case of *Brown v. Board of Education* in 1954; the resistance to black students entering Little Rock (Arkansas) Central High School in 1957; Governor Ross Barnett's attempt to block the admission of James Meredith to the University of Mississippi in 1962; and Governor George Wallace's defiant stance to prevent integration at the University of Alabama in 1963 are firmly etched in American history. Two presidents, Dwight Eisenhower and John Kennedy, had to invoke the force of the federal government to implement the Supreme Court's

---

4 In all likelihood the initial rudeness may have resulted from Kelley's attire rather than his race. As a Yale undergraduate in the 1960s, I had a similar experience with a New York bank.

ruling. The court had decided that segregated schools were inherently inferior, but its ruling offered no timetable or guidelines or mechanism for integrating the schools. How, then, did Americans, white and black, respond?

Few Americans have even the slightest understanding of the attempts to desegregate Northern schools during this period. Desegregation rulings did not mean integration. There are precious few memorials, documentaries, books, movies, or school courses about the ongoing attempts to integrate Northern schools. While directing their civil rights memorialization and remembrance to the South, Northern cities are reluctant to expose their own racial dilemmas. Northern efforts, by blacks and whites, to portray the South as the nation's exclusive racial scapegoat soothes Northern consciences but is misleading.

In his 1962 *New York Times* article "Desegregation Does Not Mean Integration," Mississippi editor (of the *Greenville Delta Democrat-Times*) Hodding Carter II outlined the obstacles to school integration in the South. Carter had received a Pulitzer Prize in 1946 for his essay on tolerance and the mistreatment of Japanese-American soldiers in the US Army in World War II. Described as a racial moderate, he advocated gradual school integration in the South. The tenets of his argument could easily have been applied to the North as well as the South. "Numerically meaningful integration," he wrote, "just isn't in the cards." Among his reasons were "residential segregation," "potential gerrymandering of school districts," "economic and physical pressures," "preferences on the part of part of Negro parents and pupils," and "vested Negro interest in school segregation." In 1962 it was blatantly apparent to Carter that in "cities in the North, school segregation will be maintained simply because of the segregation of residential districts." His realistic appraisal cautioned against enthusiasm for a smooth transition to integrated schools.

The NAACP Legal Defense Fund would ultimately have to go to court. In 1962—1963 it filed desegregation suits from coast to coast—in San Francisco, Chicago, Detroit, New York City, Philadelphia, and cities in New York, Indiana, and New Jersey. It was obvious that residential segregation had created separate school systems. The statistics in the early 1960s uniformly confirmed the situation: in Chicago, 170 schools were more than 90 percent black and 56 were totally black; more than 100 of Philadelphia's elementary schools were 99 percent black; Boston's

Roxbury neighborhood schools were more than 80 percent black; five elementary schools in San Francisco had black enrollments above 80 percent; among New York City's elementary schools, 117 had more than 90 percent black and Puerto Rican students. Nationwide only 15 percent of black children were in "non-segregated schools."

In New York City myriad commissions on integration and race—which would require volumes to describe—accomplished little. The Commission on Integration (1954) formed subcommissions on educational standards, curriculum, guidance, zoning, and community relations. The subcommissions issued a final report, "Toward Greater Opportunity." Yet in 1966, after a campaign to integrate New York's public schools, they were more segregated than they had been earlier. Integration had reached "a dead end."

One of the attempts to encourage integration in New York City was an appeal to whites in 1966 to send their children to a new school, Intermediate School 201 (IS-201), on the east edge of Manhattan's predominantly black Harlem. As such, the appeal was part of the collision course to the now infamous Ocean Hill–Brownsville teachers' strike. Officials hoped that IS-201's proximity to white Queens, across the East River, would entice parents to send their children to an integrated school. But New York's alleged multicultural and multiracial tolerance turned out to be a mirage. No white students applied. Voluntary integration was not to be a possibility. Quite the contrary, reaction was stiff. In Queens the Parents and Taxpayers (PAT) organization began in 1963 to try to control community schools in order to prevent forced desegregation by busing or other means. PAT's leaders were a Jewish lawyer, an Italian housewife, and an Irish community activist. The PAT became a "Northern lite" version of the (White) Citizens' Council to obstruct integration. And the technique spread to other boroughs.

The Ocean Hill–Brownsville teachers' strike of 1968 brought into sharp focus the issues that would plague integrated education for the next five decades. Arguably it is just as important as Little Rock Central. The event appeared to be the consequence of a mundane structural reorganization of the New York public schools, from a highly centralized operation to a decentralized approach with local community control. In reality it was a highly charged racial confrontation with conflicts over "culture," curriculum, educational standards, anti-Semitism, and employment. The battle pitted the United Federation of Teachers (UFT), heavily populated by Jews and Catholics, and its leader Albert Shanker, against the black and Hispanic school district of Ocean Hill–Brownsville with its unit administrator Rhody McCoy, a black activist and acolyte of Malcolm X.

The New York battle over decentralization of the schools was most pronounced in what are known as the outer boroughs, Queens and Brooklyn.[5] The collisions would occur in the middle- and lower-middle-class sections of the outer boroughs. Decentralization would finally win out, but the cultural boundaries that would persist for fifty years were clearly delineated in 1968.

Among the supporters of decentralization were the Ford Foundation and its president McGeorge Bundy; New York mayor John Lindsay; and John Doar, a board of education member and director of a community effort in the Bedford Stuyvesant section of the city. Many of the major players in this drama boasted of Southern civil rights connections, experience, and involvement. Doar, as a Justice Department official, had escorted James Meredith into the University of Mississippi. Albert Shanker had participated in Martin Luther King Jr.'s "I Have a Dream" event in Washington and marched in the Selma civil rights protest. Frank Nauman, a Jewish teacher and civil rights enthusiast, identified with James Meredith as an opponent of decentralization.

The Mississippi Freedom Summer seemed to provide inspiration to both sides. Like it or not, the civil rights movement was coming to New York City; no longer were blacks "at a distance." Whites in Brooklyn would resent the migration of ghetto blacks to their neighborhood. The results would be ugly.

In May 1968 Rhody McCoy was asked by the Ocean Hill–Brownsville's black governing board to terminate the employment of nineteen white teachers. (A black teacher had been mistakenly placed on the list too, but was removed.) McCoy agreed completely. According to Jerald Podair in his book *The Strike that Changed New York*, the scene in one of the district's schools, Junior High School 271 (JHS-271), had been chaotic. At the urging of African Americans, black and white teachers were separated in

---

5 New York City is composed of five boroughs. The predominantly white enclaves of Manhattan are generally isolated from racial turmoil because of wealth, residential segregation, and hypocrisy.

"cafeterias, lounges, and other common spaces." Vandalism was rampant. White teachers were assaulted by black students. Black teachers preached revolution. McCoy was outspoken: white oppression would end "only after people have resorted to violent means." He seemed predisposed to blame all problems on white racism.

Leslie Campbell, an African American Teachers Association (ATA) leader, emphasized violence and revolution, Podair noted. Campbell's classroom presentation in JHS-271 was an anti-capitalist Marxist diatribe. To illustrate revolution, his black history course highlighted Nat Turner, Denmark Vesey, and Malcolm X. If you want to steal a leather jacket, Campbell argued, "you know who to steal from. If you steal, steal from those who have it. Stop fighting among yourselves."

The UFT reaction was, as could be expected, that of a union that aimed to control its turf. But in a black community, local control meant black hiring and firing, black curriculum, and black standards. Blacks also wanted to eliminate the civil service tests required for promotion within the teaching ranks because they considered the teacher exams culturally biased against blacks. The Mayor's Advisory Council Panel, led by McGeorge Bundy, agreed; decentralization meant thirty to sixty independent school districts, with each district having "almost unfettered power to hire, fire, and grant to tenure ... " Examinations for hiring and promotion would be eliminated. The UFT viewed these proposals as a consummate lowering of standards. It rejected the infringement on its turf and organized three strikes. In September 1968, fifty-four thousand public school teachers walked off the job. By the third strike, UFT supporters were yelling "nigger scab" at a black strikebreaker and "nigger lover" at a white teacher who violated the strike.

The African American Teachers Association rejected what it considered to be white, Western norms of behavior—individualism, conformity, hard work, discipline, merit, competition, and materialism. The ATA condemned any form of testing for skill sets and "cognitive learning skills." Explicit and implicit criticism of capitalism and Western culture was aired. While there were valid reasons to include the black experience and black history in the curriculum, Western culture, as distinct from black culture, was seen as a form of cultural imperialism that embodied white Western superiority. The ATA pursued this reasoning with a vengeance. Despite the disavowal of materialism by black militants, the black population was just as attached to materialism as the white community. Mystical and romantic notions of black moral purity, devoid of materialism, was a delusion.

In the ATA's view, the white man was to be blamed for the black condition, hence Western culture must be removed from the classroom. Highly structured educational methods, combined with respect for authority—the techniques of white Western middle-class teachers— would stifle black creativity and lead black students to "misbehave and squirm." "Black children," according to JHS-271's black principal, Alton Risen, "are innovators, inventors, creators, actors and performers. They like exciting styles, fashions, colors and constant change. . . . [These] healthy bubbling energies were evidence of rare distributive talents which many whites lack" and didn't understand. Blacks' "frame of reference was concrete and spontaneous," not the Western "cold, abstract, and intellectually elitist educational culture."

In contrast to Western-style education, blacks advocated a program based on distinct black values. They professed a vague attachment to cooperation, community, and ethnic-group consciousness, with seemingly no interest in mastering reading, writing, and mathematical skills. A "unique black culture" precluded the competition inherent in a merit system and fostered a separatist, even belligerent, attitude toward whites. The word "authentic" became a workhorse description for this racially separate identity—an orientation that subordinated the individual to his or her black group affiliation. Those who did not abide by racial peer pressure were branded "traitors or Uncle Toms." There would be no compromise with white Western norms.

This refrain would crop up again, as reported by Richard Bernstein in the *New York Times* (1993), when the racial separatist Leonard Jeffries, the head of the black studies department a City University of New York, opined that whites were "ice people" and blacks were "sun people." Blacks, Jeffries continued, were viewed as "naturally creative, cooperative and intuitive," while whites were "cruel and aggressive."

The UFT did not hesitate to respond to the black cultural argument with a harsh, rational critique. To end the merit system, one UFT white teacher warned, would result in the "failure of black people to compete." Another charged the black school board of Ocean Hill–Brownsville with failing to understand the premise of a school system: to nurture "a desire to learn, and a desire to behave and a desire to advance by merit." "The [black-initiated] curriculum at Ocean Hill," argued a white UFT teacher, "is not designed to produce young American citizens well prepared to enter the job market—just well prepared to hate whitey." Albert Shanker called Ocean Hill a "cruel hoax... [blacks] were going to forget about the [standards] of middle-class values of reading, writing, and arithmetic."

African Americans' disdain for Western individualism was contra-dicted by their rationalization of the "disruptive child" problem. The UFT supported a contractual provision, the "disruptive child" clause, which would allow the teacher to "expel a seriously misbehaving stu-dent" and place him or her in a "special service" school. An incensed African American Teachers Association labeled the clause discriminatory. According to the ATA, the teacher "must accept the student's challenge to authority," even the student's use of obscenities. ATA leader Albert Vann went so far as to excuse a physical attack by blacks "on two white principals and a teacher at JHS-117." Blacks were victims, he concluded, and were merely responding to society's racism. Brooklyn's chapter of the Congress of Racial Equality (CORE) agreed that black ghetto culture was justified in tolerating this behavior. The alleged "disruptive child" was a "high-spirited non-conformist" who embodied a "highly creative imagination" and was "not willing to accept mediocre education." Black ghetto culture understood and was sympathetic to "cursing and physi-cal intimidation." The UFT, meanwhile, referred to "disruptive" black students as "young jackanapes and emotionally unstrung hoodlums."

The 1968 exchange between Ralph Rogers, the black principal of Ocean Hill's PS-144, and three white teachers with Jewish surnames revealed the chasm between black and white teachers, as recorded by Jerald Podair:

> Miss Fliss [teacher]: My children are afraid to go out of their room because they will be beaten up.
> Miss Goldstein [teacher]: There is a tendency for the older disruptive children to be troublemakers.
> Mr. Rogers [principal]: This is a community controlled school. The policy is no suspension. We do not want children in the streets.
> Goldstein: Teachers are exhausted with discipline problems. Children see others striking teachers...and nothing is done...

Fliss: A child came into my room, shouted and hit children. When I tried to take him by his arm he practically tore my arm off. The child is still in school. He slammed another child with a window pole....It happens every day.

Mr. Rubinstein [teacher]:...You cannot teach when a child comes to a teacher and uses foul language continually. Something has to be done.

Rogers: You have to devise your own method of dealing with discipline. Most of the time it is the teacher and not the child ....

Thus blacks would be on their way toward a blameless society—reluctant to critique themselves objectively, resistant to any form of accountability, and unable to cope with their own flaws. And only black teachers would both teach black children and discipline them. The "disruptive child" clause was shelved.[6]

The Ocean Hill–Brownsville strike soon degenerated into black anti-Semitism. An anonymous letter found its way into UFT teachers' mailboxes at JHS-271. It read:

If African American history is to be taught to our Black Children it Must be Done by African Americans....It is Impossible for The Middle East Murderers of Colored People [read Palestinians] to Possibly Bring To This Important Task The Insight...The Exposing of the Truth If The Years Of Brainwashing And Self-Hatred That Has Been Taught To Our Black Children By Those Bloodsucking Exploiters and Murders Is To Be Over Come....The only Persons Who Can Do The Job Are African American Brothers And Sisters, And Not the So-Called Liberal Jewish Friend. We Know From His Tricky, Deceitful Maneuvers That He is Really Our Enemy and He is Responsible For the Serious Educational Retardation Of Our Black Children.

Albert Shanker had half a million copies of the letter made and

---

6 Five decades later New York City still struggles with these issues. Elected New York City mayor in 2014, Bill de Blasio, playing the part of John Lindsay, initiated a policy to reduce the number of school suspensions. By August 2016 the number had dropped precipitously. UFT leader Michael McGrew vociferously opposed de Blasio's policy: "[T]housands of children will lose instruction as a result of these disruptions," which went unpunished, he said. The UFT worried about chaos in the classroom and the safety of teachers and students. The disproportionate number of suspended black and Hispanic students, not the validity of the discipline, was the basis of de Blasio's dictum.

distributed throughout New York City. Jews were surprised that blacks did not disavow connection with or support of it. Both Rhody McCoy and Floyd McKissick of CORE had no interest in rebuking its contents. ATA leader Campbell attacked Shanker through poetry on a radio show: "Hey Jew boy, with the yarmulke on your head / You pale faced Jew boy—I wish you were dead." The putative Jewish-black alliance, thought to be based on shared suffering and Jewish cosmopolitanism, proved to be highly exaggerated and misleading.

Another New York City confrontation, described by the social scientist Jonathan Rieder, erupted in the early 1970s between whites—mainly middle-class and lower-middle-class Jews and Italians—and blacks in neighboring Canarsie, in Brooklyn. Whites were accused of having a "culture of the blamer" and were faulted for being without "compassion." Given the circumstances of an encroaching black neighborhood that was unkempt and crime filled, it could be argued that blacks were part of a blameless culture. The economic condition of the Jews and Italians was fragile; many had left Brownsville after an influx of blacks moved there. Now with dramatically increased crime and a physical decline the Canarsie neighborhood had deteriorated. Economic conditions and high interest rates prevented them from selling, thus they were stuck.

Canarsie whites had risen from struggling immigrant status to a foothold on middle-class existence. For them, hard work and a strong family formed the basis for achievement. They considered ghetto blacks a threat to their neighborhood, schools, home values, safety, and employment. White residents of Canarsie had lived amicably with a few middle-class blacks who had moved there. A Jewish man had no problem with middle-class blacks who, he said, "were just like me.... But if you send shit from Brownsville down here, it's a different ballgame."

Many Canarsie residents had expressed support for civil rights efforts to remove overt legal segregation. But for the outer boroughs of New York City in the 1960s and 1970s, race was no longer "at a distance," no longer a problem to be viewed on television or read about in a newspaper. Race was at their doorstep and a threat to their home and school. Jonathan Rieder refers to the racial problem as one of "closeness," of black-white proximity. Yet the dynamic of crime, the deterioration of property values, and the cultural values of lower-class blacks were more damaging than physical "closeness." The lived experience of "closeness" had led middle-class and lower-middle-class whites to develop anti-black attitudes.

As poor ghetto blacks flowed into Canarsie, attitudes changed dramatically. A Jewish craftsman summarized the trajectory: "I can't help thinking of the immigrants. I mean, they tried to make a living, they sacrificed so the next generation could live a better life. They gave their family values.... My grandfather lived in Brownsville, and look what [the blacks] did there!... The niggers ruined it. They have no pride. Just because you are poor doesn't mean you have to live in filth." Canarsie could have served as a clinical trial for the sociologist James Q. Wilson's "broken windows theory," articulated in 1982. Wilson held that vandalism and an unkempt neighborhood fosters crime.

When thirty-one black students were ordered by New York's chancellor of education to be bused to the virtually all-white Bildersee Junior High School in Canarsie, a protest resulted. The neighborhood experienced racial disturbances in schools and on a playground. In 1972 and 1973 anti-busing whites staged demonstrations and boycotts.

Racial integration could get very ugly in Brooklyn. In the early 1970s, lower-class blacks from public housing projects began to arrive in numbers at the previously integrated high school. Whites began to move out of the neighborhood. There was violence. Ultimately, blacks threatened whites with knives, on what became known as "Day of Knives"–after which no whites returned to the school. During the period of increased black presence, there were five arrests per day in a student body of three thousand. A paddy wagon arrived each day. Every six weeks, a teacher was sent to the hospital; one young handicapped woman was shoved down a flight of stairs. In one five-month period, five students were either murdered or committed murder. More students appeared in the halls than in the classroom on a daily basis.

A Sober Look at an "Alliance"

The myth of the "shared suffering" alliance of blacks and Jews was exposed by the Ocean Hill–Brownsville teachers' strike, provoking resentment and outright anti-Semitism. Historically and paradoxically, blacks could attack Jews and also recommend emulating them. Jewish success, education, and work ethic were difficult for blacks to ignore. Du Bois in 1903 could refer to "unscrupulous Jews" who cheated the "black man" and later could advise blacks to develop Jewish habits of thrift and saving. Booker T. Washington told blacks to "imitate the Jew" or else "not expect any high degree of success."

Jews often emphasize their participation in the civil rights movement, illustrating their commitment by the 1964 murders of two Jewish civil rights workers in Mississippi. Blacks understood the Jewish involvement. In a *Playboy* interview with Alex Haley, Martin Luther King Jr. rhetorically asked, "How could there be anti-Semitism among Negroes when our Jewish friends" have made "sizeable contributions...and personal sacrifice." King was speaking about funding and involvement in the Southern phase of the civil rights movement. The historian Leonard Dinnerstein was even more direct. He wrote of "black leaders" who knew that Jews "bankrolled [the black] cause" and "shared their goals."

Very conscious of Jewish financial support, King spoke of the "limited degree of negro anti-Semitism," which was a "Northern ghetto phenomenon." Black anti-Semitism," he stated, "virtually does not exist in the South."

In 1965, King noted that the most common daily contact between Jews and blacks was as "some of the most direct exploiters...the slum landlords and gouging shopkeepers."

Alex Haley asked King why there was so little black philanthropic support for civil rights in contrast to Jewish support for its social-action group the B'nai B'rith. King responded that "the Negro has not developed a sense of stewardship" in the way Jews had. Here, King made his only reference to the "family unit." The Jews, spoke King, had developed unity that "started with the individual family unit." He did not address the problem of single-parent families in the black community except for a reference to slavery. There was no admonition of the urgency or need to address the problem within the black community.

King's focus was on government support of jobs and education for the "Negro." His analogy was the GI Bill and his demand was for $50 billion ($385 billion in 2017 dollars) devoted to infrastructure programs with preferential treatment for hiring blacks. King justified the amount of $50 billion by comparison to a one-year expenditure for defense. For King, large outlays of money were readily available as had occurred during wartime or the Marshall Plan. King offered no detailed outline of how to spend the money or how to create a program in which accountability was possible. Money, according to King, would bring "a spectacular decline in school dropouts, family breakups, crime rates, illegitimacy, swollen relief rolls, rioting and other social evils."

Michael Kramer wrote of black anti-Jewish rhetoric in 1985. "[T]he Jew" wrote the Brooklyn Congressman Albert Vann, "...keeps [blacks] from becoming teachers and principals and keeps our children ignorant." The African American Teachers Association issued a press release: "Jews would like us to become what they were in Hitler's Germany: spineless jellyfish." Black intellectual Harold Cruse dismissed the notion of Jewish friendship for the "Negro" as a myth.

In the early 1980s, the Louis Harris opinion poll was chronicling the nature of black/Jewish relations. In every situation, the general population disagreed with the black view. "A plurality of blacks," wrote Michael Kramer, believes that most slumlords are Jewish." Blacks, by a fifty-six to fourteen majority, thought Jews preferred money over people. Blacks, according to the poll, believed Jews were more loyal to Israel than America. The poll, on the other hand, found that Jews are "more resistant to integrated neighborhoods" and "less willing to send their children to schools with blacks" than other white Americans.

When racial issues appeared at home, however, as in Brooklyn, Jews and blacks became antagonists. Dinnerstein reports numerous anti-Semitic outbreaks in the 1960s. A black leader of a Chicago organization admitted "the Negro hates the Jew." Philadelphia blacks thought Jews were "parasites." After King's assassination in April 1968, blacks destroyed the Rockdale Temple in Cincinnati. The Boston SNCC chapter demanded that Jews hand over Temple Mishkan Tefila without a mortgage, or they would burn it. With the neighborhood changing from Jewish to African American, the Jews, intimidated, surrendered the building to African Americans free of charge.

The continuing hostility between Israel and Palestine has been a consistent source of friction between blacks and Jews to the present day. Generally, blacks, especially militants, have identified Palestine as the oppressed and Israel as the oppressor. After the 1967 Six-Day War between Israel and the Arabs, SNCC posted a cartoon with dollar signs dripping from Israeli general Moshe Dayan's uniform; another had a hand with a dollar sign and a Star of David holding up Muhammed Ali with a noose around his neck. An outbreak of black anti-Semitism erupted in 1979 when Andrew Young, the black US ambassador to the United Nations, held a prohibited private meeting with the Palestine Liberation Organization and withheld the information from the State Department. As described by Carl Gershman in *Commentary* (November 1, 1979), Young resigned under pressure, which blacks attributed to Jews. The ensuing rhetorical venom covered more than Israel; latent feelings about Jews soon emerged. The Israeli-Palestinian issue was merely a pretext for a broader black anti-Jewish attack. Ambassador Young then accused Israel of being an "expansionist power" and an "oppressor." The Southern Christian Leadership Council's Hosea Williams, wrote Kramer, bestowed the "Decoration of Martin Luther King" on Colonel Muammar Qaddafi "just before Libyan troops began killing black Christians in Chad." Reverend Williams was impressed by the Arabs: "They've got the money."

Jesse Jackson thought Young had resigned in a "capitulation" to Jewish influence. He accused Jewish banks of taking advantage of South African blacks. Going still further, Jackson placed Jews in a category with the Ku Klux Klan and the American Nazi Party as a matter for concern. Black Maryland congressman Parren Mitchell wanted a larger discussion of harmful treatment of blacks by Jewish landlords and blacks. Jews, thought conservative Roy Wilkins, were dictating to blacks: "We will define what your rights are, what your interests are, how fast you will go, who you are." Wilkins welcomed the removal of "the yoke of Jewish paternalism."

Harkening back to the days of the Bandung Conference, Andrew Young called for a "new foreign-policy constituency...made up of minorities and poor people." In an interview with ABC news in 1970, Young identified with the Black Panthers.

> *Young*: [I]t may take the destruction of Western civilization to allow the rest of the world to be free.... [A] small body of colored peoples, black people within the white West, may be the revolutionary vanguard that God has ordained to destroy the whole thing.
> *ABC*: Would you support the destruction of Western civilization if you were convinced that the rest of the world would be liberated?
> *Young*: I probably would.

The progeny of the Young affair is the Boycott, Divest, Sanction (BDS) effort, which advocates such economic actions against Israel and is aggressively supported by the Black Lives Matter movement. BDS's language and techniques are derivative of militant groups. The Movement for Black Lives platform charges Israel with apartheid and genocide against the Palestinians. It calls for the end of military aid to Israel. As before, the BDS movement, wishing to avoid conflict with American Jews, disingenuously describes itself as anti-Israel, not anti-Semitic.

The Racial Integration Muddle

Even after the *Brown* decision, resistance to school integration has been commonplace in America. Racially segregated housing has demanded other solutions, many of them obstructed by black separatism. The voluntary encouragement of whites to attend majority black schools has failed. Forcing black students to bus to predominantly white schools led to resistance in both black and white communities. The phenomena of "white fright" and "white flight" resulting from black movement into white neighborhoods were exacerbated by busing or the threat of busing. The *Brown* decision, a morally founded legal ruling, became enormously difficult to enforce throughout the country.

Busing to achieve desegregation yielded turmoil from Michigan to Massachusetts. Louise Day Hicks, a school board member, famously led the anti-busing effort in Boston. She would later be elected to Congress from her Boston district. Countering Hicks in supposedly liberal (and abolitionist) Boston, the black civil rights leader Julian Bond declared, "It's not the bus, it's us"—meaning that whites were opposed to busing only when African Americans were bused into white neighborhoods. White flight in Flint, Michigan, caused black student enrollment in DeWitt Clinton High School to increase from 10 percent in 1960 to 97 percent in 1970.

In addition to "white flight," the term "tipping" entered America's racial vocabulary in the 1960s. Tipping occurred when the percentage of blacks in a school system caused the school population to "tip" to predominantly black. In the South, alternative schools called "academies" sprung up as an alternative to full-throated racial integration. The academies would eventually accept children of middle- and upper-middle-class black families.

Arbitrary racial quotas led to confusion and an endless series of muddled court cases, some of which wound their way to the Supreme Court. The convoluted language of these decisions mirrored the lack of clarity on the issues at hand. The linguistic gymnastics of judgments on matters of integration, quotas, affirmative action, and diversity, from *University of California v. Bakke* in 1978 to the present day, are an exercise in obfuscation. Cases arising in Seattle, Michigan, Kentucky, Texas, and Connecticut attest to the national scope of the quagmire.

The all-black Dunbar High School in Washington, DC, for years had provided proof that blacks could excel in education. Dunbar students represented a cross-section of black DC, from laborers to the middle class. Observers as ideologically opposed as the Marxist Du Bois and the black conservative Thomas Sowell praised Dunbar. In 1929 Du Bois wrote of the Dunbar success as "a crushing indictment of hatred and prejudice and not a demand for further segregation." Sowell, writing in 2005, regretted the 1960s decision to concentrate school populations in local neighborhoods, for previously Dunbar had attracted students from the entire school district. Sowell called the flood of new arrivals "inadequately educated, inadequately motivated, and disruptive." Dunbar became "just another ghetto school," Sowell sadly noted.

But there were some successes. A feature story in the August 1964 issue of *Ebony* described the change at Detroit's Central High School from predominantly white to 95 percent black within only a few years. The hard-nosed principal, Charles S. Lewis, took the helm of the failed school in 1960 and refused to yield to "the gloom and despair of other secondary schools" in ghetto areas. "Tough-guy Lewis ... [weeded] out the troublemakers," reported *Ebony*. "Some 50 were sent home the first year.... Teachers relaxed and settled down to the business of teaching." The "disruptive child clause" worked. Lewis created "courses in African history and the Negro in American history"; tenth-graders read Western authors—Tolstoy, Faulkner, Sinclair Lewis, and Thomas Mann. In one year the number of college-bound students increased from 5 percent to 25 percent. These attempts would fade.

As noted earlier, by 1966 integration attempts in New York City and elsewhere had failed; beginning in 1961 they had been replaced by decentralization or a shifting of power to local communities to run their own schools. Legal segregation was demeaning, but without it blacks would struggle to understand integration and how much of it was desirable. Would the black community want token integration, self-segregation, or thorough integration?

In 1967 the research firm of Daniel Yankelovich Inc. investigated black attitudes toward school integration in thirteen cities. It found that 5 percent of the interviewees wanted no integration at all, 77 percent wanted "limited" integration, and 12 percent wanted total integration. Money, rather than integration, had become the goal, long before charter schools entered the arena. Black leaders wanted funding and jobs for black teachers. Black identity and resentment of the white community would reinforce black separatism in education.

Black Leaders, from Moderate to Militant

Robert Penn Warren, Yale professor and the only person to win a Pulitzer Prize in both fiction and poetry, was deeply concerned about race. A Kentucky native, by the 1960s, he was invested in the civil rights movement and the attitudes of blacks and whites toward it. With the narrative skill of a novelist and the probity and perspective of an historian, he captured the range of black thoughts in his memorable 1965 book *Who Speaks for the Negro?*, a series of interviews with visible blacks and a commentary on race. The range of opinion expressed by black leaders offers a thoughtful view of their situation in the midst of a tumultuous decade.

Warren's first interview was with Harlem's congressman Adam Clayton Powell Jr., the first black congressman from the state of New York, a Colgate University graduate, a Baptist minister, and an outspoken proponent of black civil rights. "I don't agree with the Black Muslims, don't believe in separation," declared Powell. "I'm an integrationist." A firm believer in nonviolence, Powell reasoned: " ... [Y]ou cannot stop nonviolence with violence.... The technique of nonviolence is the decisive factor in Negro power.... The day the Negro changes from nonviolence to violence, he is finished, and the Black Revolution has to start all over again." Like Martin Luther King Jr., Powell supported only demonstrations with a "specific target." He did not believe "Negro America" had any cultural relationship to Africa. The only "Negro" institution to survive the civil rights revolution, according to Powell, was the church. He preferred his emphasis on vocational training to Whitney Young's Marshall Plan approach or President Johnson's War on Poverty. Powell bragged about his relationship with Southern congressmen: "I have very good relations with men from the South. People...would be amazed if they knew how well we get along."

Roy Wilkins, executive director of the NAACP, was often accused by militant blacks of being too moderate, too conciliatory. The NAACP, headquartered in New York City, had a half-million members in the mid-sixties. The always practical Wilkins worked assiduously for desegregation but realized that integration was not generally feasible because of racially segregated housing. He opposed busing and "racial compulsion." As early as 1965 his goal of equality of opportunity was producing more quality schools in black neighborhoods. After the legal discriminatory obstacles were removed, Wilkins called for the "Negro" to "speed up the process of self-development and self-discipline, so that he becomes a contributing...member of society." He praised black pride and was indecisive about the potential for assimilation. He rejected characterizations of him as a moderate; his fight for "the elimination of racial segregation," he said, was truly radical.

In 1964 Whitney Young Jr. of the National Urban League challenged the United States, which had spent "$17 billion to restore Europe," to spend more than $1 billion to combat poverty in America's urban slums. In reality there was little in common between Europe's problems and those of black America. Young expressly called for self-help within the black community. "With rights," Young told Penn Warren, "go responsibilities." He elaborated in "A Cry from the Disposed":

> On our part Negro citizens must redouble their efforts to educate and train themselves for the new responsibilities which equal opportunities will require of them. They must march not only to the picket lines but to the libraries: they must prepare themselves for the stiffening competition of a no-holds-barred marketplace. They must make a special effort to eradicate the disorganization which has afflicted the lives of so many families. They must overcome not only subtle barriers of discrimination but their own shortcomings as individuals, and must make the effort incumbent on any pioneer group to move on higher emotional, spiritual and educational levels.

Class distinctions worried Young, especially the gap between the middle class and the "Negro mass." Unemployment and poverty had risen in the preceding decade even as the black middle class had grown. Depending on class, the Negro mass was sending a child to a "slum ghetto school" while the elite's kids often went to a "plush prep school." Young wanted the Urban League to play a major role in the War on Poverty version of his Marshall Plan. As reported by Robert Penn Warren, Young "generally recognizes that there is a 'Negro's negro problem'—the problem of taking responsibility to raise standards and enter competitively into the general society."

James Forman had been SNCC's executive secretary in the early 1960s before organizational dysfunction destroyed the organization. He then aligned himself with the militant Black Panthers. At New York's Riverside Church in 1969, Forman would demand $500 million in reparations from white churches, but he did not attend a similar planned ultimatum from the wealthy Temple Emanu–El in Manhattan after he was threatened by the Jewish Defense League.

The fissure between Forman and the NAACP's Wilkins was deep. Speaking after the 1964 race riots in New York, Rochester, and Philadelphia, Wilkins referred to black participants as "hoodlums, punks, foul-mouthed smart alecks" who are "undoing work of hundreds of Negro" civil rights workers. "[T]he Negro community itself," thundered Wilkins, "has just got to call a halt to violence."

Forman "accepted nonviolence as a way of life, in a sense" but was reluctant to call the slums a breeding ground for violence. Violence was just a "tactical device" to extract concessions, he said. "[E]very piece of Negro hoodlumism... [is] an indictment of the white man." Violence, merely a symptom and not the cause of a riot, was hence justified. Forman considered the black community a "special-interest group," a vehicle for "self-promotion," which by definition is unaccountable. Riots became a political tool. He thought the next step was a call for money, a "crash program—or Marshall Plan—for the Negro."

James Farmer, director of the Congress of Racial Equality, was an integrationist, dedicated to the extinction of racial segregation. Farmer's father had been a college professor; Warren observed Farmer as a man "fulfilled in himself, comfortable... ready to smile." Farmer acknowledged the debate in the black community over the proper extent of racial integration in the schools. He also knew that blacks, in many cases, did not care to live in white neighborhoods. He opposed busing. Segregated schools, whether self-segregated or legally segregated, he thought would yield excessively nationalistic and "anti-white feelings."

Like others, Farmer fretted over black identity and the potential loss of black culture. He thought that middle- and upper-class blacks neglected the black masses. Malcolm X, he said, was no man of the people but a publicity-seeking militant who "drives a new Oldsmobile...wears two-hundred-dollar suits and handmade shirts."

Ultimately Farmer's answer to the question of integration was a cliché: Blacks should strive to become a "proud and equal partner." He appeared to caution blacks about their responsibilities after the civil rights revolution: "When the thrust changes from desegregation to integration...then one of [the Negro's] chief responsibilities is to prepare himself to live in an integrated society." This approach sounds constructive, but as with Young, Wilkins, and King, the meaning of "preparation" is vague. Does it mean the acceptance of middle-class Western values as a norm? Would these giants of the civil rights movement have any influence after the revolution? Would there be a pivot within black culture toward effective preparation?

Warren's novelist's eye for detail is at work in his interview of Martin Luther King Jr. He noted King's physical "compactness and control," his "natural outgoing cordiality," his "natural grace of movement," his penchant for an inward search for answers, and, importantly, his voice—its "authority," its "mystical hold," its resonance and "rhythm." When King spoke, people listened. It was his voice that gave the young minister in Montgomery "moral superiority" to become the charismatic leader of the civil rights revolution.

King viewed integration as the road to mutual racial respect. That road would be paved with self-help, responsibility, and preparation. "We must be able to face honestly our own shortcomings," he had said in the 1950s. "We must act in a way to make possible the coming together of white and colored people on the basis of a real harmony..." His response to Warren was clear:

> After the Negro emerges in the desegregated society, then a great deal
> of time must be spent in improving standards which lag behind to a

large extent because of segregation, discrimination, and the legacy of slavery. The Negro will have to engage in a sort of Operation Boot-strap.

This was King's "third phase" of the civil rights movement. It is a view, similarly held by Whitney Young and others, that skirts very close to the much maligned but misunderstood approach of Booker T. Washington.

What did King mean by integration? He was well aware that housing segregation would prevent school integration in the major cities, North and South. He did advocate "transfer students—the busing system," but he clumsily tried to distinguish between areas where busing was convenient and where it was not. Busing students from Virginia and Maryland to Washington, DC, he thought, was impossible; busing from Westchester County or Queens to Harlem was feasible (though, in fact, the geography is no more favorable). Without integration, children white and black would not be able to understand one another. For King, the solution would arrive with a "broad level" of integrated housing.

As for assimilation, King recognized that blacks had to "absorb a great deal of white culture" in order to live in American society: "The Negro is an American. We know nothing of Africa. He's got to face the fact that he is an American." But the black cultural heritage and tradition, King thought, could exist within American assimilation. King's oft-repeated disavowal of violence needs qualifying. Just as Forman and Farmer had suggested, failure to alleviate the problems of blacks, King warned, "would inevitably lead to violence," for the urban slums were a "breeding ground" for frustration. He viewed rioting as the "result of pent-up frustration... [and] the absence of hope." He knew that for tactical reasons violence was harmful. His call for a halt to protest demonstrations in 1964 was politically motivated; violence would benefit Barry Goldwater's presidential campaign. He might have known that, despite his stature in the black community, neither he nor any other visible black leader could control an urban race riot. The 1964 disturbances that concerned him were followed by devastating riots that King was powerless to stop.

In his *Playboy* interview, King distanced himself from Malcolm X and violence in general: "I have often wished that he would talk less of violence, because violence is not going to solve our problem."

"Malcolm," King said, "...has done himself and our people a great disservice. Fiery, demagogic oratory in the black ghettos, urging Negroes to arm themselves and prepare to engage in violence, as he has done, can reap nothing but grief." The riots would have been much worse, according to King, if there had not been the discipline of nonviolence. In reality, the race riots would become catastrophic with nonviolence imposing no discipline.

King's famous hope that people "will not be judged by the color of their skin, but by the content of their character" is often cited as proof of his color-blind philosophy. But his support of a Marshall Plan for blacks and his numerous references to the damage of slavery, segregation, and discrimination are ample evidence that he had room for color consciousness.[7]

The North provided a rude racial awakening for Martin Luther King Jr. In 1963 he could poignantly juxtapose a black child in Harlem with one from Birmingham, Alabama. He could envision a "young Negro boy. He is sitting on the stoop in front of a vermin-infested apartment house in Harlem. The stench of garbage is in the halls. The drunks, the jobless, the junkies are shadow figures of his everyday world. The boy goes to a school attended mostly by Negro students with a scattering of Puerto Ricans. His father is one of the jobless. His mother is a sleep-in domestic, working for a family on Long Island."

Before his travels to the North, King had vastly underestimated the complexity of racial issues in the country at large. He was surprised when his attempt to bring the civil rights movement north was stymied. Speaking in Chicago and Cleveland in 1965, he bemoaned the fact that in the North there were no easy targets like George Wallace to use as symbols. Instead the good reverend discovered that "The Negro is not free in the North. He has the bottom of the economic ladder, often with a job and with inadequate educational opportunities."

In his *Playboy* interview, King paid a hopeful deference to the South, which had more "contact" with the "Negro" personally than the North. "The North white," according to King, "having had little actual contact with the Negro, is devoted to the abstract principle of cordial interracial relations...but the deep prejudices and discrimination...exist in

---

7 How far he would have taken color consciousness in terms of affirmative action, quotas, and busing is now a moot point. Posthumous speculation is similar to that surrounding the other two major American martyrs, Abraham Lincoln and John Kennedy. Would Reconstruction have been different if Lincoln had lived? Would Kennedy have quickly ended the Vietnam War?

hidden and subtle and covert disguises." In other words, King, like black abolitionist Samuel Ward, thought that white Northerners liked blacks best "at a distance." By contrast, he continued, "the South's prejudice has been…obvious, open, overt and glaring—which make it easier to get at…If the South is honest with itself, it may well outdistance the North in the improvement of race relations."

When asked his favorite book other than the Bible, King, a son of Western civilization, selected Plato's *Republic*.

Robert Penn Warren's conversations with black leaders pointed out differences of opinion and the use of ambiguous words—*responsibility, nonviolence, integration*. Louis Lomax thought men of King's mold were not equipped to become executives after they had led the revolution.

> Rather they are emotional men; they think in spiritual rather than prac-
> tical terms.…They can run a big Baptist church because their churches
> are, largely, personality clubs.…But faced with the task of administer-
> ing to a complex and diffuse organization…[they] flounder. Men such
> as Martin are natural born revolutionaries; they have what it takes to
> get people out into the street yelling and dying for a cause. But when
> the revolution is over, the republic would be better off if someone else
> took over the executive leadership.

Another influential black leader, Bayard Rustin, took a dim view of violence. Rustin was King's tutor for nonviolent activity. Rustin, called Mr. March-on-Washington, was instrumental in propagating nonviolent techniques. For him, nonviolent activity, unlike some demonstrations today, meant no violence. Like Lomax, he knew King could generate a crowd with his speaking ability. He nevertheless questioned King's organizing ability: "I know Martin well…he did not have the ability to organize vampires to go to a bloodbath." Rustin helped organize the 1963 March on Washington and was a strong proponent of racial integration as opposed to separation. A Communist in his youth, a committed socialist, an activist, gay, and a union supporter, Rustin evolved from activism to the political process as the proper avenue for promoting black economic advancement. In his 1970 *Harper's* article, "The Failure of Black Separatism," he denounced the violence of race riots: "To the misguided [blacks], violence, separatism, and minority ultimatums may seem revolutionary, but in reality they issue only from the desperate strivings of the impotent."

Rustin ridiculed campus militancy and some of the extremes in "programs for black studies." He thought it absurd for black Cornell students to demand a black studies course in physical education, "Theory and Practice in the Use of Small Arms and Hand Combat." He mocked a "pusillanimous university president" who authorized $2,000 in university funds to buy bongo drums for Malcolm X Day. He rejected attempts by black students to "study black history in isolation from the mainstream of American history." This, Rustin believed, would validate the attitude of white racists who held that black history was "irrelevant to American history."

Rustin disagreed with the use of black studies as "an ideological and political subject" rather than an academic endeavor. In politicizing history, the students, according to Rustin, were erroneously advocating a separatist "black nation." This, he presciently prophesied, would yield a teaching faculty based on "race, ideological purity, and political commitment—not academic competence." He denounced black students for "forsaking the opportunity to get an education." Black students were not concentrating on "the problem of teaching or learning... technical skills" for career preparation, he said. They were following an easier, frivolous path.

> If engineering requires too much concentration, then why not a course in soul music? If Plato is both "irrelevant" and difficult, the student can read Malcolm X instead. Class will [then] be a soothing, comfortable experience... like watching television.... One will have learned nothing, and the fragile sense of security developed in the protective environment of college will be cracked when exposed to the reality of competition in the world.

Rustin disagreed with black demands for financial and preferential treatment. He referred to a 1969 *Newsweek* poll indicating that "proud Negroes" rejected affirmative action "in hiring or college admissions in reparation for past injustice." Eighty-four percent of blacks had voted against such special treatment while only 10 percent had voted for it. President Ronald Reagan admired Rustin's "conviction that minorities in America could and would succeed based on their individual merit."

In the 1967 Yankelovich survey that ranked "Negro leaders," King had an astounding 83 percent approval rating in the category "Fights for What People Want" and an 82 percent rating for "Trust." The NAACP was at 70 and 67 percent, respectively; Roy Wilkins, Thurgood Marshall, and Whitney Young were huddled around 50 percent in both categories; Stokely Carmichael dropped to 32 and 20; SNCC faltered at 24 and 20; and the Black Muslims were an inconsequential 15 and 12. Eventually the separatists would exert greater long-term influence.

Racial Violence in the North

It may seem incongruous to consider the outspoken race-baiting opportunist and segregationist governor of Alabama, George Wallace, in a discussion about the influential leaders of the civil rights movement. But at least in one area, that of white Northern racial hypocrisy, he appears quite relevant. In September 1963 Kingman Brewster, acting president of Yale University, withdrew a speaking invitation to the campus for Governor Wallace. Brewster feared a violent protest by angry black New Haven residents.

One may argue that the modern incarnation of "selective free speech" began at Yale when Brewster bullied the Yale Political Union into canceling the Wallace speaking engagement. Nathan Pusey, the president of Harvard, chastised his former colleague and friend for trampling on free speech. Brewster, a former law professor, backpedaled and permitted two Yale groups to "reinvite" the governor, who never responded. Wallace allowed the patrician Brewster to wallow in his blunder.

Before Wallace's scheduled appearance in New Haven, a bomb had tragically taken the lives of four young black girls in a Birmingham church. If there were a reaction to Wallace's visit from New Haven's black community, Brewster could not count on protection from New Haven mayor Richard Lee, whose reelection bid was near.

Wallace was not intimidated by the Ivy League or New England. Like many white Southerners, he was well acquainted with Northern racial hypocrisy. He had recently engaged in a testy interchange with Connecticut governor John Dempsey, who had criticized Wallace's comportment. Wallace reminded Dempsey of Connecticut's racial conditions:

- Only two black students were among the seventeen hundred graduates in the University of Connecticut class of 1960.
- A 1961 Connecticut civil rights commission report that the state's schools were "almost wholly" racially segregated.
- The Real Estate Board of Greater Hartford rejected the application for membership of a black real estate agent. The board feared lower home prices if the agent sold a home to a black purchaser. (Recall that in 1790 New Haven and Salem, Massachusetts, had feared home prices would plummet if an influx of blacks appeared.)

One of the quieter forces behind Southern resistance to racial integration was the widespread knowledge in the South of racial hypocrisy in the North. The only disruption that occurred in New Haven in September 1963 was a disturbance over local housing discrimination.

Governor Wallace did come to the Ivy League—to Harvard, where he spoke on November 4, 1963, to a gathering of thirteen hundred students, faculty, and guests. His speech was broadcast via the Yale radio station to an off-campus site in New Haven where afterward a Yale law professor, the head of the New Haven NAACP, and a black minister held a panel discussion. Wallace would go on to speak at Dartmouth, Smith, and Brown. The entertaining governor used humor and guile to mollify his student audience; with justification he pronounced his Ivy League trip a success.

The Yale community missed an extraordinary opportunity to personally grill and confront a man who exerted significant influence on American politics in the 1960s. Was Kingman Brewster afraid that his law professors and the black clergy of New Haven could not compete with Governor Wallace? Or did he let Wallace off the intellectual hook by not allowing Yale to challenge him? Wallace's defiance, fueled by opportunism and overt segregationist views, was left unchallenged at Yale. Lest we forget, Governor Wallace in his run for president was polling more than 20 percent of the American electorate a few weeks before the 1968 election.

In the 1964 documentary film *Take This Hammer*, the angry and talented black writer James Baldwin exposed the acute level of racial frustration in an unlikely setting, San Francisco. In doing so he shredded the city's "widely advertised liberal and cosmopolitan tradition." Baldwin noted the surprising similarity between Birmingham, Alabama, and San Francisco. He wryly condemned white Northerners who thought they were paying their racial "dues" simply by not living in Mississippi. The angry retorts of young blacks in the film confirmed Baldwin's generalizations. The South is "not half as bad as San Francisco," steamed one black youth. San Francisco was "killing you with that pen and paper" by not giving you a job. Another demeaned "sit-ins": "We need violence, [and an] uprising, and a revolution."[8]

Urban racial violence during the civil rights era began in 1964 with race riots in Harlem and Rochester, New York, Philadelphia, and several New Jersey cities. These small but volatile disturbances would be the warm-up acts for full-scale urban racial warfare.

Several issues involving the riots demand emphasis. (1) There was a fundamental disconnect between the passage of the Civil Rights Act of 1964, the Voting Rights Act of 1965, and the race riots. (2) Although espousing strategic nonviolence and condemning looting and destruction, black leaders had rejected violence only for tactical reasons. (3) Black leaders were surprised by the race riots. (4) Black leaders were powerless to control what Martin Luther King Jr. called "out-of-hand demonstrations." (5) Although based on frustration and hatred of whites, the race riots for the most part destroyed property and neighborhoods

---

8 San Francisco would later experience "reverse white flight" when wealthy whites and Asians moved into the city and forced blacks out. San Francisco's black population declined from 13.4 percent in 1970 to 6 percent in 2010.

in black ghettos. They did not move into white residential or commercial areas. But white businesses in black areas were decimated.

The celebrated Civil Rights Act, fundamentally associated with the situation of blacks in the South, was signed on July 2, 1964, by President Lyndon Johnson. On July 10 a Harlem teenager was shot and killed by a white police officer, igniting disturbances in Harlem, Rochester, Philadelphia, and New Jersey. The riots were captured on film for the world to see. On July 27 Martin Luther King Jr., a staunch advocate of strategic nonviolence, recommended that black leaders seriously consider bringing an end to all demonstrations that could get "out of hand" and lead to violence. Alarmed by the Harlem upheaval, New York's Mayor Robert F. Wagner on July 24 asked King to come to New York to help curb racial tensions.

King and the nation had been caught up with the kidnapping and brutal slaying of three civil rights workers a month earlier in Philadelphia, Mississippi. The slain victims—James Chaney, Michael Schwerner, and Andrew Goodman—would be forever etched in the struggle for civil rights. Mississippi congressman Arthur Winstead, holding photos of the Harlem race riots, told civil rights workers to "go home and clean up their own mess."

Few now remember Mayor Wagner's desperate plea for King to travel ironically from Mississippi to New York for a racial peace mission. King knew very well that the riots would cause a massive white backlash in advance of the 1964 election. Racial violence in the North, King feared, would endanger President Johnson's campaign against Barry Goldwater.

In general, violence, said King, "creates many more social problems than it solves," was "impractical and immoral," and was "damaging to the movement." As a tactic, King knew that violence would damage his racial agenda. His operative phrase was "out of hand," by which he meant the loss of control that resulted from racial disruption. Furthermore he knew that the South's aggressive resistance added moral authority to his "noble cause" while race riots in the North created white fright, white flight, and a "law and order" reaction.

King referred to "well-disciplined and dignified" demonstrations in the South in contrast to the spontaneous Northern outbursts. Campaigns in the South sponsored "concrete goals," such as the removal of voter restrictions and discrimination in public accommodations. The Southern protests, he advised, were characterized by "planning prior to demonstrations." No such "specifics" or "prior planning" had accompanied disturbances in New York and Rochester. He characterized Northern riots as "generalized protests that led to violence and end up as aimless." King's "Chicago Plan" for Northern urban areas placed the first emphasis on education, then demonstrations to heighten awareness, then government legislation and support.

The emphasis on education has the appearance of a methodical approach, but there is an absence of detail. How would King approach curricula, the question of black versus white teachers, the teachers' unions, behavioral issues, skill-set goals, testing requirements, a desirable level of integration, funding, accountability of teachers and principals, parental participation, and religious involvement? He offered few specifics. Anti-discrimination legislation arrived, but the details of improved education, job creation, and the standard of living in the ghettos were beyond the grasp of the charismatic minister.

King's emphasis on nonviolent, goal-oriented activity unfortunately proved to be ineffectual for the nation at large. Many racial conflicts marred the urban landscape. Catastrophic race riots in Watts (Los Angeles), Detroit, and Newark in the mid-sixties terrified white America. Their sheer destructiveness brought chaos close to home. Americans witnessed sights familiar to a war zone. White America reacted with horror and, as King had foreseen, a desire for law and order.

Watts erupted on August 11, 1965, after Lyndon Johnson had signed the Voting Rights Act (outlawing discrimination in voting) on August 6. The fuse in Watts was lit when white police officers pulled over two blacks for a traffic violation. Alleged police brutality followed, and black protest soon erupted into full-scale war—the "out-of-hand" situation that concerned King. A hundred city blocks were destroyed, thirty-four people killed, a thousand injured, and fourteen thousand troops deployed. Arson and looting were shocking.

The year 1967 witnessed still more carnage. On July 12 the catalyst, the arrest of a black cabdriver by a white Newark policeman, and ensuing conflicting stories about abusive police behavior, detonated an urban race war. Black rioters "rampaged through downtown...chanting 'Kill the White Devils.'" "Self-service shoppers" selectively raided liquor stores, taking expensive scotch first. A local Urban League official observed hundreds of young blacks "looting and having a ball...[with] adults herding them into stores and directing them in what to take...[in] a carnival atmosphere." The results of five days of mayhem were twenty-four dead and eighteen hundred wounded. Newsreels reported New Jersey as "a state under siege."

Lyndon Johnson felt betrayed. Soon after the Newark riots, the president met with Roy Wilkins and Whitney Young Jr., whose "despair" was evident, according to White House domestic adviser Joseph Califano Jr. Johnson appointed a task force, which recognized "urbanization and discrimination, unemployment and poverty" as causes of the violence.

Meanwhile, Detroit followed. Superficially the Motor City would have seemed like an unlikely place for a race riot. The liberal white mayor, Jerry Cavanagh, had been a prime mover in securing $360 million in federal funds for various poverty programs. But on July 23 Detroit erupted when police raided several unlicensed black clubs and arrested scores of black patrons. The ensuing riots counted forty-three dead and more than a thousand injured, with almost thirteen thousand troops deployed. The US Army unit brought in was the same one that had confronted racial incidents at Little Rock Central in 1957 and the University of Mississippi in 1962. A rattled President Johnson condemned the "pillage, looting, murder, and arson...which has nothing to do with civil rights."

King and others were impotent to prevent these incendiary outbursts. King's interpretation of the riots as an "anti-police revolt" rather than an "anti-white revolt" failed to gain traction. Writing in 1968, Guy and Candie Carawan, folk musicians, described the revelations of Northern racial strife and King's limitations:

> So far the main thing [the Northern nonviolent movement] has done is to expose the racism of a northern city.... The southern campaigns begin to seem almost easy compared to the difficulty of the urban north with its complex tangle of slum-housing, chronic joblessness, poor schools and deteriorating family life. The frustrations and disappointments of Negroes caught in the ghettos...are more easily mobilized by riots and angry protests than by the reasoned words of a Martin Luther King.

King later altered his pronouncements about violence in the wake of the 1967 Detroit and Newark riots. On September 1, 1967, in an address before the American Psychological Association, he rationalized race riots as a derivation of "policy makers of white society." The South's racial system had been overturned, but "When changes were confined to the South alone, the North, in the absence of change began to seethe...and street demonstrations were not even a mild expression of militancy." King thought the violence was understandable and justified.

> Urban riots must now be recognized as durable social phenomena. They may be deplored, but they should be understood. Urban riots are a special form of violence. They are not insurrections.... They are mainly intended to shock the white community. They are a distorted form of social protest. The looting which is the principal feature serves many functions. It enables the most enraged and deprived Negro to take hold of consumer goods with the ease the white man does by using his purse.

He continues with some implausible opinions: "Often the Negro does not even want what he takes; he wants the experience of taking." (Actually, the rioters *did* want the liquor, clothes, and consumer goods they stole.) And then King bashes the concept of private property, the cornerstone of the free-market system: "But most of all, alienated from society and knowing that the society cherishes property above people, he is shocking it by abusing property rights." Thus King has justified violence as an "emotional catharsis." For King in 1967,

> The policy makers of white society create discrimination; they structured slums; and they perpetuate unemployment, ignorance, and poverty. It is incontestable and deplorable that Negroes have committed crimes; but they are derivative crimes. They are born of the greater crimes of white society.... Let us say boldly that if the violations of law by the white man...were calculated and compared with the law-breaking of a few days of riots, the hardened criminal would be the white man.

At this point the white North and South are both culprits.

King had difficulty rationalizing his toleration of violence with his adherence to nonviolence. His answer is a vague formula: "...we will have to find the militant middle between riots on the one hand and weak and timid supplication for justice on the other hand. The middle ground, I believe, is civil disobedience. It can be aggressive but nonviolent, it can dislocate but not destroy." This is a long way from his concerns in 1964 about demonstrations getting "out of hand." The ill-defined distinction between "riots" and "supplication" would result in more violence later. King's comments leave room for multiple interpretations, but the logic is clear. If civil disobedience becomes violent, destructive behavior by blacks is defensible because of past injustices—hardly a paean to strategic nonviolence.

Shaken by these destructive events, anxious politicians did what they always do: they formed a commission to evaluate and recommend constructive policies. Thus the National Advisory Commission on Civil Disorder was born in 1968 and came to be called simply the Kerner Commission for its chairman, Illinois governor Otto Kerner. The commission's instantly famous six-hundred-page report sold a hundred thousand copies in the first three days. It featured a memorable though mistaken claim: "Our nation is moving toward two societies, one black, one white—separate and unequal." In fact, two societies had existed as soon as the first black person set foot on American soil, North and South.

The Kerner Report yielded interesting information about the rioters. In both Detroit and Newark, 74 percent of the black participants were "brought up in the North." Of the black rioters arrested, 63 percent were born in the cities in which "disorder occurred." Data showed that a Southern upbringing "produced a tendency toward noninvolvement in riot situation[s]." Blacks raised in the North, however, were more prone to violence than those from the South. This tendency toward violence in the black North would conform to *Ebony* magazine's finding about the radicalization of blacks in urban environments. Further, the Yankelovich survey found that 35 percent of all blacks thought violence and rioting was necessary to achieve Negro objectives, but only 14 percent of Southern blacks thought similarly.

From the outset, the prominent black sociologist Kenneth B. Clark was pessimistic about the effectiveness of the Kerner Report. He had witnessed similar failed attempts after the 1919 riot in Chicago, the 1935 and 1943 riots in Harlem, and the Watts riot. For Clark, the report represented "a kind of Alice in Wonderland—with the same moving picture re-shown over and over again, the same analysis, the same recommendations, and the same inaction."

There was, nevertheless, action. Trillions of dollars would be spent to correct the "grievances" outlined by the Kerner Commission. The list eerily parallels the issues—poverty, inferior segregated schools, inferior integrated schools, jobs, housing, discrimination, welfare, "the abrasive relationship between the police and the minority community," and crime—and policy recommendations of the twenty-first century. In preparing the Kerner Report, commission members immediately faced a dilemma because segregated housing, school zoning, and student placement practices undermined integration. The commission chose to recommend "enrichment" programs—"smaller classes," "expanded pre-school programs," and changes "in the home environment of Negro children." This "separate but equal" approach, a rationalization of the reality of integration, was deemed an "interim action" and an "adjunct" to integration.

The commission also issued a clarion call for police reform, with a program that included "Recruitment, Assignment and Promotion of Negroes"; active "Community Relations Programs"; understanding "the use of deadly force"; "incentives, such as bonuses...to attract outstanding officers for ghetto positions"; and, of course, adequate "training." Yet a paradox lurks in the text, between an antipathy toward police and "the conviction that ghetto neighborhoods are not given adequate police protection" to combat "drug addiction, prostitution, and street violence."

Critical to the commission's agenda was an inventory of job panaceas—"consolidating and concentrating employment efforts, opening existing job structure [removing discrimination], creating one million new jobs in the public sector in three years, creating one million new jobs in the private sector in three years... encouraging business ownership in the ghetto..." Details such as "counseling in dress, appearance...hygiene, punctuality, and good work habits" were included. Today these employment goals remain unfulfilled except for the burgeoning public sector.

Payment for a vast program, according to the commission, depended entirely on "economic growth" to generate federal, state, and local tax revenues. If government revenues grew, the commission knew that there would be "competing demands." And expenditures for municipal services had already begun to spiral out of control. Public entitlements–public pension and health benefits–would soon cast a pall on budgets.

The War on Poverty

In addition to the Kerner Report, the federal government's analysis of the blacks' situation in America was completed in March 1965 with the publication of the so-called Moynihan Report. The author, Daniel Patrick Moynihan, was a sociologist serving as an assistant secretary in the Department of Labor. With his two assistants, he concentrated on the dysfunction of the "Negro family" in the urban ghettos, or what the report called "the tangle of pathology." Moynihan's work, called "The Negro Family: The Case for National Action," traced the problems of black America to the disintegration of the black family.

> The most difficult fact for white Americans to understand is that in these terms the circumstances of the Negro American community has probably been getting worse.
>
> Indices of dollars of income, standards of living, and years of education deceive. The gap between the Negro and most other groups in America is widening.
>
> The fundamental problem, in which this is most clearly the case, is that of the family structure. The evidence...is that the Negro family in the urban ghettos is crumbling. A middle class has managed to save itself, but for vast numbers of the unskilled, poorly educated city working class the fabric of conventional social relationships has all but disintegrated. There are indications that the situation may have been arrested in the past few years, but the general post-war trend is unmistakable. So long as this situation persists, the cycle of poverty and disadvantage will continue to repeat itself.
>
> At the heart of the deterioration of the fabric of Negro society is the deterioration of the Negro family.
>
> ...The family structure of lower-class Negroes is highly unstable, and in many urban centers is approaching complete breakdown.

The fundamental problem, according to Moynihan, was the inability of the black male to enter the economic mainstream, which in turn prevented his ability to be a father and husband, which in turn prevented a stable family structure, creating children ill-prepared to enter the economic mainstream. It was a vicious continuum, and it had all started with race-based slavery.

The Moynihan Report received immediate and widespread attention, especially criticism from civil rights groups. The New York City Commission on Religion and Race sought to remove mention of "family stability" from an upcoming White House conference. Yet there was nothing particularly new in Moynihan's analysis or information. As noted earlier, E. Franklin Frazier had been writing about this situation for decades. But Moynihan had an impressive platform. The call for "national action" meant removing discriminatory obstacles and providing blacks with resources to take advantage of new opportunities.

President Johnson was fully on board with a national agenda for blacks. Johnson, a shrewd Texas politician, had risen to the powerful position of Senate majority leader through a combination of ruthlessness, cleverness, and opportunism. Early in his career he had employed race-baiting rhetoric when convenient. But his ability to pass legislation through compromise and cajoling was legendary. After the Kennedy assassination, Johnson was in full command.

In June 1965 the president signaled a revolution during an address, written by Moynihan and Richard N. Goodwin, at Howard University. "Negro poverty is not white poverty," Johnson famously announced. "Many of its causes and many of its cures are the same. But there are differences [which] are solely and simply the consequence of ancient brutality, past injustice, and present prejudice.... Most of them live together—a separated people." Eradication of poverty was the goal, but blacks were a distinct priority. While civil rights legislation was aimed at the South, the "slums" of the major cities, where 73 percent of blacks lived, became the target for social legislation.

Johnson was serious. And the crusty, anti-intellectual, scotch-guzzling deal-maker had academic support. Beginning in the 1960s the concern about poverty reached popularity coincidentally with Johnson's crusade. An influential book, *The Other America*, published in 1963 by the socialist writer Michael Harrington, alleged that "between 40 million and 50 million Americans" lived in poverty. And black Americans were without doubt a large percentage of the poor and the most important priority of any program to combat poverty. At his Howard University speech, the president clearly identified black poverty as more extreme than white poverty.

In his State of the Union Address on January 8, 1967, Johnson declared "unconditional war on poverty in America" as part of his "Great Society" program. Never reluctant to think or act big, he established an anti-poverty program that was, according to the historian Daniel Boorstin, "the most self-conscious and best-organized attack on poverty in all of history." Along came a whole host of programs that included Vista, the domestic peace corps; a Job Corps for school dropouts; and Operation Head Start for children. The plethora of projects, wrote Boorstin, was dubbed by cynics the "poverty industry." The mocking terminology was nonetheless accurate.

The infused energy of idealism was rampant. Trillions of dollars were spent, but the results of the massive program were elusive at best and did not end poverty. There was even an advisory outreach body, the Community Representative Advisory Committee (CRAC), made up of representatives from local poverty groups. "Some twenty to twenty-five people," wrote Michael Gillette in *Launching the War on Poverty* (1996), "were selected...who were showing a particular skill in articulating the needs of the poor." Hyman Bookbinder, an official in the Office of Economic Opportunity, which oversaw the program, related his experience with CRAC. Before his stint at the OEO, he had risen in the ranks of the New York Laundry Workers Union to a position as labor lobbyist for the AFL-CIO to assistant to the secretary of commerce. Involvement with CRAC, gushed Bookbinder, was "psychologically, emotionally for me...the most gratifying thing that I did" at the OEO. But, Bookbinder continued surprisingly, "I can't think of a single idea or policy recommendation that emanated from the group that was of any lasting consequence." Bookbinder's emotional gratification did not compensate for the lack of substantive results. People may argue over the effectiveness of the War on Poverty, but its programs did suffer from waste, fraud, lack of accountability, and bureaucratic inefficiency. They have been replaced by programs that still attempt to solve the problems of poverty in America.

If the United States wished to confront the problems of the ghetto, there was no shortage of ideas for solutions. One of the most interesting came from the National Strategy Information Center (NSIC), a conservative, anti-Communist research group, and involved the use of military personnel. Filed under "Poverty Program" at the LBJ Library is a letter of June 20, 1967, to presidential adviser Joseph Califano Jr. from his friend Morris Liebman, a prominent lawyer and co-founder of NSIC.

The letter contains a detailed proposal for a plan to retrain "1,000 Negro officers and NCO's who have served our country in Vietnam in diversified Community Action programs...at the grassroots level...in 35-50 large centers." The scheme would "seed into metropolitan slum areas mature 'father figures' and symbols of authority—i.e., seasoned Negro officers and NCO's whose leadership abilities have been developed and tested." Clearly, part of the NSIC's motivation was to blunt the appeal of communism, Black Power, and civil disobedience. But the proposal, potentially effective in creating structure in the inner-city communities, was never realized.

The Private Sector Responds

While civil rights legislation, government programs, race riots, and law-and-order reactions were capturing attention in the 1960s, little notice was taken of corporate America's extensive and constructive response. The turbulence of the decade had awakened the private sector, which reacted with job training programs and hiring specifically geared to the black community. In 1964 the journalist Nat Hentoff wrote of American corporations recruiting Negroes. "We've found," Carl Haugen of Chase Manhattan Bank told *Newsweek* in 1964, "that we can no longer wait for Negroes to apply for jobs. We have to go and seek them out of high schools and colleges." John O. Nicklis, president of Pitney-Bowes, spoke of "relaxed testing and experience requirements for Negro applicants...and giving them special on-the-job training." Preferential hiring, though not announced as company policy, was practiced in many companies and reports given to the press. In 1963 a General Motors officer told *Business Week*, "Today, if two applicants for a job at GM have equal qualifications and one is a Negro, the Negro will get the job."

In 1968 *Fortune* published *The Negro and the City*, a book drawn from a special issue of the magazine, which described the veritable blizzard of public and private responses to the race riots and issues of civil rights. In an introduction, Robert C. Weaver, the black secretary of housing and urban development, sounded a call for public *and* private leadership to tackle the "apathy of poverty," which led to "mob violence in the streets."

"Business must reach down for the 'unemployable' Negro," wrote Max Ways, a *Fortune* editor, "by lowering standards of entry, by developing training programs, by making visible and practical the upward career paths Negroes can tread." Business did just that—by establishing numerous experiments to deal with the problems of the ghetto. William Zisch, vice chairman of Aerojet-General, proudly announced the creation of the Watts (California) Manufacturing Company geared to employ blacks. Eventually it hired two hundred people in a tent-making operation. The initial experience, 35 percent absenteeism on Monday mornings, improved, but high turnover remained a problem. Zisch eagerly sought other companies to emulate the "Watts model" and wrote to every CEO of a Fortune 500 company. He even awarded prizes to Avro, Control Data, General Dynamics, and Goodyear for their efforts in urban ghettos.

The Board for Fundamental Education (BFE) had been founded in 1948 by Cleo Blackburn, the grandson of a former slave, to educate all races. By 1968 the BFE claimed more than twenty-five thousand enrollees and a client list that included Du Pont, Olin Chemical, and Eastman Kodak. BFE and other programs were funded in part or full by federal government departments under the 1962 Manpower Development and Training Act. Corn Products operated MIND, another effort to supplement reading and writing deficiencies of the "unemployable." Equitable Life Assurance Society, with the partnership of the New York State Employment Service, embarked on a bold experiment to hire school dropouts, unmarried mothers, and those with police records. From 1962 to 1966 the program trained 121 dropouts; by 1966 only twenty-three remained employed.

Metropolitan Life Insurance was "somewhat more successful" because of a better selection process. Some 60 percent of the blacks and Puerto Ricans it hired were able to perform as clerical workers. Ford contributed to Detroit's Career Development Center, founded by "Alvin Bush, a Negro ex-bellhop ... to train Negroes for jobs"; GM worked with the Urban League to start "Project Opportunity," which would hire "several hundred so-called unemployables." It did not fire anyone "for tardiness, absence, or lack of ability," but a "follow-up committee" would go to the "malingerer's house, haul him out of bed and deliver him to the factory." SEED, a joint industry-government partnership, received funding from Western Electric, Weston Instrument, and Singer. An optimistic projection of two thousand trained employees by 1967 yielded a 50 percent initial dropout rate. Industry officials criticized the confusion generated by navigating through a labyrinth of government agencies, one state and three federal.

Joe Wilson, the CEO of Xerox in Rochester, New York, took the initiative after Rochester endured a race riot in July 1964. The proximate cause, a policeman trying to restrain a drunk black man who was fighting with his pregnant girlfriend, resulted in a riot that was confined to the ghetto, with four dead. Rochester's black population had grown from seventy-seven hundred in the 1950s to thirty-four thousand by 1964. Most of the rioting and looting occurred on Joseph Avenue, where most of the businesses destroyed were owned by Jews.

Wilson, as described by Charles Ellis, in *Joe Wilson and the Creation of Xerox,* contacted Minister Franklin Delano Roosevelt Florence, a militant charismatic leader. Working with Minister Florence, Wilson set up Operation Step Up in 1966 to train blacks for jobs at Xerox. Two years later Wilson and Florence set up Fight On, the first joint effort between government and the private sector to start a business owned by blacks. Xerox guaranteed a $500,000 purchase order for Fight On for two years.[9] These efforts were small in scope—a hundred people—and though well intentioned did not produce a revolutionary impact.

Dazzled by technological progress, the contributors to *The Negro and the City* had dreams of "model cities." The operative phase was "systems engineering," which would solve "traffic congestion" and "Negro poverty" by using the methodology of aerospace-computer-electronics companies. Virtually any human problem, viewed through a haze of technological intoxication, could be solved. The jargon is familiar: "Data, ideas, and observations... [could be translated] into mathematical models... and fed into a computer." In California, Space General, a systems-engineering company, undertook an analysis of the state's "total system of justice, from police precincts through the courts, penal institutions and parole boards to rehabilitation." The analogy seemed straightforward. A system that could launch an Apollo-Saturn rocket in 1967 could surely handle the

---

9 In 2009 Ursula Burns, a woman engineer of African descent with Panamanian parents, a strong educationally oriented mother, and a Catholic secondary-school education, became CEO of Xerox.

economic, racial, and social problems of the cities. The technologically induced model city, however, failed to achieve orbit.

Another Look at the Sixties

The 1960s produced a racial inflection. No longer did blacks face overt racial segregation. This "insult" and "badge of inferiority" was at last removed. The white North was, as it had always been, fully involved with the "Negro Problem," but now it was more apparent. Ultimately Connecticut's liberal senator Abraham Ribicoff was the national figure who called out the North's hypocritical, self-righteous racial behavior in a surprising way—by supporting legislation in 1969 sponsored by the segregationist Senator John Stennis of Mississippi.

Stennis was demanding desegregation of Northern schools if the South were forced to desegregate. Senator Ribicoff had "the greatest respect for John Stennis as a man" and realized that Stennis "made good sense." In his 1972 memoir, *America Can Make It!*, Ribicoff confessed:

> The North is guilty of monumental hypocrisy in its treatment of the black man. Without question, Northern communities have been as systematic and as consistent as Southern communities in denying the black man and his children the opportunities that exist for white people. Racism is rampant throughout the country.
>
> Perhaps we in the North needed the mirror held up to us by...Senator [John Stennis] from Mississippi, in order to see the truth ...

Hartford, a quite wealthy state capital when Ribicoff was senator, has descended into an urban ghetto whose population is 83 percent black and Hispanic. In 1989 the city was hit with a desegregation lawsuit, *Sheff v. O'Neill*. The case has been wandering through the courts for decades.

Daniel Patrick Moynihan, whose report on the dysfunctional "Negro family" caused such a stir, would advocate in 1970 a period of "benign neglect" of the issue of race. Race, for him, "has been too much talked about. The forum has been taken over to hysterics, paranoids..." He advocated ignoring the Black Panthers, who had become "cultural heroes" feted by the likes of conductor Leonard Bernstein. At the time, Moynihan, a lifelong Democrat, was executive secretary of the Council on Urban Affairs during the administration of President Richard Nixon. The problem of "female headed families," he wrote, "gets worse...The incidence of anti-social behavior among black males continues to be extraordinarily high."

By the end of the sixties, blacks were still in a quandary about their identity—was it individual, group, class, or national? The black person, like the young women at Spelman College in 1962 and 1963, would still have to ask, *Where do I fit in America?* Racial self-segregation had become a potent force.

The recognition of African heritage would become part of the American curriculum, but the hope for an African renaissance would be dashed on the rocks of tribalism, religion, dictatorship, and corruption. In the 1960s the putative unity of "people of color" fared poorly. Nigeria experienced the bloody Biafran War (1967–1970), which, among other things, pitted African Muslims against African Christians; Pakistani Muslims and Indian Hindus, too, were in conflict.

The issues raised in the sixties remain salient in the twenty-first century. Forced segregation has given way to a debate over what constitutes appropriate racial integration. Answers range from full separation to partial integration to full integration. Black leaders as diverse as Fannie Lou Hamer, Martin Luther King Jr., Roy Wilkins, James Farmer, and Malcolm X vied for attention and influence. King, Wilkins, Farmer, and Whitney Young advocated "preparation," "responsibility," and "accountability" to address the flaws of the black community—terms that would later vanish from the discussion. Would these be empty words or the language of commitment?

The white liberal editor John Fisher of *Harper's* in 1965 acknowledged the need "for the erosion of a lot of white prejudices," but he also demanded "some big changes in the habits, character and ambitions of a lot of Negroes." Blacks were not then and are not now a monolithic society. Class divisions within the black community denote different capabilities, different goals, and different attitudes. In the sixties opportunities were open to a qualified black elite and a middle class. Meanwhile racial violence raised the question of the primacy of law and order versus the frustration of the black ghetto.

The ability of the civil rights organizations to adapt to different challenges was questionable. Most revolutionaries flunk the postrevolutionary exam. Discrimination, still present, became secondary to larger social issues—family dysfunction, educational acceptance, employment eligibility, crime, poverty, accountability, and neighborhood cohesiveness. Would the civil rights organizations remain relevant in the coming decades?

The 1960s stirred up passionate anti-white, anti-Western feelings among blacks. Middle-class norms, which were the backbone of the American value system, were suspect within the black community as an infringement on black culture and in perceived opposition to it. Black America, while concentrating on grievances, did not develop a constructive and essential mechanism for self-critique.

The world is not static. Economics, technology, politics, and ideology would change in the competitive world described by Whitney Young Jr. A singular focus on race would retard the progress of black America. It would prove impossible to create a self-sufficient black economic society; an interaction with the American mainstream would be necessary. Concessions to assimilation would have to be made. The African American experience and struggle deserved significant memorialization, but that remembrance ought not to be paralyzing.

The next fifty years would test black leadership. The absence of structure—in the family, church, school, or community—would need to be corrected if mass entrance into the economic mainstream were to occur. Values rather than skin color would determine the future of black America.

1. NEW ORLEANS PORT (1860) This photograph, taken by famous New Orleans photographer Jay Dearborn Edwards, illustrates the sheer size and dynamism of the cotton world that determined the fate of black America. The economic power of slave-produced cotton blindsided the Founding Fathers, extended slavery, and caused the Civil War.

THE RIOTS IN NEW YORK: THE MOB LYNCHING A NEGRO IN CLARKSON-STREET—SEE PAGE 143.

2. CIVIL WAR DRAFT/RACE RIOTS (1863) Anti-black sentiment in New York City caused the draft/race riots, one of the most violent episodes of civil disobedience in American history. Black New Yorkers were lynched in the streets.

Department of Justice, (Freedman's Bank Building.)

3. Freedman's Savings Bank (1866) The bank was established to encourage thrift among freed slaves. Its impressive façade masked a fraudulent organization that failed. Thousands of newly freed slaves lost their savings.

WISCONSIN.

𝔚hat it offers to the 𝔍mmigrant.

AN OFFICIAL REPORT

PUBLISHED BY THE

STATE BOARD OF IMMIGRATION OF WISCONSIN.

BOARD OF COMMISSIONERS:

W. E. SMITH, Governor of State, } Ex-Officio Members.
HANS B. WARNER, Secretary of State. }

J. A. BECHER,   J. M. SMITH,   K. A. OSTERGREN.

J. A. BECHER, President.   **A. MÖNSTED**, Secretary.

CRAMER, AIKENS & CRAMER, PRINTERS,
MILWAUKEE.
1879.

4. WISCONSIN STATE RECRUITMENT BROCHURE (1879) America needed immigrants. This marketing brochure successfully enticed white Europeans to settle in Wisconsin. White America was encouraging white immigration, and white Northerners maintained a form of containment policy to keep blacks in the South.

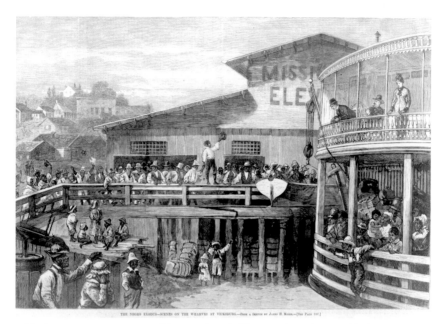

THE NEGRO EXODUS—SCENES ON THE WHARVES AT VICKSBURG.—From a Sketch by James H. Moser.—[See Page 297.]

5. Exoduster movement to Kansas (1878) This was the only mass black migration attempt north between 1865 and World War I. Strong resistance by white Kansans curtailed the effort.

6. Liverpool Cotton Exchange invitation (1906) The invitation for the opening of the new Liverpool Cotton Exchange building graphically portrays the export dominance of cotton. The implications for black American cotton laborers were straightforward.

Ford English School

This is to Certify that

having completed the Course of Study prescribed by the

Ford English School, is entitled to receive this

A course of study in the Ford English School covering a period of nine months gives a man the ground work in English speech, enables him to understand the English language, to write it and read it within certain limitations

DIPLOMA

It gives him a definite comprehension of the rudiments of Government, National, State and Municipal, and fits him to become a Citizen of the United States, and to understand the obligations thereof.

Given at Detroit, U.S.A. this_____ day of_____ A.D. 19___

Ford Motor Company

Henry Ford
President

Edsel B. Ford
Vice-President

Educational Department

7. Ford English language school diploma (1915) America had to accommodate the millions of non-English-speaking white immigrants—essential for industrial growth. Ford Motor Company and many companies established their own internal language schools to facilitate necessary work efficiency.

8. Americanization Day parade (1915) Assimilation was promoted by enormous parades featuring patriotic symbols. Six thousand Ford Motor Company employees participated in the parade depicted in the photograph.

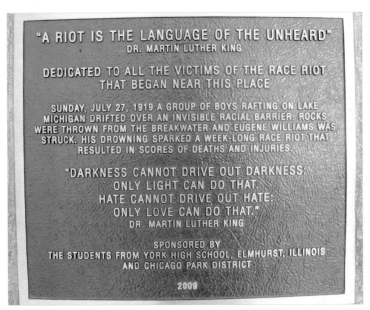

9. CHICAGO 1919 RACE RIOT PLAQUE (2009) The Northern movement of blacks during the Great Migration resulted in race riots. The plaque belatedly and insufficiently commemorates the largest of these massive disturbances. Martin Luther King Jr. would also say at the Stanford speech in 1967 that "riots are socially destructive and self-defeating." "I am still convinced," he remarked in 1966, "that for the Negro to turn to violence would be both impractical and immoral."

10. RHINELANDER COURT CASE (WHITE PLAINS, NEW YORK, 1925) The wealthy Rhinelander family prompted a lawsuit to have their son's marriage to Alice Jones, a dark-skinned woman, annulled. The disputed issue was deception—a failure to disclose that she was possibly black. Alice Jones consented to partially disrobe in the jury room to "prove" that there was no deception. This composograph image used actors rather than actual people to imagine the scene in the jury room. The black press was outraged.

11. POLAND JEWISH EDUCATION (1920S) Poor Jewish children living in a Polish ghetto attended religious schools. The Jewish cultural tradition of education allowed the descendants of Jews who immigrated to America to prosper.

12. *BUSINESS WEEK* COVER (1930) The American racial context of the period tolerated this blatant racial slur on the cover of a national publication.

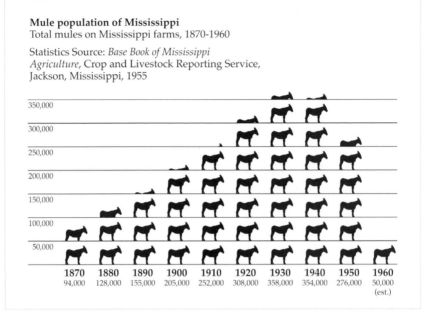

Mule population of Mississippi
Total mules on Mississippi farms, 1870-1960

Statistics Source: *Base Book of Mississippi Agriculture*, Crop and Livestock Reporting Service, Jackson, Mississippi, 1955

	1870	1880	1890	1900	1910	1920	1930	1940	1950	1960
	94,000	128,000	155,000	205,000	252,000	308,000	358,000	354,000	276,000	50,000 (est.)

13. MULE GRAPH The decline of the mule population evidenced the displacement of black and white farm works by mechanization. This occurred simultaneously with the civil rights movement, and its impact parallels the later deindustrialization phenomenon.

14A. (*opposite*) **AND 14B. NEW YORK CITY SCHOOL BOYCOTT FLYER**
(1964) These represented 464,000 black and Hispanic students who boycotted classes because of inferior education. Chicago held a similar boycott in October 1963. The Northern racially motivated school boycott coincided with the 1964 Mississippi Freedom Summer's educational outreach effort.

SWEEP AND CLEAR—Guardsmen and Los Angeles police officers march down Avalon Blvd. at 43rd St. in an action designed to free the streets of rioters and looters.
Times photo by Don Cormier

15. Los Angeles race riot (1965) This massive conflagration occurred soon after the Civil Rights Act of 1965. Urban race riots would become a defining feature of the 1960s.

16. Senator Robert Kennedy (March 1966) Senator Kennedy is speaking to five thousand people at the University of Mississippi. The enthusiastic reception contrasts starkly to the hostility felt toward the Kennedy brothers three and a half years earlier during the violent racial integration of the school.

17A. AND 17B. MISSISSIPPI CIVIL RIGHTS MARKERS The state of Mississippi has memorialized the civil rights activists and events of the civil rights movement. There is a national need to expand memorialization of the black experience.

WHAT'S IN A NAME?

At Milwaukee demonstration, young Commando (left) makes symbolic break with "white" words and images by shredding copy of Webster's New World Dictionary of the American Language. Playwright Ossie Davis has said that English language is the black man's enemy. At Black Power Conference in Newark (right), the youth section led fight against continued use of the word "Negro."

BY LERONE BENNETT JR.

Malcolm X played pivotal role in downgrading the word "Negro." After leaving the Muslim movement, he organized the Organization of Afro-American Unity. Since his assassination, he has become something of a patron saint of the pro-black movement.

National controversy rages over proper

"When I use a word," Humpty Dumpty said in a rather scornful tone, "it means just what I choose it to mean—neither more nor less."

"The question is," said Alice, "whether you can make words mean so many different things."

"The question is," said Humpty Dumpty, "which is to be master—that's all."

—Lewis Carroll, *Through the Looking Glass*

MORE concretely, within the context of the racial looking glass, the question is whether one can make the word "Negro" mean so many different things or whether one should abandon it and use the words "black" or "Afro-American."

This question is at the root of a bitter national controversy over the proper designation for *identifiable* Americans of African descent. (More than 40 million "white" Americans, according to some scholars, have African ancestors.) A large and vocal group is pressing an aggressive campaign for the use of the word "Afro-American" as the only historically accurate and humanly significant designation of this large and pivotal portion of the American population. This group charges that the word "Negro" is an inaccurate epithet which perpetuates the master-slave mentality in the minds of both black and white Americans. An equally large, but not so vocal, group says the word "Negro" is as accurate and as euphonious as the words "black" and "Afro-American." This group is scornful of the premises of the advocates of change. A Negro by any other name, they say, would be as black and as beautiful—and as segregated. The times, they add,

---

18. BLACK MILITANT SHREDDING WEBSTER'S DICTIONARY (*EBONY* MAGAZINE, 1967) In an article, "What's in a Name? Negro vs. Afro-American vs. Black," *Ebony* highlighted the identity confusion of black Americans. A Milwaukee scene features the symbolic destruction of an English dictionary, a publication deemed racist. Militant blacks had put Western civilization on trial.

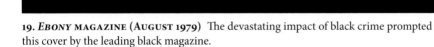

19. *EBONY* MAGAZINE (AUGUST 1979) The devastating impact of black crime prompted this cover by the leading black magazine.

PERSONAL INJURY AND MENTAL PAIN

More Blacks Killed On Streets Than In Vietnam

MORE BLACKS were killed by other Blacks in the year 1977 than died in the entire, nine-year Vietnam War. Most of the 5,734 Blacks killed on the battlefields of Black America in 1977 could have survived Vietnam, since the Blacks who died there (5,711) averaged only 634 per year. These astounding figures only begin to underscore the seriousness of Black on Black crime, for nearly 87 percent of the robberies, rapes and assaults on Blacks are committed by other Blacks, reports the Law Enforcement Assistance Administration. Most of these personal crimes of violence are against lone victims on streets, in parks, on playgrounds and school grounds, or in parking lots; are more likely to be reported to the police than crimes involving theft; and are less likely to be reported by males than females, according to University of Maryland criminologist, Dr. Julius Debro. He also finds that Black households are more likely than White households to be burglarized; that, contrary to widespread belief, households headed by persons over 65 have the lowest rates of all types of household crime, and that the larger the household, the greater the chance of victimization.

The criminologist estimates that actual crime volume is at least three times larger than the total compiled by the FBI's annual Uniform Crime Reports. "We know that if we are going to attack crime," he continues, "we must now concentrate our efforts on young people and try and get them to report incidents of criminal behavior. It is important for old people to know that they are relatively safe within their own homes and that it isn't necessary to barricade themselves in their homes for further protection."

Debro notes that perceptions of Black crime vary in different sections of the country. "In the North," he reports, "violence is still seen as a way of life . . . on the East Coast [perceptions lead] to a feeling that the victim is just waiting to be victimized because there is no other choice . . . On the West Coast, the perception . . . is not one of fear for Black on Black crime but one of acceptance that it will occur and that very little will be done to combat [it] . . . In the Southwest, both in Houston and in Dallas the fear of crime [is] not as strong as the fear of police

. . . Most Blacks [see] the police as an occupying force which [has] little concern for human lives among Blacks and Mexicans."

The South, however, differs markedly from the rest of the nation, Debro continues, since it is "generally a place in which citizens can walk the streets at night without worrying about the fear of crime." He notes that crime has decreased in Atlanta since (and because) its political leadership changed from White to Black. Debro relates this reduction and the fact that juvenile gangs do not exist in the city to "a) a Black concerned police department, b) the relationship of the police department with tenants and tenants' associations, and c) the police department acting as a referral service." All of this suggests that the ultimate solution of Black on Black crime will require extensive Black leadership.

Dead victims of crime like the one being removed from street by Chicago policeman (right) were more numerous in Black communities in one year than all the Blacks killed (a total of 5,711) in entire Vietnam War (below), which lasted nine years.

20. *EBONY MAGAZINE (AUGUST 1979)* Black-on-black murders prompted a dramatic comparison with the number of blacks killed in combat during the Vietnam War.

21. *EBONY MAGAZINE (AUGUST 1979)* (*opposite*) The photograph illustrates the desperate reaction of blacks in Chicago to the scope and severity of the drug traffic. Demands for stronger drug law enforcement came from the black community.

STOP CODDLING THE HOODLUMS

'GOING EASY ON CRIMINALS ENCOURAGES CRIME'

By Winston E. Moore

The author, Winston E. Moore, chief of security for the Chicago Housing Authority, is an authority on Black on Black crime which, he says, could be reduced drastically if the Black community would begin to "come down hard" on Blacks who prey on other Blacks. Until assuming his present post two years ago, Moore, a trained psychologist, was executive director of the Cook County (Chicago) Dept. of Corrections (nine years) and warden of Cook County Jail (two years).

IT is my conviction that we will never put an end to the mounting problem of Black on Black crime until we stop coddling the hoodlums. By "coddling the hoodlums," I am referring to the Black community's extraordinary tolerance toward the growing army of Black criminals who have turned life in the nation's urban ghettos into a veritable hell. Not only are these criminals allowed to prey on their law-abiding Black brothers and sisters with virtual impunity, they have attained bona fide hero status among many young Blacks not unlike that of the legendary gunslingers of the old West.

What is urgently needed today is a massive campaign to re-educate Blacks to see Black criminals among them for what they are, not heroes but deadly enemies—cowardly, two-bit punks who cheat, rob, maim and murder and in general make decent people's lives miserable. We Blacks should begin by serving notice to our elected and appointed government officials, both Black and White and on all levels, that we will no longer tolerate their traditional misguided leniency toward the Black on Black criminal. We must make it unmistakably clear to these officials that we will no longer put up with the prevailing racist, White-controlled dual criminal justice system which comes down hard on Black criminals when their victims are White but lets them off with a slap on the wrist for a comparable crime whenever the victims are Black. A grim statistic will illustrate my point. Less than five percent of all Blacks currently on Death Row throughout the United States are there for murdering Blacks. The remaining 95 percent are on Death Row for murdering Whites.

What in effect the upholders of this dual system—the police, states' attorneys, judges, probation officers, parole boards, etc.—are saying is that a Black life has less value than a White life, that a Black person's limbs are less valuable than a White person's limbs, that Black pain is less painful than White pain, that violating a Black woman is a lesser crime than violating a White woman, that Black property is less important than White property.

The historical roots of this dual system of "justice" can easily be traced to the plantations of the antebellum South. To jail or kill a slave who had murdered another slave was not in the best interest of the slaveowner since such punishment would have deprived him of two slaves instead of only one. Consequently, such murders were treated lightly—not because of compassion for the killer but because of the slaveowner's economic interest. The same was true for rape among slaves, which was not considered a crime but frequently encouraged since it produced additional valuable slaves. Only when the victim was White was the full fury of the slave code unleashed—usually to nauseating extremes of cruelty in the form of lynchings.

Today, the racist, dual plantation justice system of antebellum days is still very much with us throughout the United States. Although modified and somewhat refined, it still tells the Black criminal that as long as he confines his criminal activity to the Black community, he can count on leniency from the law should he get caught.

Since a large percentage (approximately 70 percent) of all Black on Black crime is drug-related, i.e., committed by individuals under the influence of some kind of drugs, we should start our crackdown by demanding severe punishment for those who push dope in our communities. As it stands, we seldom hear or read about a Black drug pusher getting arrested, convicted and receiving a severe prison sentence. Quite to the contrary, dope pushers are being worshipped and hard drugs have become a way of life in the Black community. This must change. Law enforcement authorities must be pressured to stop treating Black dope pushers like petty thieves. They are deadly criminals and should be dealt with as such. By dealing realistically with the dope pusher, we can reduce the flow of drugs into the Black communities and thereby substantially reduce Black on Black crime.

Next to drugs, the fastest growing crime in the Black community is rape. But conviction of rape is less than five percent. The reason for this is that law enforcement officials prefer to believe a convicted rapist rather than accept the word of an honorable Black woman with an excellent reputation, an attitude which, as I mentioned earlier, goes back to slavery. Even some Black policemen who have been part of the plantation justice system for a long time tend to have difficulty believing that somebody had to rape a Black woman, since Black women are often thought of as being promiscuous. To encourage Black rape victims to report the rape, a step without which conviction of rapists is impossible, law enforcement officials—through community action—must be made to cease their insulting attitude toward Black rape victims. Until that has been accomplished, the rapists have every right to feel that the law is on their side.

22. *EBONY* MAGAZINE (AUGUST 1979) A black law enforcement official demands stricter penalties for black criminals.

COMMUNITY INVOLVEMENT

CITIZENS MUST FIGHT BLACK ON BLACK CRIME

Sam Nolan, acting chief of the Chicago police, was deputy superintendent of the department's Bureau of Community Services in 1974 when he addressed a church audience as part of efforts to encourage cooperation with the police by the public. Many policemen contend that the control of crime is the basic responsibility of citizens.

Police cannot solve problems alone, warns Atlanta's chief
By George Napper

23. *EBONY* MAGAZINE (AUGUST 1979) Pleas arose for help from black communities to assist the law enforcement efforts.

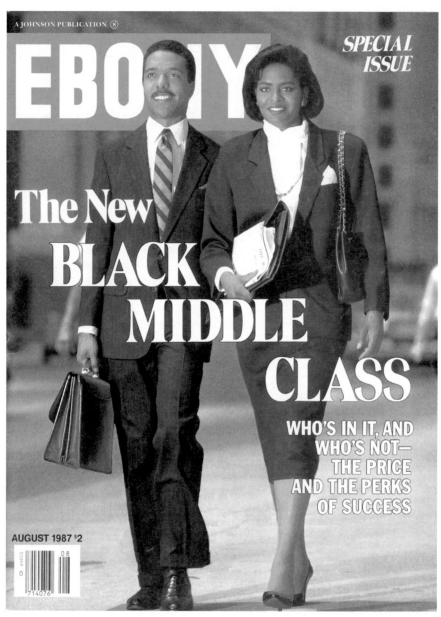

24A. AND 24B. *EBONY* **MAGAZINE (AUGUST 1987, AUGUST 1993)** The magazine promoted middle-class norms for black America.

AUGUST 1993 $2

SPECIAL ISSUE

EBONY The New

BLACK FAMILY

▶ **DETERMINED**

▶ **DYNAMIC**

▶ **DIVERSE**

A JOHNSON PUBLICATION ®

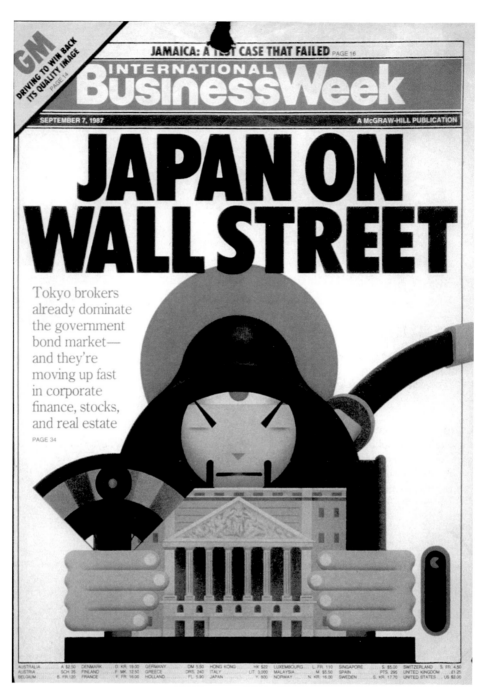

JAMAICA: A TEST CASE THAT FAILED PAGE 16

INTERNATIONAL BusinessWeek

SEPTEMBER 7, 1987 — A McGRAW-HILL PUBLICATION

JAPAN ON WALL STREET

Tokyo brokers
already dominate
the government
bond market—
and they're
moving up fast
in corporate
finance, stocks,
and real estate

PAGE 34

25. *BUSINESS WEEK* (SEPTEMBER 7, 1987) The current narrative describes the unity of "people of color." This cover depicts the economic prowess of Japan. As such, it exemplifies the distinct experiences, culture, and degrees of economic success among non-white, non-Western nations, rather than their commonality.

26. Sunflower, Mississippi (2005) In 1967, New York politicians journeyed to Sunflower for photo ops to promote voter registration. Manhattan borough president Percy Sutton's visit to Sunflower, as contained in the text, is a case in point. He never returned to Sunflower or to aid the black community there. After the drama of the civil rights movement subsided in Sunflower and other Southern venues, Northerners rarely returned. There was no long-term commitment to the black population or the fate of Sunflower. This vacant street represents the decline when economic displacement occurs.

27. President Obama viewing Norman Rockwell New Orleans school integration painting (1964) A pensive President Obama studies the image in 2011. The iconic painting is permanently on display in Stockbridge, Massachusetts. Less than an hour's drive away from Stockbridge, a racial school desegregation has been in the court system for Hartford, Connecticut, since 1989. De facto school segregation has existed in Northern communities both before and after the *Brown v. Board of Education* (1954) desegregation case.

Chapter Five

The Enduring American Dilemma

More Blacks Killed on Streets Than in Vietnam
                                    —*EBONY*, AUGUST 1979

Police Cannot Solve Problems Alone, Warns Atlanta's African American
Chief
                            —GEORGE NAPPER, *EBONY*, AUGUST 1979

...[B]lack-on-black murder...the leading cause of death in black males
fifteen to forty-four....There is nothing more painful to me...than to
walk down the street and hear footsteps and start thinking robbery.
Then [I] look around and see someone white and feel relieved....The
killing is not based on poverty; it is based on greed and violence and
guns....We've got the power...to stop killing each other....There is a
code of silence, based upon fear. Our silence is a sanctuary for killers
and drug dealers....The victim has to rise up.
                                    —REVEREND JESSE JACKSON, 1993

African American children have special needs in this Eurocentric
wasteland of lily-white lies and outright distortions.
    —JEREMIAH A. WRIGHT JR., SENIOR PASTOR AT TRINITY UNITED CHURCH
        OF CHRIST, CHICAGO (BARACK OBAMA, CONGREGANT), 1995

Obama Elected President as Racial Barrier Falls
                            —*NEW YORK TIMES*, NOVEMBER 4, 2008

What is needed is a kind of Marshall Plan for the Abandoned [black
America]—massive intervention in education, public safety, health, and

other aspects of life, with the aim being to arrest the downward spiral.
Otherwise, that phrase which I detest—permanent underclass—will
become our permanent reality.
—EUGENE ROBINSON, PULITZER PRIZE–WINNING BLACK JOURNALIST, 2010

[I] would rather handle everything that the Germans, Italians and
Japanese can throw at me than to face the trouble that I see in the
Negro question.
—GENERAL GEORGE C. MARSHALL
(FOR WHOM THE MARSHALL PLAN IS NAMED), 1943

We have drifted away from basic principles as a people.... I fault integration as part of the reason for us drifting apart as a people.... We
must learn to control our communities, especially economically, and
not depend on outsiders... We are not spending our resources wisely;
maybe instead of drinking eight or nine quarts of beer weekly, it should
be cut down to one.
—DAVID L. JORDAN, BLACK FORMER MISSISSIPPI STATE SENATOR, 2014

Black poverty: 10,020,000 (24.1 percent of African Americans).
3,651,000 (32.9 percent of African American children).
—INCOME AND POVERTY IN THE UNITED STATES, 2015,
UNITED STATES CENSUS BUREAU

Black spokesmen often use a train-ticket metaphor: they demand a
ticket to enter the economic mainstream. But the economic train
does not stop for passengers; it is constantly moving. And blacks are more
severely affected by economic change because they have little ability to
roll with the punches. When America gets a cold, black America gets
pneumonia—the adage has always had validity.

Beginning in the 1970s there were shocks to the American economy,
the first of which was the "oil shock," the consequence of rising oil and
gasoline prices directed by the Middle East oil cartel. The decade also gave
birth to a new term, "stagflation," the deadly combination of economic
stagnation and inflation that sapped America's confidence. The most
vulnerable segment of American society, black America, was hardest hit.
The key to understanding economic change is adaptability, which allows

physical, social, and economic mobility. Underpinning this mobility is education, a requisite especially for African Americans. How would black America respond to these challenges?

The United States in the 1980s would fear a real but exaggerated economic threat from non-Western, nonwhite Japan, whose economic assault brought the leviathan General Motors to its knees. No longer did GM face government scrutiny for market dominance; rather, the critical engine of American growth turned to the government for aid. China succeeded Japan as another non-Western economic competitor. But the computer age catapulted the United States into technological leadership in the 1990s and powered an economic boom.

The twenty-first century began with the devastating attack on New York's World Trade Center. Radical Islamic terrorism grew as an international force. Involvement in another two Iraq wars revealed yet again the complexity of dealing with Islam and oil money in the nuclear age. In 2008 a severe recession destabilized the economy and undermined the country's confidence. The 2008 presidential election propelled an African American into the White House.

The new economy produced winners and losers—cities, states, and corporations. Detroit, Arsenal of Democracy, was a loser. It succumbed to foreign competition, government mismanagement, and, in 2013, debt default. Reeling from its demise, the city underwent a humiliating restructuring process. African Americans who comprised 83 percent of Detroit's population bore the brunt.

Public pension fund indebtedness, not a concern in the 1960s, began to create havoc for state and local budgets. New York City's 2016 school budget, as noted earlier, was $29.6 billion, of which a whopping $6.5 billion was designated for teacher pensions and benefits. (People have forgotten New York City's insolvency in 1975.) Controversy over the power and impact of teachers' unions entered the racial domain. A battle royal, with enormous racial implications, is now joined between the teachers' unions and their non-union competitor, charter schools. Police unions have squared off against black communities in championing their own respective interests.

The all-male, virtually all-white undergraduate Yale College of the 1960s changed dramatically, as did other schools. Despite aggressive recruitment and the accommodation of blacks, racial tension has plagued

Yale, a bastion of power and wealth. With its unlimited resources and exclusively progressive faculty and administration, the school would seem to be the ideal place to cultivate racial harmony. Yale has a $26 billion endowment; by contrast, the top ten endowments at HBCUs together do not reach $2 billion. When a black student enters Yale, that student instantly becomes part of a privileged set. Blacks comprise 12 percent of the class of 2021.[1] In the mid-1960s Yale offered just one course in African American history, a seminar called "The Negro in American History," and three courses in African studies. By 2016 a student could find forty-nine courses in African American studies and forty-five courses in African studies.

The Marshall Plan:
The Coattail Effect on Black America

Discussions about race usually lead to requests for money. When speaking about the needs of the black community, black spokesmen in particular resort to an analogy with the Marshall Plan, the economic aid program funded by the United States to promote the recovery of Europe after World War II. For several years beginning in 1948, almost $13 billion was loaned or given to Western European countries. The funds were used to purchase imports (mainly from the United States) and rebuild the shattered industrial complexes of Europe. The Marshall Plan was used to restore the economic systems of countries that had once enjoyed functioning economies.

Over the years, however, the Marshall Plan became a useful analogy in requesting money for large-scale economic programs in the United States, even though such programs bore no resemblance to the circumstances of the Marshall Plan.[2] Black leaders are not alone in

---

1 Yale's category "black" does not explicitly state whether it consists solely of African Americans or includes those of African descent, i.e., Africans and Caribbean blacks. In 2003, Henry Louis Gates Jr. noted that as many as two-thirds of Harvard University students, classified as blacks, were of West Indian and African descent or biracial rather than African American, i.e., "in which all four grandparents were born in America, descendants of slaves."

2 The Marshall Plan has an indirect link to race via cotton: the blueprint for the famous plan was heavily influenced by William Clayton, a partner in Anderson, Clayton, and Company, the world's largest cotton brokerage firm. Because of his sophisticated knowledge of international trade, Clayton was appointed assistant secretary of state for economic affairs in the Truman administration. His background enabled him to formulate a highly workable program for Europe's

inappropriately hopping on the Marshall Plan bandwagon. A partial list of other hopefuls would include calls by conservatives and liberals in 1999 to rebuild the Balkans; to provide money and technical support to developing countries in 2001–2002 and allow them to reduce poverty; to combat terrorism in the Middle East in 2002; and to support a democracy-building project in Iraq in 2003. John Kerry could not resist riding the coattails of the Marshall Plan. In an early 2017 interview, the secretary of state called for a Marshall Plan to aid the youth of the Middle East when the context was inappropriate. It is surprising that the Marshall Plan has not been converted into a verb form—*the United States should Marshall-Plan Country X*, or *Country Y should be Marshall-Planned*.

Blacks, and a few white spokesmen, sought an identification with the Marshall Plan's success in order to obtain funds for various initiatives. Whitney Young Jr. recognized the advantages of such a program. "A nation that invested $17 billion to restore a Europe ravaged by World War II," wrote the director of the National Urban League in 1964, "should be able to create a domestic Marshall Plan to enable Negro citizens to compete in the free enterprise marketplace." Martin Luther King Jr. followed: "The National Urban League, in an excellent statement, has underlined the fact that we find nothing strange about the Marshall Plan... [helping] our own handicapped black multitudes." In 1982 the *New Yorker* writer Ken Auletta recommended "a domestic Marshall Plan... as many civil-rights leaders have advocated." The black writer Anthony Walton in 1999 suggested a technological Marshall Plan to aid black students. In 2010 the black journalist Eugene Robinson was quite specific: "What is needed is a kind of Marshall Plan for the Abandoned—massive intervention in education, public safety, health, and other aspects of life, with the aim being to arrest the downward spiral. Otherwise, that phrase I detest—permanent underclass—will become our permanent reality."

An expenditure well beyond the scope of the Marshall Plan did occur during the fifty years following the civil rights movement of the 1960s. Trillions of dollars were spent on black education, health, and community

---

reentry into the commercial world. George C. Marshall, as secretary of state, announced this enormous undertaking at the Harvard University commencement in June 1947. In fact, the outline of the plan had been circulated a month earlier by Secretary of State Dean Acheson to the Delta Council, a group of cotton growers, on the campus of Delta State University in the Mississippi Delta town of Cleveland.

life. Still, reforms advocated by black groups continue to concentrate on raising money from governments, foundations, individuals, and corporate sources. What has been the result? Has there been accountability?

In 2016 black spokesmen still blame white institutional racism for the problems facing black America. Even the definition of racial integration remains in flux between the black desire for separation and a functional assimilation. Impatient with the income and wealth gap between the races, with actual and perceived discrimination, with police/community friction, many Americans want policy recommendations: "What should we do?" What program or what grand scheme will succeed if so many efforts have not closed the economic gap or elevated the black underclass?

Blacks bear some responsibility for failing to follow the 1960s advice of Whitney Young Jr., Martin Luther King Jr., and Roy Wilkins. Each of these leaders was at the forefront of the civil rights movement. Each made demands of black people to overcome their "shortcomings." In 2008 Senator Barack Obama spoke: "We also have to demand more from ourselves... [and] to realize that responsibility does not end at conception, that what makes them a man is not the ability to have a child but the courage to raise one." Following this pronouncement, the Reverend Jesse Jackson famously criticized presidential candidate Obama for "talking down to black people." "I want to cut his nuts off," Jackson added. In 2015 as president, Obama omitted the word "responsibility" from his speech to the NAACP. Today there is little talk of responsibility and more talk of grievances, without the crucial process of self-criticism.

The programs aimed at support for blacks following the race riots of the sixties and the 1968 Kerner Report did not fulfill their grand promises and expectations within twenty years. Yet another commission, the 1988 Commission on Cities, produced a scorecard, "Quiet Riots: Race and Poverty in the United States," evaluating the effectiveness of the Kerner Report. Because twenty years had passed, readers had to be reminded of the magnitude of the race riots: "The severity of the riots [1965-1969]," wrote one of the contributors, John Hebers, "[is] little remembered by most Americans." He recounted the statistics: "250 killed—far more than died in two decades of nonviolent protest in the South—12,000...injured, 83,000...arrested." If by 1988 some had forgotten, by 2016 almost everyone would have to be reminded of the catastrophic nature of the riots. The increased "sophistication" of the police and the damaging reaction to the riots recognized by black leaders put a halt to the degree of these disturbances.

One of the cornerstones of the Kerner Report, the relationship of police to black urban communities, has never been resolved. The paradox—the hostility of ghetto dwellers toward the police and the absolute need for adequate police protection in these high-crime areas—still festers. The Kerner recommendations—more black policemen and officers, community service, proper grievance and complaint procedures—are still put forward today. In August 1979 an *Ebony* magazine article identified an exception: the dual standard of justice whereby blacks in 1968 felt that police were too lenient toward black-on-black crime. "If a black man kills another black man, the law is generally enforced at its minimum," testified a journalist. "Violence of every type runs rampant in a ghetto."

The few bright spots of progress in black communities since Kerner may be covered quickly. A significant number of urban blacks moved into the middle class—still a fragile status. The "coalitions" between "government and businesses" provided a "glimmer of hope" regarding employment (though there was extensive voluntary cooperation between the government and the private sector beginning in the 1960s, well before the Kerner Report). The scorecard on Kerner cited a surge in black elected officials.

The title of the 1988 report, "Quiet Riots," was meant to contrast the urban ghettos of that day to those of the violent race riots of the 1960s. It referred to the worsening condition of unemployment, poverty, social disorganization, segregation, family disintegration, housing and school deterioration, and crime: "Poverty is worse than it was twenty years ago.... There is a large and growing urban underclass in America, made up of blacks and Hispanics in the central cities. They are more economically isolated, more socially isolated, than ever before." These conditions, declared the editors, Fred Harris and Roger Wilkins, were *more* destructive of human life than the race riots of the 1960s.

The term "black underclass," infrequently used before the Kerner Report was written, by 1988 had become commonplace. The situation had gone from "bad to worst" despite the "Great Society programs..., the sweeping anti-discrimination and affirmative-action legislation." What's more, "Quiet Riots" conveniently downplayed the huge sums of money expended on programs for blacks by allowing simply that the government did "throw money at the problems." Discussions of the pathology of the ghetto always enumerated the same items—"crime, family disruption, teenage pregnancy, drugs, joblessness, failing schools, and dilapidated housing."

"Quiet Riots" proposals—more money for similar programs—have a familiar ring from the 1960s to the twenty-first century. Job training was the "greatest need." After that, desegregation, affirmative action, health, and child development. The welfare system was failing. Even liberal senator Edward Kennedy in 1978 had been appalled by its results. "We say to this child," lamented Kennedy, "wait, there is a way, one way you can be somebody to someone. We will give you an apartment and furniture to fill it. We will give you a TV set and a telephone. We will give you clothing, and cheap food, and free medical care...and in return, you only have to do one thing: just go out and have a baby. And faced with such an offer, it is no surprise that hundreds of thousands have been caught in the trap that our welfare system has become."

Like the Kerner Report, "Quiet Riots" made no reference to personal responsibility, preparation, or "shortcomings." These words from black leaders of the 1960s were buried. Instead by 1988 the entire blame for black social conditions was seen to be the system imposed by white America. "The problem," wrote one of the authors of "Quiet Riots," "is not a problem of defective people; the problem is a problem of a defective system." Veering away from statistics, "Quiet Riots" quotes the sociologist Lee Rainwater, who blamed the plight of inner-city blacks on "white cupidity."

If hopes and dreams had not materialized twenty years after the Kerner Report, almost fifty years later the same problems remain. In 2016 one city of particular interest was Milwaukee, the subject of a 1967

Ebony article titled "Miracle in Milwaukee" and the scene of racial tension in the 1960s. Beginning in July 1967 this city, then of 750,000 with 85,000 blacks (11 percent), had suffered a race riot with three killed and a hundred injured.

The *Ebony* story concentrated on a militant NAACP movement in Milwaukee comprising of black youths with the unlikely leadership combination of Prentice McKenney, a nineteen-year-old angry black, and an equally outraged Father James E. Groppi, a white Catholic priest highly committed to the black cause. The youths called themselves Commandos. Their goal was open housing and an end to housing discrimination. McKenney's rhetoric was unabashedly anti-white: "You've got to threaten these crackers...only a massive show of force by black people will make whitey act right." Father Groppi sanctioned the use of violence by blacks "if other techniques don't work." Mayor Henry Maier, fearing white flight, opposed open occupancy. In protest, two thousand NAACP militants marched across Kosciuszko Bridge into the Polish section of Milwaukee, asserting their pride and revolutionary zeal. Soon a fight between teenagers escalated into a full-scale riot.

Years later, racial violence erupted in Milwaukee in August 2016 when a black policeman, Dominique Heaggan-Brown, shot a black armed suspect. Several days of racial violence followed. Looting, fires, gunshots, and a police show of force rattled the ghetto. Brown was charged with first-degree reckless homicide. Given the obvious facts of the case, it seems apparent that he would have been charged even without the destructive riot that ensued.

Fifty years after the civil rights era, Milwaukee's black population had grown to 238,000 (40 percent) in a city of—thanks to white flight—fewer than 600,000 residents. The statistics are grim. Seventy-five percent of black students attend schools that are 90 percent black. Fewer than 16 percent of public school children tested at grade level in reading while only 20 percent were proficient in math. The overall black unemployment rate was 17.3 percent, that of whites 4 percent. Black male unemployment was even higher. Single-parent families made up 70 percent of the black population. High school student suspensions for blacks were at 56 percent (4 percent for whites).

Class distinctions within black America were also evident in *Ebony*. Hillsborough, California, a wealthy San Francisco suburb, is a long way from the Milwaukee ghetto. In November 1967 *Ebony* had profiled Karen Hutchison, a fourteen-year-old black pianist from Hillsborough. The prodigy had been raised by her mother, who was a graduate of the Music Institute of San Jose, and her father, a successful physician. Karen Hutchison, a student at Notre Dame High School, was mastering Bach, Mozart, and Chopin. The *Ebony* article mirrored the reality of differences that would become more pronounced as elite blacks distinguished themselves from the larger black community.

Jobs

The elimination of poverty in the black community, as elsewhere, depends on job readiness and job availability. Myriad federal programs have failed to transform employment for blacks in the workforce. By the 1980s unemployment for the black underclass remained dire, and it remains so today. Despite a massive effort, penetration in the private sector is severely lacking. Black ownership of businesses has improved but is hardly stellar. Despite government and corporate programs, why didn't the efforts work on a large scale?

One example, among many, of government-sponsored programs is described in Ken Auletta's 1992 book *The Underclass*. (The author worried that his use of the term "underclass" was somehow racist.) Auletta tried to find out why money, time, and energy produced feeble results and few hard numbers or accountability. He did it by investigating a single job-training program, the Manhattan-based Manpower Demonstration Research Corporation. The MDRC, formed in 1974, was specially geared toward helping youths train for jobs. It received federal support for a five-year program that enrolled ten thousand young people. Two-thirds did not finish the program; one-third did complete the program and enter the workforce, but their subsequent job performance was not tracked.

The MDRC received $21.5 million from the federal government and the Ford Foundation. The entire government Job Corps program for training, according to Auletta, was spending $13,000 per person annually for 41,500 enrollees, a total of $539.5 million. The MDRC program, wrote Auletta, "had some success, but it is expensive." His description of "some success" included no data; instead he meandered into a discussion about the stifling impact of arbitrary budget limits. It is difficult to see how the MDRC could be called a success. In many cases the statistical impact of such large programs is either ignored or subject to politically induced inflation. The need to track results is absolutely essential to enforce accountability.

Auletta discusses the overall condition of the black underclass, offering familiar statistics. The dysfunctional family in 1979, for example, included more than 70 percent of black families in urban ghettos that were "maintained by a single woman."

As to solutions, Auletta could only suggest more government expenditures. He noted the possibility of a government Marshall Plan, "a vast increase in federal funds spent on public jobs, subsidized housing, and other entitlements for the poor." A "guaranteed income and a decent national welfare standard" were also mentioned. Interestingly, with the US economy in shambles in the early 1980s, Auletta acknowledged the appeal of West German and Japanese models of centralized government control and the symbiosis of the public and private sectors. But unlike the United States, Japan and West Germany are highly homogeneous countries, and, in the case of Japan, extremely hierarchical. Their concepts and practices do not travel well to these shores.

In the twentieth century the figures show a growing black middle class and an elite segment of the black population that has excelled in every aspect of American life. A few black senior business executives have become household names. A partial list would include Richard Parsons (Citicorp, Time Warner), Kenneth Chenault (American Express), Ursula Burns (Xerox), and Kenneth Frazier (Merck). While the black middle class has expanded, its economic status is precarious, supported by a relatively small asset base. Black unemployment and poor housing remain at crisis levels. The racial wealth gap has increased. The Institute of Policy Studies and the Corporation for Enterprise Development reported in August 2016 that the average wealth of white families had increased three times the rate of black families' wealth over the last thirty years. Penetration of the marketplace is dismal for black-owned businesses. In 2014 black-owned firms comprised only 2 percent of American firms with paid employees.

America's corporations are clamoring for black employees; business schools are eagerly attempting to recruit black students. Every major corporation has a diversity department whose task is to increase black and minority employment and shepherd its progress. Affirmative action, initiated by private companies in the early 1960s, continues. General Mills in 2016 demanded that its advertising firms be staffed by 50 percent women and 20 percent minorities. Still, such efforts over the last five decades evidently have not worked. The difficulty remains the small pipeline of qualified applicants. The inability of blacks to enter the private sector is based on several factors—education, some reluctance to enter the business world, the lack of a commercial tradition, poor choice of career paths in business, and, in many cases, a separatist mentality. A segregated background, whether forced or by choice, is a distinct hindrance for blacks. The problem, if it exists at all, is far less pronounced among Asians and Asian Americans.

Deference to assimilation and proper guidance will substantially increase black access to and success in the private sector, and thus reduce the racial income and wealth gap. After interviewing a select group of black Harvard Business School graduates and black participants in the A Better Chance (ABC) enrichment program, the black journalist Ellis Cose in 2011 reported optimistically about the prospects of blacks. Cose clearly recognized the pivot from an earlier generation's struggle: "I remember my paternal grandmother say, 'Get your education. It's the one thing they can't take away.' They were trying to prepare us for a world in which everything wasn't fair. I think the message to our children now changes...you can't blame white people for whatever failures you may have. It's what you are capable of doing. It's what your values are. It's how hard you work."

One of Cose's respondents reported the obvious, that a Harvard degree "made the workplace easier to navigate." Another remarked on the need to "give up some blackness or appear to have given up 'being black.'" Others mentioned the need to fit in but did not elaborate: "If you're willing to talk like a white guy, if you're willing to completely assimilate, you will be successful." What does talking and writing like a white man mean? Is it a form of discrimination or an acceptance of Western middle-class values? This same graduate warned blacks not to be "pigeonholed" into "diversity positions." Cose advised blacks to work in areas that have revenue streams and are "quantifiable." One fifty-year-old woman thought young blacks were "extremely" naive in not valuing "contacts and networks." In addition to a black network, white networks and mentors, according to Cose, were essential. "I found older white men to be my best mentors and sponsors," said one graduate. The identity aspect never vanishes for anyone, especially blacks. We all have multiple identities and must learn how to steer accordingly. This does not mean negating cultural, family, or regional heritage; it does mean avoiding hypersensitivity. Cose quoted the black historian Manning Marable, who highlighted the "paradox of integration." For Marable, integration into the mainstream meant disrupting racial solidarity across social and economic lines. Marable was wrong. This is not a paradox; it is a natural phenomenon.

The choice of careers and college majors, either through lack of understanding or aversion to the private sector, widens the racial wealth gap between blacks and whites. One way to close the gap is to encourage graduates to choose a high-paying job in the private sector. At one end of the spectrum, black Harvard MBAs in 2009 had a median starting salary of $134,000. Even in this highly educated segment of the black community, choice of careers, rather than race, skews income. Fifty-four percent of Harvard MBAs worked in the private sector, but only 35 percent of the ABC alumni worked for corporations. Nine percent of the Harvard graduates worked for nonprofits versus 21 percent of the ABC alumni. Sixty percent of the Harvard MBAs earned more than $200,000 annually; only 15 percent of the ABC alumni had incomes of more than $200,000 by their mid-forties. Of note is that 72 percent of the Harvard MBAs came from middle- or upper-middle-class families, but 55 percent of the ABC alumni came from poor neighborhoods. If income gap is an important problem, preparation for a private-sector career is paramount.

In the course of reporting on Harvard MBAs, Cose endorsed the "cultural and values-oriented [behavioral] norms" of a Chicago-based charter school approach. At the core of Perspectives Charter Schools is "a disciplined life," including "perseverance, hard work, and time management." Race-neutral middle-class values matter.

In 2016 Georgetown University produced a compelling study, "African Americans: College Majors and Earnings," which detailed the concentration of blacks in "lower-paying majors." They were underrepresented in the "fastest-growing, highest-paying occupations."

African Americans account for only 8 percent of general engineering majors, 7 percent of math majors...only 5 percent of computer
engineering majors [and] 7 percent of finance and marketing majors.
In health majors, they account for 10 percent but clustered in the
lowest-earning detailed major: 21 percent are in health and medical
administrative services, compared to only 6 percent in the higher-
earning detailed major of pharmacy, pharmaceutical science, and
administration. African Americans are also highly represented in
majors associated with serving the community which tend to be low
earning—human services and community organization (20%) and
social work (19%)....[Even worse,] since 2009...the percentage of
African Americans with industrial and...engineering technologies
majors decreased by 4 percentage points and 3 percentage points,
respectively. [The representation in majors for lower-paying jobs] saw
a slight increase...by 3 percentage points.

This observation is not news. The black writer Anthony Walton
described the historical impact of technology on African Americans in
a 1999 article in the *Atlantic*. He warned of dire consequences if blacks
did not focus on education and technology. He cited the "shockingly
low percentage of blacks who earned PhDs in computer science (1.8%),
engineering (2.1%), physical sciences (1.5%), and mathematics (0.6%)"
in 1995. Walton concluded that "by tolerating and not questioning the
folkways that encouraged it, blacks are [keeping] themselves...out of the
mainstream once again." By "folkways" he meant black culture, which
determined "aspiration and behavior." Walton was blunt: "[B]lacks must
change....Otherwise they will be unable to cross the next technological
threshold that emerges in human civilization." Wealthy technology giants
Bill Gates and Larry Ellison, according to Walton, should generously
finance math and science education in elementary schools. This appeal
for private funds is directly opposed to Black Lives Matter's declared goal
of eliminating private support of public education.

Historically Booker T. Washington was the most effective black
spokesman for the prioritization of economics and business. The Wizard
of Tuskegee was severely restricted by white America's racial policies
and attitudes and by blacks' failure to emphasize business. Washington's
attempt to develop a self-sufficient black economy at the turn of the

twentieth century was ultimately doomed. But by the end of the century his advocacy and understanding of a financial stepping-stone approach, from modest business ventures to major corporate and financial power, proved to be indeed prescient and practical. The limitations of the segregated world, whether legal, de facto, or self-imposed, have given way to opportunities in an integrated world. It is time to revisit Washington's dream of economic stature.

Booker T. Washington's influence was manifest in the rise of Aaron Henry, head of Mississippi's NAACP in the 1960s. Henry's father, Ed Henry, had decided to follow Booker T. Washington's example. He left his sharecropping life on a farm near the Delta town of Clarksdale in 1927 and opened a shoe repair shop in Webb, Mississippi, a majority black town of a thousand people. Through his connection with the Southern Leather Company, he became a business entrepreneur with white as well as black customers. He gained economic independence. His son Aaron went to school and became a pharmacist in Clarksdale. Familiar with the Delta's racial mores, Aaron Henry knew how to navigate between blacks and whites. He had developed close friendships with poor whites on the farm, and he also bore the brunt of indignities, firebombing, and gunfire, but he never became bitter or lost sight of his integrationist goals. He chose the biracially oriented NAACP and the Mississippi Freedom Democratic Party over the militant, separatist Student Nonviolent Coordinating Committee. In interviews he abhorred the violence of the 1960s urban race riots. Today Aaron Henry is remembered in Mississippi with biographies and historical plaques. The Booker T. Washington–influenced independence of his father surely contributed to Aaron Henry's private-sector success and his achievements.

From the black underclass to the middle class to the elite, a variety of factors plague African Americans' full participation in the benefits of the economic mainstream. Many of these employment-related issues are race neutral; all derive from educational performance, societal preference, and individual choice. The much-discussed impact of de-industrialization on black employment could be mitigated by education and/or vocational training. There needs to be a regimented approach to training the black underclass. To date there has been little understanding of why programs have not been effective. Necessary accountability over an extended period of time is sorely lacking. Fifty years after the racial pivot of the 1960s, America is still dealing with many of the same issues described in the Kerner Report.

A noticeable change from the 1960s is the current hypersensitivity to actual or perceived job discrimination. The Equal Employment Opportunity Commission (EEOC) reports an astounding thirty-one thousand racial discrimination complaints filed in 2015. In April 2016 even the *New York Times* was hit with a racial discrimination lawsuit. But such litigation offers no solution to the chronic employment predicament of black America.

Still Seeking a Better Education

One generation, approximately twenty-five years, after the *Brown* decision, racial integration in school systems, community-based school districts, busing, and funding were still in question. Without an adequate educational background, the mass of the black underclass has no hope of entering the economic mainstream. Among the elite, the various segments of the middle class, and the underclass, a close examination reveals problems in all sectors. One bright spot is the performance of black women in universities, where 69 percent of the black students who entered graduate school in 2015 were black women.

The courts have been wading through cases of racial integration in secondary education for decades. Even the desirability of complete racial integration remains in doubt. *Brown*, a great victory, removed the stigma of forced segregation, but it did not provide a blueprint for effecting integration. Residential segregation in the North and South proved to be a rude awakening for America: the difficulty of busing black children out of their neighborhoods and into white schools was virtually insurmountable.

Thus the Congress of Racial Equality in 1970 recommended rejection of "extensive busing" in favor of decentralized community schools controlled by blacks—a scheme diametrically opposed to integration. Further attraction to self-segregation followed. In 1979 *Brown* was reinterpreted by Robert Carter, an NAACP lawyer who had tried the case, to mean educational opportunity rather than racial integration. This was part of a demand for more money for black schools. The influential Derrick Bell, the first black to teach law at Harvard, and an NAACP attorney, had doubts about the "emphasis on racial mixing" and turned his attention to the "creation and development of 'model' all-black schools." According to Bell, "model all-black schools" might be better than racially mixed schools:

> ...Rather than beat our heads against the wall seeking pupil-desegregation...[we] could have organized parents and communities to ensure effective implementation of equal funding...mandates.

Bell even expressed his unambiguous separatist intent through his fictional character Geneva: "We need...to push for more money...in all-black schools rather than exhaust ourselves and our resources on ethereal integration in mainly white suburbs." The educational fight became one over funding, not integration. In 1977 the Supreme Court allowed funding for "programs in the inner city, predominantly minority schools, as an alternative to racial mixing." Many black parents agreed that neighborhood schools were preferable to busing to integrated ones. As funding moved to the top of the black agenda, controversy followed over changes in local tax laws and the raising of taxes.

Teachers' unions have gained considerable power, and their benefits, regulations, and political sway are now major parts of educational decisions. The power of the unions has been channeled into politics and education. Reform after reform has been attempted; none has succeeded on a massive scale. Budget considerations and population shifts brought school closings in cities like Chicago, where blacks suffered job losses in the process. When New Orleans converted to charter schools after Katrina, one of the explicit arguments against the move was the loss of 20 percent of the black teachers. The Bill and Melinda Gates Foundation and the Broad Foundation were heavily involved in the transition; hence they were singled out for condemnation in the Movement for Black Lives platform. A similar reaction had appeared in the North when integration threatened the existence of racially segregated schools in the late nineteenth and early twentieth centuries. In all these situations black children have served as the pawns in political gambits.

A battle is now being waged by the teachers' unions against charter schools, which are publicly funded and non-unionized, and aimed at educating minorities in the cities. Entrepreneurial charter schools arose because of the deficiencies of traditional public schools, which simply failed to educate poor blacks and Hispanics. The teachers' unions and their allies counter with complaints of underfunding and unfair competition from charters. They accuse the attractive charters of being highly selective in their choice of students, of suspending students for disciplinary infractions, and of an inordinate concentration on test scores. The closely watched results of charters are generally superior to those of public schools. Test scores of black and Hispanic students have improved. Predictably, some charter schools have failed. The teachers' unions, in a fit of rhetorical excess, accuse charter school advocates of trying to privatize education.

The question remains whether charter schools can, with their logistical problems, change the course of black secondary education or even influence public schools. Particularly difficult is the rapid turnover of charter school teachers, who often wilt under the pressures of the job. But the charter schools do represent constructive competition for public schools beset by sclerotic behavior. A guildlike civil service attitude permeates much of the education establishment. Performance benchmarks, such as high school graduation rates, have often become a fraudulent exercise, with undeserving students being graduated in order to pad statistics. The rules on early teacher retirement encourage a civil service attitude, as if schools are a war zone where it is necessary to limit combat duty. In truth the classroom environment, for many social reasons, is often not conducive to teacher engagement. Lest we forget, President Barack Obama's daughters have enjoyed the benefits of the exclusive private Sidwell Friends School (tuition $34,000 plus) in Washington. By example the Obamas have shunned the public school system, just as the black elite is disconnected from the inner-city educational system. Obama's former education chief, Arne Duncan, sent his children to schools in suburban Virginia, where he had chosen to live.

For charter schools, black and Hispanic students are the prize. Charter schools point to exceedingly large applications as a strong indicator of demand. But if there had been a groundswell of support, and if education in the black community was an important priority, voting patterns in local, state, and federal elections would have shown it. This has yet to happen. Segments of the black community, including the NAACP, Black Lives Matter, politicians, and black teachers' union members, are vociferously opposed to charter schools and to voucher programs that would pay parents to choose schools for their children. The enormous past success of parochial schools is buried in an ideological disdain for religious schools.

On October 15, 2016, the NAACP approved a resolution calling for a moratorium on charter schools. Chiefly interested in control and funding, the organization rationalized its stance by criticizing an allegedly harsh student suspension policy, diversion of funds away from public schools, and a selection process that enrolled the best students while leaving the difficult applicants to the public system. As an aside, the NAACP mentioned the racially segregated aspect of charter schools. Notably, the teachers' union contributed $400,000 to the NAACP.

The NAACP's action was really about jobs, pensions, benefits, and tenure protection for black teachers, not the education of children. In a sensationalist attack, the NAACP invoked a misplaced historical analogy:

> [R]esearchers have warned that charter school expansions in low-income communities mirror predatory lending practices that led to the sub-prime mortgage disaster, putting schools and communities impacted by these practices at great risk of loss and harm ...

Charter schools should be given a chance but should also be subject to rigorous examination. Another factor, racial integration, is a deliberate casualty because charter schools are designed for low-performing black and Hispanic children. Given that racially segregated housing is anchored in cement, the segregation endemic to charters is an almost unavoidable alternative, as realistic NAACP lawyers recognized about "model black schools" beginning in 1970.

Myriad government and private-sector enrichment programs have failed to pull education out of the racial quagmire. Currently the *New York Times* and the *Wall Street Journal* regularly cheerlead and highlight a small, somewhat successful school, class, program, or teacher perceived to be capable of large-scale replication. Money is certainly available for these efforts. On August 13, 2016, the *Wall Street Journal*

profiled one such educator, the middle-school principal of Mott Hall
Bridges Academy in Brooklyn, established by Nadia Lopez. Her school
now has three hundred students. The Robin Hood Foundation, composed of Wall Street super wealth, will pounce on any educational
proposal in the New York area that can be explained with compelling
metrics. Unfortunately, no revolution derives from their commendable largesse. Fixing an inner-city school system is not the same as
investment speculation, technological innovation, entrepreneurship,
or investment prowess—or luck. Facebook founder Mark Zuckerberg
alone shoveled $100 million into the Newark, New Jersey, school system
with no results. The celebrity Zuckerberg considered his expensive foray
into Newark education a learning experience.

Examples abound of well-funded specialized programs that have
proliferated. Both Prep for Prep (a New York City program with one hundred and fifty students per year) and A Better Chance (which has some
regional offices) find students as early as the fourth grade, place them in
private schools, monitor their progress, supply enrichment programs, and
follow their path through college. These programs can be highly labor
intensive and costly; the tracking of even this small number of students
can be difficult. The imaginative Young Women's Leadership Network
(YWLN) can handle larger numbers of students because it supplements
existing school programs with a dedicated and well-organized staff.
YWLN, which currently has a presence in twenty-four schools—throughout the nation but mostly in New York City—cannot transform a large
urban school system, but its model is efficient and effective.

The behemoth of educational reform programs, Teach For America,
which had a $321 million operating budget in 2014, has existed since 1989
without making a major impact on black inner-city or rural educational
prospects. TFA scatters college graduates to a variety of schools with
large enrollments of black and Hispanic children, from New York to the
Mississippi Delta to Los Angeles. The eager, bright TFA teachers represent
cheap labor where teacher recruitment is difficult. One of TFA's main
justifications is its role in leading college students into the educational
field; certainly many have followed careers in education, but the schools
in which they teach have not been transformed. Many of these highly
labor-intensive programs are commendable but limited in addressing the
enormous scope of underclass black education. It should be noted that

the Black Lives Matter platform specifically calls for eliminating Teach For America.

Of the many school issues—politics, funding, unions, decentralized community control, and private support of public schools—racial identity and racial control are among the most contentious. Black values and black culture are generally invoked. The uniqueness of black culture in opposition to white middle-class behavioral norms was specifically encountered, as we have seen, in the 1968 Ocean Hill–Brownsville battle. At the time the African American Teachers Association denounced what it perceived as white middle-class values—individualism, competition, materialism, elitism, and capitalism. These values are now formalized succinctly as "acting white," which some blacks regard as the present-day version of passing for white. Instead a black principal in 1968 called for "egalitarianism, mutualism, spontaneity … and moving talents." The teachers had to be black and "identify with and speak the language of the black [inner city] community." Today blacks want someone "who looks like them" as a teacher or mentor. On trial are the middle-class skill sets—reading, writing, arithmetic, work ethic—taught in a traditional manner.

The concept of discipline remains of paramount importance in programs for black education. Blacks and whites have disagreed about it from the "disruptive child clause" argument in 1968 over the United Federation of Teachers contract in New York, to the school suspension controversy of 2016. A provision to eliminate school suspensions is part of the Black Lives Matter platform—likely motivated to some degree by the prospect of job creation. (In lieu of suspensions, BLM advocates more black teachers.) In the 1960s blacks reasoned that suspensions were discriminatory. Moreover, disruptive behavior in black children was seen as positive—"the sign of a non-conformist" and evidence of a "highly creative imagination." CORE went so far as to argue that "cursing and physical altercations" should be excused. Talking back to figures of authority was permissible. The twenty-first-century interpretation blames suspension for the high rate of black incarceration.

The highly praised Harlem Children's Zone (HCZ), founded by the charismatic Geoffrey Canada in the 1990s, was quickly forced to confront the seemingly eternal questions of assimilation, middle-class values, and discipline. The HCZ experiment covered almost a hundred blocks in Harlem and connected HCZ schools with social issues in the community. By 2013 it had grown to more than twelve thousand students with a $101 million budget. Much of the program is privately funded. Its results and its ability to measure them are not clear, but the effort illustrates that large sums of private money are available for such projects.

As described by the writer Paul Tough, Geoffrey Canada learned the perils of separation at Bowdoin College, which he entered in 1970. Canada observed self-segregation on campus at the Afro-American Center, which was closed to white students after 5 p.m. If black students failed to attend weekly meetings at the center, they were ostracized. Black students congregated on one dorm floor, named the Ghetto.

These deterrents to interaction with white students served to restrict postgraduate connections. Nevertheless, Canada understood the need for assimilation and the importance of interaction with whites and was able to attract billionaire hedge fund manager Stan Druckenmiller and a bevy of Wall Street benefactors to bankroll the Harlem Children's Zone.[3]

Canada, an enthusiastic proponent of middle-class aspirations, found lack of discipline his most glaring problem. Effectiveness could be blocked by disruption; the school's greatest obstacle at the start was behavior. Instilling "appropriate behavior" was deemed necessary to enter the "mainstream working world." Druckenmiller advocated "intense monitoring and shaping of behavioral patterns" in a "military style, real rote-learning, [and the] rote-behavior thing" copied from a charter school. The billionaire benefactor, in a politically incorrect moment, categorized disruptive students as "bad apples."

Canada did not want blacks to "reject completely the values and habits of Harlem," but he did not define the values and habits he admired. When he retired in 2014, his valedictory remarks reflected Western middle-class values. The HCZ, he said, "is about working hard, focusing on college, being responsible, delaying pregnancy and childbearing until you're a professional."

---

3 Self-segregation is present. Despite the discredited example of Bowdoin, in March 2016 the University of Oregon, bowing to pressure from black students, announced the establishment of a separate black residential community on campus and invited six black fraternities to locate there.

Another education program, the SEED School of Baltimore, unlike the HCZ, takes inner-city students out of the toxic environment of their ghetto. As described by Thomas Friedman in the *New York Times*, the kids live in a dormitory during the school week and return home for the weekend. The physical separation, according to President Obama's secretary of education, Arne Duncan, from a dysfunctional or nonexistent family and gangs was deemed necessary to instill proper values.

Self-Examination

Joel Klein, chancellor of New York City schools in the early years of the twenty-first century, believed that confidence in a child derived from "core academic education." Klein considered grades more important than the contrived empathetic promotion of individual self-esteem. The "cold reality of a report card," rather than a "feel good" campaign, he said, "breeds genuine confidence." Nadia Lopez presented straightforward goals for her students: "They need to know how to make money and how to get into industries where they're underrepresented as a group.... They don't need to be saved." This echoes the advice of the civil rights giants of the 1960s regarding preparation for citizenship—and goes even further back to Booker T. Washington.

One reason this approach gains ground so painfully is that self-examination is virtually absent in black society. The destructive aspects of black culture or values are denied, rationalized, or treated sympathetically rather than realistically. Take single-parent families, for example. The black journalist Eugene Robinson does acknowledge the detrimental behavioral norms of the urban ghetto, but he softens the message. In his book *Disintegration* (2010) he wrote that the astronomical levels of black single parenthood were given too much emphasis. But he recommended that black preachers "hammer home" the need for marriage. Typically, he viewed single-parent families as a "society-wide phenomenon," thereby excusing blacks.

The black CNN newscaster Don Lemon reaped a harvest of criticism in 2013 when he dared condemn single parenthood among blacks. "Black people," Lemon declared, "if you really want to fix the problem, here's just five things that you should think about doing." The No. 1 item

on that list—"and probably the most important," he said—had to do with
out-of-wedlock births.

> Just because you can have a baby, it doesn't mean you should. Especially
> without planning for one or getting married first. More than 72 per-
> cent of children in the African American community are born out of
> wedlock. That means absent fathers. And the studies show that lack
> of a male role model is an express train right to prison, and the cycle
> continues.

Lemon was soundly reprimanded by blacks. One black blogger blasted him for daring to criticize the black community and for demanding
that blacks be responsible. "If Lemon really wanted to help the black community," the blogger complained, "he could start by adopting a deeper
understanding of the history." In other words, blacks are immune from
self-examination. In this narrative the thrust of any coverage of blacks
should be solely about grievances, without any mention of irresponsibility. Lemon had violated a covenant. In this sort of intellectual vacuum,
objectivity is utterly lost.

It is common for blacks to blame single parenthood on the excessive
incarceration of black males. But, as we have seen, black women were
having difficulty finding "eligible black men" in the 1930s and 1950s,
before mass incarceration. Violence is also excused by pointing to the
"great majority of African Americans…who are law-abiding, church-
going citizens." Nevertheless the crime rate in the inner cities, despite
the upright blacks who may live in the ghetto or the suburb, is a huge
problem.

The underlying causes of black denial are the denigration of middle-
class values, the tendency to fall back on past injustices, and the disproportionate emphasis on black group identity for political purposes.
Robinson knows full well the crippling effect of the "acting white" accusation among blacks: "Those [blacks] who cannot live in both worlds, who
do not understand both sets of values, are all but lost." By "both worlds"
he means black and white, but in fact Western middle-class norms are
color neutral. Robinson understands the cohesive power and influence
of the church; as such, he should be much more emphatic in bringing the
message to the preachers. He should preach to the preachers. Instead he

expresses an amorphous demand for a massive program, which he associates with the Marshall Plan, to fund "education, public safety, health, and other aspects of life." All roads lead to government money.

Perhaps the best example of the life-altering impact of racially neutral middle-class values was offered by an icon of black culture, the movie director, producer, and writer Spike Lee. At a speech before thousands of black students (and the author of this book) at Jackson State University, the Historically Black school in Mississippi, Lee recounted his college experience. During his undergraduate years, he recalled, he would write to his mother who would promptly correct the grammar and content of his letters in red ink and send the improved letter back to him. Lee went on to criticize the absence of fathers generally, and when asked by a student for job contacts, he told him to find his own.

The refusal to engage in self-examination or self-critique is epitomized by the writer Ta-Nehisi Coates in his *Between the World and Me*. For him, the past is an uncomplicated attempt to pursue an ideological purpose. He calls it "weaponized history." Blacks, according to Coates, share no responsibility for black-on-black crime. Coates views the phrase as "deception": "To yell black-on-black crime is to shame him for bleeding." In reality, Coates has allowed the black individual no free will; he or she is controlled by an environment. Coates's ideology would lead blacks into a mindset of perpetual victimhood.

The Integration Muddle

Desegregation and school integration have become more complicated in the sixty years since *Brown*. The judicial system has found it difficult to define a legally responsible formula for integration. In 1989 blacks and Hispanics in Hartford, Connecticut, filed a desegregation suit, *Sheff v. O'Neill*; seven years later the Connecticut Supreme Court finally ruled by a narrow four-to-three majority that Hartford must desegregate its schools. The court used an arbitrary formula in stipulating that 47.5 percent of blacks and Hispanic students should attend "reduced isolation schools"—defined as those with not more than 75 percent black and Hispanic enrollment, nor less than 25 percent. By 2016, 44 percent of black and Hispanic students were enrolled in such schools, some of which were magnet schools. These numerical ratios are more convoluted than complex—how did the court arrive at them? Comprehensive performance data has not been released. The case has not been settled since a 1996 state court in a split decision mandated that the Hartford schools be desegregated. Twenty-eight years after *Sheff*, the *Hartford (CT) Courant* headline on March 18, 2017, read, "Frustration at Pace of Change," about the still racially segregated school system of the city. After the expenditure of $3 billion on *Sheff*-related expenses, thousands of students, according to the *Hartford Courant* "remain in poverty-stricken, racially segregated institutions."

James E. Ryan, dean of the Harvard School of Education, has noted the peculiar circumstances of *Sheff v. O'Neill*. Connecticut's population in 2010 was 77 percent white, 10 percent black, and 13 percent Hispanic; the black-Hispanic components were clustered in the major cities—Hartford, New Haven, and Bridgeport—all of which were de facto segregated. Hartford was officially considered to be 83 percent black and Hispanic. The court's ruling, according to Ryan, should have been applied to New Haven and Bridgeport as well. "Where have the lawyers been?" asked Ryan. "When southern states...dragged their heels, lawyers for the NAACP Legal Defense Fund dragged them to court to insist that they were governed by *Brown*. Why haven't lawyers done the same in Connecticut and insisted on the application of *Sheff* throughout the state?" This is the same language that Governor George Wallace used in 1963 and that Connecticut's senator Abraham Ribicoff used in 1969 and 1972 to describe the North's racial hypocrisy.

In a 2016 decision dripping with frustration, Judge Thomas Moukawsher of the State Superior Court condemned Connecticut for inadequately educating "students of poor districts." He called for the wealthy state's legislators to offer a plan within 180 days to alter the school funding process, recast the virtually nonexistent methods of teacher evaluation, and set new standards for high school graduation. The judge considered this a "constitutional" matter. He demeaned existing teacher evaluation as "little more than cotton candy in a rainstorm"; he considered graduation rates meaningless and quoted the Bridgeport school superintendent's observation: "[a] functionally illiterate person could get a Bridgeport high school degree." This observation could be applied across America. It also illustrates the danger of using statistics to evaluate performance: if high school graduation rates are the measure, schools from Connecticut to Mississippi to California will lower standards to enhance results.

Moukawsher's decision immediately ran afoul of the powerful Connecticut teachers' union and Governor Daniel Malloy, who appointed the judge and is beholden to the union. Not only in Connecticut, politically entrenched parties may be found at every level of the education mess. Every state is grappling with similar issues while the burden of educating black students falls solely on a broken school system.

Other bastions of liberalism, New York State and City, remain mired in racial segregation. "New York has the most segregated schools in the country," reported a highly influential study in 2014. "New York seems to turn away when race issues come close to home." Specifically, 90 percent of black students in New York City attend schools with more than 50 percent black and Hispanic majorities; 75 percent of black students attend schools with more than 90 percent black and Hispanic majorities; 30 percent of black students attend "apartheid schools" with less than 1 percent white enrollment.

Ambivalence and resistance to racial integration by whites and blacks continues. New York's Upper West Side, a self-described tolerant, diversity-conscious, progressive neighborhood, is the scene of one integration battle. In 2016 the city proposed new school district zoning to move predominantly white, prosperous students closer to the Amsterdam public housing complex, which includes poor black and Hispanic children. Whites adamantly resisted. A year earlier another plan—to send some students from low-scoring, black, and Hispanic PS-191 to high-scoring, white PS-199—"drew such fierce complaints," according to the *Wall Street Journal*, that "the idea [was] scrapped." After the new zoning proposal, a sign warning residents about children attending a school near a housing project was posted in the upscale, predominantly white Schwab House apartments. It advised that the change (i.e., racial school integration) "Can Greatly Impact the Value of our Homes." According to the *New York Times*, white New York liberal Democratic politicians Linda B. Rosenthal, Jerrold Nadler, Brad Hoylman, and Scott Stringer opposed racially integrating the two schools. This same fear of black proximity, as we have seen, existed in Connecticut and Massachusetts in the 1790s. Black abolitionist Samuel R. Ward's observation that whites liked blacks best at a distance may be applied to the Upper West Side in 2016. How times have not changed.

Meanwhile, the performance of black students in the New York City public schools is of serious concern. William McGurn, in the *Wall Street Journal* (February 27, 2017), reported the dismal results. Only 20 percent of black students from grades three to eight passed the state's math test; only 27 percent were proficient in English for their grade level. "As a general rule," wrote McGurn, "the longer New York City kids stay in traditional public schools, the worse they do." This occurs while New York City is "spending $23,516 per pupil this year, among the most in the U.S." New York touts its graduation rate, which is an unreliable number because of incentives to boost performance at the expense of reality. The job-ready or college-ready numbers reduce the significance of graduation rates substantially.

The segregation issue is not entirely one-sided, for blacks, too, have concerns—about the percentage enrollment of white students in a class. Research, including the Coleman Report, indicates that poor black students do better when exposed to middle-class white classmates. This is a strong endorsement for Western middle-class values. But what is the appropriate percentage of middle-class white students? In a *New York Times* article, the white principal of an elementary school in a gentrifying area of upper Manhattan decided that "20 to 25 percent" white students was "good." Confronted with these figures, a black mother worried that her child's school would "turn all white." The very thought of trying to establish racial percentages boggles the mind. In contrast, a significant number of blacks in the inner city have shown enthusiasm for charter and "model" all-black schools, both of which are racially segregated. The black population is quite conflicted over the issue of racially segregated or racially integrated schools, with a strong whiff of "separate but equal" in the confusion.

Diversity for diversity's sake has replaced merit-based tests as a wedge to place black students in New York City's better schools. The NAACP Legal Defense Fund has lodged complaints against the highly selective Stuyvesant, Bronx Science, and Brooklyn Tech public schools. Admissions to these schools are determined by a single test. The Legal Defense Fund wants multiple qualifications to be used in the application process. While the educational excellence of these schools is universally admired, the NAACP believes that increased diversity—the admission of more blacks and Hispanics—should be an appropriate goal in and of itself. In 2015, of the 5,103 students who were admitted to these schools, 5 percent were African American, 7 percent Hispanic, 52 percent of Asian descent, and 28 percent white. In the most selective school, ten African Americans were admitted in a class of 953. In its argument the NAACP relied on the "racially disparate impact" theory, which holds that only equivalent percentages of students are relevant—blacks and whites should occupy approximately the same number of places. In practice this generally applies only when blacks are perceived to be at a disadvantage. For New York City's specialized schools, the 5 percent of blacks who were admitted was considered too low relative to whites and Asians. Hence admissions requirements, according to Sherrilyn Ifill, president of the Legal Defense Fund, should be changed and test scores de-emphasized.

Most black students do poorly on standardized tests as compared to whites, Asians, and Hispanics. Eugene Robinson identifies this problem but gives no reasons for the deficiency. The 2015 results of the Scholastic Aptitude Test (SAT) showed a widening gap between the scores of blacks and whites dating from 2006; the average score for 252,566 blacks who took the ACT in 2015 was lower than any other racial group, including whites, Hispanics, American Indians, and Pacific Islanders. Predictably, the NAACP and the Legal Defense Fund consider standardized tests like the SAT and the American College Testing (ACT) culturally biased. Actually, if culturally biased they are discriminatory and candidates for a lawsuit from the NAACP Legal Defense Fund.

Often blacks blame poor scores on cultural differences. But do these cultural differences reflect cultural bias or a culture in need of change? Disparities of wealth are also proposed by blacks as a reason for poor test scores or academic performance. But the well-known work of the late black anthropologist John Ogbu disputes this theory: "[B]road cultural attributes among blacks—such as parental style, commitment to learning, and work ethic—bear a heavy responsibility for the black-white educational gap." The cultural resistance to education is manifested by the phrase "acting white"—a pejorative term connoting abandoning black identity in order to achieve in the classroom.

Ogbu was explicit about the necessity of colorblind Western middle-class norms:

> [T]he way to help [black students]…is to show them the following school rules of behavior for achievement (for example, regular school attendance, doing school and homework, paying attention in class, etc.) does not require them to give up their own minority cultural frame of reference. We do not help these young people by telling them that we admire and encourage their "resistance" to the system. Rather, we show them how to succeed by practicing accommodation, not assimilation.

Ogbu's distinction between *accommodation* and *assimilation* is a matter of semantics rather than difference. Ironically, *accommodation* was the precise word used pejoratively to criticize Booker T. Washington, as an appeaser of the white majority.

In other words, an exclusive attention to the income gap needs to be supplemented by an objective look at the behavioral habits of black society.

The phenomenon of reverse racism—or black racism as opposed to white racism—is an uncomfortable concept for many blacks. When they reject the idea, it can lead to some indefensible situations, as in the case of the white attorney Morris Dees, founder of the Southern Poverty Law Center in Montgomery, Alabama. The intrepid Dees, a stalwart defender of black rights in the 1960s, was not afraid to tackle discrimination in Montgomery. He brought many desegregation lawsuits, including cases that integrated juries, the local YWCA, the Montgomery County Commission, and the Alabama state legislature. He also bankrupted Ku Klux Klan groups via a lawsuit and sued the state of Alabama to remove the Confederate flag from the state capitol.

Fifty years later, in a 2012 article in the *Montgomery Advertiser*, Dees attacked reverse racism. He had filed lawsuits against Macon County, Alabama, and Alabama State University, a Historically Black institution, charging racial discrimination. In the nation's first reverse-discrimination case, he sued Macon County's all-black school board for terminating all of its white bus drivers and teachers whose children attended the all-white Macon Academy. This blatant attempt to hire blacks by firing whites is reminiscent of Rhody McCoy's replacement of eighteen white teachers by blacks in Ocean Hill–Brownsville in 1968. Dees sued Alabama State University for refusing to give tenure to white professors. He won both cases. The formidable attorney then blasted the black-majority Montgomery County Commission for electing a black Democratic chair and co-chair strictly on racial and party lines. Previously a white Republican majority had appointed a black Democratic chair and a white co-chair.

Political power, in Dees's view, ought to be shared. Having battled white racial discrimination, he was not about to tolerate black racial discrimination despite cries of "traitor" from some blacks. Quoting Martin Luther King Jr., Dees cautioned against "raw political power" dictating that "these good-paying jobs should go to blacks who hold power, regardless of the injustices." Evidently Alabama State did not learn its lesson, for it was again sued in April 2015 when faculty search committees were instructed to hire only blacks.

In the world of 2016, Morris Dees would be accused of a microaggression by Sheree Marlowe, the black diversity director at Clark University in Massachusetts. According to the *New York Times*, Marlowe "questioned the validity of reverse racism." In a spasm of twisted logic, she argued that "racism is a system in which a dominant race benefits from the oppression of others." The visible black writer Ta-Nehisi Coates is in agreement with this opinion—in direct opposition to that of Morris Dees. According to this reasoning, blacks may discriminate against whites because blacks are oppressed. Under Marlowe's dictum, Morris Dees would be guilty of racial insensitivity. Thus a form of racial immunity from blame, i.e., black privilege, is established. Self-criticism, so vital to constructive adaptation and progress, is nowhere to be found.

Some relics survive in the racially desegregated world; one is the Historically Black College and University (HBCU). What role does an Historically Black college now play? In the past the HBCUs played a critical role; today they face competition for talented black students in a society where blacks can go to any school and are sought by predominantly white universities.

One has only to look at a glaring success story to understand the past importance of the HBCUs. A black male born in 1948, one of ten children with only a mother as a parent, was raised in the inner city of Nashville. After a transformative summer program at Fisk University, he entered another HBCU, Tennessee State University, and graduated in 1972 with a degree in electrical engineering. A master's degree followed from Stanford. He then became the first African American from an HBCU hired by AT&T's Bell Laboratories, where he became a star innovator in wireless communication systems. He is best known for commercializing a moribund product, the cell phone. As manager of the wireless unit, he met with his all-white group and immediately discovered the problem and solution to the cell phone puzzle. Unfettered by conventional wisdom, he led the way to innovations and a score of patents. This confident, fearless businessman is Jesse Russell. In interviews he credits the nurturing environment of Tennessee State for a major role in his success. Today, with other options available, is his experience still relevant?

Racial integration has taken its toll on HBCUs. The athletic programs at HBCU schools are a shadow of their former greatness because black athletes may now play in the major college sports arena. Grambling University is no longer an incubator for the National Football League, just as the Negro baseball leagues disappeared after the integration of professional baseball. In a recent football contest, the HBCU South Carolina State lost to its larger integrated opponent, Clemson University, by a score of 59 to 0. The referees attempted to shorten the game because of the embarrassment. Clemson's team was well stocked with black players who years ago would probably have been playing for an HBCU. The HBCUs, proud of their status in the NCAA's Division I, are reluctant to move to the less competitive and less expensive Division II. They are willing to suffer humiliation for a big payday.

If the mission of the HBCUs is definitely not to defeat Ohio State or Alabama on the gridiron, what *is* their mission? Many private HBCU's are facing financial challenges. Fully 89 percent of HBCU students participate in federal loan programs; the comparable figure for predominantly white universities is 55 percent, and 18 percent of Yale's student body have a Pell government loan. Endowments at predominantly white colleges dwarf those at HBCUs. The top 10 HBCU endowments range from $34 million to $659 million; at the top predominantly white schools the lowest number is $6 billion and the highest is $32 billion—and this gap has doubled in the last twenty years. Graduation rates in six years at seven of the HBCUs is 20 percent or lower. Meanwhile the black elite who enter Ivy League schools have graduation rates between 87 percent and 97 percent. The Movement for Black Lives wants more government financial support for HBCUs.

If America's goals are the benefits of assimilation—a comfort level of association between blacks and whites, exposure to a competitive environment, social and commercial contacts, and easier access to the economic mainstream—how can HBCUs justify their existence? The conundrum of the survival of an all-black institution goes to the heart of the preference for separation or integration. At its core, an HBCU is a product of group and individual identity. And the cost of operating an HBCU, when consolidation is an option, becomes a racially charged rather than a rational discussion.

The separatism represented by HBCUs can lead to some strange situations, as in the 1992 case of *Ayres v. Fordice*. Jake Ayres, a black man, filed suit against the state of Mississippi on behalf of the three public HBCUs in Mississippi—Jackson State University, Alcorn State University, and Mississippi Valley State University—in 1975. He charged discriminatory funding. Mississippi had grossly underfunded the HBCUs relative to the state's public white universities during the period of de jure segregation. The US Supreme Court decided in favor of the plaintiff and awarded compensation. In so doing, the court was placed in the uncomfortable position of fostering segregation by acknowledging the legality of a segregated institution. The enrollment of the three HBCUs by the mid-1980s was 91 to 99 percent black.

The court wiggled its way through the obvious contradiction of preserving segregation. Justice Clarence Thomas, in a sympathetic concurring opinion, noted the paradox but personally claimed to understand the need to assist the institutions: "It would be ironic, to say the least, if the institutions that sustained blacks during segregation were themselves destroyed in an effort to combat its vestiges." Part of the compromise embedded in the $500 million settlement required the three schools to attain a "10 percent other-race enrollment" before receiving money for their endowments. By 2005 the three schools had almost achieved this requirement with the aid of "diversity scholarships" to white students, the recruitment of Russian tennis players and Canadian baseball players, and online courses. With five predominantly white universities and three HBCUs, Mississippi has eight public institutions of higher learning, which it can ill afford. Consolidation would have greatly enhanced the efficiency and quality of education and surely would have provided the benefits of assimilation into the mainstream economy.

In order to increase the numbers of African American students, predominantly white universities aggressively search for and recruit black applicants. The effort has increased black enrollment at the eight Ivy League schools by 35 percent in a decade. The Ivy League class entering in 2016 was up 1,503 from 1,110 ten years earlier. Note that the increase is 393 students—hardly a dent in the racial educational universe. American universities, from the Ivy League to smaller liberal arts colleges to well-regarded public and private schools, compete fiercely for eligible graduates from the feeder organizations. Yet the numbers are small. When they are well organized, college prep programs can attract private sources of funds. Major obstacles in the programs are the labor-intensive nature of the process and the need for charismatic, focused leadership. Overall, these well-publicized efforts, though certainly worthwhile endeavors, have not been measurable in their ability to influence the mass of black students.

A great many well-intentioned enrichment programs, private and public, serve the black community. One successful effort, Camp Sherwood Forest, a summer camp near St. Louis under the extraordinary leadership of Mary Rogers, has been able to supplement children's experiences during the school year. In 2015 Camp Sherwood accommodated three hundred youngsters from poor backgrounds, most of whom were black. It operated with a $1.5 million budget. Within the group, a leadership training program can be tracked because three-quarters of the participants maintain contact. Figures reveal a 100 percent high school graduation rate and a 94 percent matriculation rate into a stable career. The camp is funded by local St. Louis philanthropies. The dedicated Ms. Rogers has been with the camp for fifty years.

While the success of many African Americans and the growth of the black middle class and the elite are often cited as progress, the fact of lagging black educational performance, particularly in the lower class, remains glaring, undeniable, and seemingly impervious to change. The education wars have resulted only in a political war between public school advocates, charter schools, and racial interest groups. The goal is control and money rather than instilling a desire for learning, a bedrock skill set in math, reading, writing, and critical thinking, and a work ethic.

Why hasn't a constructive set of middle-class values permeated black society? Revisiting the 1960s will offer some clues, for the educational battleground features many of the same earlier skirmishes and highlights society-wide problems. Black society, certainly not a monolith, nevertheless monolithically points to poverty and discrimination as the causes of the education gap and votes as a bloc. Both of these factors, according to blacks, have created personal, psychological, and health-related impediments for black students. Solutions call invariably for increased spending, local community control, less emphasis on testing, disciplinary counseling rather than suspension, and more concentration on black history.

These demands by the black community today are in many ways similar to those made in the Ocean Hill–Brownsville strike, which pitted New York City's majority Jewish teachers' union against the black community and the African American Teachers Association. Blacks wanted a separate value system that rejected what they regarded as "white middle-class" norms for a distinct but ill-defined black cultural system. An emphasis on "cooperation and egalitarianism" and a black ethos were needed to combat perceived white norms—"individualism, materialism, competition, work ethic, mastering basic skill sets." At the time, whites countered with the need for the very traits that were denigrated by blacks. In a practical sense, whites maintained that a proper entrance into the workplace required the "so-called" white middle-class approach, an approach already adopted by much of the black middle class. Discipline was a very sticky point and still is.

The "disruptive student clause," vigorously supported by whites in the 1960s, continues to be disputed in 2016 by blacks who prefer therapy. Valerie Jarrett, President Obama's adviser, in September 2016 called for a lenient approach to the discipline of black children, a "trauma-informed" approach. Jarrett's background is elitist—Stanford University and the University of Michigan Law School. Her father was a noted physician at the University of Chicago Medical School, and her father-in-law, Vernon Jarrett, was a prominent black journalist. Her husband's family lived in the Rosenwald complex, a black apartment building with a group of black professionals. The Rosenwald complex, which had its own nursery school and activity center, had little contact with the surrounding neighborhood. The black social elite, members of the Jack and Jill and Links, were disconnected from the black underclass by the 1940s.

Jarrett enumerated the causes of "unhealed trauma," which she called the major retardant for black children: "neglect, abuse, family dysfunction...absence of a loved one due to incarceration or death." She inferred discrimination because black boys and girls were expelled and sent to the juvenile justice system more often than whites or any other group. At work here is the "disparate impact" theory, in which underlying causes are irrelevant. Jarrett then blamed excessively harsh discipline for "unplanned pregnancies, dropping out of school" or entrapment in the juvenile justice system. The child who committed destructive classroom behavior in the 1960s was said to be a "high-spirited nonconformist." The African American Teachers Association did not suggest how a teacher might conduct a class under such circumstances. Likewise, the Justice Department has rebranded "juvenile delinquent," now called "justice-involved youth." Yet Geoffrey Canada of the Harlem Children's Zone knew full well that no school can function without discipline.

Nowhere does Valerie Jarrett demand any responsibility from black families, black communities, or black churches. The black immunity mindset omits any criticism of black society. The government alone is charged with correcting black cultural ills.

A very small pipeline of excellent black students exists for matriculation to the leading universities. Otherwise, junior colleges, city colleges, and other schools must often accommodate a black student body that is vastly in need of remedial attention. According to recent statistics, 56 percent of black high school graduates need remedial work versus 35 percent for white students. Only 6 percent of black students were considered ready for college in all four subjects—English, math, reading, and science. A recent study revealed that at half of the HBCUs, only 34 percent of the students graduated.

The courts have responded to the universities' dilemma with a dissension-packed affirmative-action debate. Should the United States afford special treatment for black students? The first significant case, *Regents of the University of California v. Bakke* in 1978, involved the challenge of a white student to the affirmative-action policy of the University of California Medical School at Davis. The Supreme Court's ruling allowed for admission consideration based on diversity but did not approve quotas. Gone were the unanimous days of *Brown*: the court's ruling was five to four with multiple opinions. *Grutter v. Bollinger* (2003), involving the University of Michigan Law School, prompted Justice Sandra Day O'Connor to assume that affirmative action would be limited to twenty-five years. (One is reminded of Malcolm X's prediction that government financial aid targeted to blacks would last only twenty-five years.) In *Fisher v. University of Texas at Austin* (2016) the court upheld the university's race-conscious admissions program.

All these decisions disavow quotas but allow for circumvention to foster diversity, i.e., some form of affirmative action. The bottom line is that there is not a sufficient number of qualified black applicants for the better schools. The rationale of the courts and the universities embraces racial diversity as now a fundamental part of higher education. White plaintiffs argue that they are being denied access to school for reasons of race rather than merit.

The twenty-first century's hypersensitivity to race, ethnicity, gender, religion, and sexual orientation has been fully adopted by black students. This exaggerated reaction to actual or perceived slights, no matter how insignificant, is extremely damaging to black students and leads to an unwarranted distraction from academics and a retreat to racial separation—the antithesis of assimilation. Black students at a variety of American universities, from the University of Missouri to Yale, have expressed their discontent with alleged widespread racism on campus.

The protesting black student at the University of Missouri was the son of a millionaire black businessman. The protesting black student at Yale was the daughter of an upper-middle-class family.

Black students admitted to Yale are competitive, achievement oriented, and resilient, surely part of a select class. Like their fellows at other Ivy League and prestigious schools, they and their white counterparts are perceived as different. Once a student, any student, walks onto the Old Campus at Yale his freshman year, he acquires an added identity. The newly minted Yale student of any race or ethnicity becomes privileged and is recognized as a Yalie in job applications, business or academic circles, and social settings. Doors are opened, networks are available. Prestigious museums, for example, like the Museum of Modern Art in New York, are well aware of Ivy League graduates as potential candidates for board membership. One needs only to recall the experience of William Melvin Kelley, the black Harvard student who entered a staid Boston bank dressed as a summer construction worker and was treated condescendingly—until his Harvard affiliation emerged.

Yet racial disturbances intrude. Much more research needs to be done on the experience of blacks at Yale and other well-endowed progressive schools, their career choices, and life after the Ivy League. Graduation statistics need to be supplemented by texture.

The confluence of race, today's hypersensitivity, and the submergence of individual to group loyalty has yielded an extreme vulnerability to slights or perceived slights. The expectations of black students at better schools are greater than those of students at other schools. The "coddled" atmosphere on campus encourages fragility, tribalism, insecurity, narcissism, an inability to deal with confrontation, and appeal to narrative rather than analysis, and a repugnance to diverse ideas. While these feelings may affect many students, black students are most affected because of their psychological anchor to race-based slavery and overt legal segregation. In either case, the overall educational process suffers, but especially for black students.

The professors Christakis affair at Yale provides a disturbing example. Nicholas Christakis, a prominent physician and sociologist, served as master of Silliman College, a residential college within Yale. (The master, now called head, is the social and organizational leader of approximately five hundred students who live and dine at a residential college within Yale.) His wife, Erika, herself a child psychologist, objected to a Yale administration email providing guidelines for student Halloween costumes. Yale officials were afraid of costumes that racial or ethnic groups might find offensive. Erika Christakis, who taught a course called "Concept of the Problem Child," is a liberal Democrat who voted for Barack Obama in both presidential elections. Her message was simply that an administration should not be monitoring this level of student activity. Instead she suggested that an offended student confront the person wearing a perceived insensitive costume, mention the offense, and initiate a dialogue.

There ensued an uproar on campus. Black and a few Hispanic students angrily and disrespectfully confronted Nicholas Christakis in the courtyard of Silliman College. Shouting students surrounded him in a small-scale version of a gladiatorial contest in the Roman Coliseum. A video of one episode pitted an emotionally distraught student, Jerelyn Luther, facing a cowering, befuddled Christakis. She screamed:

> Why the fuck did you accept the position?! Who the fuck hired you?! You should step down! If that is what you think about being a master, you should step down! It is not about creating an intellectual space!...Do you understand that? It is about creating a home here....You are disgusting.

Ms. Luther, the African American daughter of upper-middle-class parents, had been a member of the committee that had selected Christakis as master. Her behavior was emulated by others.

This was a mob scene captured on publicly available video for half an hour. The video should be viewed by psychologists, parents, and students, and afterward discussed. In one scene a black male defiantly moves a couple of feet away from Christakis and dresses him down. A quaking Christakis continues to apologize for the pain he has caused by not remembering some of the students' names during this his first year as master. When he is absurdly accused of "creating a violent space," he finally disagrees. The group tantrum reminds one of the African American Teachers Association and the Congress of Racial Equality supporting student cursing and physical confrontation in the 1968 racial imbroglio in Brooklyn. During all of this show of rage, demand for an apology, and irrational discourteous behavior, many of the black women students began crying in their outrage, a display that definitely separated them from the Black Power participants of the 1960s. The coddled students of the twenty-first century expressed themselves through tears.

Erika Christakis and her husband were forced to resign from Silliman College and subsequently took a sabbatical from Yale. They received no support from the administration or the majority of the faculty or student body in this principled stand for free speech and the proper way to foster adolescent growth. In no way had Erika's response to the administration's email harmed any ethnic group.

Did the offended students need a hermetically sealed, cozy environment or an intellectually stimulating adventure? What was the black students' previous experience where blacks were a minority? Was the racial adjustment overwhelming? Would their response be to self-segregate on campus or to integrate? Would the choice of courses or majors gravitate to African American studies? To what extent would the perception of affirmative action be a stigma? These are questions that might arise with black students at a predominantly white school. Does this mean that black students would be more comfortable at an HBCU? Does the socioeconomic background of black students lead to different levels of assimilation at an Ivy League school or a public university?

On October 17, 2016, the Graduate and Professional Student Senate at Yale issued its report on "Race, Diversity and Inclusion." Seventy-two percent of the black graduate students who responded to a survey cited "bias" in the classroom. Bias was never defined; no specific examples of bias were cited. Of note, only 17 percent of the graduate student body responded to the survey, indicating a substantial degree of apathy about the subject. Only 44 percent of the black students had a faculty mentor—was that Yale's fault or the students'?

The survey included a less than penetrating question: "Has a faculty member ever called you by the wrong name?" There was no follow-up question about the student's action in response to such a circumstance. Presumably a simple correction would be in order. But in this atmosphere any form of individual confrontation, no matter how inconsequential, evidently should be avoided in favor of an institutional response or complaint.

The report's recommendations included more diversity among faculty, mental health support for minorities, more emphasis on non-Western courses, and more money for minority cultural centers. Yale's faculty is the very essence of political correctness, as are most other university faculties. Yet accusations of pervasive racism are to be found in schools across the country. At Yale, in any event, the graduate students had not built a case for their demands.

Yale became the scene of another flash point when a question arose about one of its residential colleges bearing the name of Yale graduate John C. Calhoun (1782–1850). This highly visible congressman and senator from South Carolina, as well as secretary of war, secretary of state, and vice president of the United States, was a staunch supporter of slavery among myriad other political and social issues in the years before the Civil War. Calhoun owned slaves on his South Carolina farm. Both as an undergraduate and a law student at Yale, he had many friends from his college days. In 2016 the black Yale group Next Yale, which purports to speak for various disadvantaged ethnic and racial groups, demanded the renaming of Calhoun College.

The Yale Corporation, the school's governing body, went through a lengthy strained process to justify changing the name of Calhoun while leaving Yale College unchanged. Ultimately, in February 2017 the Yale Corporation changed the name of Calhoun College to Gracie Hopper College, a white woman graduate student who became a pioneer in computer science.

But there's a catch: Elihu Yale, for whom Yale is named, was extensively involved in the eighteenth-century slave trade, and Yale president Peter Salovey has refused even to consider changing the name of the university itself. Yale is, after all, a brand name. It is virtually inconceivable that Yale's faculty, student body, or administration would abandon the prestige associated with the name of Yale, despite the blatant hypocrisy of possibly removing Calhoun and allowing Yale to stand. President Salovey offered a flimsy but telling materialistic distinction between John Calhoun and Elihu Yale: Elhu Yale made a donation to Yale, whereas Calhoun had no "similarly strong association with our campus." Black and white students at Yale seem to have no problem retaining the name Yale, even with its slave-trading past. One wit wrote to the *Wall Street Journal* about the Yale community's reluctance to accept an alternative name, College of Southern Middle Connecticut. The point is that political correctness has no obligation for consistency and always succumbs to money or notoriety.

In a further nuance of the 2017 version of multiculturalism, two non-white women students did object to the selection of a white woman, rather than a black woman—especially since the announcement was made during Black History Month. For them, "[W]hite femininity has often been used as a tool to enforce racist and colonialist structures...As such...this decision constitutes 'whitewashing' to the wider Yale community." Their logic is akin to shredding *Webster's* dictionary in the 1960s to remove the influence of Western civilization, a civilization that has given these two students an educational opportunity. Race, by these standards, supersedes gender.

Black students and students "of color" at Yale and in more than seventy universities have demanded reparations for slavery in the form of diversity initiatives. The group Next Yale demanded an ethnic studies course requirement; mental health professionals in each of four cultural centers (Afro-American, Native American, Hispanic, and Asian American); an annual $2 million increase in the operating budgets of the cultural centers; five full-time staff members in these centers; and an increase in "diversity" faculty. Most of these items, implicitly or explicitly, involve cash. Yale has plenty of money in a $26 billion endowment. So, even before Next Yale's demands, Yale had allocated $50 million to an initiative to increase faculty diversity. This does not mean immediately recruiting, hiring, and supporting "emerging" faculty, because there is a limited number of qualified black and minority professors. Nor is it clear what these additional "diversity" faculty members should teach. Currently Yale has twenty-four tenured African American faculty members. Almost all of them teach African American-related subjects. The new hires presumably will teach African American-related courses. Recall that both the journalist Louis Lomax in 1960 and the historian John Hope Franklin in 2005 worried about the association of black teachers purely with black subjects.

Other schools have bought into the diversity sweepstakes with cash: Brown, $165 million; Columbia, $85 million; the University of Cincinnati, $40 million; Johns Hopkins, $25 million, and so on. The "disadvantaged" groups are asking Yale for still more money, given the size of the university's endowment.

Related to the diversity effort is a concurrent initiative to eliminate white English poets as a requirement for an English major at Yale. "The Major English Poets [a required course]," says a petition from Next Yale, "…creates a culture that is especially hostile to students of color.… It's time to decolonize—not diversify course offerings." (In 1967 *Ebony* magazine published a photo of a black militant student shredding *Webster's* dictionary, which was deemed racist and a relic of imperialism.) Western civilization is being demonized and run out of the curriculum. A hodge-podge of ethnic, racial, and nationality courses are offered as substitutes.

As each student group expresses itself, some strange things happen. At Yale, tribal warfare broke out between self-identified Navajos and the self-identified Lakota, or Sioux. A lawsuit, *John Doe v. Yale University*, resulted. In 2012 the Yale Navajo students planned a coup to rid the Native American Culture Center of its Sioux dean and the dean's supporter. The complaint alleges that the Navajos engaged a Navajo woman student to entrap a Sioux undergraduate by seducing him and then claiming rape. She did this and filed a sexual assault charge, which resulted in Yale's expulsion of the Sioux student. The complaint filed by the Sioux is currently in a federal district court in Connecticut. It alleges that the sexual act was consensual and that Yale has caused significant harm to the Sioux student because he has been unable to gain admission to other colleges.

These events at Yale are generic to most American campuses. The question of identity arises. To what extent is a student an individual, or part of a racial or ethnic group? Will an extreme identification with a group lead to separatism and inhibit a free flow of ideas among all types of students? This inability to communicate, a self-imposed restriction on free speech, is already occurring. In a sense, the move to separatism and the response by administrations is just the form of tokenism that Malcolm X mocked. As always, looking at the world exclusively through a racial lens leads to mistakes. For Malcolm X, the racial lens allowed him to see Egypt and Ghana as models for the future of black America. The economic disarray in Africa, as opposed to the ascendancy of the West and Asia, should give pause to blind racial pride. A black student, or any student, is composed of multiple identities, some more important than others. There is room for cultural heritage, but the bedrock of America lies on a foundation of Western civilization, which is capable of adapting.

Recasting Memorials

The controversy over historical memorials and symbols gained traction particularly after the tragic murders of nine black congregants during a prayer service at the Emanuel African Methodist Church in Charleston, South Carolina, in June 2015. The assailant, a deranged white youth, had posted a Confederate flag on a website, thus connecting his actions to slavery, Jim Crow, and associated symbols. The Confederate flag was soon removed from its flagpole at the state capitol by the governor and the state legislature.

A reevaluation of race-related memorials, statues, and monuments has begun in earnest. The removal or renaming process is prompted by echoes of slavery, the Confederacy, or actual or perceived anti-black attitudes at the local, state, and federal levels. Colleges, cities, states, and the federal government are asking what should be memorialized and what should be changed, discarded, or amended. Amid this controversy the mammoth new National Museum of African American History and Culture has opened in Washington, DC.

The replacement of the Confederate flag as an official symbol is obvious. But other decisions can be complicated. *New York Times* columnist David Brooks recommended that Confederate general Robert E. Lee's name be kept on "institutions that reflect postwar service, like Washington and Lee University." But, he added, "we should remove Lee's name from most schools, roads, and other institutions"—a contorted distinction.

At Appomattox, General Ulysses S. Grant referred to Lee as a foe who fought valiantly. Grant, as he recorded, then fell into a long conversation with General Lee. Grant requested a pardon for Lee, and later as president he hosted Lee at the White House. Why would Grant dignify Lee and pardon his most formidable adversary? Why would America be oblivious to Grant's decisions that were devastating to recently freed slaves? The judgment of symbols is indeed a slippery slope and requires a consistent methodology informed by history. And a concentration on symbols may create a distraction from real structural problems.

If slaveholding alone is a criterion, attention would include more than John C. Calhoun, Robert E. Lee, and Jefferson Davis. George Washington and James Madison were also slaveholders, and they were important participants in the Constitutional Convention of 1787, which permitted slavery to exist in the legal system. Northerners were also complicit in their desire to create a nation. Do these facts imperil Washington Square and Madison Avenue? The slave compromises were brokered by Connecticut delegates Roger Sherman and Oliver Ellsworth. Should these Connecticut delegates be recognized for their complicity? As Roger Kimball points out, Elihu Yale's conduct was "far more egregious" than that of Calhoun.

The professors of the University of Ghana in September 2016 demanded that the recently dedicated statue of Mahatma Gandhi be removed from the campus and returned to India. Gandhi, as a young lawyer in South Africa in 1896, wrote disparagingly of blacks, even using the slur *Kaffir*: "A general belief seems to prevail in the Colony that the Indians are little better, if at all, than the savages or the Natives of Africa. Even the children are taught to believe in that manner, with the result that the Indian is being dragged down to the position of a raw Kaffir." Gandhi advocated separate entrances to public buildings for Africans and Indians. There is no evidence, according to Ashwin Desai and Goolam Vahed, that Gandhi was "concern[ed] with the social, economic and political circumstances of Africans in South Africa." Nevertheless, they write, he "continues to be wrapped in the halo of an anti-racist, anti-colonial fighter on African soil."[4]

An embarrassed Ghanaian Foreign Ministry wants merely to move the Gandhi statue within Ghana. He is, after all, revered for creating the strategy of nonviolence that was adopted so successfully by Martin Luther King Jr. for the civil rights movement. Should statues of Gandhi in America, such as the one standing in the southwest corner of Union Square Park in New York, be removed or amended? Do Americans want a racist symbol greeting people as they emerge from the Union Square subway station?

The complexity of dealing with race-related memorials and words can produce highly selective and hypocritical decisions. White Americans are confused by the extensive use of the N-word by blacks. The black comedian Larry Wilmore, at the 2016 White House correspondents' dinner,

---

4 Gandhi's racial attitudes are a salient example of the fictional unity of "people of color." This is a question of identity. What does an African or an African American have in common with an Indian? All have different heritages and live under different political and economic systems.

apparently referred to President Obama as "my Nigga," to which President Obama smiled, thumped his chest, and hugged Wilmore. Some blacks view this as permissible, a form of legitimate code or "ownership"; other blacks disapprove but do little to prevent its use.

Most antebellum white Northerners and even abolitionists expressed anti-black attitudes, ranging from hatred to estimates of inferiority, to containment in the South, to indifference to the removal of blacks entirely. The implications of white Northern racial views would become consequential after Emancipation. As noted earlier, William Henry Seward was conspicuously anti-slavery but was also conspicuously anti-black. There is a statue of Seward at the southwest corner of Madison Square Park in New York City. Should the description on Seward's statue be amended to reflect his attitude toward black America? Theodore Roosevelt rides astride his horse on a statue in front of New York's Natural History Museum. His opinions about blacks would be anathema today, especially his aside that blacks were responsible for lynchings. Should a caption on TR's statue reflect his attitude toward blacks? Grant's decision not to send troops to Vicksburg, Mississippi, in 1875 was a fatal blow to black suffrage. The valiant general in the 1863 Battle of Vicksburg surrendered in the 1875 Battle of Vicksburg. Should Grant's Tomb note this catastrophic failure? The Republican Party consistently reminds African Americans that Abraham Lincoln, the first Republican president, ended race-based slavery—without acknowledging his flawed approach to black equality and egalitarian status. Historians have rationalized and excused his refusal, replacing the real Lincoln with an evolving icon of heroic racial enlightenment. Rather than confront Lincoln's racial flaws, historians rationalize Lincoln as "Big Enough to Be Inconsistent," the title of George Fredrickson's book.

And what about memorializing some people and events that have been purposely forgotten? The North has deliberately avoided memorializing much of its racial history. Many racial events need to be brought visibly to the public's attention. In July 1863, as part of the so-called Draft Riots, white New Yorkers burned the Colored Orphanage Asylum; black New Yorkers were lynched and hung from lampposts. A plaque should be appropriately placed as a reminder of New York's racially troubled past.

The gatekeepers of our heritage might consider applying a notation, an asterisk, to mark a compromised historical figure or event. In sports the practice is already established. When a record-breaker is thought to have used performance-enhancing drugs, his accomplishment is diminished with a qualifying asterisk. If applied to history, an asterisk would accompany the mention of the Constitutional Convention of 1787 and the US Constitution for enshrining slavery in the fabric of American society. Abraham Lincoln, the man who saved the Union and ended slavery, would also have an asterisk. No statute of limitations would be allowed; every situation would be judged by present-day considerations.

To date the major American civil rights museums have been created entirely in the South. The National Civil Rights Museum, a part of the National Park Service, is located in Memphis, Tennessee. Because it depicts events that occurred predominantly in the South, it is really a regional and not a national museum; the National Civil Rights Museum should be renamed. The current historical racial narrative is exclusively about the South and fails to prosecute the North. White Northerners, of course, prefer to neglect their unseemly past and would rather memorialize the Underground Railroad, the Amistad slave revolt, or Lincoln's New York City Cooper Union speech ("A house divided against itself cannot stand"), all of which are designed to show the North in a positive light. A realistic understanding of race in America demands full disclosure by the North.

The current portrait of America as an oppressive Western society is obsessively concerned with grievances. All nations are flawed. The genuine greatness of America is lost in the vilification exercise that now prevails in the academy and popular culture. America is the grand experiment in the making of a large-scale multi-ethnic nation, as Lincoln cogently put it, "the last best hope of earth." The scars should be recognized, but the true genius of America should be fully exhibited.

Watching the Movies

Ideas flow through popular culture, particularly movies, which are at the same time profit ventures, entertainment, and a substitute for the serious study of complex themes. They are often carriers of ideas and capture the spirit and context of the times. The general public gathers much of its information from popular movies and absorbs the material uncritically. The film usually gains credence from the use of dubious modifiers—"based on" or "inspired by" a true story. Often the drama is embellished with episodes that did not occur in real life but could have happened or did occur elsewhere. When it comes to matters of race, it is useful to subject a movie to examination of fact, fiction, context, and appeal.

In the latter half of the twentieth century, the most influential race-themed movie is arguably *To Kill a Mockingbird* (1962), based on Harper Lee's Pulitzer Prize–winning book. Praise for the movie was biracial. Almost a million books have been sold annually since the movie appeared, even in the twenty-first century. The story, set in 1930s Alabama, featured a gross miscarriage of justice involving a black man, Tom Robinson (played by Brock Peters), who was defended by a local lawyer, Atticus Finch (played by Gregory Peck). Robinson, falsely accused of the rape of a poor white woman, was found guilty and subsequently was killed when he tried to escape from prison. Atticus Finch's eloquent but failed courtroom defense was the centerpiece of the movie, but the star was the narrator, Finch's beloved daughter Scout.

Praise, as well as controversy, has followed the book and the movie. "I remember starting [the book in the eighth grade]...and just devouring it, not being able to get enough of it," wrote Oprah Winfrey in 2010, "because I fell in love with Scout....I wanted to be Scout and I wanted a father like Atticus Finch....I think *To Kill a Mockingbird* is our national novel." Andrew Young, black congressman from Georgia, ambassador to the United Nations, and mayor of Atlanta, thought the book "inspires hope in the midst of chaos and confusion." At a screening of the movie in January 2014 at the New York Historical Society, Sherrilyn Ifill, president of the NAACP Legal Defense Fund, attributed her interest in law to Atticus Finch. In his presidential farewell address on January 10, 2017 in Chicago, President Obama honored Atticus Finch for considering issues from someone else's point of view.

In a scene not included in the movie, Harper Lee injects the reality of racial separation in an encounter at a black church. Calpurnia, Finch's devoted cook, housekeeper, and surrogate mother for Scout and her brother Jem, took the children to her Sunday church service. Harper Lee puts Calpurnia, who in Roman history was the name of Julius Caesar's second wife, in a prominent household role. Upon a peaceful entrance into the church, Calpurnia is confronted by Lula:

"I wants to know why you bringin' white chillum to nigger church."

"They's my comp'ny," replied Calpurnia.

"I reckon you's comp'ny at the Finch house durin' the week.... You ain't got no business bringin' white chillum here—they got their and we got our'n," Lula persisted.

"It's the same God, ain't it?" Calpurnia retorted, thus ending the fight with Lula leaving.

Calpurnia, who spoke normally in grammatically correct English, in this episode reverted to colloquial black dialect. The language shift illustrated the dual character of blacks who operated in two worlds, one white, one black.

Judged in the context of the twenty-first century, *Mockingbird* appears paternalistic, racially condescending, and offensive in its use of "nigger," the most inflammatory word in the English language when used by whites but apparently acceptable when used by blacks. Today the human interaction between the characters of the story has been overshadowed by its depiction of 1930s overt legal segregation. In the current hypersensitive environment, it remains to be seen whether—despite these racial accusations and the discovery of a first manuscript of *To Kill a Mockingbird*, which contains a harsher racial treatment than the original—the historical significance and popularity of the book will survive.

The 2011 race-themed book and movie *The Help* inherited the popularity of *Mockingbird*—ten million copies of the book sold, $216 million gross in movie box office receipts, and winner of an Oscar. Thus far it is the biggest financial success among the race-themed movies. The author, Kathleen Stockett, had three characters in her novel *The Help* read *Mockingbird*. The story line, which is the struggles of black maids during the civil rights era of the early 1960s, evokes an emotional response. The white heroine, Skeeter Phelan, adds a biracial dimension in this thoroughly feminist fictional story. The result is a feel-good portrayal of the tragic side of the African American experience.

The Help's one-dimensional characters are a far cry from the nuanced reality of personal relationships between the races. The true connections between whites and blacks ran the gambit from genuine closeness to paternalism, to condescension, to harsh treatment. The two races lived cheek to jowl in smaller Southern towns and rural areas. Black maids were well aware of the differing attitudes of white Southerners. "Good white people" was a common descriptive term used by blacks when distinguishing among whites. Racial codes were observed by both sides who had daily contact. One has only to read Kathryn Stockett's own words at the end of her book, where she issues a nonfiction *mea culpa*: "...there was so much more love between white families and black domestics than I had the ink or time to portray."

The Help is derivative. Most of the background for the story came from *Telling Memories among Southern Women* by Susan Tucker. This collection of oral histories by "domestic workers and their employees" reveals a carefully selective use of material. Stockett was well aware of the success of *To Kill a Mockingbird*, whose formula, a white hero and a black victim, she borrowed.

What accounts for the astounding mass appeal of *The Help*? The book and movie provide a clear catharsis for America—"a bit healing," said the *Detroit News*. Good and evil are clearly identified. The white South is America's racial scapegoat. A white Southern woman who has experienced a conversion to racial tolerance gives voice and hope to black maids. The script is soothing to white guilt and at the same time appealing to some African Americans who interpret the story as protest.

Many blacks, however, recoiled from the movie. The director of the Association of Black Women Academics charged that "[It] distorts, ignores and trivializes the experiences of black domestic workers." And blacks objected to yet another depiction of a white savior, in this case Skeeter Phelan. Other blacks criticized the lack of "authenticity"—a code for suspecting any description or analysis by anyone other than a black person. The racial guild approach holds that only blacks can discuss blacks—a theory that would disturb the journalist Louis Lomax or the historian John Hope Franklin, neither of whom wished to be slotted as black specialists.

A whiff of jealousy also underlies the black criticism of a white author's colossal hit. Kathryn Stockett was accused of poaching on racially exclusive territory. "Cultural appropriation" is the new term applied to allegations of the "theft" of black culture for artistic fame and fortune.

The implications are clear: an author or actor must stay within their own ethnic, racial, national, or gender boundaries. By these rules,

Leontyne Price should not have sung Italian opera, Wynton Marsalis should not play Mozart, Denzel Washington should not have been Shakespeare's *Richard III*, and Kazuo Ishiguro, born in Nagasaki, should not have written an English drama like *The Remains of the Day*. The celebrated playwright August Wilson (1945-2005) rejected colorblind casting—the practice of using black actors to play traditional white roles. As such, the black separatist Wilson would have objected to Denzel Washington's performing Shakespeare. The talented Washington would be restricted to black productions. Washington both coincidentally and ironically is currently starring in the movie adaptation of Wilson's *Fences*. One wonders what Wilson would think of the Founding Fathers being played by a non-white cast in the smash hit musical *Hamilton*. Cultures interact; the results are often magnificent.

Conversely, in a spirited debate with Wilson, the prominent drama critic and educator Robert Brustein countered, "I believe that America will only begin to fulfill its promise when we acknowledge that we are individuals first, Americans second, and tribalists third." Brustein continued: "In 1997 you are no longer slaves,... [yet, you] talk about yourself as if you are standing on the ground of the slave quarters...representing yourself as a 300 year old man. The fact is things have changed over the course of the last 300 years."

Other race-themed movies have followed *The Help*. In 2013 the star-studded cast of *The Butler* included Oprah Winfrey. The movie traced the life of Eugene Allen, whose tenure as a butler in the White House spanned presidents from Harry Truman to Ronald Reagan. The film is a highly fictionalized account of the extraordinary experience of Allen (played by Forest Whitaker as Cecil Gaines, a fictionalized Eugene Allen) and grossed $176 million.

Another important movie rendition of the black experience, *12 Years a Slave*, dramatized the antebellum story of Solomon Northrup, a free black captured in New York State, sent to a cotton farm in Louisiana, and freed with the aid of white abolitionists after twelve years of captivity. That the film enjoyed a $187 million gross testifies to its popularity.

The account of Northrup's ordeal was first published in book form in 1853. The details of his journey in the South, the names of his slave owners, and the places he visited have been "validated" by research. The book purports to be an autobiography, which it is not. According to the

Louisiana archival detective Sue Lyles Eakin, the book was written in three months by a white ghost writer, David Wilson, who had no verifiable connection to abolition. The haste for publication was a reaction to the commercial popularity of Harriet Beecher Stowe's *Uncle Tom's Cabin*, published in 1852. Stowe's first three months of royalties earned her $10,000, an important inducement; no wonder *12 Years a Slave* was dedicated to Harriet Beecher Stowe.

Eakin researched Northrup's story for decades before publishing the "first authenticated edition" of the book in 1968. Her work continued until in 2007 she produced the most recent edition, which contains a critical analysis of fact and fiction. Hollywood embellished this otherwise remarkable tale. It is worth noting that there is no record of Solomon Northrup after he was freed; no one knows where he was buried. This obscurity parallels the white North's lack of interest in black America after slavery had been abolished.

The movie *Selma*, a 2014 account of the march led by Martin Luther King Jr. from Selma across the Pettus Bridge to Montgomery, Alabama, in 1965, graphically displayed the racial injustice of overt legal segregation and its attendant violence in the South. The movie's alleged diminution of the role of Lyndon Johnson caused the late president's former chief domestic adviser, Joseph Califano Jr., to criticize the movie. Even more troubling to blacks and their supporters was the failure of the movie to win an Oscar. One observer rationalized the snub as a consequence of the film's failure to include a "white do-gooder." *Selma* grossed a disappointing $66 million.

Another well-anticipated movie, *Birth of a Nation*, chronicled the 1831 slave rebellion led by Nat Turner in Virginia. It was released in October 2016. The history of slave rebellions is vital to our understanding of the African American experience. *Birth of a Nation* is a composite, not a documentary. The movie's destiny is complicated by the trial of its writer, director, and actor, Nate Parker, for rape as a college student at Pennsylvania State University in 1999.

The difference between the cultural experience of a drama-enhanced movie and that of a museum are stark. The background for the Mississippi Civil Rights Museum (2017) illustrates the temptation to fictionalize in search of drama. The exhibition company proposed an image of a black nose behind a whites-only drinking fountain, but this idea was rejected by a black independent scholar who said that nobody was lynched for drinking water from a whites-only fountain. Segregation, he pointed out, was cruel in itself without the need to fictionalize. He was concerned about valid challenges to this exaggeration. Films don't have to worry about stories that digress from historical fact.

The Portability of Education

Education is the prerequisite for intellectual, physical, and economic mobility. It is portable, flexible, and the basis of individual and group self-esteem and confidence. Those societies that prize education have succeeded.

We have multiple examples of cultures that have evolved from illiterate agrarian peasantry to mass literacy and subsequent entrance into the economic mainstream. At the turn of the century Japan, a homogeneous, hierarchical society, attained mass literacy in one generation. It was accomplished through a rigid system that dictated policy and implementation. Japan's goal was Western-style literacy, which it achieved by borrowing Western techniques and people. The homogeneous populations of European countries also achieved literacy through Western norms. A heterogeneous population in a country without a hierarchy, like the United States, would be unable to duplicate Japan's accomplishment using the apparatus of a federal government.

Jews were able to create a literate society after the destruction of the second temple around 70 A.D. when a religious sect, the Pharisees, took control and dictated laws to foster education. Even before, the Pharisees had decreed that teachers of children be appointed in every city for boys aged six and seven. The Pharisees understood that study and teaching were necessary for proper worship both inside and outside the synagogue. In other words, literacy made religion and Jewish identity portable. It also provoked an occupational shift by which Jews would become bankers, doctors, lawyers, and scientists from an exclusively agricultural base. When the Jews were expelled from Spain and other European countries, the firmly rooted appreciation for education was maintained. The tradition continued during the Middle Ages. As recounted by the historian Ivan Marcus:

> At age five or six, a Jewish boy living in medieval Germany or France
> began his formal schooling by participating in a special ritual.... The

boy is seated on a teacher's lap, and the teacher shows him a tablet on which the Hebrew alphabet is written...and encourages the boy to repeat each sequence [of the exercise] aloud. The teacher smears honey over the letters on the tablet and tells the child to lick it off...the teacher leads the boy down to the riverbank and tells him that his future study of the Torah, like the rushing water in the river, will never end.

For Jews, America was the Promised Land. Nothing better illustrates this than President George Washington's 1790 visit to the Touro Synagogue in Newport, Rhode Island, and his defining letter to the Jews of Newport on August 18, 1790:

> May the children of the stock of Abraham who dwell in this land continue to merit and enjoy the good will of the other inhabitants—while every one shall sit in safety under his own vine and fig tree and there shall be none to make him afraid.

The letter was signed simply "G. Washington." When Jews refer to the "shared suffering" of blacks and Jews, they should reflect upon this letter. Blacks came to America in shackles. Just three years before Washington's visit to Newport, the new American Constitution had sanctioned slavery, albeit with the assumption by most delegates that the peculiar institution would wither. By contrast, the most powerful man in America, the hero of the American Revolution and a nation builder, had welcomed Jews, who would prosper as never before. Occasional slights and religious-inspired injustices are of little relevance when considered in the totality of the American Jewish experience.

Jewish education was portable. Jews could adapt. When penniless Eastern European immigrants landed in America, they may have settled in the tenements of New York's Lower East Side, but they became America's most successful immigrant group in terms of material prosperity and intellectual accomplishment. Culture triumphed over poverty. America's assimilation process allowed Jews to thrive. Jews were not alone in fostering education through religious institutions. The Catholic parochial school lifted millions of lower-class Italian and Irish children into the economic mainstream through a strict approach to education.

Singapore, the city state with 5.5 million people, is another instructive case. Its heterogeneous population, 75 percent Chinese and the remainder Malay and Indian, is fully literate and enormously successful. In 1965 the per capita GDP was $56; it is now more than $56,000. The autocratic founder, Lee Kuan Yew, a graduate of Cambridge University, realized that survival of his country required English as the national language. Local dialects and national languages could be preserved for cultural reasons, but English would assure national cohesion and competitive-ness in global business. Resorting to ethnic dialects, he reasoned, would lead to strife and tribalism. The priority was clear. Bilingual education in Singapore meant that English was the "first language and the mother tongue the second."

The United States is the only large-scale experiment in the via-bility of a heterogeneous country in which millions were accepted and absorbed via assimilation. The currently maligned "melting pot" approach worked while diverse groups were assimilated and yet main-tained their ethnic heritage. The major exceptions, of course, were blacks and American Indians. Race-based slavery and white America's discriminatory laws and customs prevented black matriculation into the economic mainstream before the 1960s. Now the obstacles for black America need to be reevaluated so that blacks may be fully incorporated into the American economy. After centuries of race-based prejudice, a Western values system has replaced color as the access to the economic mainstream. The tragedy of American Indians is a textbook case in the flaws of tribalism.

The examples above reveal the context of educational and economic success. The culture of each model is different—homogeneous and het-erogeneous, large and small, autocratic and egalitarian, rich in natural resources and poor in natural resources. But commonalities stand out: strong family units and a cohesive national identity that transcends ethnic groups.

Current issues over immigration in the United States concentrate on national and individual identity. Homogeneous societies like Japan and Europe have an advantage in cohesive action but a disadvantage in integrating foreigners. Thus far Japan has shown no intention of encouraging immigration by other ethnic or national groups; Western Europe's difficulty in absorbing immigrants is being tested in an extreme case—Muslim immigrants both past and present who strongly resist assimilation. America's current definition of multiculturalism leads to divisiveness.

Police and Community

Racial violence, then and now, may be triggered by a single incident. In August 1991 a racial melee exploded in the Crown Heights section of Brooklyn when a black youth was accidentally hit and killed by a car driven by a Hasidic Jew. Later a black man, Lemrick Nelson, in a fit of revenge, stabbed a Jewish student, Yankel Rosenbaum, to death. Blacks then participated in several days of "raw anti-Semitic rioting," according to Fred Siegel. A black-majority jury acquitted the obviously guilty Nelson of criminal charges. Afterward the jury celebrated Nelson's acquittal at a victory party. Nelson served time for violating Rosenbaum's civil rights and later admitted to the stabbing.

Four years after "Quiet Riots" had pronounced ghetto race riots a thing of the past, Watts in April 1992 experienced a massive racial eruption. In 1964 the National Urban League's statistics had erroneously described Los Angeles as "the best for black employment, housing, and income." Then Watts 1965 came along. In 1973 Los Angeles elected its first black mayor, Tom Bradley, a former police officer, who served as the city's highest-ranking official until 1993. Still, racial turmoil was present when Watts produced America's first "multicultural" riot. Prosperous Korean businesses, which had replaced Jewish-owned stores in black areas, were the target of black bitterness as exploiters of the black community. Before the riot of 1992 a black teenager was shot and killed by a Korean store owner in a physical altercation over shoplifting. The Korean was given a suspended sentence.

The spark for the tumultuous main riot was a video showing a black man, Rodney King, being beaten by police. They had tried to stop the intoxicated King, a parolee who had served time for robbing a Korean store, for speeding. King, afraid he would be jailed for breaking parole, led the police on a high-speed chase. After apprehending King, their abusive treatment of him was captured on film. When the police were acquitted after trial, Los Angeles blacks and Hispanics began an orgy of looting and arson.

A white truck driver, Reginald Denny, who happened to be driving through Watts, was beaten by Damian Williams and three other gang members, the L.A. Four. Cameras recorded the incident. Then fifty mostly Hispanic and Asian immigrants were attacked on a street corner by blacks. The tally for the riot was enormous—more than fifty killed, two thousand injured, and more than two thousand arrested.

The militant black community interpreted the race riot as a justifiable response to racial injustice. When the four gang members who pummeled Reginald Denny were tried and treated leniently, the court results were greeted enthusiastically by the black community. Most charges were dismissed by the jury. The black community, noted Fred Siegel, treated the L.A. Four "either as heroes, modern-day Nat Turners...or 'scapegoats' for a white racist criminal-justice system." The accused Damian Williams was regarded as heroic, not because he was innocent but, wrote John Taylor, because he actually was guilty of "smashing a brick into a white man's head." Ironically, blacks had simultaneously condemned white racism and Korean exploitation. The unity of "people of color" was yet again exposed as a fiction.

The black congresswoman Maxine Waters, co-chair of Bill Clinton's presidential campaign, supported the L.A. Four and suggested that violence "drew attention to the victimization of blacks by white society." It was as if the black race, rather than individuals, was being tried. Yet another tradition of individual responsibility, the criminal act, disappeared in the haze of past injustice. "If we don't get justice," warned Maxine Waters, "we're going to have a civil war." Intimidation meant leverage. She was right: henceforth disruptive demonstrations, violence, and the threat of violence were considered legitimate tactics.

The anger and resentment leading to violence in Watts was partly aimed at nonblack businesses in the neighborhood. Again the collateral question is, why were Jews and Koreans, not blacks, owners of businesses in their own neighborhoods? Why did blacks, as David Levering Lewis observed at an earlier time in Harlem, "miss the significance of the role of proprietor"—especially for stepping-stone businesses?

Koreans in black communities of New York City experienced the same friction in the 1990s. The Koreans had pooled their resources in a constructive effort of group unity to finance businesses. Tom Shachtman describes one function of the "close-knit Korean business community in New York." Jung-ok Hwang, a Korean businessman, who had saved money from previous entrepreneurial efforts, moved to New York in the mid-1970s. Although he had no knowledge of the liquor business, he wanted to buy a small liquor store in the Chelsea neighborhood. First he located a shop that interested him, then worked for the owner and took a wine course. Soon he purchased the going concern. Each morning and evening a representative of the nineteen Korean-American families who owned liquor stores said a prayer for every proprietor in the group. Each owner contributed at least one dollar to a fund for each prayer. Part of the proceeds, which amounted to $10,000 annually, became a scholarship for a Korean-American youth. All of Hwang's five children went to American colleges, the youngest graduating from the Massachusetts Institute of Technology.

Why had blacks not followed the example of Jews and Koreans? This brings to mind Jews as the model for savings cited by Frederick Douglass, Booker T. Washington, W. E. B. Du Bois, and Louis Armstrong. Black leadership had observed Jewish habits of saving for the future. In a rather bizarre explanation for blacks' disregard of savings, the noted black writer Thomas Sowell blamed Southern whites for the lack of thrift—and most other faults—among blacks who, he thought, emulated Southern whites. But the Connecticut Survey of 1800 also described free blacks in the North as profligate, and Connecticut's early-nineteenth-century black population had no contact with Southern whites.

Today, black hostility remains. The events of Orlando, Ferguson, New York, Baltimore, Milwaukee, Charlotte, and other places where blacks were killed by police or a private guard have prompted mass protests either immediately after the incident or after an acquittal of the accused. The facts of each case are different such that interpretation and proper adjudication vary. In one incident, an ethnic Chinese policeman in New York City was convicted, much to the consternation of New York's Asian community. In Milwaukee a black suspect was shot by a black policeman. In Minneapolis a black suspect was shot by an Hispanic officer. In Charlotte, which has a black police chief, a black suspect was shot by a black police officer.

In their diatribe against white America, black activists now gloss over the race of the black policemen. Because activists can no longer use the racial theme of a white cop shooting a black suspect, the mantra is "police" rather than "white police" who are abusing blacks. President

Obama and various black leaders pay lip service to peaceful demonstrations while joining in the chorus of vilification for past and perceived present injustices. In no way does the black community remind the rioters that alleged wrongs need to be adjudicated through a criminal justice system, not in the streets. In addition to images of people marching in protest, the film of the Charlotte protest captured scenes of street violence and looting, people being beaten, and a black man shot by the rioters— just the kind of mayhem that black leaders of the 1960s condemned.

Baltimore experienced an outburst of racial violence in April 2015 when a black man died in a police van. Six police officers, black and white, were indicted for murder and negligent behavior by the black prosecutor in a city with a black mayor and a black police chief. The presiding black judge, who had a civil rights background, acquitted the police officers. Kurt Schmoke, the former black mayor and a Yale (1971) graduate, called his native Baltimore "a tale of two cities."

Schmoke, now president of the University of Baltimore, is an excellent example of the ascendancy of blacks in the twenty-first century. A Rhodes Scholar, graduate of Harvard Law School, and former member of the Yale governing body, he helped defuse the Black Panther confrontation in New Haven during his student years. Despite such formidable credentials, awards, and positions of power, Schmoke and other black leaders have had little sway over crime and the endemic issues of black inner-city culture.

Policy recommendations from the Kerner Report have a familiar ring today: add more black police, improve police conduct and patrol practices, justify the conditions of deadly force, set up community relations programs. Technology, in the form of body cameras, would be a twenty-first-century addition. And differing circumstances would include the influence of special-interest police unions, which have grown immensely; at times the police union can inhibit an investigation of police conduct. In 2016, too, budgetary constraints for municipalities are structural rather than cyclical. Public pension funds, benefits, and debt service have restricted expenditures for many public service departments.

Violent racial unrest lurks just below the surface. The law-and-order response to the 1960s race riots should be a lesson. Instead, some viewed the law-and-order goals as overly restrictive and racially motivated. The desire for "law and order," wrote the historian Garry Wills about Chicago's racial turbulence in 1968, "is nothing so simple as a code word for racism: it is a cry, as things begin to break up, for stability, for stopping history in mid-dissolution." Blacks react to law and order as the preservation of an unjust system; they want monetary compensation, have no compunction about destruction, avoid working through the system even when blacks are in positions of authority, and refuse to analyze events of the last fifty years objectively. Although the facts of each of the recent accusations of police abuse have been different, Black Lives Matter and others view all as indistinguishable acts of police brutality. The drama and resulting turmoil have generated publicity that vividly illustrates the persistent racial divide.

Through movies, books, articles, and the media, Black Lives Matter and similar groups draw false analogies between past events and police abuse. The ire relates to the deaths of blacks at the hands of police, the lack of prosecution of alleged mistreatment, the perceived disrespect of the black community. Their references are the best-known historical trials—the Scottsboro boys in 1931, Emmett Till in 1955, and the three murdered civil rights workers in Philadelphia, Mississippi, in 1964—all of which typified gross miscarriages of justice. The equating of these tragedies to the twenty-first-century situations involving blacks—Trayvon Martin in Orlando; Michael Brown in Ferguson, Missouri; Freddie Gray in Baltimore; and others—is highly misleading in the current world of black mayors, police chiefs, police officers, and prosecutors, and the scrutiny of the media.

Then there is Chicago 2016. The city has experienced 762 homicides of which 80 percent are black-on-black and over four thousand shooting-related episodes. Chicago's public school system is broken; its finances are dismal; its police/community relationship is dreadful. The most public example of friction occurred when an unarmed black man, Lequan McDonald, was shot repeatedly by a cop. Angry demonstrations ensued. All but forgotten is the gang-related murder of nine-year-old Tyshawn Lee at roughly the same time. Two higher profile gang murders—the cousin of basketball star Dwyane Wade and the grandson of Congressman Danny Davis—received some attention. In all of 2016, the police have accounted for only twenty-five of the shootings. To ascribe the problem wholly to lax gun control laws and poverty is to avoid a share of the responsibility. Chicago's roster of well-known leaders includes President Barack Obama, Jessie Jackson, Reverend Jeremiah Wright,

Valerie Jarrett, Mayor Rahm Emmanuel (President Obama's former chief of staff), and Arne Duncan (former superintendent of Chicago Schools and President Obama's former secretary of education). This line-up clearly had little influence on Chicago's state of affairs. Chicago's gang problems have a long history. In 1966, Republican senators Charles Percy (Chicago) and Jacob Javits (New York) tried to co-opt the leadership of one gang, the Blackstone Rangers, to work together with Republicans for the betterment of the city. This effort was short-lived.

The failure of the black ghetto community to cooperate with the police, particularly in cases of black crime, makes the neighborhood more unsafe than it already is. Criminals roam with little or no fear or apprehension because blacks do not help identify or testify against them. Often the neighborhood is afraid of retaliation if they assist police. *The New Yorker* in September 2016 carried the story of a young man in Chicago, Romaine Hill, who identified and testified against the man who had shot him in 2013. The culprit was convicted and sentenced to fifteen years in prison. Within a year, Romaine Hill was assassinated while walking through a park on his way to work. This is precisely the type of retaliation that *Ebony* exposed in 1967 when witnesses to the murder of Joey Thomas in Harlem had to be moved to another community for their safety. A "code of silence," whether out of fear of retaliation or hostility toward police, is irrational when the safety of a community is at stake.

Reverend Jesse Jackson was very much aware of the problems in his law-and-order stance in 1993, as reported by the journalist Mike Royko. "[B]lack-on-black murder," spoke Reverend Jackson, "[is] the leading cause of death in black males." He famously continued, "There is nothing more painful to me...than to walk down the street and hear footsteps and start thinking robbery. Then [I] look around and see someone white and feel relieved." "The killing," he asserted, "is not based on poverty; it is based on greed and violence and guns.... We've got the power...to stop killing each other." He then slammed blacks for refusing to speak out and to cooperate with police: "There is a code of silence, based upon fear. Our silence is a sanctuary for killers and drug dealers.... The victim has to rise up."

The facts, circumstances, and context of each case of police abuse are different and bear no relationship to the highly visible racial injustices of the past. Each case should be examined and tried on its merits; aberrant behavior will be recognized and punished. Otherwise a racialized evolution of the justice system will lead to equally wrong decisions—see, for example, Damian Williams in Watts and Lemrick Nelson in Brooklyn—as blacks cheer.

The singular concentration on alleged police abuse also becomes a distraction to the overall safety of the black community. While vilifying police, the black community at the same time wants more protection, which means more police. New York City has added a thousand new police officers; Chicago plans to add a thousand, which are slated to initially cost $130 million. That cost will surely rise sharply when pensions are activated. A black or white child born today will shoulder an enormous burden when fully loaded pension fund benefits become due.

The Kerner Commission faced the same contradiction—"the hostility between police and ghetto communities" and the "conviction that ghetto neighborhoods are not given adequate police protection." These conflicting facts remain ever present—except that since the 1970s cities have had black mayors, black police chiefs, and black police officers. The usual discriminatory accusation—white cops killing black citizens—is no longer valid. Black officials can now be responsible for black deaths in the line of duty.

The rift between police and the community is further complicated by the police union. Many states have enacted "decertification" regulations and statutes. These, with a varying degree of strength, can take away the license of a police officer who is guilty of serious misconduct. According to expert law professor emeritus Roger Goldman in the *Atlantic* (April 9, 2017), some blue states, i.e. progressive states, like Massachusetts, California, Hawaii, and Maryland, either have no "decertification" laws or have weak ones. "This should be an indication," he continues, "that opposition" is coming from police unions. California has moved from having "decertification" to not having any. New York passed a "decertification" regulation, not statute, in October 2016, but the nature of the enforcement remains to be seen. The nexus between politics and the public service unions, just as in the education arena, is on display in the "decertification" issue. Even if tough "decertification" laws existed, what are the safeguards against politicization of the process?

In 2014 the black Yale sociologist Elijah Anderson blamed the police for "abdicating their responsibilities, as high rates of homicide and violence are tolerated..." He never mentions the increase of black police at all levels in urban environments. For Anderson, the police should be more, not less, vigilant in black ghettos. Without police protection, Anderson asserts, "street justice" fills the vacuum left by police inaction, bringing greater violence and higher homicide rates. Ghetto conditions, he says, are the result of poverty based on job dislocation and "slashed" welfare rolls. In this analysis, the black individual is again stripped of free will. But attitudes expressed by black law enforcement officers are different. Winston E. Moore, the first black executive director of the Cook County (Chicago) Department of Corrections, thought that poverty was no excuse for black-on-black crime: "I am tired of this argument because, again, it says that blacks are innately irresponsible and unable to make rational decisions between right and wrong."

On the surface, both of these black men advocate strict enforcement of the law. But one, the Yale professor, denies black agency, and the other, a highly placed officer of the law, believes in individual responsibility. Do their opposing views of free will merely reflect a generational difference (Moore operated in the 1970s) or a gigantic shift in values?

Protests following the killing of Trayvon Martin in Florida gave birth to Black Lives Matter (BLM), a social-media-fueled movement that has surpassed older black organizations in zeal and public attention. First identified with a response to police "brutality," it quickly moved to a broader, more ambitious program. Black Lives Matter uses the drama and publicity of street violence to promote its real agenda, which is radical change in America. Today, Black Lives Matter and other black activist groups selectively avoid the vastly more harmful debacle of black-on-black crime.

Major funding has now arrived for Black Lives Matter. George Soros, the billionaire hedge fund manager, has given $33 million; the Ford and Borealis Foundations are raising $100 million. In conjunction with other like-minded groups, BLM has formed the Movement for Black Lives and the related fund recipient, the Black-Led Movement Fund. The organization has intensified its attack on alleged white supremacy and oppression.

Black Lives Matter is a manifestation of the racial divide and a proxy for looking not only at actual or perceived abusive police conduct but at a panoply of racial issues. BLM and a large segment of America's black population believe that institutional racism, racial discrimination, systemic racism, white privilege, and oppression are pervasive. Slavery and overt legal segregation demand monetary compensation—that is, reparations. Any means, including violence, is justified in obtaining funding and an equal share of America's wealth. Sole blame for black poverty and inadequate housing, health, education, and black crime is placed on white racism, capitalism, colonialism, and Western civilization.

BLM has been a major divisive factor in the social fabric. In 2015, according to the Southern Poverty Law Center, the number of black militant and anti-white hate groups increased by 59 percent to 180, a direct consequence of the racial tension fomented by Black Lives Matter. With its purely separatist goals, the group takes credit for creating protests that lead to violence, which it considers an effective method of intimidation. Black Lives Matter does not touch the sacrosanct area of behavioral norms. It advocates a conversation in which activists demand and government responds. This is not a recipe for dialogue and objectivity.

Blacks resent the characterization of a monolithic black society. Yet the black middle and upper classes would appear to be in complete sympathy and agreement with BLM's philosophy. Even privileged blacks have not disagreed with BLM. Are they afraid? Is this an example of racial solidarity or group peer pressure? The BLM platform is readily available for inspection, yet there has been little attention paid by the black elite.

The violence of street riots, in today's context, is enormously effective in generating intimidation under the guise of activism. "It is an age of enlightenment," wrote the *New York Times* columnist Charles Blow. But both Lyndon Johnson and the early Martin Luther King Jr. condemned violence. While black militants subscribed to violence, law and order advocates, such as Morris Liebman in 1964, thought that "grievances must be settled in the courts and not in the streets." The law is amenable to change.

President Obama asked benignly for peaceful protest and better relations between the police and the black community, but he failed to denounce destruction and criminal behavior. His 2015 speech to the NAACP was more conciliatory to the people in the streets than to law enforcement officials. Jesse Jackson had accused Senator Obama of "talking down to black people" when as a presidential candidate he had dared to criticize blacks. President Obama had digested the advice and thereafter avoided criticism of black behavior.

One of BLM's young leaders, DeRay Mckesson, in his seminar at the Yale Divinity School in October 2015, used the essay "In Defense of Looting" to show diverse points of view. Mckesson wanted to illustrate the tension between protest and property. The "Looting" article, written by Willie Osterweil, a member of the punk band Vulture Shit, was included in Mckesson's reading list. Osterweil, following in the intellectual footsteps of Malcolm X and the African American Teachers Association, proclaimed looting a positive good:

> The mystifying ideological claim that looting is violent and non-political is one that has been carefully produced by the ruling class.... [T] here is a practical benefit to looting.... [The looters] might just be feeding their family.... They might just be expropriating what they otherwise buy—liquor...—but it still represents a material way that riots and protests help the community: by providing a way for people to solve...immediate problems of poverty.... When, in the midst of an anti-police protest movement, people loot...they are getting straight to the heart of the problem of the police—property and white supremacy.

Osterweil's defense of looting and denigration of private property in some ways parallels that of the later Martin Luther King Jr. in 1967. Yale, obviously worried about donors, was quick to dissociate itself from the seminar's reading list. A Yale spokesman explained that "no one in the audience spoke out in favor of looting." The justification of looting and street violence, as acceptable civil disobedience, represents a real threat to society and is counterproductive to achieving black economic and educational momentum.

Like the BLM program, the platform for Movement for Black Lives is a harangue against white supremacy, oppression, capitalism, exploitation, colonialism, and discrimination. Its main thrust is a multifaceted demand for money from government entities and corporations in the form of reparations for slavery and past injustices. The platform calls for an "immediate passage of HR-40," the bill introduced by John Conyers since

1989 and tabled. It would authorize a commission to study all reparations proposals. The platform also demands an end to all private funding of schools. Bill and Melinda Gates, the Walton Family, and Eli and Edythe Broad, because of their enormous grants to education, are accused of "denying Black people their human right to an education…[depriving] Black people of the right to self-determine the kind of education their children receive." Instead the group wants a federal government grant of $165 billion for a "full and free" college education for all blacks. All black student college debt would be abolished. A guaranteed "livable minimum income" would be granted to all black people. "Reformer programs" such as Teach For America and the Broad Superintendents Academy would be eliminated. Presumably no privately funded scholarships for black students would be allowed. School endowments—Harvard, $36 billion; Yale, $27 billion; Princeton, $23 billion; Stanford, $22 billion—would be fair game for the wealth-tax proposals of Black Lives Matter. Other demands include:

- Place a moratorium on charter school and school closings.
- Put a moratorium on all out-of-school suspensions.
- Shut down all juvenile detention centers.
- Remove police from schools and replace them with positive alternatives to discipline and safety.

Movement for Black Lives also advocates community control of schools, as in the Ocean Hill–Brownsville battle. It would put local communities with equal funding provisions in charge of every aspect of running a school district. Funding increases would go to Historically Black Colleges, black media, and cultural, political, and social institutions. The movement wants "retroactive decriminalization, immediate release and record expungement of all drug-related offenses and prostitution," with reparations to compensate.

To finance this mind-boggling list of demands, taxes would be universally raised. The personal income tax would gradually move to 80 percent; estate, capital gains, and corporate rates would rise. A wealth tax would be imposed. Tax deductions for mortgage interest payments would be eliminated.

While accepting money from foundations, the Movement for Black

Lives prefers to receive funding from the federal government, hence higher taxes. Political pressure could force continuing government grants with no substantive oversight. One movement demand confusingly states, "Debt of elimination of Black municipality," which might mean some form of expunging municipal debt that specifically relates to blacks.

This prodigious list of demands is a naked grab for money. Any form of accountability is absent. No analysis of existing or former programs is ever mentioned. There is not a trace of concern for individual responsibility or performance criteria. The platform, despite its emphasis on historical injustice, is ahistorical in ignoring all past efforts specifically directed toward blacks. Without an objective look at the effectiveness of these endeavors, no appropriations can be intelligently authorized. Black Lives Matter advocates self-segregation without elaborating on the role of racial integration, without touching the sacrosanct subject of behavioral norms.

Nor are semantics free from the oversight of Black Lives Matter. It has mandated de facto copyright protection for a broad category of labels, including All Lives Matter, whose use it prohibits. Enforcement is strict at every level; intimidation is effective. In November 2015 the Democratic Congressional Campaign Committee instructed its staff never to say "all lives matter." On a less exalted level, the gullible University of Houston Student Government Association (SGA), by a thirteen-to-two vote, severely punished Rohini Sethi, its executive vice president, for posting the phrase "all lives matter" on her Facebook page. Stunned, Sethi received a "50-day suspension from SGA, was required to attend a diversity workshop, was compelled to attend three campus cultural events each month, was obliged to write an apology letter, and was forced to give a public presentation about her transgression."

After riding roughshod over free speech, the SGA president, Shane Smith, said that the First Amendment does not prohibit "workplace discipline," which he imposed. Rohini Sethi, as is apparent by her name, is of Indian descent and therefore a person "of color." Black Lives Matter and other black groups pay lip service to people "of color" but reserve special status for themselves. Including other groups as victims of discrimination is merely a pretext for gaining support without conferring equal rank. Some groups, to paraphrase George Orwell, are more equal than others.

Black Leadership

Black leaders responded in substantially different ways to the riots of the 1960s and Watts in 1992 than to the smaller violent demonstrations of 2015 and 2016. The early Martin Luther King Jr., Roy Wilkins, and Whitney Young Jr., while understanding the frustrations of the ghetto, were opposed to violence and looting, though they were powerless to control the disruptions. The influential giants of black leadership of a half-century ago have not been replaced. King's heroics are displayed for the world to see through the media, books, movies, and museums. His words survive in articles, journals, and books. But his principles and attitudes are now subject to interpretation.

History acknowledges, too, the efforts of Charles Hamilton Houston, Walter White, Roy Wilkins, and Thurgood Marshall. Whitney Young Jr.'s contribution through the National Urban League is memorable. Today, can anyone name the recent leaders of the rudderless NAACP and the National Urban League? When a racial event occurs, the media often interview officers of the NAACP and the Urban League as representatives of the black community. When an act is perceived to be discriminatory, the NAACP is ready to broadcast discrimination before facts are adjudicated. The alphabet black organizations—SNCC, SCLC, and COFO (Council of Federated Organizations)—have either dissolved or lost force after the elimination of concrete and visible legal injustices. Complex racial issues of education, income, or politics are still expressed in the language of the civil rights movement, but the attempt to associate today with the 1960s has failed to achieve pervasive resonance.

By 1992 the founding fathers of the civil rights revolution of the 1960s had been supplanted by politicians, particularly black mayors and almost fifty members of the congressional Black Caucus. Among black mayors, Carl Rowan (Cleveland, 1968), Coleman Young (Detroit, 1974), Marion Barry (Washington, DC, 1979), Richard Arrington Jr. (Birmingham, 1979), Andrew Young (Atlanta, 1982), Harold Washington (Chicago, 1983), David Dinkins (New York, 1988), and Willie Herenton (Memphis, 1991) comprise a partial list. In addition, the Internet has given wide national visibility to a variety of black activist and community groups competing for local, state, and national attention. The election of numerous black officials to public office is often cited as progress, which in a certain sense it is. But black mayors have not fulfilled promises of a revolutionary transition to black prosperity. "A black mayor," Bayard Rustin observed, "is not Nirvana." The problems are deeper. Many of the 950 black elected officials in Mississippi represent economically moribund communities with a huge black voting majority.

The fantasy of a postracial society arrived with the 2008 election of Barack Obama to the presidency. Democratic Party leaders—Senate Majority Leader Harry Reid and then Senator Joe Biden—accepted candidate Obama as an elite black person who embodied assimilation. Reid liked Obama because he was "light-skinned" and spoke "with no Negro dialect, unless he wanted to have one." Biden saw Obama as "the first mainstream African American who is articulate and bright and clean and a nice-looking guy." The young Ivy League African American, however, did not usher America into a peace of racial harmony. Quite the opposite occurred. By the end of his eight-year presidency, race relations were worse than before his election.

President Obama's biography cannot be a model for troubled black youth. He was raised by a family that was deeply committed to his education; he went to private schools; and he was not subject to the destructive peer pressures of the inner city. He serves as the most prominent example of what an African American *can* become in America today. Nevertheless, he cannot replace a father, teacher, or religious leader as an aspirational influence on a child, nor did he try to change the behavioral norms of the black underclass. As an opportunistic ambitious politician, he embraced Chicago's visible blacks, including Jesse Jackson and the Reverend Jeremiah Wright. When they became liabilities outside the confines of the black Illinois electorate, he jettisoned both. The racial crossover candidate emerged. Other popular black politicians—former Newark mayor and current US senator Cory Booker and former Massachusetts governor Deval Patrick—are cut from the same integrationist fabric.

Quite apart from these black heroes, where are the structures of family, community, or church that will implement the necessary policies to deal with employment, crime, and education? Currently they do not exist. The dysfunctional nature of much of the black underclass is well known and well documented. It is difficult to see how the public school system can rectify the damage created by the single-parent family and the absenteeism of the black father. There has been no sense of urgency by the black community to instill a value system that will encourage an intact family. The lack of eligible husbands had been noted in the 1930s before the incarceration of blacks became widespread. The journalist Eugene Robinson dismisses the importance of marriage but lamely leaves the task to "every preacher, in every pulpit." President Obama, who is a committed family man, rarely mentions the responsibility of fathers. In his presidential valedictory speech President Obama emphasized the role of political activism but neglected any mention of the importance of a two-parent family structure.

The family is the first incubator of behavioral norms that foster education, hard work, and citizenship. The probability of proper child-rearing with such a huge percentage of poor single-parent families is very low. A study in Connecticut by a former high school superintendent and current professor of education, David Title, measured the correlation of test scores for children based on three factors—family income, per pupil expenditure, and single-parent families. The most prominent factor affecting negative performance on test scores was the single-parent family, not family income or per pupil expenditure. We need more studies analyzing the correlation between single-parent families and educational performance. Moreover, intervention with social programs must start as early as possible, even prenatal.

What community-based organizations now exist to channel energy constructively? Where are the voluntary groups that might promote community goals? Since the 1960s scores of public and privately funded programs have been formed to address issues in the black community. Do we know what they have accomplished, how the funds were employed, and what happened to the people who administered the funds and to their beneficiaries? We do know that chronic problems, frustration, and anger persist despite massive expenditures, so any call for new grants should be predicated on what has happened in previous efforts. History does matter.

Particularly in urban areas one can find numerous social activists and organizations that operate under the banner of social justice. They analogize their work and role to those of the civil rights movement of the 1960s, but this is most assuredly not the case. Suffrage, the judicial removal of overt legal discrimination in public accommodations, and the removal of legal school segregation are objectives distinctly different from the kinds of challenges presented by today's complex social issues. Black commentators sometimes refer to the 1960s reforms as the easy part of the black struggle.

The language and methodology of the civil rights era has been hijacked irresponsibly by today's social activists and commentators. The demonstrations, often violent, following each perceived incidence of abusive behavior is a harmful conditioned response that serves no purpose. It is a misapplied relic of the civil rights era. The identification of many of today's racial issues with those of the 1960s is a harmful myth in need of shattering. The title of the popular book *The New Jim Crow: Mass Incarceration in the Age of Colorblindness* is a false analogy that employs the coattail effect by associating the subject with an emotionally charged phrase. The musician, actor, and civil rights activist Harry Belafonte sees "parallels between the roadblocks and successes of the 1950s and '60s and those of today." A closer look would show the differences.

The refusal to discuss black behavioral norms is especially damaging. The black "Many Rivers to Cross" festival in Atlanta in October 2016 advertised three themes—voting, mass incarceration, and the relationship between community and law enforcement. Nowhere did the program tackle education, family, employment, and black-on-black crime. The ubiquitous accusation of racism and its alternative form, institutional racism, provide a convenient excuse for avoiding objectivity. Separatism, rather than integration, is given full vent. Black movements from Marcus Garvey to Malcolm X to the Student Non-Violent Coordinating Committee to the Black Panthers to Black Lives Matter are essentially espousing a separate racial society.

Confusion reigns in the black community, which aspires to the fruits of assimilation but demands the separatism implicit in the current iteration of multiculturalism. The ghost of the Black Panther movement lurks in the corners of multiculturalism. The integrationist goals of the NAACP, dating to the early twentieth century, are subordinated.

The practical task facing America is the economic elevation of the black community—desperately for the underclass and significantly for the fragile middle class. Despite the economic gains, civil rights attainment, and political power, since the civil rights era, overall statistics are problematic—especially in the underclass—24.1 percent of all African Americans and 32.9 percent of all black children below the age of eighteen live below the poverty line; average wealth of white families has increased by three times that of black families in the last thirty years; blacks score lower on the American College Testing Program's ACT than any other racial or ethnic group; blacks are concentrated in "lower paying [college] majors" and underrepresented in "fastest-growing, highest paying occupations."

Questions of race relations, race progress, and racial identity in America remain of paramount concern. The enormity of change is evident, but statistics, emotions, demonstrations, movies, memorials, and attitudes point to the continuing difficulty of assimilating and incorporating the black underclass into the economic mainstream. The goals of the Kerner Report have not been met. The beginning of the twenty-first century signals yet another inflection point in American race relations. The burden now, as Eli Ginzberg wrote in 1956, "for improving the Negro's preparation for work falls on the Negro community itself.... It is too much to ask of the school that it make up for all of the deficiencies in the home and the community.... [L]eaders of the Negro community [should] speed the assimilation of Negroes into American society."

Chapter Six

From Dream to Reality

Contrary to optimistic expectations, a postracial America did not follow the election of Barack Obama to the presidency. Racial divisiveness is more evident now than it was when Obama took office. America's cities are still ubiquitously described in the famous language of the Kerner Report (1968): "two societies—one black and one white—separate and unequal." To be sure, we now have a much larger black middle class (with a vulnerable asset base) and a visible black elite. But we also have a large black underclass. The fourth-grade black girl in the Mississippi Delta who can't read and the "functionally illiterate" black high school graduate in Bridgeport, Connecticut, are still with us despite major corrective attention and funding.

The policy impasse over "what to do" about this continues primarily because of a black mindset. Blacks and many whites place the blame for black problems almost exclusively on poverty, discrimination, and wide-spread racism. These are the causes, they say, of the plight of the black underclass and the restrictions of the black middle class. This analysis, however, has led only to frustration, immunization from self-examination, greater demands for financial intervention, and sanction for violence in the streets under the guise of peaceful protest. In this scenario, black separatism appears with a nostalgic nod to the Black Power movement of the 1960s. Black attraction to a separate society is an impediment to full participation in the American mainstream. Assimilation, without question, weakens group identity, but the benefits are overwhelming for the individual and the specific ethnic community. Moreover, the by-product of national cohesion strengthens all.

Before we can achieve any major, broad-based improvement in the social and educational status of blacks, they must develop a frank process of self-examination to replace the current unwillingness to look objectively at destructive behavioral norms. Otherwise the myriad programs designed specifically to aid blacks will fail to achieve a large-scale transformation. This particular burden—of facing themselves—lies squarely on the black community.

Any analysis of today's racial problems must recognize the racial and economic world of 2017, which is quite different from that of the 1960s. Municipal, state, and federal budgets are constrained by debt and low growth. Unlike those of the 1960s, today's financial and economic problems are structural. Legacy entitlements—benefits and health care—are an enormous burden unknown in the sixties. The public pension crisis was not on the horizon fifty years ago. Ferocious global business competition was a nonfactor in post–World War II America. Any proposal to deal with social problems must face the realities of government expenditures and economic growth—they are no longer abstractions.

Economic advancement must be the number one goal for black Americans while they pursue an appropriate approach to social justice.

National economic growth is the prerequisite for economic advancement for both blacks and whites. Historically, education, social choice, and a growing American economy have provided stepping-stones for the rising lower classes. Preparation, a responsibility well understood and well expressed by black civil rights leaders in the 1960s, is the *sine qua non* of economic, physical, and intellectual mobility. Today preparation is absent from black dialogue.

The institutional framework—church, family, community, school, and government—for fostering requisite norms among blacks is dysfunctional. Some form of discipline must be practiced. If black family structure continues in its present form, educational and vocational obstacles may be virtually insurmountable. According to the most recent US Census, as reported in the *Journal of Blacks in Higher Education*, only 38.7 percent of black children under the age of eighteen live with both parents (74.3 percent for whites), and one-third of black children under the age of eighteen live with mothers who have never been married (6.5 percent for whites). The consequences should be made clear: two-parent families generally have higher incomes than single-parent families; more supervision, structure, attention, discipline, and interaction with teachers and parents occur when two parents are present. The vocabulary deficit of children in poor single-parent families is well established.

Most disturbing is the seeming lack of urgency in confronting the debacle of the black family. The very mention of the single-parent family as an issue is often regarded by blacks as racial condescension. The problem is barely acknowledged and certainly not confronted. Instead the drama of a confrontation with police generates vast media coverage.

The broad substitution of public schools and social programs for parenting is a speculative experiment that has shown little promise. Because of teachers' unions, troubled school systems should be challenged from the outside by voucher programs and charter schools. These efforts are not intended to replace public schools; their role, like that of any entrepreneurial endeavor, is to find a better way. The process of choice should force a constructive reaction from the public school system.

For the black underclass, the church remains the major institutional vehicle for dealing with behavioral norms and adequate parenting. This role demands the active involvement of black church members with congregants and with families and children who are not church members. Both blacks and whites should bring pressure to engage the black church. Without a serious effort to change elements of black culture, children may escape a dismal fate, but large numbers will be trapped in poverty or in a persistent income gap.

A movement—not a protest action but an organized effort—can instill constructive values. But it requires both white and black participation. Every socioeconomic class of the black community must be involved. Narrowing of the income gap between middle-class blacks and whites is also a function of educational choices. Private-sector employment should be emphasized; the kind of major a college student decides on will usually influence their income. Without adequate preparation, however, a major with high earning potential will be illusive.

Segregated housing severely restricts the normal channels of racial interaction among elementary and secondary school children. To some extent, colleges provide an opportunity for integrated exposure and a transition to the workplace. At every level for whites and blacks, the classroom should emphasize the practical advantages of assimilation while continuing to foster cultural heritage. The parallel societies advocated by some blacks are a nonstarter for mass movement into the economic world.

Emphasis on racial interaction and organization at the community level is paramount. Federal intervention was essential in eliminating overt legal segregation, but a concentration on education and business, in order to be effective, must be local. Even federal programs must succeed or fail on the state and local levels. Large government social programs are plagued by inefficiency, bureaucracy, politics, logistics, accountability, and the tendency to become employment agencies with little impact. The most important role models, whether parents, teachers, or religious leaders, are local.

Highly visible efforts to reform education have been transient, not transformational. Although widely praised and memorialized, the educational component of the Mississippi Freedom Summer of 1964 had little lasting effect. Teach For America has had an important presence in predominantly black Mississippi schools for years, yet no school district has been profoundly affected. In 2016 the thirteen Mississippi school districts that were classified as failing were all majority black. All had mostly or entirely black leadership.

Accountability in social and educational programs has been severely lacking. Funding should be contingent on performance; experimentation should be encouraged. Tracking is essential and must extend for many years. Short-term blips in educational performance are often mistakenly presented as successful trends in order to gain future grants from foundations and government. Data on children's experience should extend from preschool to postcollege to determine successful matriculation into a stable career. High school graduation rates are often too easily manipulated to be a reliable indicator of progress.

America has drifted away from the ideal of a color-blind society toward an exaggerated notion of color-consciousness. A few in the black community have objected. The actor Morgan Freeman had a testy interchange in 2005 with CBS journalist Mike Wallace, in which Freeman rejected the idea of Black History Month. He then asked Wallace, who was Jewish, if he favored a Jewish History Month. A stunned Wallace replied no. Freeman, who wanted to be considered a man, not a black man, then violated the racial notation dictum: "I'm going to stop calling you a white man, and I'm going to ask you to stop calling me a black man. I know you as Mike Wallace. You know me as Morgan Freeman." Freeman's goal was to be identified as an individual, not a member of a group. The late tennis great Arthur Ashe similarly hoped for a world of individuals without racial implications: "I look forward to the day when a white man can look across the room at a black man and say without guilt, 'I don't like him'—without it having to do with race.... And a black man should be able to do the same thing. Then we'll have real equality."

There is a room for both color-blindness and color-consciousness in the American conversation. Color-blind Western norms are necessary to give most students, black and white, the tools for individual economic self-sufficiency, cultural growth, a sense of place in America, and a recognition of the proper balance between individual and group identity. But the interest in, appreciation for, support of, and participation in black heritage, black history, and black arts are constructive elements of color-consciousness. This is not to say that black ideology should dominate the interpretation of American history. The tragedies of that history must be fully revealed, like its triumphs. For the most part, American history as currently taught and told by blacks is a litany of grievances that paralyze and do not account for change. Today's classrooms should concentrate on critical analysis, which means free speech, exposure to different and conflicting interpretations, and navigation between different points of view. This is a journey for students of all races and ethnicities.

The study of Abraham Lincoln is a case in point, involving distinct racial interpretations. Should he be canonized as the Great Emancipator or relegated to the mortal status of a president "forced into glory"? Without Lincoln, warts and all, America might resemble the debilitating fragmentation of the Balkans.

In discussions of race, the racial attitudes of white Northerners should be included in addition to those of the white South. While studying America's actual or perceived flaws, the full force of American idealism and exceptionalism should be compared to the performance of other nations. The continued massive immigration to America, with little emigration from its shores, is a testament to the nation's promise. History shows how the economic system has worked and how the principles of the Founding Fathers created a government with the capacity to adapt.

The reinterpretation of American history as one extended nightmare of grievances is psychologically retarding, leading to a state of perpetual paralysis characterized by an absence of free will among the aggrieved. During the "unutterable woe of human slavery," historians found black "agency" or personal initiative; now blacks' community, regardless of wealth or status, are regarded as victims with no agency. Too many success stories contradict the idea that blacks have no free will.

A hypersensitive racial climate, especially on college campuses, diverts our attention from the dire statistics of black life. The individual is forced into a black group-think of conditioned responses, peer pressure, intimidation, and a want of contact with diverse ideas. In its current iteration, the multicultural approach on campus leads more likely to separation than to integration. A black student who requests black roommates, who self-segregates in black fraternities or at meals, whose main cultural affiliation is with a black cultural center, and whose major concentration is African American studies has chosen uniformity, not diversity. Under the pretext of fostering inclusion and diversity, universities in many ways are encouraging separatism.

Alternatively, the white student or adult may see the black person only as an abstraction. For whites to avoid exposure to African Americans, black history, or racial policies is to ignore and avoid America's most significant social issue.

Discussions, disagreements, and confrontations are inevitable and are constructive if conducted respectfully, frankly, and with knowledge. The individual's ability to deal with day-to-day confrontation—person to person—is a desirable quality. Too often today's students rely on institutional (or social media) crutches—government, a conflict resolution specialist, a college official, or artificial group security—to resolve their problems. The tactic encourages separation and an unhealthy dependency; it drains self-reliance. Human contact dissipates lack of trust. The overuse and misuse of legal remedies and guidelines that purport to be ethical dictates stifle the process of maturation and create a litigious quagmire.

The author asked a black minister in Mississippi, the Reverend Edward Thomas, if it made a difference whether a white or a black adult spoke to a black youth. Reverend Thomas responded, "I can say things that you can't, and you can say things that I can't." Such is the constructive exposure to different perspectives.

Martin Luther King's understanding of the importance of contact between people was inadvertently vindicated at a Yale class reunion in June 2016. Psychology professor John Dovidio in the midst of a presentation on "unconscious bias" described the lack of trust between a black patient and a white doctor. When the author asked him if that was the first visit of the patient to the doctor, professor Dovidio replied, "yes." When the author asked what happened after subsequent visits, the Yale psychologist said that the lack of trust resolved.

Black leaders need to tackle the social problems that have persisted since the struggle for freedom was won. The revolution is over. The pantomime of civil-rights-era tactics—in language, demonstrations, and violence—must give way to constructive engagement with existing institutions. The daily grind of running a school or teaching is far less glamorous and requires much more patience and dedication than involvement in a protest. Mass incarceration can be dealt with through existing legal channels and an effort by the black community to exert leadership on social issues. Accusations of police abuse should be followed not by street demonstrations but by a sober analysis of complex facts.

Ultimately, America's racial dilemma will be resolved, in practical terms, only when black citizens are assimilated and set on a path toward economic prosperity. This goal has eluded the mass of black America, but now racial obstacles have been sufficiently removed. Values count more than race in today's economic picture. Faith in our ability to adjust allows us to confront our most profound challenge: to integrate a people brought to America in slavery.

Notes on Sources

Preface

Samuel P. Huntington's *Who Are We?: The Challenges to America's National Identity* (2004) provides a good overview of the quest for unity among different ethnic groups. He outlines the concepts that originated with the Founding Fathers. Marcus Hansen's *The Immigrant in American History* (1940) deals effectively with early immigration and American culture. For a collection of speeches at the 1890 national discussion of the state of black America, see *the First Mohonk Conference on the Negro Question, Held at Lake Mohonk* (2015 ed.) edited by Isabel C. Barrows.

Chapter One: Racial Attitudes in the North, 1800–1865

Specific state and city studies offer useful accounts of the vastly underappreciated antebellum experience of free blacks. The negative attitudes of white Northerners toward free blacks were critical in determining black destiny after the Emancipation. Views in Philadelphia may be found in Gary B. Nash's *Forging Freedom: The Formation of Philadelphia's Black Community, 1720–1840* (1988). His *Race and Revolution* (1990) provides a more general view. *Freedom's Prophet* (2008) by Richard Newman recounts the experience of Philadelphia's Bishop Richard Allen of the AME Church. *Black Bostonians* (1999) by James Oliver Horton and Lois E. Horton is a thorough account. Of special and underappreciated significance are two volumes of *Voices of the Republic: Connecticut Towns 1800–1832* (2003) edited by Christopher P. Bickford and Howard R. Lamar. They contain the Connecticut survey that asks about the values and work ethic of free blacks. Horatio T. Strother's *The Underground Railroad in Connecticut* (1962) describes the era well. *Free Blacks in America, 1800–1860* (1970) edited by John Bracey Jr., August Meier, and Elliott Rudwick offers interesting accounts. Joan D. Hedrick's biography *Harriet Beecher Stowe: A Life* (1994) is useful; for a full picture, see Stowe's *Uncle Tom's Cabin* (1994 ed.), *Palmetto Leaves* (1999 ed.), and "Our Florida Plantation" (*Atlantic Monthly*, May 1879).

The distinction between Northern attitudes toward race and slavery is exemplified by William Henry Seward, the New York politician whose influence was more important than is generally recognized. His biographers include John M. Taylor, *William Henry Seward: Lincoln's Right Hand* (1991), Frederic Bancroft, *The Life of William Henry Seward* (1900), and Walter Stahr, *Seward: Lincoln's Indispensable Man* (2012). Of special importance is Ernest N. Paolino's *The Foundation of the American Empire: William Henry Seward and U.S. Foreign Policy* (1973), which reveals the centrality of commerce in the American mind. Commerce, not black equality, was the goal of America after the Civil War. Seward's speeches are readily available in print.

The black experience in New York is well explored by Edgar J. McManus's *The History of Slavery in New York* (1996), Leslie M. Harris's *In the Shadow of Slavery: African Americans in New York City, 1626–1863* (2003), and especially Gunja SenGupta's *From Slavery to Poverty: Racial Origins of Welfare in New York, 1840–1918* (2009). Leon Litwack offers general coverage in *North of Slavery* (1961). Both Eugene H. Berwanger's *The Frontier Against Slavery: Western Anti-Negro Prejudice and the Slavery Extension Controversy* (1967) and V. Jacques Voegeli's *Free But Not Equal: The Midwest and the North During the Civil War* (1967) are indispensable guides to Northern racial animosity.

The two volumes of *Northern Editorials on Secession* (1942) edited by Howard Cecil Perkins supply a comprehensive view of press attitudes. Another perceptive treatment of racial attitudes may be found in several essays by C. Vann Woodward in his *American Counterpoint: Slavery and Racism in the North–South Dialogue* (1971 ed.). Harriet E. Wilson's *Our Nig, or Sketches from the Life of a Free Black* (2011 ed.), first published in 1859, is the first novel published in English by an African-American woman. Wilson tells the story of the brutal treatment of a black domestic by a white family in New England. *Twenty-two Years a Slave and Forty Years a Freeman* (1857) by Austin Stewart describes Wilberforce, Canada, and the difficulty of creating a self-sufficient all-black town.

Lee Kuan Yew's interviews on the necessity of diffusion, which relate to Abraham Lincoln's views, are in *The Grand Master's Insight on China, the United States, and the World* (2013), edited by Graham Allison and Robert D. Blackwell, and in his memoir, *Lee Kuan Yew: My Lifelong Challenge* (2012). Sources on Lincoln are endless; David Herbert Donald in "Getting Right with Lincoln" (*Harper's*, April 1951) cited 1,079 pages of published works about Lincoln before 1939. A sampling pertinent to this study would include *Abraham Lincoln: Selected Speeches, Messages, and Letters* (1962 ed.) edited by T. Harry Williams, *Lincoln's Plan of Reconstruction* (1967 ed.) by William B. Hesseltine, and *Lincoln and the Economics of the American Dream* (1994 ed.) by Gabor S. Boritt. To understand a neglected aspect of his life as a corporate lawyer, see the pamphlet "Abraham Lincoln: An Illinois Central Lawyer" (February 1945) by Elmer A. Smith. *Forced into Glory: Abraham Lincoln's White Dream* (1991) by the black journalist Lerone Bennett Jr. questions Lincoln's motivation in racial matters. The title *Big Enough to Be Inconsistent: Abraham Lincoln Confronts Slavery and Race* (2008) by George M. Fredrickson indicates how historians rationalize Lincoln's racial views. Robert Penn Warren asked black leaders in *Who Speaks for the Negro* (1965) what they thought about Abraham Lincoln. The adoption of Abraham Lincoln as a "patron saint" by the white Citizens' Councils is covered in Neil R. McMillen's *The Citizens' Council: Organized Resistance to the Second Reconstruction, 1954–1964* (1994 ed.).

In his *Personal Memoirs* (1999 ed.), General Ulysses S. Grant poignantly recollects his conversation with General Robert E. Lee at the Confederate surrender at Appomattox. C. Vann Woodward's equation of Northern and Southern attitudes toward black equality are contained in his essay "The Price of Freedom," published in *What Was Freedom's Price?* (1978) edited by David G. Sansing.

Chapter Two: The Containment of Blacks in the South

My book *Cotton and Race in the Making of America* (2009) describes the containment policy. A fundamental America trait—mobility, whether physical, economic, or educational—was severely restricted and often denied for black Americans. The intriguing saga of the inability of the

United States to prosecute Confederate president Jefferson Davis after the Civil War is well told by R. F. Nichols in "United States vs. Jefferson Davis, 1865–1869" in the *American Historical Review* (April 1926). See also *Jefferson Davis, American* (2000) by William J. Cooper Jr. The role of Senator Ben Wade is the subject of Hans L. Trefousse's *Benjamin Franklin Wade: Radical Republican from Ohio* (1963) and his article "Ben Franklin and the Negro" in the *Ohio Historical Quarterly* (April 1959). For an account of Edward Atkinson, see Harold Williamson's *Edward Atkinson: The Biography of an American Liberal, 1827–1905* (1934) and Atkinson's pamphlet "Cheap Cotton, Cheap Labor" (1861). For an accurate account of the fate of the "forty acres and a mule" saga, read John David Smith's essay "The Enduring Myth of 'Forty Acres and a Mule'" (*Chronicle of Higher Education*, February 21, 2003).

W. E. B. Du Bois's work figured prominently during this period with his 1934 book, *Black Reconstruction, 1860–1880* (1992 ed.). Also see "The Freedmen's Bureau" in the *Atlantic Monthly* (March 1901). Du Bois's novel *The Quest for the Silver Fleece* (1911) shows the centrality of cotton in America and in the black experience. His *The Souls of Black Folk* (1961 ed.) attempts to define the identity of blacks. *The Negro American Family* (1908) and the 1914 report "Morals and Manners Among Negro Americans" offer Du Bois's views on black family life and illegitimacy at the beginning of the twentieth century. Du Bois could be direct: "Without doubt the point where the Negro American is furthest behind modern civilization is his sexual mores." His *The Philadelphia Negro: A Social Study* (1995 ed.) is a pioneering work of sociology. Du Bois's *The Education of Black People: Ten Critiques, 1906–1960* (1973) edited by Herbert Aptheker is a penetrating view of black education over a long time span. Each of the essays in *The Negro Problem* (1903), edited by Du Bois, provides a period view of blacks by black writers. His own contribution, "The Talented Tenth," looks at the career choices of black college graduates; "The Characteristics of the Negro People" by H. T. Kealing outlines group "failings." Note also Jonathan Levy's *Freaks of Fortune: The Emerging World of Capitalism and Risk in America* (2012) for an account of the Freedmen's Bank. David Levering Lewis's two-volume biography of Du Bois is a comprehensive factual account. Also noteworthy is *W. E. B. Du Bois: Black Radical Democrat* (1986) by Manning Marable.

Eric Foner's celebrated *Reconstruction: America's Unfinished Revolution* (2002 ed.) and his shorter version, with Joshua Brown, *Forever Free: The Story of Emancipation and Reconstruction* (2005), consider black accomplishments during Reconstruction. John Hope Franklin's *Reconstruction After the Civil War* (1961) remains important. *Yankee Stepfather: General O. O. Howard and the Freedmen* (1994 ed.) and *Frederick Douglass*, both by William S. McFeely, are essential reading. Frederick Douglass's memoir, *Life and Times of Frederick Douglass: Written by Himself* (1969 ed.) is a good introduction to this giant of American history, and his article "The Negro Exodus from the Gulf States" (*Journal of Social Science*, May 1880) offers insights into his political and economic views. Two valuable studies, *The Racial Attitudes of American Presidents from Abraham Lincoln to Theodore Roosevelt* (1972 ed.) by George Sinkler, and *The Betrayal of the Negro from Rutherford B. Hayes to Woodrow Wilson* (1965 ed.) by Rayford W. Logan, concentrate on the presidents.

Lawrence N. Powell's *New Masters: Northern Planters During the Civil War and Reconstruction* (1980) explores the important but underappreciated attempt by Northern farmers to exploit the cotton market. The *Life and Letters of Henry Lee Higginson* (1921 reprint) by Bliss Perry explores the fascinating story of a prominent Bostonian and former Union officer's failed attempt to win a fortune in cotton. The marvelous tale of Mississippi's Montgomery family is well told in Janet Sharp Hermann's *The Pursuit of a Dream* (1981). *Black Property Owners in the South, 1790–1915* (1997 ed.) details a significant economic story. Nicholas Lemann in *Redemption: The Last Battle of the Civil War* (2006) describes how the Reconstruction governor Adelbert Ames frittered away his time rather than seriously engaged the whites who literally ended Reconstruction in Mississippi. Both memoirs of black Mississippi congressman John R. Lynch, *The Facts of Reconstruction* (1970 ed.) and *Reminiscences of an Active Life: The Autobiography of John Roy Lynch* (1970 ed.) are well worthwhile. *Lucius Q. C. Lamar: His Life, Times, and Speeches, 1825–1893* (1896) by Edward Mayes, and *Lucius Q. C. Lamar: Secession and Reunion* (1935) by Wirt Armistead Cate explore the career of this fascinating Southern politician, educator, and associate justice of the Supreme Court. A chapter of John F. Kennedy's *Profiles in Courage* (1964 ed.) is devoted to Lamar. Neil R. McMillen's Dark Journey: Black Mississippians in the

Age of Jim Crow is a worthwhile study of one state. David Blight covers remembrances of the period in Race and Reunion: The Civil War in American Memory.

The Exoduster movement, the only significant attempt by blacks to migrate north during Reconstruction, is described in *Exodusters: Black Migration to Kansas After Reconstruction* (1986 ed.) by Nell Irvin Painter and *In Search of Canaan: Black Migration to Kansas, 1879–1880* (1978) by Robert G. Athearn. Little attention is given to the failure of the movement, which confirmed the force of the containment policy.

For the legal interpretation of race, see Peter Irons's *A People's History of the Supreme Court* (1999) and the cases themselves. Booker T. Washington's *Atlanta Exposition Speech* (1895) is a pragmatic statement of economic priorities and his recognition of the limited role of blacks. Often criticized, Washington played the hand he was dealt and built an institution. His memoir, *Up from Slavery* (1995 ed.), is an essential document of American history, along with Frederick Douglass's autobiography and the numerous contributions of W. E. B. Du Bois. Louis Harlan's *Booker T. Washington: The Making of a Black Leader, 1856–1901* (1975 ed.) and *Booker T. Washington: The Wizard of Tuskegee, 1901–1915* (1986 ed.) provide a detailed account of the life. See also Washington's *Black Diamonds* (1969 ed.). James D. Anderson's *The Education of Blacks in the South, 1860–1935* (1988) makes an important contribution in describing the white philanthropic role in black education. Davison M. Douglas's *Jim Crow Moves North: The Battle over Northern School Segregation, 1865–1954* (2005) is a comprehensive and enlightening study of racially segregated education in the North. I have relied extensively on the factual material in Douglas's work. Owen Wister's *Roosevelt: The Story of a Friendship* (1930) is an interesting look at Theodore Roosevelt's correspondence with a friend about race. *Theodore Roosevelt and the Idea of Race* by Thomas G. Dyer investigates Roosevelt's support of his black appointees. Harvard professor Albert Bushnell Hart writes matter-of-factly of the inferiority of the mass of blacks in *The Southerners' South* (1910), yet he marvels at the progress of Japan and China in *The Obvious Orient* (1911). Hart, a friend of Theodore Roosevelt, clearly distinguished between these "people of color" and American blacks. The meeting and friendship in 1893 in New York of Varina Davis, wife of Confederate president Jefferson Davis, and Julia Dent Grant, wife of the Union general, is featured in *First Lady of the Confederacy: Varina Davis's Civil War* (2006) by Joan E. Cashin and *Varina Howell: Wife of Jefferson Davis* (1998 ed.) by Eron Rowland. The story is an expressive reminder of North–South reconciliation.

Chapter Three: The Great Migration: The Reception of Blacks in Northern Cities

A city-by-city look at the black migration north reveals a fairly common experience. For Chicago, see Allan H. Spear, *Black Chicago: The Making of a Negro Ghetto* (1970 ed.); William M. Tuttle Jr., *Race Riot: Chicago in the Red Summer of 1919* (1996 ed.); and Carl Sandburg, *The Chicago Race Riots, July 1919* (2013 ed.). Of special significance is the classic *Black Metropolis* (1945) by St. Clair Drake and Horace R. Cayton, with its valuable introduction by Richard Wright. *The Land of Hope: Chicago, Black Southerners, and the Great Migration* (1991 ed.) by James R. Grossman offers an overview.

Interesting aspects of Detroit's racial experience may be found in *Internal Combustion: The Races in Detroit, 1915–1926* (1976) by David Allan Levine and in two books by Dominic J. Capeci, *Race Relations in Wartime Detroit* (1984) and *Layered Violence: The Detroit Rioters of 1943* (1991). Thomas J. Sugrue's *The Origins of the Urban Crisis: Race and Inequality in Postwar Detroit* describes the background of Detroit's racial turmoil. The Ford Motor Company pamphlet "Helpful Hints and Advice to Employees" (1915) gives a detailed picture of labor practices in one of the engines of Detroit's economy. *Sand Against the Wind* (1966), the memoirs of John C. Dancy, the head of Detroit's National Urban League during the period, is a useful account by a prominent black leader of Detroit. The essays in *The Rise of the Ghetto* (1970), edited by John H. Bracey Jr., August Meier, and Elliott Rudwick, focus on a wide range of black migration topics. *Darrow: A Biography* (1979) by Kevin Tierney reviews the role of one of America's leading attorneys in the racially and historically significant Detroit trial of Ossian Sweet.

David Levering Lewis's essay "Harlem My Home" in *Harlem Renaissance: Art of Black America* (1987) is a lively account of the noted black community in New York City. Lewis identifies the consequences of black failure to follow the Jewish commercial tradition in his essay "Parallels and Divergences: Assimilationist Strategies of Afro-American and Jewish Elites from 1910 to the Early 1930s," in *Bridges and Boundaries: African Americans and American Jews* (1992) edited by Jack Salzman. As a general study of the period, Lewis's *W. E. B. Du Bois: The Fight for Equality and the American Century, 1919–1963* (2000) is comprehensive.

The *Chicago Defender* and *Ebony* magazine, both black publications, are critical sources for the black perspective. The works of the prolific black sociologist E. Franklin Frazier form a library in themselves. For this study, these of his books are relevant: *The Negro Family in Chicago* (1932), *The Negro Family in the United States* (1949 ed.), *Black Bourgeoisie* (1997 ed.), and *The Negro in the United States* (1949). The relationship of Ben Burns, white editor of black publications; John Johnson, founder and publisher of *Ebony*; and Richard Wright, novelist, provides an almost theatrical account of racial matters. Two memoirs—Ben Burns, *Nitty Gritty: A White Editor in Black Journalism* and John H. Johnson (with Lerone Bennett Jr.) *Succeeding against the Odds: The Autobiography of a Great American Businessman*—are revealing stories of their voyages in black journalism.

In 1945 Richard Wright searched for an identity and a place to call home in *Black Boy* (2006 ed.), which purports to be autobiographical. But even his editor cautions, "One could question the reliability of Wright's memory, [and] try to discriminate between fact and fiction in this densely woven texture of the autobiography ... [nevertheless it] was a work of stunning imagination and mythic power." Wright's most noteworthy novel, *Native Son* (1968 ed.), conveyed his anger and frustration over the plight of blacks in Chicago's racial ghetto. See also *Conversations with Richard Wright* (1993) edited by Keneth Kinnamon and Michel Fabre, and Hazel Rowley's biography, *Richard Wright: The Life and Times* (2001). Wright's *The Color Curtain: A Report on the Bandung Conference* (1994 ed.), with a foreword by Gunnar Myrdal, describes his misleading view of the unity of "people of color." For a perspective on the black elite, see Lawrence Otis Graham, *Our Kind of People: Inside America's Black Upper Class* (2000) and *Member of the Club: Reflections on Life in a Racially Polarized World* (1996).

For a view of middle-class black families in Greenville, Mississippi, in the 1940s and 1950s, see *Separate, But Equal: The Mississippi Photographs of Henry Clay Anderson* (2002), a book praised by the power broker

Vernon E. Jordan Jr. The lawyer and confidant of President Bill Clinton waxed nostalgic: "During my formative years in Atlanta, Georgia, my family and I lived in a segregated world, but it was not an unhappy world. We knew the system was unjust, but that didn't mean we didn't live our lives to the fullest.... It was a world of structure and organization that enabled us to move forward with our lives." For Jordan, the middle-class blacks photographed by Anderson in Greenville reminded him of his life in Atlanta. What happened to that "structure and organization" when blacks migrated to the urban North?

The extraordinary Rhinelander court case, about racial intermarriage in New York, is the subject of *Love on Trial: An American Scandal in Black and White* (2001) by Earl Lewis and Heidi Ardizzone. Both *The History of Black Business in America: Capitalism, Race, Entrepreneurship* (1998) by Juliet K. Walker and *The Negro as Capitalist: A Study of Banking and Business among American Negroes* (1936) by Abram L. Harris have useful information about blacks in the private sector. To contrast a white immigrant's Americanization experience with that of black migrants, see Michael Pupin's memoir *From Immigrant to Inventor* (1923) and his essay "The Revelation of Lincoln to a Serbian Immigrant" in the *Lincoln Centennial Association Papers* (1926). *The Negro Status and Race Relations in the United States, 1911–1946* (1948) by Anson Phelps Stokes describes the white philanthropic efforts of the Phelps-Stokes Fund. Extremely important is *The Negro Potential* (1956), a summary of the story of integration in the armed forces by Eli Ginzberg, the economist who was instrumental in the process of dismantling racial segregation. *The Rebellious Life of Mrs. Rosa Parks* (2013) by Jeanne Theoharis should be read not only for an account of this hero of the civil rights movement but also to understand her sad descent into financial problems and her personal experience with crime in the Detroit ghetto. Books by the adventurous journalist Louis Lamb—*The Reluctant African* (1960) and *The Negro Revolt* (1962)—offer an opinionated account of the period by a contemporary. On the forceful entrance of black separatist groups into the landscape, see the synopsis by Jesse Russell and Ronald Cohn for "The Hate That Hate Produced" (1959) by TV producers Mike Wallace and Louis Lomax, and view the video at https://archive.org/details/ PBSTheHateThatHateProduced, which vividly reports on the Nation of Islam diatribe against whites. The Nation's language may be found in many later sources, including Derrick Bell's *Faces at the Bottom of the Well: The Permanence of Racism* (1992).

Chapter Four: The 1960s: Civil Rights and Civil War

The American Challenge (1964) by J.-J. Servan-Schreiber offers a convincing account of post–World War II American economic preeminence. Essential reading for the period are two seminal studies: Daniel Patrick Moynihan's "The Negro Family: The Case for National Action" (1965) in *The Moynihan Report and the Politics of Controversy* (1967) by Lee Rainwater and William L. Yancey, and the "Report of the National Advisory Commission on Civil Disorders" (1968), the so-called Kerner Report. *Mirror to America: The Autobiography of John Hope Franklin* (2005) relates the life story of this prominent black historian against the background of his times. For Staughton Lynd's encounter with the confused world of black identity, see *Stepping Stones: Memoir of a Life Together* (2009) by Alice and Staughton Lynd; *From Here to There* (2010) by Staughton Lynd; and *The Admirable Radical: Staughton Lynd and Cold War Dissent, 1945–1970* (2010) by Carl Mirra. My interview (November 11, 2011) with Alice and Staughton Lynd (my former teacher) provided insights into the experiences of this remarkable couple during the Mississippi Freedom Summer of 1964. Doug McAdam's *Freedom Summer* (1988) is a general account. Additional material on the civil rights activities in the 1960s may be found in Clayborne Carson, *In Struggle: SNCC and the Black Awakening of the 1960s* (1982 ed.); the Mississippi minister Ed King, and Trent Watts, *Mississippi: Behind the Scenes of Freedom Summer* (2014); John Dittmer's excellent *Local People: The Struggle for Civil Rights in Mississippi* (1995 ed.); and Charles M. Payne, *I've Got the Light of Freedom: The Organizing Tradition and the Mississippi Freedom Struggle* (2007 ed.). *Aaron Henry: The Fire Ever Burning* (2002) by Aaron Henry with Constance Curry is a thoughtful memoir by the head of the Mississippi branch of the NAACP. Also, Henry's oral histories shed light on the activities of this long-term participant in Mississippi's civil rights struggle. *Mississippi from Within* (1965) by Shirley Tucker is a collection of period newspaper clippings well worth reading. Guy and Candie

Carawan's *Freedom Is a Constant Struggle: Songs of the Freedom Movement* (1968) has relevant text.

Malcolm X: The Last Speeches (1989) edited by Bruce Perry covers the final period of his life. The courageous journey of James Meredith is described in his *A Mission from God: A Memoir and Challenge for America* (2012), with William Doyle, and in my conversations with Meredith. An audio recording of Robert Kennedy's speech at the University of Mississippi is available from the school's archive department. W. E. B. Du Bois's attitude toward James Meredith's integration of Ole Miss is in Conor Cruise O'Brien's *Memoir: My Life and Themes* (2000 ed.). The story of the remarkable civil rights activist Fannie Lou Hamer is well told in *This Little Light of Mine: The Story of Fannie Lou Hamer* (1993) by Kay Mills, and in *For Freedom's Sake: The Life of Fannie Lou Hamer* (2000 ed.) by Chana Kai Lee. William Melvin Kelly's article "The Ivy League Negro" (*Esquire*, August 1963) offers a stark contrast in temperament and class to the experience of Fannie Lou Hamer.

The collection of essays in *Integration vs. Segregation* (1964) edited by Hubert H. Humphrey offers a clear contemporaneous view of school desegregation issues. Nat Hentoff's cogent *The New Equality* (1964) surveys the racial scene, including integration, with perception. I relied extensively on the factual account of the 1968 New York City teachers' strike in *The Strike That Changed New York: Blacks, Whites, and the Ocean Hill–Brownsville Crisis* (2002) by Jerald E. Podair. The 1960s liberal panacea of community school districts, according to the *New York Times* (June 21, 2017), was "distinguished by cronyism and corruption more than by pedagogical experience." Mayors across the political spectrum—from Rudy Giuliani and Michael Bloomberg to Bill de Blasio—have lobbied for centralized mayoral control of the school system. Jonathan Rieder describes the racial confrontation in another section of Brooklyn in *Canarsie: The Jews and Italians of Brooklyn Against Liberalism* (1985).

For a sober view of the "alliance" between blacks and Jews, see the comprehensive *Anti-Semitism in America* (1994) by Leonard Dinnerstein, and essays by Hasia R. Diner, Winston C. McDowell, Joe M. Trotter, Walda Katz-Fishman, and Jerome Scott, and V. P. Franklin in *African Americans and Jews in the Twentieth Century* (1998) edited by V. P. Franklin, Nancy L. Grant, Harold M. Kletnick, and Genna Rae McNeil. Michael Kramer's *New York Magazine* article "Blacks and Jews:

How Wide the Rift?" (February 4, 1989) points to the 1960s as well. Background on anti-Semitism in America may be found in *A Scapegoat in the New Wilderness* (1994) by Frederic Cople Jaher. Note also two essays by Jonathan Karp: "Philosemitism in African American Culture" in *Philosemitism in History* (2011) edited by Jonathan Karp and Adam Sutcliffe, and "Blacks, Jews, and the Business of Race Music, 1945–1955" in *Chosen Capital: The Jewish Encounter with American Capitalism* (2012) edited by Rebecca Kobrin. The opinion of an influential black radio announcer about Jews is contained in *Burn, Baby! Burn!: The Autobiography of Magnificent Montague* (2003). One must be careful when reading *Shared Dreams: Martin Luther King Jr. and the Jewish Community* (1999) by Rabbi Marc Schneier. Rabbi Schneier quotes an anonymous passage from "Letter to an Anti-Zionist Friend" (*Saturday Review*, August 1967), which he attributes to Martin Luther King Jr.; but research casts doubt on King's authorship. Carl Gershman's "The Andrew Young Affair" (*Commentary*, November 1, 1979) is a thorough account of the racially charged events surrounding Andrew Young's resignation as ambassador to the United Nations.

In 1991 Professor and Black Studies chairman Leonard Jeffries of the City College of New York was accused of rampant anti-Semitism after a speech at the Empire State Black Arts and Cultural Festival. In it the showman professor accused "rich Jews" of financing the slave trade. In fact some Jews did finance the slave trade, but Jeffries's wild exaggeration encompassing *all* "rich Jews" renders the remark inaccurate. He then accused Jewish movie moguls and Italians of a conspiracy to orchestrate "a system of destruction for Black people" via the film industry. While Jews did have a disproportionate influence in the movie industry, as described in Neal Gabler's *An Empire of Their Own* (1988), there was no conspiracy. Jews were reflecting American attitudes, not a shared allegiance based on oppression. Jews were no better or worse than other white Americans. Jeffries then blasted Assistant Undersecretary of Education Diane Ravitch for her role in revising a draft of a syllabus on Afro-centrism. Ravitch, he exclaimed, was "a Texas Jew" and an "ultimate, supreme, sophisticated, debonair racist—pure and simple." Like Ravitch, he continued, "Many people who happen to be Jewish have blinded us on the attack coming from the Jewish community—systematic, unrelenting."

Some of the school integration issues in the North are explored in *Sweet Land of Liberty: The Forgotten Struggle for Civil Rights in the North* (2008) by Thomas J. Sugrue. Thomas Sowell's *Black Rednecks and White Liberals* (2005) discusses the historically important all-black Dunbar High School's role in black education. Daniel Yankelovich's survey, "What Negroes Think" (1967), outlines black attitudes toward racial integration. The Yankelovich poll is included in the essay "The New Negro Mood" by Roger Beardwood in *Fortune* magazine's *The Negro and the City* (1968). Robert Penn Warren provides an invaluable portrait of black leaders in the early 1960s in *Who Speaks for the Negro?* (1966 ed.). The versatile novelist, poet, and essayist captures the period and the participants from the perspective of a white Southerner who for decades had been invested in the racial experience. Thoroughly conversant with the racial hypocrisy of the North, Warren pilloried a Vermont newspaper for discouraging black migration to the state: "Vermont has no Negro problem. Furthermore, Vermont does not intend to have any." Warren's earlier book, *Segregation: The Inner Conflict in the South* (1957), is a collection of absorbing conversations with Southerners.

James R. Ralph Jr. provides a factual account of Chicago's struggle with race in *Northern Protest: Martin Luther King Jr., Chicago, and the Civil Rights Movement* (1993). Of special interest is King's realization of Northern racial discrimination. King himself offers a clear explanation of his views in *Why We Can't Wait* (1964 ed.). For an early biography of King, see *Crusader Without Violence* (1959) by L. D. Reddick, who ends his book presciently: "Montgomery has given Martin Luther King Jr. to all men everywhere. Someday *all* of Montgomery will be proud of him." The archived videos of King's TV interviews are extremely valuable in assessing his ideas and his rhetorical skills. For an assessment of King's limitations, see *Negro Revolt* (1962) by Louis Lomax. See also Alex Haley's interview with King in *Playboy* (January 1965). *Playboy* describes the interview as the longest interview that King had ever given to a publication. King's understanding of the importance of contact between people was inadvertently vindicated at a Yale class reunion in June 2015.

For the rescinding of George Wallace's invitation to speak at Yale, see the *Yale Daily News* (September 20, 1963). For an account of George Wallace, see Dan T. Carter's unauthorized *The Politics of Rage: The Origins of the New Conservatism and the Transformation of American Politics*

(2000 ed.), or two sympathetic biographies: *George Wallace: American Populist* (1994) by Stephen Lesher, and *The Wallace Story* (1966) by Bill Jones, Wallace's press secretary. The testy debate between William F. Buckley Jr. and George Wallace on Buckley's TV show *Firing Line* (January 1968) pitted the traditional conservative against the populist Wallace.

I relied on the comprehensive factual account of the race riots in *Law and Order: Street Crime, Civil Unrest, and the Crisis of Liberalism in the 1960s* (2005) by Michael W. Flann. See also Clay Risen's *A Nation on Fire: America in the Wake of the Assassination* (2009). The 1966 attempt to co-opt the support of black gangs in Chicago by Republican senators, and harness their influence constructively, is described in *Rule and Ruin* (2012) by Geoffrey Kabaservice. Videos of and commentary on the race riots, which were extensively covered by the TV networks, are readily available. Of particular interest, note the potential use of black military veterans in the inner cities in Morris Liebman's proposal to Joseph Califano Jr., "Political Stability, National Goals and the Negro Veteran" (1967), available in the LBJ Library. *Urban Choices: The City and Its critics* (1966) by Roger Starr cleverly and astutely analyzes the racial dynamic of New York City. The James Baldwin documentary *Take This Hammer* (1964) highlights racial frustrations in San Francisco, a city "widely advertised [for its] liberal and cosmopolitan tradition." Within a generation San Francisco would lose a substantial portion of its black population. Bayard Rustin's *Harper's* article, "The Failure of Black Separatism" (January 1970), expresses the views of a highly regarded black leader who is thoroughly opposed to street violence. John D'Emilio's biography, *Lost Prophet: The Life and Times of Bayard Rustin*, is especially informative. Of special significance is Rustin's proposal for a "Freedom Budget" in 1966 particularly for black America. He wanted $100 billion ($764 billion in 2017) to elevate blacks to equality. The expenditure, he wrote, would be paid for by a $400 billion economic growth dividend without raising taxes. This reliance on economic growth rather than tax hikes would ironically conform to conservative philosophy. The "Freedom Budget" failed to gain sufficient traction.

The attempt by private corporations to hire black employees in the 1960s is explained in Time-Life's *The Negro and the City* (1968) and in Charles D. Ellis's *Joe Wilson and the Creation of Xerox* (2006). Daniel

J. Boorstin's insightful essay "Cities Within Cites: The Urban Blues" in his *The Americans: The Democratic Experience* (1974 ed.) captures the racial experience of "Negro Americans." For a punctuation mark, read Connecticut governor and senator Abraham Ribicoff's indictment of racial hypocrisy in the North in his *America Can Make It!* (1972).

Chapter Five: The Enduring American Dilemma

The widespread use of the Marshall Plan as an analogy in confronting America's racial issues prompts a discussion of the original plan, in which humanitarian motives combined with economic designs. For the proper use of analogies, as opposed to the employment of analogies for ideological justification, consult David Hackett Fischer's Chapter XI, "Fallacies of False Analogies," in *Historians' Fallacies: Toward a Logic of Historical Thought* (1970). *Our Finest Hour: Will Clayton, the Marshall Plan, and the Triumph of Democracy* (1993) by Gregory A. Fossedal describes the economic origins of the fabled effort. For the South's role in the Marshall Plan, see *Dixie Looks Abroad: The South and U.S. Foreign Relations, 1789–1973* (2002) by Joseph A. Fry. European customers of Southern cotton motivated some Southern politicians to assist in the reconstruction of Europe. Whitney Young's thoughts on black preparation and his appeal for a Marshall Plan are contained in "A Cry from the Dispossessed," *Christian Century* (December 1964). *Quiet Riots: Race and Poverty in the United States* (1988) edited by Fred R. Harris and Roger W. Wilkins discusses the failures of the Kerner Report's recommendations. The Edward Kennedy welfare quote is contained in "Blacks and Jews: How Wide the Rift" (*New York* magazine, February 4, 1985) by Michael Kramer. Ken Auletta's *The Underclass* (1982) explores the meager results of a government-sponsored job-training program while using the Marshall Plan analogy to request greater government funding. The economic racial gaps bear close attention. As reported in the *Journal of Blacks in Higher Education*, the US Census Bureau 2015 reported a drop in black home ownership from 49.1 percent to 41.5 percent from 2014 to 2015. The racial gap thus widened to 30 percent.

Ellis Cose tries to explain the opportunities for black graduates of the Harvard Business School and the A Better Chance (ABC) program

in *The End of Anger: The New Generation's Take on Race and Rage* (2011).
For Cose, elite blacks had entered a new era of vocational possibilities. Anthony Walton's article "Technology Versus African-Americans"
(*Atlantic*, January 1999) presciently warned blacks to "change" or miss
occupational opportunities in technology. Derrick Bell's pessimistic views
on integration and racism are expressed through his fictional characters
in *Faces at the Bottom of the Well: The Permanence of Racism* (1992). In
his epilogue, Bell assigns free will to slaves who "carve[d] out a human-
ity," but he removes self-determination from twentieth-century blacks
who are "imprisoned by the history of racial subordination." Oddly, this
well-known professor includes himself among the imprisoned. For him,
there is no difference in experience between a black professor at New
York University and the black inhabitant of an urban ghetto. Without
free will, the black person in Bell's scenario is not responsible for black-
on-black crime.

> Blacks continue to react negatively to exhortations about individual
> responsibility. In a 2017 Jackson State University publication, the politi-
> cal scientist D'Andra Orey compared responses by blacks to President
> Obama. If the president, rather than "Joe Biden, Colin Powell, or Bill
> Clinton...blamed black males for failure" to take responsibility for
> racial "inequities," blacks with a strong racial identity, claimed Professor
> Orey, would discount Obama's position. But blacks supported Obama's
> position if he "blamed the system."

The journalist Paul Tough enters the world of black education in
*Whatever It Takes: Geoffrey Canada's Quest to Change Harlem and
America* (2008), a sympathetic account of the highly visible founder of
the Harlem Children's Zone. *Lessons of Hope: How to Fix Our Schools*
(2014) by Joel Klein, New York City's chancellor of education in the
Michael Bloomberg administration, persuasively argues that a student's
confidence and success derive not from empathic treatment but from
mastery of a "core academic education." The prolific journalist Eugene
Robinson understands its severity but fails to confront the single-parent
family crisis, nor does he attempt to understand the racial gap in educational testing in *Disintegration: The Splintering of Black America* (2010).
Ta-Nehisi Coates's *Between the World and Me* typifies the purest form of
responsibility-avoidance language.

New York's racially segregated school system is well documented in "New York State's Extreme School Segregation, Inaction and a Damaged Future" (2014) by John Kucsera, published by the UCLA Civil Rights Project. The late Nigerian-born anthropologist John Ogbu directly indicts black culture as the basis for the poor educational performance of black students in *Black American Students in an Affluent Suburb: A Study of Academic Disengagement* (1992). Ogbu's foreword in *Black Resistance in High School: Forging a Separate Culture* (1992) by P. Patrick Solomon emphasizes standard Western color-blind behavioral norms but recognizes cultural distinctiveness. His advocacy of the partial use of African American vernacular language (Ebonics) to acquire standard American English is controversial. The *Journal of Blacks in Higher Education* is a critical source for recent studies of black enrollment, achievement, and relative performance.

Woody Brittain's hope for a return of the debate format on the Yale campus was indeed realized, not by the Afro-American Cultural Center but by the Yale's William F. Buckley Jr. Society, which instituted a form of the *Firing Line* TV debate program associated with the society's namesake, William F. Buckley Jr. *South African Gandhi: Stretcher-Bearer of Empire* (2015) by Ashwin Desai and Goolam Vahed describes Gandhi's sojourn in South Africa and his attitudes toward black South Africans. Harper Lee's seminal *To Kill a Mockingbird* (1960 ed.) has been the touchstone for praise, popularity, and controversy in its unparalleled inclusion in racial dialogue. *Scout, Atticus, and Boo: A Celebration of To Kill a Mockingbird* (2010) by Mary McDonagh Murphy is a collection of stories by well-known people about the influence of *Mockingbird* on their lives and careers. Kathryn Stockett's commercially successful *The Help* (2009) owes a large debt to *Mockingbird* and to *Telling Memories Among Southern Women: Domestic Workers and Their Employers in the Segregated South* (1988) edited by Susan Tucker. *Twelve Years a Slave* (2013 ed.) is the inspirational basis for the movie of the same name. The notes by researcher Sue Eakin are essential to following the story.

The origins of Jewish education and its impact on occupations is well told in *The Chosen Few: How Education Shaped Jewish History, 70–1492* (2012) by Maristella Botticini and Zvi Eckstein. *Rituals of Childhood: Jewish Acculturation in Medieval Europe* (1996) by Ivan G. Marcus relates the poignant anecdote of a Jewish boy exposed to lifelong learning. *Polyn: Jewish Life in the Old Country* (1999) by Alter Kacyzne graphically depicts Jewish schools in the midst of abject poverty in 1920s Poland. The historian Oscar Handlin tells his story of the transition of Jews from the ghettos of Europe to Brooklyn in "Being Jewish: The Endless Quest," *American Scholar* (Summer 1997).

Fred Siegel's *The Future Once Happened Here* (1997) captures the racial tension and violence of life in New York, Washington, and Los Angeles. The continuing influence of the 1960s is well described in *The Dream and the Nightmare: The Sixties Legacy to the Underclass* (1993) by Myron Magnet. The entrepreneurial role of a group of Koreans in New York City is the subject of *Around the Block: The Business of a Neighborhood* (1997) by Tom Shachtman. Koreans, like the Jews before them, were resented by blacks because of their business presence in black neighborhoods.

Index

Page numbers followed by n indicate notes.

Accommodation, distinguished from assimilation, 244

Accountability: needed for blacks, x, xv, 113, 181, 214; needed for government programs, 185, 201, 208, 213, 220, 224–225, 230, 281, 290

Acheson, Dean, 218–219n2

"Acting white," as pejorative, 235, 238, 243

Adams, Charles Francis Jr., 87

Aerojet-General, 210

Affirmative action, 125, 188, 196–197, 222, 226, 251, 254

Africa: Lomax and, 157; repatriation of blacks to, proposed, 130, 154. *See also* Ghana

African American Teachers Association, 185, 235, 249, 250

"African American," use of, 159

"African Americans: College Majors and Earnings" study, 227–228

African Civilization Society, 19

African Free Schools, 19

"Afro-American," use of, 159

Alabama State University, 244–245

Ali, Muhammed, 186

"All Lives Matter," copyrighted, 281

Allen, Richard, 4

Alvord, John W., 62

America Can Make It! (Ribicoff), 212

American Challenge, An (Servan-Schreiber), 151

American Colonization Society (ACS), 9

American Dilemma, An (Myrdal), xii, 125, 147

American Teachers Association (ATA), criticism of capitalism and Western culture, 178–180, 182

Americanization, of immigrants in Detroit, 113–118

Ames, Adelbert, 55

Amsterdam News, 110, 125, 126, 132

Anderson, Elijah, 276–277

Andrew, John, 28, 30

Antebellum North, distinction between its abhorrence of race-based slavery and its disdain for free blacks, 1–40; Civil War and policy of containment of freed slaves in South, 27–35; colonization and fear of black movement north, 9–12, 19, 24–26, 31–32, 34, 35, 38; economics of slavery and, 2–3, 16; examples from fiction, 10–14; Lincoln's racial attitudes, 35–38; policy of containment of freed slaves in South, 27–35; separatism and, 3–9, 12–13; Seward and, 14–17; suffrage and, 10, 16–17, 23, 24, 34–36; westward expansion and, 21–25, 32; white European immigration and, 34–35

Anti-Semitism: in Chicago, 128; in New York City, 129, 180–182. *See also* Jews

Appeasement of whites, Booker T. Washington and, 71, 82, 244

Appomattox, VA, end of Civil War and, 38–39

Arkansas, 29

Armstrong, Louis, 131, 272

Arrington, Richard Jr., 282

Assimilation: accommodation distinguished from, 244; benefits of, 247, 287; black middle class and, 134; blacks excluded from, in Detroit, 118–120; cultural adaptation and, 145; Du Bois and, 73; economic advancement and, 96; education and, 236–237; Ford Motor Company's encouragement of, 113–118; importance of, while retaining cultural heritage, 289; by Jews, 131; jobs and middle class values, 226–227; King on, 193; Obama and, 283; as path toward economic prosperity, 293; as priority for blacks, ix–x; proper use of term, ix; slavery and blacks as exception to, x–xii; white culture and, 125; white refusal to encourage blacks, 47, 86–89

Association of Black Women Academics, 264

Atkinson, Edward, 45

Atlantic, 228, 276

Auletta, Ken, 219, 224–225

Ayres, Jake, 247

Ayres v. Fordice, 247–248

Bacon, Leonard, 9

Baldwin, James, ix, 199

Bandung Conference, 112, 113, 157, 186

Barnard, Frederick, 117

Barnett, Ross, 162, 174

Barry, Marion, 282

Barrymore, Ethel, 109n5

Beauty Star cosmetics, 105

Beecher, Henry Ward, 45

Belafonte, Harry, 285

Bell, Derrick, 231

Beman, Reverend Jehiel C., 12

Benjamin, Judah P., 50

Bennett, Lerone Jr., 37–38, 158

Bernstein, Richard, 179

Berwanger, Eugene, 23

Better Chance, A, 234

Between the World and Me (Coates), 239

Biden, Joe, 37, 283

Bilbo, Theodore G., 130

Binga, Joseph, 94–95n1

Bingham, John A., 26

Birmingham, AL, bombing and death of young girls in, 197

Birth of a Nation (film), 266

Black, Hugo, 160

Black Bourgeoisie (Frazier), 133–134

Black Boy (Wright), 99, 101–102

Black culture: denigration of middle-class values, 238–239; education enrichment programs and, 233–235; immunity to self-criticism, xv; self-examination lacking in, 237–239, 245, 287–288

Black History Month, 256; Freeman on, 290–291

"Black laws," 10, 23, 30, 31

Black Lives Matter movement, 187, 228, 277–281; copyrights owned by, 281; false analogies of past and current police behavior, 274; opposition to Teach For America, 235; tension fomented by, 278; unions and, 235. *See also* Movement for Black Lives

Black Metropolis: A Study of Negro Life in a Northern City (Drake and Cayton), Wright's introduction to, 100, 102

Black Muslims, 129–130, 146, 197

Black nationalism, 129–130, 134

Black P. (Pharaoh) Stone Nation gang, in Chicago, 141

Black Panthers, xv, 156, 186–187, 191, 212–213, 285

Black Power movement, 156, 158–159, 167, 209, 254, 287

Black studies programs, 158, 179, 196

Blackburn, Cleo, 210

Black-Jewish alliance, 182–183; blacks able to both attack and emulate Jews, 183–187

Black-Led Movement Fund, 277

Black-on-black crime, xv, 140–142, 146, 155, 221, 239, 274, 275, 277

Blackstone Rangers, 275

Blessey, Gerald, 161, 162

Blow, Charles, 278

Blumstein's, 129

Board for Fundamental Education (BFE), 210

Bookbinder, Hyman, 208

Booker, Cory, 283
Boorstin, Daniel, 120–121, 208
Borealis Foundation, 277
Boston, MA, 85, 175–176
Boutwell, George S., 47
Boycott, Divest, Sanction (BDS)
    movement, 187
Bradley, Joseph, 67–68
Bradley, Tom, 270
Brewster, Kingman, 197, 198
Brinkerhoff, Jacob, 32
"Broken windows theory," 183
Brooke, Edward, 108
Brooks, David, 258
Brown, Henry B., 68–69
Brown, John, 45, 50, 66
Brown, Michael, 274
Brown University, 256
Brown v. Board of Education of Topeka
    (1954), xi–xii, 66, 69, 123–125, 145,
    174–175, 230–231, 239
Brownsville, TX, 87
Bruce, Blanche K., 57, 158
Brustein, Robert, 265
Bryan, Guy, 59
Bunche, Ralph J., 126
Bundy, McGeorge, 177, 178
Burns, Ben, 92–93, 95, 100, 103–108, 110,
    141
Burns, Esther, 105, 107
Burns, Ursula, 211n9, 225
Bush, Alvin, 210
Busing policies, 6, 124, 145–146, 176, 183,
    187, 190, 192, 193, 230–231
Butler, Benjamin, 32
Butler, The (film), 265
Buttrick, Wallace, 71

Cahan, Abraham, 131–132
Calhoun, John C., 255
Califano, Joseph Jr., 202, 208–209, 266
California, 67
Camp Sherwood Forest, 248
Campbell, Leslie, 178, 182
Campbell, Nora, 170
Canada, 31, 33
Canada, Geoffrey, 235, 250
Canarsie, NY, 182–183

Capeci, Dominic J. Jr., 132
Capitalism: American Teachers
    Association criticism of, 178–180, 182;
    blacks and rejection of, 113, 154–156
Carawan, Guy and Candie, 202
Carmichael, Stokely, 156, 167–168, 197
Carnegie, Andrew, 70–71
Carson, Clayton, 167
Carter, Hodding II, 175
Carter, Robert, 230–231
Cavanaugh, Jerry, 202
Cayton, Horace, 94–95n1, 102
Chaney, James, 200
Charter schools, 217, 227, 231–233, 236,
    249, 289
Chase, Salmon P., 32, 50
Chattel slavery, 79
Chenault, Kenneth, 225
Chicago, IL: Ben Burns' writing and, 95,
    103–108; black boycott of schools in,
    166; black-on-black homicides and,
    274; black-police tensions and, 141,
    276; *Ebony* magazine and, 105, 108–
    112; education of blacks and, 85, 97;
    employment conditions, 97; family
    structures and, 98–99, 99n3; gangs
    in, 141; in Great Migration era, 93,
    94–113, 124; housing and segregation
    in, 95–96, 98; Jewish businesses
    in, 128; race riots in, 97–98, 98n2;
    Richard Wright's writing and, 99–103;
    schools in, 175, 274
Chicago Defender, 92–93, 95–96, 99,
    103–104, 111, 159
Chicago Tribune, 29, 66, 94–95
Child, Lydia Maria, 20
Child Development Group of
    Mississippi (CDGM), 170
Chiriqui Improvement Company, 26
Christakis, Erika, 253–254
Christakis, Nicholas, 252–254
Chronicle of Philanthropy, 135
Churches, 133–134, 189, 238, 288; black
    behavioral norms and, 73, 289;
    "freedom schools" and, 166; political
    power and, 135
Cincinnati, OH, 85, 99
Cincinnati Enquirer, 32

Citizenship: blacks and second-class, 46, 60, 70–71, 83; Ford Motor Co., Detroit, and goals of, 114–115, 118; Fourteenth Amendment and blacks, x; Lincoln and freed slaves, 36; Naturalization Act and whites, x; reconstruction legislation and, 48–49, 52; responsibilities and expectations of, x, 7–8, 237, 284
Civil disobedience, 203–204, 209, 279
Civil Rights Act (1875), 53, 67
Civil Rights Act (1964), 146, 164, 199, 200
Civil rights era (1960s), 149–214; black-Jewish relationships and, 156, 183–187; civil rights movement highlights, 163–173; class and "Ivy League Negro," 173–174; desegregation and integration highlights, 174–183; economic context, 151–152; education sector's separatism and resistance to integration, 187–189; government programs, costs, and results, 206–209; integration, self-segregation, and black identity, 153–159; integration and Meredith at Ole Miss, 159–162; Japan and "people of color," 152–153; language and methodology "hacked" in 21st century, 285; political context, 151; private sector programs and results, 209–212; racial violence in North, 197–205; still-relevant issues of, 212–214; Warren's interviews with black leaders, 189–197
Civil rights movement (1960s), 163–173; "aura" of, xv; dollars spent after and outcomes of, 219–220, 222; Freedom Summer and, 160, 164–166; Hamer and, 166–172; industrial farming and displacement of black workers, 172–173; Jews and, 131, 184; military veterans and, 144; separatism and, 167–168; violence against workers, 163–164, 200
Civil War, 38–40; economics, legal status, and politics after, 48–60; fate of confederates after, 48–51; Northern

policy of containing freed slaves in South, 27–35
Clapp, Channing, 76
Clark, Kenneth B., 204
Clark, Mark, 143
Clark, Peter, 31
Clayton, William, 218n2
Cleveland, Grover, 81
Cleveland, OH: black-police tensions and, 141; education in, 85; Great Migration and population growth, 94; school segregation and, 122–123
Cleveland Leader, 84
Clinton, Bill, xii, 136
Clinton, Hillary, 135–136
Coates, Ta-Nehisi, 103, 239, 245
Cohn, David, 6–7
Cole, Raymond E., 114
Coleman Report, 242
Coles, Edward, 23–24
Colonization: antebellum Northern attitudes toward blacks and fear of movement north, 9–12, 19, 24–26, 31–32, 34, 35, 38; proposed during Reconstruction, 42–43, 48, 64
"Colored," use of term, 158–159
Colored Home of the City of New York, 19–20
Colored Orphanage Asylum, 19
Columbia University, 256
Columbus Crisis, 33
Commentary, 186
Communism, 100–101, 103, 111–112, 113, 195, 209. *See also* Marxism
Community Representative Advisory Committee (CRAC), 208
Confederate flag controversy, 258
Congress of Racial Equality (CORE), 180, 182, 230, 235
Congressional Black Caucus, 282
Conkling, Roscoe, 52–53
Connecticut: antebellum attitudes toward blacks and, 6, 7–10, 12; desegregation and, 84, 239–241. *See also* New Haven, CT
Connecticut Academy of Arts and Sciences, 7

Connecticut Journal, 7

Constitution, of US: First Amendment, 281; Thirteenth Amendment, 52, 67; Fourteenth Amendment, x, 50, 53, 59, 67–69; Fifteenth Amendment, 9, 17, 53

Containment, of freed slaves in South, 27–35, 89; expediency rationalization of, 47, 59; during Reconstruction, 46–48, 52–53, 82

Conyers, John, 75n1, 279–280

Cornell University, 196

Corporation for Enterprise Development, 225

Cose, Ellis, 226–227

Cotton: Carnegie on need for, 70–71; economy of South during Reconstruction, 44–46, 48; industrial farming and displacement of black workers in 1960s, 172–173; Marshall plan and, 218n2; Northerners' raising of, during Reconstruction, 75–78; Southern economy before Civil War, 2–3, 6–7, 12–13, 17, 21, 25

Council of Federated Organizations (COFO), 282

Cox, Earnest Sevier, 130

Cox, Minnie Lee, 87

Crain, Jeanne, 109n5

Crandall, Prudence, 10

Crime: black activists' justification of, 154–155; blacks and police and, 141; Burns on, 107–108; urban life and social disintegration, 139–140. *See also* Black-on-black crime

Crisis magazine, 72, 104, 110, 126–127

Crowe, Milburn, 83

Crum, William, 87

Cruse, Harold, 185

"Cultural appropriation," 264–265

Cumming v. School Board of Richmond, County, Georgia (1899), 69

Daily Worker, 103

Dana, Richard, 49

Dancy, John C., 110, 119, 120

Dandridge, Dorothy, 109n5

Daniel Yankelovich Inc. survey, 189, 197, 204

Dark Princess (Du Bois), 94

Darrow, Clarence, 119–120, 138

David, Joseph, 78–80

David, Lee Parsons, 110

Davis, Garrett, 26–27

Davis, Jefferson, 48–50, 78–80

Davis, Ossie, 158

Davis, Varina Howell, 89

"Day of Knives," in New York City, 183

De Blasio, Bill, 181n6

De Voe, Thomas, 18

"Decertification," of police, 276

Dees, Morris, 244–245

Degler, Carl, 132

Democratic National Convention (1964), 164, 169

Dempsey, John, 198

Denny, Reginald, 270–271

Dependence: on government, in Great Migration era, 133; on government welfare, crime, and, 139–140; philanthropy and, 137–138

Desai, Ashwin, 259

Detroit, MI: black-police tensions and, 141; in Great Migration era, 113–120, 124, 132, 133–134; race riots in, 98, 101, 201, 202, 204; in 21st century, 217

Dicey, Edward, 4–5

"Diffusion," Lincoln and, 25, 26–27, 27n1

Dinkins, David, 282

Dinnerstein, Leonard, 184, 185

Discipline: education and, 235–237, 249–250; success and, 227

Disintegration (Robinson), 237

"Disparate impact" theory, 243, 250

"Disruptive child program," 179, 180–181, 181n6, 188, 235, 249–250

Dittenhoefer, Abram, 49

Diversity: for diversity's sake, 242–243; educational institutions and, 248, 256. *See also* Affirmative action

Dix, John, 28

Doar, John, 177

Donald, Cleveland, 161

Doolittle, James R., 34

Dorrough, C. M. "Fisty," 171–172

"Double consciousness," of Du Bois, 73, 92

Douglas, Davison, 84, 121, 124

Douglass, Frederick, 12, 43, 89, 108; after Civil War, 60–65; on antebellum separatism, 4–5; Exoduster movement and, 66; Isaiah Montgomery and, 81; Jews as models for, 131; on Lincoln, 65; Lincoln's self-help philosophy and, 36, 37; Santo Domingo and, 42; saving habits and, 272; on Stowe, 11

Dovidio, John, 293

Draft Riots, in New York City (1863), 20, 260

Drake, St. Clair, 94–95n1, 102

Druckenmiller, Stan, 236

Du Bois, W. E. B., 4, 46, 69, 74, 94, 110, 113, 160, 167; appeal of Japan and Germany during World War II era, 92–93, 113; blacks and economics and education, 69, 71–74; "double consciousness" and, 73, 92; Dunbar High School and, 188; Freedmen's Bureau failure and, 63; Hart and, 88; hatred of America and capitalism, 113; Jews and, 184; Madam C. J. Walker and, 127; Meredith and, 160–161; move to Ghana, 74, 154, 160; on Reconstruction, 42; saving habits and, 272; segregation in Great Migration era and, 122; "The Talented Tenth" and, 73, 88; use of "Negro," 158

Dukes, Hazel, 142

Dunbar High School, Washington, DC, 188

Dunbar National Bank, 134

Duncan, Arne, 232, 237, 275

Durham, NC, 134

Dwight, Timothy, 7

Eakin, Sue Lyles, 266

Eastland, James, 162

Ebony magazine, 108–109, 141, 147, 204, 221, 256, 275; avoidance of negative stories, 104–108; circulation of, 110–111; interracial marriage as topic for, 105, 108–109; Milwaukee and, 223–224; "passing as white" as topic for, 105, 108, 110; on philanthropy and dependence, 137–138; on successful integration, 188; on terminology for blacks, 158–159. See also Burns, Ben

Economic free enterprise system: blacks need to enter, ix, xvi. See also Capitalism

Economics: adaptation to change and, 216–218; assimilation as path toward prosperity, 293; government programs, costs, and results, 288; industrial farming and displacement of black workers in 1960s, 172–173; Jewish building ownership and black businesses, 126–132; national need to elevate underclass blacks, 286, 288; personal independence and, 36, 83, 104; reasons for Great Migration north, 93–94; Reconstruction and race, 44–45, 69–75; saving habits and economic success, 62, 131, 134, 184, 272; at time of civil rights movement, 151–152. See also Self-sufficiency

Education: alternative schools in South, integration and, 187; Booker T. Washington and, 70–71; charter schools and, 217, 227, 231–233, 236, 249, 289; Chicago and New York City school boycotts and, 166; in Chicago during Great Migration, 97; continuing failures of, 287; cost of higher education in 1960s, 152; denial of school for blacks in Connecticut, 9–10; desegregation and integration and, 121–125, 174–183, 239–244; Dwight on blacks and, 9; economic prospects and, 267–270; enrichment program and black culture, 233–235; freed slaves and, 31; of freedmen, during Reconstruction, 83–85; Freedom Summer and, 164–167; Hayes and, 59; hypersensitivity on college campuses, 251–257; jobs and middle-class values, 226–227; King and lack of detail about approach to, 201; in Milwaukee, 223; NAACP and lack of black attorneys, 138–139; as path to black assimilation, 144–145; performance, middle-class values, and "unhealed trauma," 249–250; philanthropy and school funding, 136–137; racial integration and, 46; Reconstruction and race, 48; remediation and, 250–251; resistance to integration and promotion of separatism, 187–189; 21st century concerns, 230–237; vocational school of blacks proposed by Douglass, 12; white culture and, 125. See also *Brown v. Board of Education of Topeka* (1954)

Eisenhower, Dwight D., 142, 174

Eliot, Charles W., 87–88, 136

Elite blacks, 37, 86, 126, 134, 191, 224, 225, 283, 287; black militants and, 278; Du Bois and, 71–73, 88; economics and, 229; education and, 230, 232, 247, 249–250; Great Migration and, 133–134; 1960s and, 213, 224

Ellington, Ed, 161

Ellis, Charles, 211

Ellison, Keith (Keith E. Hakim), 156

Emancipation Proclamation (1863), 26, 38

Emanuel African Methodist Church, murders at, 258

Emmanuel, Rahm, 94n1, 275

Employment: in Chicago during Great Migration, 97; middle-class values and, 226–230; private sector and, 225–227, 289; preparation needs for, 144; 21st century concerns, 224–230

Enforcement Acts, 54, 67

English language: assimilation and, 115–116; English poets excluded from college curricula, 256

Equal Employment Opportunity Commission (EEOC), 230

Equitable Life Assurance Society, 210

Esquire, 173

Evarts, William H., 49, 50

Evers, Medgar, 163

Exoduster movement, 65–66

Expediency, containment and, 47, 59

Family structure: crime and, 139–142; employment prospects and, 225; Hamer and, 172; Moynihan Report and, 165, 206–207, 212–213; need for stable, 72, 282–284; single-parent families, prevalence of and attitudes toward, xv, 99n3, 144, 184, 223, 237, 283–284, 288–289; and urban life during Great Migration, 98–99, 99n3; value systems and, 144–145

Farmer, James, 191–192, 193, 213

Farming, Douglass' advocating of, 63

Farrakhan, Louis, 146–147

Fifteenth Amendment, to US Constitution, 9, 17, 53

First Amendment, to US Constitution, 281

Fisher, John, 213

Fisher v. University of Texas at Austin, 251

Florence, Franklin Delano Roosevelt, 211

Foner, Eric, 26, 45

Forced into Glory: Abraham Lincoln's White Dream (Bennett), 37–38

Ford Foundation, 277

Ford Motor Company, 113–116, 210

Forman, James, 191, 193

Forten, James, 18

Fortune, 209–210

"Forty acres and a mule" experiment, 74–75, 75n1, 76

Forward, 131–132

Founding Fathers: assimilation's importance to, x, xi; memorials to, 258–259

Fourteenth Amendment, to US Constitution, x, 50, 53, 59, 67–69

Franklin, Benjamin, xi, 5, 117–118

Franklin, John Hope, 38, 158, 256, 264

Frazier, E. Franklin, xii, 98–99, 108, 132, 133–134, 141, 144, 155

Frazier, Kenneth, 225

Frederick Douglass' Paper, 60

Fredrickson, George M., 25, 260

Free Produce movement, 19

Free speech, college campuses and, 162, 197–199

Free Speech Movement, 165

Free will, as subordinate to legacy of slavery, xv

Freedmen's Bank, 61, 62–63

Freedmen's Bureau, 16, 27, 61, 62, 79

Freedom Farm, 170

Freedom Schools, 164–167

Freedom Summer, 163, 164–166, 177, 290

Freeman, Morgan, 290–291

Friedman, Thomas, 237

From Immigrant to Inventor (Pupin), 118

Fusion political movement, 57

Gandhi, Mahatma, 259, 259n4

Garnet, Henry Highland, 19, 159

Garrison, William Lloyd, 30

Garvey, Marcus, 129–130, 154, 158

Gates, Henry Louis Jr., 108, 218n1

General Education Board (GEB), 71, 136

General Mills, 225

General Motors, 151, 209, 210, 217

Georgetown University, 227–228

Gershman, Carl, 186

Ghana, 167, 257, 259; Du Bois and, 74, 154, 160

Gillette, Michael, 208

Ginzberg, Eli, 142–145, 286

Glazer, Nathan, 124

Glory (film), 28

Goldman, Roger, 276

Goldwater, Barry, 155, 193, 200

Goodman, Andrew, 200

Goodwin, Richard N., 207

Gordon, Mittie Maude Lena, 130

Gordon, Robert, 18–19

Government programs, 99n3, 165, 207–208; accountability needed for, 185, 201, 208, 213, 220, 224–225, 230, 281, 290

Grace, William Russell, 57

Graham, Lawrence Otis, 108–109, 133–134

Grant, Julia Dent, 89

Grant, Ulysses S.: during Civil War, 55,

260; Lee's surrender and, 38–39, 48; pardons for Confederates, 75; parole of Lee, 39, 258; as president, 51, 52, 53–56, 64

Gray, Freddie, 274

Great Migration, North's responses and blacks' experiences, 91–147; adjustment from rural to urban life, 139–142; blacks isolated by blinders of race, 92–93; in Chicago, 93, 94–113; in Detroit, 94, 113–120; development of racially separate societies, 145–147; economic reasons for migration, 93–94; in New York City, 94, 120–136; philanthropy's effects on, 134, 136–138; World War II's effects on segregation, 142–145

Great Society, cost and results of programs of, 207–208

Greater Liberia Act (1938), 130

Greeley, Horace, 49

Green, Benjamin, 80

Greenberg, Cheryl, 128

Greenberg, Jack, 131, 139

Gregory, Ilya, 105

Grievances, of blacks: counterproductive, 113, 156–157, 205, 214, 220–221, 238; courts and laws and, 278; history as taught today and, 261, 291–292

Groppi, Father James E., 223

Grutter v. Bollinger, 251

Haley, Alex, 184

Hall, Butler, 117

Hall, J. C., 35

Halliwell, Henry J., 84–85

Hamer, Fannie Lou, 164, 166–167, 168–173, 213

Hamid, Bishop Amiru Al-Minin Sufi Abdul, 128

Hampton Institutes, 136

Hanson, Marcus, xv

Harlan, John Marshall, 69

Harlem. See New York City

Harlem Children's Zone (HCZ), 235–237, 250

Harper's Weekly, 69, 196, 213

Harrington, Michael, 207

Harris, Fred, 221

Harrison, Benjamin, 68

Hart, Albert Bushnell, 88

Haugen, Carl, 209

Hayes, Arthur Garfield, 138

Hayes, Rutherford B., 58–60, 70

Heaggan-Brown, Dominique, 223, 224

Hebers, John, 221

Help, The (book and film), 263–264

Henry, Aaron, 144, 229

Henry, Ed, 229

Hentoff, Nat, 209

Herbert, Bob, 146

Herenton, Willie, 282

Hicks, James L., 125

Hicks, Louise Day, 6

Higginson, Henry Lee, 76–77

Higginson, Ida Agassiz, 76–77

Hill, Romaine, 275

Historically Black College and
    University (HBCU), 244–245, 251;
    current role and regulation of,
    245–248

History of Black Business in America, The
    (Walker), 63

Hoar, George, 68

Hopper Home, 19

Horne, Lena, 108, 109n5

Housing, segregation and, 95–96, 98,
    119–121, 124, 175–176, 190

Houston, Charles Hamilton, 138–139,
    282

Howard, Jacob M., 35

Howard, Oliver Otis, 61–62

Hoylman, Brad, 241–242

Hughes, Charles Evans, 123

Humphrey, Hubert, 169

Huston, Charles Hamilton, 123

Hwang, Jung-ok, 271–272

Ifill, Sherrilyn, 243, 262

Ile Vache, Haiti, 26

Illinois: exclusion laws in, 23–25, 29–30;
    desegregation and, 84

Illinois State Journal, 25

Immigrant in American History, The
    (Hanson), xv

Immigrants: America's national identity
    and, x–xi; assimilation and, 89, 159,
    269; Detroit and, 113–118; employers'
    needs for, 66; Northern integration
    and, 182–183; white Europeans
    welcomed, 34–35

"In Defense of Looting" (Mckesson), 279

Incarceration, of blacks, xv, 108, 235, 238,
    250, 284, 285, 293

Indiana: education of blacks and, 85;
    exclusion laws in, 23, 24, 30

Inferiority, of blacks: belief in, 7, 15–17,
    20, 24–25, 32, 35, 46, 71, 142–144;
    disproved, 137; *Plessy v. Ferguson* and,
    68–69

Ingalls, John J., 66

Institute of Policy Studies, 225

Institutional Investor magazine, 151

Integration: beginnings of still
    unresolved issue and, 83–85; black
    identity in civil rights era and,
    153–159; "paradox of," 227. *See also*
    Education

Internal Combustion (Levine), 115

Interracial marriage: anti-miscegenation
    laws overturned, 109; as *Ebony*
    magazine topic, 105, 108–109; Lamar
    and, 58; Northerners' fear of, 20,
    23–24. *See also* Education

Iowa, exclusion laws in, 24, 30, 34

Israeli-Palestinian conflict, blacks' anti-
    Israel stance, 185–187

"Ivy League Negro," 173–174

Jack and Jill of America, 133, 250

Jackson, Reverend Jesse, 142, 186, 220,
    274, 275, 279, 283

Jamaica, 43

Japan, 217, 269; economics after World
    War II and "people of color," 152,
    152n1; literacy and, 267; Meredith and
    values of Japanese, 159–160, 160n2

Jarrett, Valerie, 249–250, 275

Javits, Jacob, 275

Jay, John, 5

Jefferson, Thomas, xi

Jeffries, Leonard, 179

Jews: black-Jewish relationships and, 156; as business owners in black neighborhoods, 126–132, 270, 271–272; Du Bois and Nazi treatment of, 113; education, assimilation, and success in US, 267–268; George Washington and, xi; myth of shared suffering with blacks, 182, 183–184, 268; as role model for blacks, 65, 131. *See also* Anti-Semitism

Jim Crow Moves North: The Battle over Northern School Segregation, 1865–1954 (Douglas), 84

Job Corps program, 208, 224–225

Jocelyn, Simeon S., 9–10

Joe Wilson and the Creation of Xerox (Ellis), 211

John Doe v. Yale University, 257

John Hopkins University, 256

Johnson, Andrew, 16, 49, 52, 75

Johnson, Charles, 122

Johnson, Eunice, 105, 107

Johnson, James Weldon, 121, 137

Johnson, John, 99, 104–107, 111, 134

Johnson, Lyndon, 164, 169, 190, 200, 201, 202, 207, 266, 278

Johnson, Reverend John H., 128

Johnson Publishing Company, 38, 99

Jones, Alice, 109–110

Jones, Reverend Absalom, 4

Journal of Blacks in Higher Education, 288–289

Julian, George, 26, 32

Kansas, 65–67

Karp, Jonathan, 130

Kelley, William Melvin, 173–174, 252

Kemp, Washington, 62

Kennedy, Edward (Ted), 162, 222

Kennedy, John F., 151, 160, 161, 162, 174

Kennedy, Joseph, 151

Kennedy, Robert F., 160, 161–162

Kerner, Otto, 98, 204

Kerner Report. *See* "Report of the National Advisory Commission on Civil Disorders" (Kerner Report)

Kerry, John, 219

Kimball, Roger, 259

King, Annie Mae, 170

King, Martin Luther Jr., ix, xiv, 184, 185, 189, 213, 219, 245, 259, 266, 278, 279, 282, 293; expectations of others, 220; Hamer and, 169; "I Have a Dream" speech, xiv, 163, 177; "people of color" and, xiv–xv; private property concept and, 203; Rustin and, 195–196; support of jobs and education, 184–185; and "third phase" of civil rights movement, 192–195; violence and race riots in 1960s, 199–204

King, Rodney, 270–271

Kirkwood, Samuel, 29

Koch's Department Store, 128–129

Kock, Bernard, 26

Korean War, 143–144

Koreans, as business owners in black neighborhoods, 270, 271–272

Kramer, Michael, 185, 186

Ku Klux Klan, 53, 54, 118, 160, 244

L.A. Four, 271

La Guardia, Fiorello, 132, 133

Lamar, L. Q., 54–56, 57–58

Launching the War on Poverty (Gillette), 208

Law-and-order measures, 146, 200, 201, 213, 273–274, 278

Leaders, black: from Chicago, 274–275; in earlier eras, 282; fantasy of post-racial era and, 283; in 21st century, 282–286, 287

Lee, Chana Kai, 168

Lee, Harper, 262–263

Lee, John, 116

Lee, Richard, 197

Lee, Robert E.: Grant's parole of, 39, 75; memorials to, 258; surrender to Grant, 38–39, 48

Lee, Spike, 239

Lee, Tyshawn, 141, 274

Legal Defense Fund, of NAACP, 108, 139, 160, 175–176, 240, 242–243

Lemon, Don, 237–238

Levine, David Allan, 115

Lewis, Charles S., 188
Lewis, David Levering, 126, 271
Liberia, 9, 11, 19, 35, 66, 130. *See also* Colonization
Liebman, Morris, 208–209, 278
Lincoln, Abraham, 49, 61, 117–118, 291; colonization and, 12, 24–26, 38; diffusion and, 25, 26–27; Douglass and, 60, 65; racial attitudes of, 21, 35–38, 260, 261; Seward and, 14–16
Lincoln, Robert Todd, 88
Lindsay, John, 177
Little Rock Central High School, 174
Little Rock Nine of Harlem, 125
Litwack, Leon, 36
Lomax, Louis, 129, 131, 141, 157–158, 195, 264
Looting, called positive good, 279
Lopez, Nadia, 234, 237
Louisiana, 29, 36, 54
Louisiana Purchase (1803), 21
Lovejoy, Owen, 24, 26
Loving v. Virginia, 109
Luther, Jerelyn, 253
Lynch, John R., 55–58, 68
Lynd, Alice, 165
Lynd, Staughton, 153, 163–166

MacArthur, Douglas, 152
Madam C. J. Walker Beauty Culture, 127
Maier, Henry, 223
Maine, 28, 84
Malcolm X, xv, xvi, 38, 146, 166, 167, 213, 251, 257; Farmer on, 192; Hamer and, 168, 169; King on, 193–194; Meredith and, 160; separation with reparations and, 154, 156–157
Malloy, Daniel, 241
Malvin, John, 31
Manpower Demonstration Research Corporation (MDRC), 224–225
Manpower Development and Training Act, 210
"Many Rivers to Cross" festival, in Atlanta, 285
Marable, Manning, 227
Marcus, Ivan, 267–268

Marlowe, Sheree, 245
Marshall, George, 218–219n2
Marshall, Louis, 138
Marshall, Thurgood, 108, 123, 139, 155, 160, 197, 282
Marshall Plan: after World War II, 218, 218n2; proposed for blacks, 185, 190, 191, 194, 218–224, 225, 239. *See also* Reparations, for slavery
Martin, Trayvon, 274, 277
Marxism, 72, 113, 167–168, 178, 188. *See also* Communism
Massachusetts: abolitionists' disdain for freed blacks, 77; antebellum attitudes toward blacks and, 6–7, 27, 28–29, 30; desegregation and, 84
McAdam, Doug, 165
McCoy, Rhody, 245
McDonald, Lequan, 274
McDougall, Winston C., 128
McFeeley, William, 61
McGrew, Michael, 181n6
McGurn, William, 242
McKenna, Joseph, 69
McKenney, Prentice, 223
Mckesson, DeRay, 279
McKinley, William, 69, 136
McKissick, Floyd, 182
McManus, Edgar, 18
McMillen, Neil, 82
Meier, August, 139
Member of the Club (Graham), 108
Memorials to historic persons, controversies over, 255, 258–261
Meredith, James, 159–161, 163, 174, 177
Messenger, 126
Metropolitan Life Insurance, 210
Mexican War, 21
Michigan: exclusion laws in, 23, 24, 30, 35; desegregation and, 84
Middle class, blacks and, xvi, 107–108, 133, 145, 159, 188, 191, 213, 221, 225, 230, 249, 287, 289
Middle-class values and behavior (race-neutral), xvi, 133–134, 180, 192, 214, 226–227, 235–236, 238–239, 242; denigration of, in black culture, 238–239; education and, 236–237,

249–250; employment prospects and, 226–230

Military: as assimilation and education model, 165n3; segregation and integration in, 142–144

Mills, Isaac, 110

Mills, Kay, 166, 168, 171

Milwaukee, WI, 222–224

Minnesota: exclusion laws in, 23, 30, 33; desegregation and, 84

Miscegenation. *See* Interracial marriage

Mississippi: after Civil War, 48, 54–58; freed slaves and, 29

Mississippi Civil Rights Museum, 266–267

Mississippi Constitutional Convention (1890), disenfranchisement of blacks and, 81–82

Missouri, 67

Mitchell, Parren, 186

Monroe, James, 141

Montague, Nathaniel "Magnificent," 130

Montgomery, Benjamin, 78–80

Montgomery, Isaiah, 78, 80–83

Montgomery Advertiser, 244

Moore, Winston E., 277

Morgan, Charles, 130

Morse, Charles, 76

Mott Hall Bridges Academy, 234

Moukawsher, Thomas, 240–241

Moulton, Samuel W., 52–53

Mound Bayou, MS, 78, 80–83

Movement for Black Lives, 187, 277; historically black colleges and, 247; opposition to charter schools, 231, 233; platform, demands, and financing of, 279–281

Movies, 261–267

Moynihan, Daniel Patrick, xii, 124, 206, 207, 212

Moynihan Report. *See* "Negro Family: The Case for National Action" (Moynihan)

Muhammad, Elijah, 130, 146, 156

Muhammad, Wallace Ford, 130

Multiculturalism, separatism and divisiveness of, xv, 256, 270, 285

Muslim immigrants, 269–270

Myrdal, Gunnar, xii, 125, 137, 147

Myths, about race and racism: aura of civil rights movement, xv; "lost cause" of South, 44; "people of color" and, xiv–xv; race as solely Southern problem, xiv

NAACP, 72, 103; adoption of black babies and, 109; assimilation and, 146; black-on-black crime and, 142; *Brown* decision and, 123; Darrow and, 119–120; Hamer on, 169; opposition to charter schools, 233; restrictive covenants and, 95–96; 21st-century leaders and, 282; use of term "colored," 158; use of white lawyers, 138–139. *See also* Legal Defense Fund, of NAACP

Nadler, Jerrold, 241–242

Nasser, Gamal Abdul, 157

Nation of Islam, 130, 146–147, 156

National Advisory Commission on Civil Disorder, 204–205. *See also* "Report of the National Advisory Commission on Civil Disorders" (Kerner Report)

National Association of Real Estate Boards, Code of Ethics, in 1924, 119

National Museum of African American History and Culture, 258

National Rights Museum, 261

National Strategy Information Center (NSIC), 208–209

Native Americans, x, 54, 243, 257, 259, 269

Native Son (Wright), 99, 100–101, 102, 105–106, 141

Naturalization Act (1790), x

Nauman, Frank, 177

"Negro," use of term, 158–159

Negro and the City, The, 209–210, 211

"Negro Convention" (1848), 36

Negro Digest, 104, 105

Negro Family in Chicago, The (Frazier), xii, 98–99

"Negro Family: The Case for National Action, The" (Moynihan), xii, xvii, 99, 99n3, 124, 155, 165, 206–207, 212

Negro Potential, The (Ginzberg), 142–145
Negro Revolt, The (Lomax), 157–158
Nelson, Lemrick, 270
New Hampshire, 84
New Haven, CT, 6, 8–10, 12
New Jersey, 85. *See also* Newark, NJ
New Jim Crow: Mass Incarceration in the Age of Colorblindness, The, 285
New York City: assimilation and middle-class traits, 133–136; black boycott of schools in, 166; black businesses and self-confidence, but lack of economic foundation, 126–132; education and segregation in, 121–125, 146, 177, 177n5, 241–242; in Great Migration era, 94, 120–136, 121–122, 125–133; housing and segregation in, 120–121, 124; police and, 276; racial violence in, 132–133; union costs and, 217
New York City Colonization Society, 19
New York City Commission on Religion and Race, 207
New York Manumission Society, 19
New York State: antebellum attitudes toward blacks in, 16–20; education of blacks and, 85; freed slaves and, 29
New York State Convention of Colored Citizens, 18
New York Times, 17, 37, 89, 110, 135, 141, 233, 242, 245; change in terminology regarding blacks, 137; on Lynch, 57; Montgomerys and, 80; Reconstruction and, 45–46, 69
New Yorker, 275
Newark, DE, 98, 101
Newark, NJ: race riots in, 101, 201–202, 204; schools in, 234
Next Yale, 256–257
Nicklis, John O., 209
"Nigger," use of term by blacks, 259–260, 263
Nkrumah, Kwame, 167
North: hypocritical racial behavior, 197–199, 212; need to acknowledge racial past and attitudes of, 291. *See also* Antebellum North; Reconstruction
North Carolina, 54
North Star, 60

Northrup, Solomon, 265–266

Oakland, CA, 84
Obama, Barack, xii, 37, 94, 135, 173, 220, 260, 262, 274, 284; education of daughters of, 232; fails to denounce criminal behavior, 278–279; fantasy of post-racial era and, 283, 287; racial protests and, 272–273
O'Brien, Conor Cruise, 74
Ocean Hill–Brownsville, NY, 176, 179–180, 235, 245, 249, 280
O'Connor, Sandra Day, 251
O'Conor, Charles, 49
O'Dwyer, Paul, 173
Office of Economic Opportunity (OEO), 208
Ogbu, John, 243–244
Ogden, Robert, 71, 136
Ohio: education of blacks and, 84, 122; exclusion laws in, 23, 30–33; during Reconstruction, 42
Operation Head Start, 208
Oregon, 22
Osterweil, Willie, 279
Other America, The (Harrington), 207
Ottley, Roi, 110
Our Nig; or, Sketches from the Life of a Free Black (Wilson), 13–14
Owen, Robert, 78–79

Packard Motor Car Company, 115
Palmer, John M., 24
Palmetto Leaves (Stowe), 12–13
Parker, Nate, 266
Parks, Rosa, 146
Parsons, Richard, 225
"Passing as white," as *Ebony* magazine topic, 105, 108, 110. *See also* "Acting white," as pejorative
Patrick, Deval, 283
Patterson, Orlando, 108
Peace Movement of Ethiopia (PME), 130
Pension funds, impact of costs on business and education, 151, 217, 273, 276
"People of color": African wars and, 213; aura of civil rights movement,

xiv–xv; fictional unity of, 259n4; King
    and, xiv–xv; Wright and, 112–113
Percy, Charles, 275
Perspectives Charter Schools, 227
Phelps-Stokes Fund, 135, 137
Philadelphia, PA: black entrepreneur in,
    18; desegregation and, 84–85, 175; free
    blacks in, 4–5; in Great Migration
    era, 124; illegitimate births in, 99
Philanthropy, effects of paternalistic, 19,
    134, 136–138
Phillip, Wendell, 12
Pierrepont, Edwards, 55
Pig Bank (farm cooperative), 170
Pigs' Feet Mary, 127
Pinky (movie), 109n5
Pitney-Bowes, 209
Pittsburgh, PA, 84, 85
Plessy, Homer, 68
Plessy v. Ferguson (1896), 68–69, 70, 123
Podair, Jerald, 177–178, 180–181
Police: paradox of hostility toward police
    and need for protection, 275–277;
    police unions and decertification of
    officers, 276; tension with blacks, 141,
    221, 270–281
Powell, Adam Clayton Jr., 38, 132–133,
    189–190
Prentiss, Seargent S., 2–3
Prep for Prep, 234
Private property, denigration of, 279
Private sector: employment and,
    225–227, 289; programs to assist
    blacks, 209–212
Property Owner's Journal, 95, 96
Pugh, Billy W., 139–140
Pupin, Michael, 117–118
Pusey, Nathan, 197

Qaddafi, Muammar, 186
Quest for the Silver Fleece, The (Du Bois),
    72
"Quiet Riots: Race and Poverty in the
    United States," 220–222, 270
Quota systems, xvi, 14, 123, 125, 155, 188,
    251

Race relations, as continuing American
    dilemma (1960s to 2016), xiv,
    215–286; black leadership and, 274–
    275, 282–286; common economic
    shocks, 216–218; economic success
    and education, 267–270; education
    concerns, 230–237; employment
    conditions, 224–230; historical
    memorials and symbols, 255, 258–261;
    integration concerns, 239–257;
    Marshall Plan proposals, 218–224;
    movies and popular culture, 261–267;
    need for constructive community-
    based organizations, 284–286; racial
    violence and community policing,
    270–281; reverse racism and,
    244–245; self-examination needed,
    237–239
Racial violence, 270–281; Black Lives
    Matter movement, 277–281; black
    militants and, 146–147; in Detroit in
    Great Migration era, 120; dichotomy
    of hostility toward police and need
    for protection, 275–277; examples of,
    270; in 1940s, 102; in NYC in Great
    Migration era, 132–133; and race riots
    in 1960s, 199–204; riots defended as
    justifiable and legitimate, 202–203,
    271, 272–273; riots in Chicago during
    Great Migration, 97–98, 98n2; riots
    in civil rights era, 101, 193–194,
    199–204, 211, 220–221; sanctioning of,
    223, 278–279, 287
Rainwater, Lee, 222
Rangel, Charles, 142, 173
Reagan, Ronald, 197
Reconstruction, and North's
    containment of blacks in South,
    41–89; black suffrage and, 42, 58–59;
    conditions in South after Civil War,
    48–60; containment policies, 46–48,
    52–53, 82; creation of inferior roles
    for blacks, 42–48; Douglass and,
    60–65; economics of race and, 44–45,
    69–75; education of freedmen and,
    83–85; legislation and legal rights,

52, 67–69; Montgomery family, cotton, and black self-sufficiency, 78–83; Northern opinions of black inferiority and refusal to assimilate them, 47, 86–89; Northerners, cotton, and freedmen as employees, 75–78

Regents of the University of California v. Bakke, 188, 251

Reid, Harry, 37

Reider, Jonathan, 182–183

Reluctant African, The (Lomax), 157

Reparations, for slavery, 11, 75n1, 156, 191, 196–197, 256, 278, 279–280

"Report of the National Advisory Commission on Civil Disorders" (Kerner Report), xii, xvii, 98, 204–205, 273, 276, 286, 287; evaluation of, 220–222

Reverse racism, 244–245

Rhinelander, Leonard "Kip," 109–110

Rhode Island, 28, 84

Ribicoff, Abraham, 212, 240

Riddle, Albert G., 32

Ridgway, Matthew, 143–144

Rise of David Levinsky, The (Cahan), 132

Risen, Alton, 179

Rivera, Lino, 132

Robeson, Paul, 85

Robin Hood Foundation, 234

Robinson, Eugene, 219, 237, 238, 243, 284

Rochester, NY, 211

Rockefeller, John D. Jr., 136

Rockefeller, John D. Sr., 71, 134, 136

Rogers, Mary, 248

Rogers, Ralph, 180

Roosevelt, Eleanor, 38, 107

Roosevelt, Franklin Delano, 38, 133, 151, 211

Roosevelt, Theodore, 37, 65, 78, 136, 260; Booker T. Washington and, 70; opinions on black inferiorities, 86–87

Rosenbaum, Yankel, 270

Rosenfield, Adolph B., 128

Rosenthal, Linda B., 241–242

Rosenwald, Julius, 131, 136–137

Rowan, Carl, 282

Royko, Mike, 275

Rudwick, Elliott, 139

Rugaber, Walter, 173

Russell, Carlos, 142

Russell, Jesse, 246

Russell, Richard, 27n1

Rustin, Bayard, 195–197, 283

Ryan, James E., 240

Salovey, Peter, 255

San Francisco, CA, 84, 176, 199, 199n8

Sand against the Wind (Dancy), 110

Sandburg, Carl, 95, 98

Sanders, Bernie, 135

Santo Domingo, 42, 64

Saving habits, economic success and, 62, 131, 134, 184, 272

Savio, Mario, 165

Schlesinger, Arthur Jr., 151

Schmoke, Kurt, 273

Schurz, Carl, 59

Schwerner, Michael, 200

Scottsboro Boys, 274

Sealy, Lloyd, 140

SEED, 210–211

SEED School, 237

Segregation: civil rights era and black identity, 153–159, 174–183; education and, 121–125, 174–183, 239–244; housing and, 95–96, 98, 119–121, 124, 175–176, 190; during Reconstruction, 48; World War II's effects on, 142–145. *See also* Colonization; Integration

Self-segregation. *See* Separatism

Self-sufficiency: B. T. Washington's call for, xvi; Montgomery family and, 78–83

Selma (film), 266

Semmes, Raphael, 50–51, 75

Separatism: antebellum Northern attitudes toward blacks and, 3–9, 12–13; blacks and rejection of capitalism and justification of violence, 154–156; of blacks during Great Migration, 145–146; blacks' lack of material success after Civil

War and, 63–64, 69; civil rights movement and, 153–159, 167–168; as destructive path, 158; encouraged as multiculturalism, xv; in higher education, 292; as holding back black economic progress, 287; Nation of Islam and, 146–147; in 21st century, 236n3, 285. *See also* Colonization
Servan-Schreiber, Jean-Jacques, 151
Sethi, Rohini, 281
Seward, Henry, 14
Seward, William Henry, 14–17, 260
Shachtman, Tom, 271
Shanker, Albert, 177, 180, 181–182
Shaw, Robert Gould, 45
Sheff v. O'Neill, 212, 239–240
Sherman, John, 32
Sherman, William Tecumseh, 28, 61, 74–75
Siegel, Fred, 270, 271
Sillers, Walter Sr., 83
Singapore, education and success in, 268–269
Single-parent families, 225, 237–239, 283–284, 288–289
Skipper, Joseph, 146
Slaughterhouse Cases (1873), 67
Smith, Gerrit, 49, 50
Smith, Shane, 281
Smith, Stephen, 18
Society for the Relief of Worthy, Aged, Indigent Colored Persons, 19–20
Soros, George, 277
Souls of Black Folk, The (Du Bois), 73
South: economics, legal status, and politics after Civil War, 48–60; fate of confederates after Civil War, 48–51. *See also specific states and topics*
South Carolina, 54
Southern Christian Leadership Conference (SCLC), 169, 186, 282
Southern Nonviolent Coordinating Committee (SNCC), 164–169, 185, 282
Southern Poverty Law Center, 278
Sowell, Thomas, 8–9, 188, 272
Space General, 211–221

Speed, James, 49
Spelman College, 136, 153, 213
Spingarn, Arthur, 131
Stanton, Edwin, 29–30
Stapleton, Roosevelt, 171
Stennis, John, 212
Stevens, Thaddeus, 32, 52, 75
Stewart, Austin, 18
Stockett, Kathleen, 263–264
Stowe, Harriet Beecher, 9, 10–13, 266
Strike that Changed New York, The (Podair), 177–178
Stringer, Scott, 241–242
Succeeding against the Odds (Johnson), 104
Suffrage, for blacks: antebellum Northern attitudes toward blacks and, 10, 16–17, 23, 24, 34–36; Joseph Davis and, 80; Mississippi and disenfranchisement of blacks, 81–82; Northern containment of blacks during Reconstruction and, 58–59; T. Roosevelt and, 87
Sumner, Charles, 27, 30, 56
Supreme Court, of US, 67–69, 109, 160, 174–175, 188, 231, 251
Sutton, Percy, 172–173
Sweet, Dr. Ossian, 119–120, 138
Sweet, Henry, 119–120

Take This Hammer (film), 199
Taylor, John, 270
Teach For America, 234–235, 280, 290
Teachers' unions, 177, 178, 179–180, 181, 181n6, 231–234, 289
Telling Memories among Southern Women (Tucker), 264
Temple Emanu-El, 191
Temple Mishkan Tefila, 185
Tennessee, 29, 67
Texas, 19
Thackston, Frank, 161, 162
Thirteenth Amendment, to US Constitution, 52, 67
Thomas, Clarence, 108, 247
Thomas, Edward, 171, 292
Thomas, Franklin, 108

Thomas, Joey, 275
Thomas, Lorenzo, 30
Tilden, Samuel J., 58
Till, Emmett, 193, 274
Timbuctoo colony, 50
Tinnin, Bill, 171
"Tipping," 187
Title, David, 284
To Kill a Mockingbird (book and movie), 262–263
Tobey, Edward, 45
Tocqueville, Alexis de, 37
Tough, Paul, 236
Toure, Sekou, 167, 168
Townsend, Pascol Jr., 171
Truman, Harry S., 142
Trumball, Lyman, 24
Tucker, Susan, 264
Turner, Alexander, 119
Turner, Nat, 266
Tuskegee Institute, 70–71, 127, 136
Tuttle, William, 94
12 Years a Slave (film), 265–266
Tyler, George M., 67

Uncle Tom's Cabin (Stowe), 9, 10–11, 266
Underclass, The (Auletta), 224–225
Underground Railroad, 33
Underwood, John, 49
United Federation of Teachers (UFT), 177, 178, 179–180, 181, 181n6
United Negro Improvement Association, 158
United States v. Cruikshank (1876), 67
Universal Negro Improvement Association (UNIA), 129–130
University of Alabama, 174
University of Cincinnati, 256
University of Ghana, 259
University of Mississippi (Ole Miss), 159–161, 163, 174
Urban League, 109, 126, 131, 191, 210, 219, 282

Vahed, Goolam, 259
Vanderbilt, Cornelius, 49

Vann, Albert, 180, 185
Vermont, 84
Violence. *See* Racial violence
Vista program, 208
Voegeli, V. Jacque, 25
Voting Rights Act (1965), 199, 201
Voucher programs, 233, 289

Wade, Benjamin Franklin, 42
Wade, Dwyane, 274
Wagner, Robert F., 200
Waite, Morrison, 67, 68
Walker, Juliet E. K., 63
Walker, Madam C. J., 127, 134
Wall Street Journal, 233–234, 241, 242, 255–256
Wallace, George, 161, 174, 194, 240; and selective free speech at Yale, 197–199
Wallace, Mike, 290–291
Walton, Anthony, 219, 228
War on Poverty, 152, 190
Ward, Benjamin, 141
Ward, Samuel R., 77, 195, 242
Warren, Robert Penn, 38; interviews with black leaders, 189–197
Washington, Booker T., 13, 36, 59, 193, 244; appeasement and, 71, 82, 244; assimilation and, 138; Du Bois and, 74; economic power's importance and, 63, 69–71; educational priorities of, 83, 228–229; Isaiah Montgomery and, 82; Jews and, 131, 184; Madam C. J. Walker and, 127; philanthropy and, 136; preparation for citizenship, 237; saving habits, 272; self-help of blacks, 78; T. Roosevelt and, 86
Washington, DC, 122–123
Washington, George, x, xi, 268
Washington, Harold, 282
Waters, Ethel, 109n5
Waters, Maxine, 270
"Watts model," 210
Watts riots, 101, 201, 204, 270, 271
Ways, Max, 210
Weaver, Robert C., 209–210
Webster, Noah, 7, 8, 9
Weinstein, Morris, 129

Western Civilization, criticism of, xvi, 178–180, 182, 186–187, 214, 257, 278

Westward expansion, antebellum Northern attitudes toward blacks and, 21–25, 32

White, Walter, 103, 108, 121–122, 138, 282

White flight: in civil rights era, 187–188, 200; during Great Migration, 93, 95–96, 121, 124, 125, 145–146; reverse flight, 199n8; in 21st century, 85, 223

Who Speaks for the Negro? (Warren), 189–197

"Why I Choose Exile" (Wright), 107, 112

Wilder, Douglas, 108

Wilkins, Roger, 221

Wilkins, Roy, 38, 104, 146, 155, 169, 186, 190–192, 197, 202, 213, 220, 282

Willey, Waitman T., 27

Williams, Damian, 271

Williams, Eugene, 97

Williams, Hosea, 186

Williams, John Jr., 5

Williams v. Mississippi (1898), 69

Wills, Garry, 273–274

Wilmore, Larry, 259–260

Wilmot, David, 21–23

Wilmot Proviso (1846), 21–22

Wilson, August, 265

Wilson, "Daddy," 62

Wilson, David, 266

Wilson, Harriet, 13–14

Wilson, Henry, 27

Wilson, James Q., 182–183

Wilson, Joe, 211

Winfrey, Oprah, 262, 265

Winstead, Arthur, 200

Wisconsin, 23, 30, 33–35, 84

Wisconsin State Colonization Society, 34

Wister, Owen, 86

Woodson, Carter G., 31

Woodward, C. Vann, 39, 152n1, 158

World War I, labor shortages and black employment, 25, 46, 93, 97, 143

World War II, effects on segregation and integration, 142–144

Wright, Bruce, 142

Wright, Jeremiah, 135, 274, 283

Wright, Richard, 141, 147, 157, 167; bitterness about America, 111–112; Johnson and, 105–106; responsibility for blacks' problems and, 102–103; writing during Great Migration era, 99–103

Xerox, 211, 211n9

Yale, Elihu, 255–256, 259

Yale University, 152, 163–164, 173–174; "black" category, 218n1; Christakises and, 252–254; hypersensitivity and multiculturalism, 252–257; named buildings at, 255–256; Osterweil and looting defense, 279; racial tensions at, 217–218; Wallace and free speech, 197–199

Yates, Richard, 24–25, 29

Yew, Lee Kwan, 27n1, 269

Young, Andrew, 186–187, 262, 282

Young, Coleman, 282

Young, Whitney Jr., 190–193, 197, 202, 213, 214, 219, 220, 282

Young Women's Leadership Network (YWLN), 234

Zisch, William, 210

Zuckerberg, Mark, 234

Photo Credits

01. **Loading steamboats at New Orleans, ca. 1860.** The Historic New Orleans Collection

02. **The Riots In New York : The Mob Lynching A Negro In Clarkson-Street.** Picture Collection, The New York Public Library, Astor, Lenox and Tilden Foundations

03. **Department of Justice, Freedman's Bank Building.** Library of Congress Prints & Photographs Division [LC-USZ62-100429]

04. **Wisconsin State recruitment brochure, 1879.** Wisconsin Historical Society, WHS-62557

05. **The negro exodus—scenes on the wharves at Vicksburg.** Library of Congress Prints & Photographs Division [LC-USZ62-127755]

06. **Liverpool Cotton Association invitation for opening of New Cotton Exchange, 1906.** International Cotton Association

07. **Ford English School diploma.** From the Collections of The Henry Ford. Gift of Ford Motor Company.

08. **Foreign-born employees of Ford Factory in "Americanization Day" parade, Jul 5, 1915.** From the Collections of The Henry Ford

09. **2009 race riot plaque, Chicago. York High School, Elmhurst, IL.** courtesy Gene Dattel

10. **New York Evening Graphic's composite image of Alice Rhinelander disrobing, Nov 25, 1925.** Composograph of Alice Rhinelander, 1925. Photographers unknown. Composite image by Harry Grogin and Emile Gavereau, New York Evening Graphic.

11. **Jewish boys school in Lublin, Poland. 1924.** From the Archives of the YIVO Institute for Jewish Research, New York

12. **BusinessWeek magazine cover, "Is There A Nigger?", Mar 19, 1930.** *BusinessWeek*

13. **Mule population on Mississippi farms, 1870–1960.** Adam Fanucci

14a. **Flyer from School Boycott, Freedom Day, Feb 3, 1964.** Elliot Linzer Collection, Department of Special Collections and Archives, Queens College, City University of New York

14b. **"Change the Status-Crow" boycott poster, New York, Mar 16, 1964.** Change the Status-Crow Flyer, March 1964, Box 1, Folder 8, Elliot Linzer Collection, Department of Special Collections and Archives, Queens College, City University of New York

15. **Los Angeles Times front page, Aug 15, 1965.** ©1965. Los Angeles Times. Reprinted with Permission.

16. **Bobby Kennedy delivering speech at University of Mississippi: Image 10.** Ed Meek and Meek School of Journalism and New Media Collection (MUM00739). The Department of Archives and Special Collections, J.D. Williams Library, The University of Mississippi.

17a. **Mississippi Freedom Trail sign—Aaron Henry.** ©2015 by Mark Hilton (HMdb.org)

17b. **Mississippi Freedom Trail sign—"Black Power" Speech.** ©2015 by Mark Hilton (HMdb.org)

18. *Ebony* **Magazine, November 1967, interior page 46 "What's in a Name?".** Courtesy EBONY Media Operations, LLC. All rights reserved.

19. *Ebony* **Magazine, Aug 1979, COVER "Black on Black Crime".** Courtesy EBONY Media Operations, LLC. All rights reserved.

20 *Ebony* **Magazine, Aug 1979, interior page 38 "Personal Injury and Mental Pain".** Courtesy EBONY Media Operations, LLC. All rights reserved.

21. *Ebony* Magazine, Aug 1979, interior page 119 "dope is a known killer". Courtesy EBONY Media Operations, LLC. All rights reserved.

22. *Ebony* Magazine, Aug 1979, interior page 118 "Going Easy on Criminals Encourages Crime". Courtesy EBONY Media Operations, LLC. All rights reserved.

23. *Ebony* Magazine, Aug 1979, interior page 113 "Citizens Must Fight Black on Black Crime". Courtesy EBONY Media Operations, LLC. All rights reserved.

24a. *Ebony* Magazine, Aug 1987, COVER "The New Black Middle Class". Courtesy EBONY Media Operations, LLC. All rights reserved.

24b. *Ebony* Magazine, Aug 1993, COVER "The New Black Family". Courtesy EBONY Media Operations, LLC. All rights reserved.

25. International *BusinessWeek* magazine cover, "Japan on Wall Street", Sep 7, 1987. *BusinessWeek*

26. Deserted downtown of Sunflower, Mississippi, 2005. Kim Rushing/Delta State University

27. President Obama studying Norman Rockwell painting of 1960 New Orleans School integration. White House Photo